THE SPACE OF APPEARANCE

The MIT Press
Cambridge, Massachusetts
London, England

GEORGE BAIRD

The Space of Appearance

This book was set in Perpetua and Helvetica Neue by DEKR Corporation and was printed and bound in the United States of America.

Library of Congress Cataloging-in-Publication Data

Baird, George.
    The space of appearance / George Baird.
      p.   cm.
    Includes bibliographical references and index.
    ISBN 0-262-02378-4 (alk. paper)
    1. Signs and symbols in architecture.   2. Structuralism.
  3. Architecture, Postmodern.   4. Deconstructivism (Architecture)
  I. Title.
  NA2500.B24   1995
  720′.1—dc20   94-40180
                                                            CIP

CONTENTS

PREFACE

The work of preparing this text has had support from a number of institutions and individuals. First of all, I wish to acknowledge the support of the Graham Foundation. Second, I extend my gratitude to the Getty Center for the History of Art and the Humanities, where I was a Visiting Scholar for a strategically useful period of time. At an earlier stage, the support of the Social Sciences and Humanities Research Council of Canada permitted initial research to be undertaken.

Detlef Mertins, Brigitte Shim, and Mark Wasiuta have been of enormous assistance in the research necessary for the work; they have also been among my most tenacious and persistent coaches. Doug Cogger, Brigitte des Rochers, and Jovi Cruces assisted me in the compilation of illustrations.

Every effort has been made to trace the copyright ownership of the illustrations in this volume. In some cases this has not proven possible, and I would welcome the opportunity to repair any omissions in future editions. I am grateful to the many organizations and individuals who have cooperated so readily in giving their permission to reproduce photographs and drawings.

Thanks are due to several generations of students of architecture at the universities of Toronto, Princeton, and Harvard, all of whom heard out partially formed versions of the arguments that follow.

I should like to express my gratitude also to Marc Baraness, Brian Boigon, K. Michael Hays, Edward Jones, Michael Kirkland, Wayne Lawson, Larry Richards, Edward Robbins, Tony Scherman, and Anne Stevens, who read early drafts of the manuscript and made helpful suggestions. During my stay at the Getty, Thomas Huhn gave me a personal introduction to the work of Theodor Adorno. Joy Gordon assisted me in the translation of certain texts originally published in French. Roger Conover and Matthew Abbate at MIT Press assisted me strategically to bring the text to a final stage.

The extended period of time it has taken me to complete it puts me in mind of some very long-term obligations. To start with I should like to mention Robert Maxwell, who started me out, many years ago, on the intellectual track that has led to the present text. I also want to cite the name of Peter Eisenman, whose recent production is criticized in the text that follows, but whose contribution to architectural discourse in our time is, in my view, without parallel. He gave me extraordinarily generous support before we had even met, and continued it long after that. To Joseph Rykwert I owe the greatest intellectual debt, as his constant support of my intellectual endeavors has sustained me longest of all.

Lastly, I want to express my gratitude to Barry Sampson, who has been my partner in architectural practice for a decade and a half; who has supported the production of the present work by making good my absences from our joint professional commitments; who has offered constant psychological support to its production, even at the cost of his own professional equanimity; and who has made strategic criticism of the evolution of its arguments.

And to Elizabeth Baird, for her faithful forbearance of me, as I have been engaged in this protracted effort to be architectural practitioner, theoretician, and husband all at the same time.

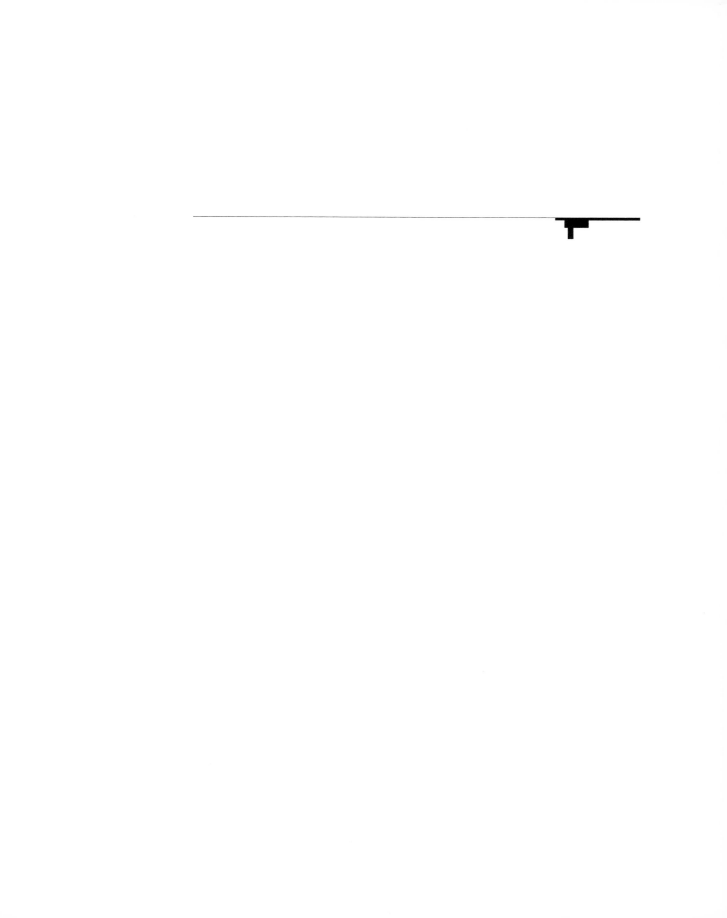

INTRODUCTION

*Action needs for its full appearance the shining brightness we once
called glory, and which is possible only in the public realm.*

Hannah Arendt, 1958

*Architecture worthy of human beings thinks
better of men than they actually are.*

Theodor Adorno, 1965

It is some quarter of a century since 1968. As time passes, that eventful year increasingly appears to have constituted a major watershed in the history of architecture in the twentieth century. And this is not just a matter of the direct impact of the '68 "events," as they were called, on architectural practice and education at that time. From the vantage point of the present day, it is possible to see how 1968 also constitutes a sort of pivot point in the whole twentieth-century evolution of ideas about human affairs, which has in turn influenced the most important theorizing about and criticism of architecture during the same period of time. Indeed, an overall historical pattern of two tiers of such influence—one focused on a series of particular controversies in architecture, and the other on a longer-term theoretical backdrop to those controversies—forms one major theme of this book.

Even a cursory examination of the influence on architecture of the various social and political tendencies that came to a head in 1968 reveals their startling impact. The process began with the dramatic disintegration of the entire body of ideas and practices that architects had hitherto accepted from their mentors in the first generation of so-called modern masters. For the public at large, this disintegration was the result of its increasingly hostile response to the visible impacts of modern architecture on the forms of existing cities around the world. Inside the discipline, the disintegration took a more intense and more politicized form, particularly during 1968 itself. For practicing architects—and even more particularly for students—architecture's capacity almost automatically to confer benefit on society, so long taken virtually as a given, suddenly came into grave question.

Of the subsequent developments both in theory and in practice, probably most visible has been the rise to ascendancy of the architectural tendency that has become known as postmodernism—a tendency whose advocates, at least according to them, had learned the error of their ways and committed themselves instead to a new architecture that would be more responsive to public concerns and public taste. To be sure, this tendency was paralleled by a dramatic rise in the level of public interest in and discussion about architecture, even if both continued to be more negative about the discipline than its varied protagonists would have liked. As a result, we have even seen such prominent nonarchitects as the popularizing author Tom Wolfe and Britain's Prince of Wales become influential arbiters of architectural taste.[1]

One might have expected these various tendencies by now to have created a new set of circumstances within which architecture would have regained a secure and integral social role for itself, such as was called for by the leading protagonists of postmodernism, from the very earliest days of their own attacks on modernism a quarter-century ago. Yet architecture's broad public role, as well as the moral and theoretical conviction of its practitioners, are hardly any more assured today than they were in 1968. In fact, it is possible to note that even as early an instance of postmodern architecture as Charles Moore's Piazza d'Italia of 1975 already provoked a discernible sense of public unease on account of its blatantly scenographic qualities.[2] It was as though Moore had evoked, almost in spite of himself, some barely articulate yearning amongst some part of his project's audience for some more materially "authentic" form of honorific architecture than it offered. Moreover, the characteristic motifs of postmodernism having by now become so ubiquitous a part of the routine commercial architecture of our era, it is clear that the sense of unease among the public is far from having abated.

Then, too, it is significant that inside the architectural academy, architectural postmodernism has been in disrepute for some time. Many leading theoreticians hold it in contempt, and a majority of students in the most prominent schools eschew it, seeing its residual public popularity as almost ethically compromising. At the same time, many members of a younger generation of teachers have for several years now promoted a mode of praxis that seeks to dismantle the normative social premises seen to underlie postmodernism, and proposes instead an architecture of critique. Yet relatively few executed projects embodying this mode of praxis have been achieved, and it now appears that the momentum of the critical tendency, evidently so potent only a year or so ago, may soon itself be exhausted. The tendency appears to have succeeded in destroying the moral confi-

I.1   A view of the Piazza d'Italia in New Orleans, by Charles Moore. In the lower left lies the artificial map of Italy, which forms a series of islands in the pool in the base of the fountain. Surrounding it are various more vertically iconographic elements of the design, including the notorious waterspouts based on a self-portrait of the architect (on the face of the arch at the far left). (Photograph © Marc Treib.)

dence of postmodernism—at least in the eyes of the most discriminating of today's architecture students—but it does not appear to have succeeded in replacing it, as a form of professional praxis in the larger world.

Not coincidentally, this quarter-century of controversy and anxiety in architecture manifests the distinct influence of ideas from outside architecture. The body of ideas at the beginning of the period in question was one that became generally known, particularly in North America, by the name "structuralism"; the parallel one shaping so much of the discussion today has now taken on, again for American audiences in particular, the rather parallel name of "poststructuralism."

In the structuralist philosophical atmosphere of the late 1960s and 1970s, young architectural critics and theorists became fascinated with ideas such as those of the French critic and theorist Roland Barthes, and of his mentor the anthropologist Claude Lévi-Strauss.[3] From Barthes, the young critics learned that a wide variety of social and cultural phenomena—not just traditional art forms—could be bracketed at arm's length and interpreted as systems of signification. From Lévi-Strauss they learned that even such large-scale social constructs as, let us say, western European civilization were historically relative ones, which could not be thought entitled to any automatic priority in the larger human scheme of things.

Having also learned from Barthes the new techniques of semiotics, whereby it was possible to treat architecture according to a linguistic analogy, the young generation of critics and theorists soon began to interpret the hitherto unquestioned projects and theories of modernism with similar detachment. Having understood from Lévi-Strauss the relative status of western European civilization as a whole, they easily also began to see the body of ideas and practices constituting modernism as similarly relative. Thus, when modernism's universal applications began to falter, the structuralist approaches of the younger generation radically undermined the unquestioned intellectual confidence it had previously enjoyed. Similarly, when more symbolically deliberate modes of designing began to be explored instead, semiotics was there to buttress the case for them. By the time of Charles Jencks's *Language of Post-Modern Architecture* in 1977, the deep influence of structuralist theories on postmodernism in architecture was indisputably clear.[4]

Some two decades later, a younger generation has looked to the ideas of a group of theorists broadly known as poststructuralist, including such figures as Jean-François Lyotard, Jacques Derrida, and Jean Baudrillard.[5] The pattern of differences and similarities of influence is a remarkable one to examine, reflecting as it does the complex pattern of similarities and oppositions that marks the broader relationship of the two generations of philosophers and social scientists. Notwithstanding the parallels that can be drawn between the two, the younger generation of figures cited is, for example, far less certain of the objective status of "reality" than the older one was. From Lyotard the new generation of critics and theorists has learned not just that western European civilization is a "relative" construct, but that even such intellectual conceptions as "history" or "Marxism"—at least insofar as they have been portrayed as capable of total explanation—really constitute unsupportably totalizing "master narratives." From Derrida they have gathered not just that any given text must be seen as variably interpretable, but that those interpretations may well vary extremely. From Baudrillard, they have come to understand that the possible series of secondary or tertiary readings of any given signifier is so limitless, especially in the era of the multiplicity of media in which we now live, that there can no longer be thought to exist original meanings in any consequential way. For Baudrillard, all social and cultural referents today are simulations that have lost any relationship to any original they might once have been thought to possess. Not only that, the new generation of critics and theorists has also had pointed out by him the relative ease of social and political manipulation to which such labile simulations are now susceptible.

It is not surprising, then, that the generation of critics and theorists who took up the ideas of poststructuralism felt obliged in turn strongly to dissent from what they saw as the too easy and untrustworthy affirmations of postmodern architecture. Indeed, they sought to reinforce the sense of "unease" about postmodernism among the public, and made a central tenet of their own design praxis the "deconstruction" of preexisting architectures, and the unmasking of their hitherto unrevealed significances and effects. In a variety of forms, in different parts of the world, the confrontation of the precepts of poststructuralism with the tentatively established but now so ubiquitous motifs of postmodernism comprised, up until recently, a central theme in pressing theoretical discussion in architecture.[6]

For the moment, I want to shift away from the barricades of recent architectural battles, to a consideration of certain terminological ambiguities in the current territory of cultural theory. The first of these begins right inside architectural discussion, and it has to do with the apparently obvious opposition between the terms "modern" and "postmodern." We are all quite familiar with this distinction, established in the writings of such figures as Charles Jencks and Robert A. M. Stern;[7] indeed, I have employed the terms thus far in a fashion consistent with Jencks's and Stern's well-established usage. In it, "modern" is seen characteristically to have to do with the abstract, the universal, and the anonymous, and "postmodern" with the metaphorical, the symbolic, and the particular. Yet the farther one moves outside the specific sphere of architectural discussion, the less this apparently clear distinction holds. In the larger realm of cultural theory, the characteristic usages of "postmodern" broaden dramatically. For Fredric Jameson, for example, John Portman is a "post-modern" architect.[8] For Jameson's colleague Anders Stephanson, the characteristic features of postmodernism are "fragmentation," "heterogeneity," and—interestingly enough—"surfaces *without* history" (my italics).[9]

Evidently, before such figures as these can workably be brought into the discussion, the characteristic usages of the terms inside architecture will have to be recontextualized so that the differing terminological nuances at stake can be even provisionally reconciled. But of course, the existence of nuances of such significance can also be seen as symptomatic of a larger ambiguity: that between the terms modern and postmodern as they have been employed by the two whole generations of cultural theorists cited above. For figures such as Lyotard and Baudrillard, for example, the category of the postmodern (more or less consistent, for them, with the era of poststructuralism) would constitute a quite decisive break with the older and now (in their view) obsolete category of the modern. For others—Albrecht Wellmer, for example—such a decisive break simply doesn't exist. While conceding much to the critiques of modernism by Lyotard and Baudrillard, Wellmer nevertheless argues that modernism and postmodernism remain necessarily intertwined in the most compelling cultural theory of our time. As Wellmer puts it:

> I shall argue that postmodernism at its best might be seen as a self-critical—a skeptical, ironic, but nevertheless unrelenting—form of modernism; a modernism beyond utopianism, scientism and foundationalism; in short, a post*metaphysical* modernism.[10]

Now of course, in making such a claim, Wellmer could be (and has been) dismissed as a too loyal ally of his senior German colleague Jürgen Habermas.[11] But it is interesting to note that admirers of Habermas are not the only ones to continue to insist on some sort of consequential linkage of modernism and postmodernism in our time. Andrew Ross, for example, has commented that

> we have come to see post-structuralism as a belated response to the vanguardist innovations of high modernism. Post-structuralism is the critical revolution that was delayed; it is the continuation of modernism by other means.[12]

Decon as continuity of Modern revolution delayed by Po-Mo

Such differences of opinion are themselves a function of the historical relationship of structuralism and poststructuralism.[13] To the structuralist generation of critics and theorists of the 1960s and 1970s, architecture, like language, was acknowledged first of all to be a social construct. It was in this sense that they saw the linguistic analogy—as it was represented by the newly fashionable discipline of semiotics—as being pertinent in the first place. Semiotics was seen by its (principally French) progenitors as having had its origins in the early twentieth-century work of the pioneering linguist Fernand de Saussure, according to whom any semiological system would comprise three basic polar dimensions. First of all, such a system would comprise both a *langue* and a *parole*. The *langue* would be the collective, unconscious dimension of the system of meaning (such as a language), and the *parole* would be its corresponding aspect of individualized expression. Then too, each component of the system would consist of a "signifier" (the sign or symbol in the system in question) and a "signified" (that for which the signifier in question stood). Following from researches on many different languages and on other symbol systems, Saussure had realized that in any elaborated system such as a language—or, as we would have it, such as architecture—the fundamental relationship of signifiers to their signifieds is in the first instance an arbitrary one. It is in this elementary sense that we all understand that the words *arbor* in Latin, *arbre* in French, and *tree* in English—three different signifiers—all stand for the same signified. Finally, Saussure also noted how the components of any such system of signifiers possessed two distinct mechanisms available for utilization, one having to do with their combination, and the other to do with their characteristic ways of being substituted one for another.[14] It was a sharpened understanding of these aspects of semiotics that opened the

1.2   A view of a part of the courtyard at Michael Graves's library at San Juan Capistrano, from 1982. (Photograph © Peter Aaron/Esto.)

way to the exploration of systems of symbolic expression in architecture by the early postmodernists such as Robert Stern, Michael Graves, and Charles Moore, all eventually to be compiled by Jencks in his 1977 text.

We may now turn to the corresponding implications of poststructuralism for the next generation. Insofar as Lyotard had argued against the hegemony of any "master narratives" in human affairs, the new generation of critics and theorists in architecture began to formulate resistance to what they saw as obvious systems of "hierarchy" in architecture. Insofar as Derrida had argued the opacity and fluidity of the semantic content of language, the young generation developed formal interests in architecture that emphasized seriality and juxtaposition instead of symbolic reference. Insofar as both these thinkers had argued for a quite heterogeneous model of reality, their architectural followers developed interests in architectural inversions and in deliberate, often aggressive discontinuities. Finally, those followers responded to imputations of the "unreality" of perceived signifiers, such as Baudrillard had so strenuously warned of, by employing aggressive, decentering strategies to deconstruct and to unmask received meanings in architecture—meanings likely to show up as inconsequential or, even worse, as hegemonic.

If we take the example of such a putatively poststructuralist project as Bernard Tschumi's Parc de La Villette, we can see how Tschumi's neutral grid of objects disposed across a field could be seen to subvert hierarchy, how its seriality and lack of programmatic content enable it to resist predictable semantic readings, and how its aggressive material and color palette may be thought to encourage subversive social speculations.[15] A parallel account can be given of Peter Eisenman's Wexner Center at Ohio

I.3   A view across the landscape of the park of La Villette, looking toward one of the pavilions designed by Bernard Tschumi. (Photograph © J.-M. Monthiers.)

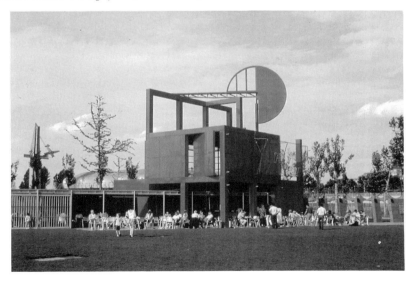

State University. In this case, it is the inversion of the customary disposition of its program—the entrance leads one down to galleries apparently underground—that first stated its decentering intention. The relentless abstraction of its grids provided an evidently neutral semantic field, and its visual defiance of conventional architectonic readings (the column that does not meet the ground) declared its ambition to thwart even elementary visual common sense.[16]

On the face of it, then, two different sets of philosophical influences seem to have provoked two different sets of architectural responses. Yet the matter cannot be left at that. I have already noted the historical relationships some have detected between the ideas of the generation of structuralist theorists of the sixties and those of their currently topical poststructuralist successors. It is not difficult, for example, to draw a clear lineage from Roland Barthes's wry and aloof interpretations of consumer products in the 1960s to Jean Baudrillard's more recent and more melodramatic commentaries on Disneyland and contemporary media events.[17] It is no more difficult to trace a line from Claude Lévi-Strauss's cautions regarding the easy temptations of anthropological enthnocentricity, first expressed in the 1960s, to the analogous cautions being put to the contemporary sociologist by Pierre Bourdieu, cautions that have influenced the wide-ranging cultural critiques of such poststructuralists as Andrew Ross.[18]

I cite these two lineages in particular since the intellectual issues they bear on seem to me directly relevant to architecture. Let us take the lineage from Barthes to Baudrillard, to start with. A key part of Barthes's theoretical apparatus was of course the fundamental conceptual relationship of the signifier to the signified; and fundamental to that relationship was its arbitrariness. In fact, we can say that it is this arbitrariness that gives symbol systems within society, such as language, their vast social flexibility and fluidity. This same arbitrariness makes their relationship contingent, highly susceptible to manipulation and to semantic erosion. And of course it is this last aspect that has so preoccupied Baudrillard, focusing as he has so often done on the role of symbols in a society saturated with media. But

I.5   A view of the foyer of Peter Eisenman's Wexner Center, illustrating the much-discussed column that does not meet the ground. (Photograph © Jeff Goldberg/Esto.)

I.4   A view of the exterior of Peter Eisenman's Wexner Center at Ohio State University in Columbus. In the foreground can be seen reconstructed elements from the nineteenth-century Armory Building, which occupied the same site. Beyond these can be seen parts of the large, three-dimensional white grid that is the principal design component of the project. (Photograph © Jeff Goldberg/Esto.)

where Barthes's critiques were both acute and exemplary in their modes of revelatory disclosure, Baudrillard's have become progressively more apocalyptic, to the point where his theory of the precession of simulacra eventually brings him to deny any palpable reality at all to systems of signification in our time.

Now this is a major shift in the use of semiotic models as they have been passed on from, say, Saussure to Barthes to Baudrillard. For Saussure, the signifier could admittedly only point to the signified: precisely on account of its initial arbitrariness, it was limited to this form of relation. But this "pointing" was the sole assurance of reality that such sign systems have ever been able to offer. Thus it seems to me that Baudrillard's melodramatic warnings have to be seen as problematic in their overstatement. Indeed, his warnings of the perceived unreliability of simulacra have the strange effect of actually contributing to that unreliability. The partial, contingent, admittedly only relative reliability of the relationships of signifiers to signifieds—on which the elementary conduct of all our lives depends—receives no comparable acknowledgment from him.[19]

This overlooked zone of contingent reliability in human affairs leads to my second point. For what the line from Lévi-Strauss to Bourdieu to Ross embodies, above all, is a moot circumspection on the part of the actor/analyst in relation to the social construct he is engaged in analyzing. Insofar as architecture too constitutes a social construct in these terms, the architect necessarily positions him or herself in a highly strategic ethical place in respect to it. We know the familiar remark of Walter Benjamin that architecture is "consummated by a collectivity in a state of distraction."[20] One might also cite the observation of Bernard Huet that "architecture and the city both situate themselves inside a body of conventions, and these conventions undergo a very slow evolution."[21] It is my view that this complex intellectual pattern, involving both constants *and* shifts of position, is of the profoundest importance for the current state of architectural theory and practice. The broad philosophical parallels that link poststructuralism to its immediate intellectual predecessor seem to me to have certain cautionary implications for any possible poststructuralist architecture. At the very least, they would seem to suggest serious ultimate limitations of the frequently avant-gardist gestures common in poststructuralist architectural circles. Unless they are brilliantly strategic in their form of intervention, such gestures are likely to fail; to generate simply confusion *De-con* and trauma for the public at large, rather than liberation; or even to strengthen the hegemonic social structures they ostensibly seek to challenge.

I don't think it is coincidental that projects such as Tschumi's pavilions for the Parc de La Villette and Eisenman's Wexner Center both manifest such a profound ambiguity in respect to the role of the "object" in human affairs. Of course they both embody "objecthood" in some sense of the term, and must even be seen to do so quite aggressively. Indeed, it appears to be part of the obligation the authors of these projects have taken on to recast normative social assumptions, to have their buildings assume a quite intrusive role in respect to the consciousness of the observer who happens upon them. Neither La Villette nor the Wexner, as far as I can tell, is intended in any way to be "appropriated in a state of distraction." Rather, they seem to propose a quite declaratory "objective" presence.

Yet it is also a fact that both authors curiously deny many possible "object" qualities their buildings possess. In both cases, for example, a radical continuity of perceptible surface—however diverse material components of the architecture may be—suppresses any strong reading of materiality that might be made; both projects—despite the authors' aggressive psychic assaults on the perception of the observer—render difficult any easy reading of their ultimate spatial limits: La Villette by a strategy of radical dispersion of its components, and the Wexner by a parallel one that obscures the building's actual relationship to its immediate physical context.

In their profound common ambiguity on this point, both Tschumi's and Eisenman's projects seem to me to be more traditionally "modern"—in the old-fashioned sense of the term—than might be supposed. For I would argue that in this ambiguity, they both betray a mistrust of the historic status of the "object," as though the object itself were to be suspected of "hegemonic" ambitions in history. Both projects manifest an implicit allegiance to an older tradition in cultural theory that mistrusted the "things of the world" as manifestations of "reification." This is the term that has been employed in left organicist theory from Marx through Jameson, to encapsulate a characterization of the products of industrial production as alienated and lifeless. In a remarkable way, then, these projects bring to the fore a key aspect of the cultural dilemma of the "things of the world" in our time. For they show, I think, how urgently we yearn for worldliness at the same time that we fundamentally lack confidence in it.

This dilemma may serve as an introduction to the arguments of this text as a whole. For I seek to address a whole range of the predicaments of modernity and its progeny in architecture, as they have surfaced in a series of anguished theoretical debates from 1900 to the present. I have striven also to elucidate the striking tendency of many of these predicaments to come to the surface of architectural controversy more than once—seemingly suggesting that modernity and postmodernity in architecture, as some of the cultural theorists already cited have stated in their own fields, still have some characteristics in common. The architectural debates are presented in considerable detail, yet I attempt also to ground them in a larger context of issues in cultural theory. The relation of specificity of architectural argument to general cultural pertinence, in my view, lends them both their poignance and their broad historical significance.

Earlier I cited Andrew Ross, who has argued for a clear linkage of modernism and postmodernism, notwithstanding the arguments of many of his own generation of critics and theorists. Interestingly enough, in the same text in which he described poststructuralism as "the continuation of modernism by other means," Ross also stated:

> Increasingly . . . the claims of post-structuralism have been placed in a larger context or "condition," of which they have been seen equally as a symptom and as a determining cause. This larger condition—post-modernism—addresses a whole range of material conditions that are no longer consonant with the dominant rationality of modernism and its technological commitment to finding *solutions* in every sphere of social and cultural life.[22]

What particularly interests me is how Ross's schema echoes a statement by the German-American political philosopher Hannah Arendt, made some years before the advent of structuralism, let alone poststructuralism. In her 1958 text *The Human Condition,* Arendt essayed a remarkably comprehensive criticism of what she called the "outstanding characteristics of the modern age." Among them, she said,

> from its beginning to our own time we find the typical attitudes of *homo faber:* his instrumentalization of the world, his confidence in tools and in the productivity of the maker of artificial objects; his trust in the all-comprehensive range of the means-ends category, his conviction that every issue can be solved and every human motivation reduced to the principle of utility; his sovereignty, which regards everything given as material and thinks of the whole of nature as of "an immense fabric from which we can cut out whatever we want to resew it however we like."[23]

MAX
FRISCH

Modernist doubt being as deeply rooted and as broadly shared amongst the intelligentsia of the past half-century as this brief citation has indicated, and architecture being so inescapably "social" an art form, it should perhaps not be surprising that the pervasive "doubt" in question has so radically invaded its own central body of theory and praxis.

For my own part, I propose to look again at the ideas of the controversial political philosopher Arendt. Her reputation has been a complicated one. Even during her lifetime, her work provoked more dissent than commendation. Disavowed by Marxist as well as neo-Marxist intellectuals on account of her very early disaffection with both Soviet communism and its revisionist western European variants, she failed also to satisfy mainstream American academic propriety—both its historical and its sociological variants—on account of her scorn for empiricist methodologies. Last but not least, she eventually also provoked severe criticism from the major groups who spoke for American Jewry on account of her deeply disconcerting account of the 1960 trial of Adolf Eichmann in Jerusalem, and of the fateful relations between European Jews and their oppressors that led to it.[24]

For a decade or so after her death in 1975, Arendt's reputation languished, continuing to be of interest only to a relatively small group, including such close personal colleagues as Mary McCarthy and Hans Jonas; intellectual protégés such as Elizabeth Young-Breuhl and Michael Denneny; and architectural theorists and critics, such as Kenneth Frampton and myself.[25] More recently, however, it has become possible to discern an increasing interest in her life and her work. This revival probably initially became most sharply focused with the 1984 publication of Young-Breuhl's comprehensive biography *Hannah Arendt: For Love of the World* and reached a new threshold with the just-published *Hannah Arendt/Karl Jaspers Correspondence 1926–1969.*[26]

From the early 1980s forward, she has also increasingly served as a source of inspiration to a younger generation of French political philosophers, one example being Claude Lefort.[27] She has also gained stature in the eyes of Heidegger scholars such as Reiner Schurmann and younger political theorists such as Bonnie Honig.[28] Then, too, her thinking appears an increasingly significant source of ideas in respect to the burgeoning new interest in the concept of "civil society," which has arisen out of a worldwide fascination with the various democracy movements in eastern Europe in the late 1980s. In Jean Cohen's and Andrew Arato's recent *Civil Society and Political Theory,* for example, Arendt is ranked with such figures as Jürgen Habermas and Michel Foucault as a seminal contributor to the redefinition of "civil society" in the political theory of our era.[29] Given the central relevance of such a concept to architecture—a topic I shall address in chapter seven—a consideration of Arendt's thinking will also be germane to an appropriate redefinition of the role of architecture in the same period.

My own title *The Space of Appearance* derives from a phrase in Arendt's *The Human Condition.* Something of the title's intended significance may be gleaned from the evocative passage within which it occurred:

> Action and speech create a space between the participants which can find its proper location almost any time and anywhere. It is the space of appearance in the widest sense of the word, namely, the space where I appear to others as others appear to me, where men exist not merely like other living or inanimate things but make their appearance explicitly.[30]

Now this "widest sense of the word" will prove to even the most cursory reader of Arendt rather quickly to encompass architecture. To be sure, it was her view that "the space of appearance" was in the first instance the creation of "action" and of "speech," not of any such phenomenon as architecture. Yet she was well aware at the same time how utterly reliant on "tangibility"—to use her word—the space of appearance is. As she put it,

> The whole factual world of human affairs depends for its reality and its continued existence, first, upon the presence of others who have seen and heard and will remember, and, second, on the transformation of the intangible into the tangibility of things.[31]

And that architecture constitutes an essential component of the tangible "world" was equally evident to her:

> The reality and reliability of the human world rest primarily on the fact that we are surrounded by things more permanent than the activity by which they were produced, and potentially even more permanent than the lives of their authors. Human life, in so far as it is world-building, is engaged in a constant process of reification, and the degree of worldliness of produced things, which all together form the human artifice, depends upon their greater or lesser permanence in the world itself.[32]

regarding ideas as things— materializing

i.e. will need history & context.

In such remarks, Arendt can be seen to be taking up a philosophical position that fundamentally and strategically interrelates the concepts of "reification" and "worldliness"—a position that situates her uniquely within the overall territory of modern and postmodern cultural theory.

Like many of her philosophical peers in the twentieth century, Arendt was profoundly influenced by the nineteenth-century work of Karl Marx. For her, his wide-ranging and revolutionary theory of labor was particularly fundamental. Her own pivotal work in this area is both an homage to and a critique of his pioneering work. In particular, she ascribed to him the "powerful discovery" that

> the laboring activity itself, regardless of historical circumstances . . . possesses indeed a "productivity" of its own, no matter how futile and non-durable its products may be. This productivity does not lie in any of labor's products but in the human "power," whose strength is not exhausted when it has produced the means of its own subsistence and survival but is capable of producing a "surplus," that is, more than is necessary for its own "reproduction."[33]

Yet Arendt demurred at Marx's unquestioning assumptions of an almost self-sufficient connection—one she saw not just Marx but the whole "modern age" as having made—between "productivity" and the "life process."

> When Marx defined labor as "man's metabolism with nature," in whose process "nature's material [is] adapted by a change of form to the wants of man," so that "labor has incorporated itself with its subject," he indicated clearly that he was "speaking physiologically" and that labor and consumption are but two stages of the ever-recurring cycle of biological life.[34]

As Arendt saw it, Marx's assumption of this "incorporation," as a part of his intellectual system, had profoundly problematic consequences for the "worldliness" of "things."

> Within a completely "socialized mankind," whose sole purpose would be the entertaining of the life process—and this is the unfortunately quite unutopian ideal that guides Marx's theories—the distinction between labor and work would have completely disappeared; all work would have become labor because all things would be understood, not in their worldly, objective quality, but as results of living labor power and functions of the life process.[35]

For her, this was a conclusion that was unwarranted in the exclusivity of its emphasis on the "organicism" of the life cycle in human affairs. Not that she questioned the primacy, on its own terms, of "life."[36] The degree of primacy that ought, in modern culture, to be ascribed to the "organic," and to "process," has been a continuing controversy in modern cultural theory, a controversy in which Arendt has herself been a vigorous participant—albeit one who acknowledged her minority position. As the comments just cited indicate, she saw the characteristic disposition to give overriding primacy to an organicist model of the "life process" within human affairs as an intellectual bias shared by the whole Enlightenment tendency from Condorcet to Bentham, out of which Marx himself sprang. Given this, it should hardly be surprising that during the period between Marx's major works and the present, a disposition to ascribe primacy to some "organic" model of the "life process" has been held in common by philosophers, politically speaking, of the right (Herbert Spencer), the center (Lewis Mumford), and the left (Georg Lukács).[37]

Of course, in speaking of Arendt's unique advocacy of "worldliness" in modern cultural theory, we encounter the complex influence on her of her first intellectual mentor: Martin Heidegger. It was from him that she learned her phenomenology, firsthand, as a student in the mid-1920s. And it was the astonishing hybrid of his thinking, blended with that of Augustine, Dante, Machiavelli, and Marx, that she was eventually able to formulate—in the process managing to leave behind his wary skepticism of the world—in favor of a Dantean affirmation of "worldliness." Appropriately enough Young-Breuhl subtitles her biography *For Love of the World.* None of Arendt's philosophical predecessors nor any of her contemporaries has matched the depth of her passionate engagement with "the things of the world." It is this engagement, in my view, that makes her particular twentieth-century phenomenology so distinctive, so personally attractive, and so especially pertinent to architecture. It was her own deep conviction, in this regard, that led her to her almost archaic defense of "the human artifice," and to the role of *homo faber*—that is, of man the maker of things—notwithstanding her sweeping criticism of the "characteristics of the modern age."

> Acting and speaking men need the help of *homo faber* in his highest capacity, that is, the help of the artist, of poets and historiographers, of monument-builders or writers, because without them the only product of their activity, the story they enact and tell, would not survive at all.[38]

To be sure, passionately engaged with the world though she was, Arendt quite readily acknowledged the acute limitations of reification, remarking, for example, that

> reification and materialization, without which no thought can become a tangible thing, is always paid for, and . . . the price is life itself: it is always the "dead letter" in which the "living spirit" must survive, a deadness from which it can be rescued only when the dead letter comes again into contact with a life willing to resurrect it.[39]

If her conclusion has been a sound one, our acutely ambiguous current attitude to the "object" in the modern world might well benefit from a careful reconsideration of it. This would point to the possibility of our once again assuming a stance vis-à-vis the "things of the world" that would acknowledge their "brittle" status (to use Adorno's word), but would not go so far as to fetishize them. Should we assume such a reconsidered stance, then it will also follow that contemporary phenomenologies that seek to underscore the liberatory potential of "subjectivity," and the architectural praxes that follow from them, will need to make their case with caution. For it is difficult, in the light of these particular arguments, not to suppose that "deconstruction," taken as an utterly unmediated methodology vis-à-vis "the things of the world," would lead over time to a condition of radical subjectivity, in which men were indeed freed of the oppression of the "reified world," but at the cost of losing at the same time the reality and reliability that would enable their stories to survive. What is at stake after all is "the whole factual world of human affairs," which, we have already noted, depends both on "the presence of others"—a condition that individual subjectivity cannot meet—as well as on "the transformation of the intangible into the tangibility of things"; that is to say, on architecture among other things.

I shall not pursue this particular argument any further here. Still, it is important to acknowledge how my commentary so far has seemed to ascribe importance, in respect to "the space of appearance," only to the tangibility of things. For Arendt, of course, important as such tangibility was, it nevertheless remained secondary to her primary conviction that "the space of appearance" was created by "action" and by "speech." The latter may seem to be of less significance to architectural debate than her views concerning "the things of the world," but this is not so. A brief consideration of her concepts of "action" and "speech" will show why. For Arendt,

> Human plurality, the basic condition of both action and speech, has the twofold character of equality and distinction. If men were not equal, they could neither understand each other and those who came before them nor plan for the future and foresee the needs of those who will come after them. If men were not distinct, each human being distinguished from any other who is, was, or will ever be, they would need neither speech nor action to make themselves understood.[40]

Moreover, for her, "speech and action reveal this unique distinctness. . . . In acting and speaking, men show who they are, reveal actively their unique personal identities and thus make their appearance in the human world."[41] And these views led her in turn to her almost uniquely optimistic view of the human possibilities arising out of "action."[42] This engagement of hers is unreservedly manifest in the passage quoted as the epigraph to this introduction:

PLURALITY.
c.f. Schorske's
work on
Vienna

> This revelatory quality of speech and action comes to the fore where people are
> *with* others and neither for nor against them—that is, in sheer human togetherness.
> . . . Because of its inherent tendency to disclose the agent together with the act,
> action needs for its full appearance the shining brightness we once called glory,
> and which is possible only in the public realm.[43]

This passage is significant for my own emerging *parti pris* in three distinct respects. First, it powerfully reevokes the image of Arendt herself, in her role as mentor to her graduate students in political theory at the University of Chicago in the sixties; students who enthusiastically went on to put her lessons to work in all the varied and often unexpected modes of "action" that have typified cultural and political activity in the intervening years. These modes have stretched from the citizen activism and grass roots campaigns following 1968 through such unexpected events as the newly militant campaigns for ethnic minority and gay liberation, as well as a whole series of highly creative and intellectually rigorous reinterpretations of American popular culture.[44] In retrospect, it seems to me that it has been Arendt's provocative linkage of the political concept of "action" to so many varied modes of liberatory praxis in our era that makes the overall body of ideas she formulated in the late fifties and sixties so relevant to current concerns. What is more, this relevance appears likely in many ways to exceed that of the often quite parallel theoretical positions of Arendt's contemporary Adorno, given the rather Olympian bleakness of his personal temperament as contrasted with her decisively engaged one. Then too, it also links her, in a surprising fashion, with certain of the more affirmative modalities of poststructuralism itself.

Finally, there is her astonishing reference to the "shining brightness that we once called glory," which reminds us that "action" turns out to depend for its "full appearance" on the existence of a "public realm." Thus the perhaps unexpected relationship of "action" to architecture can be seen to become apparent, after all. As she put it,

> the reality of the public realm relies on the simultaneous presence of innumerable
> perspectives and aspects in which the common world presents itself and for which
> no common measurement or denominator can ever be devised. For though the
> common world is the common meeting ground of all, those who are present have
> different locations in it, and the location of one can no more coincide with the
> location of another than the location of two objects. Being seen and heard by

[margin handwritten note:] if a tree falls & no one hears it, it hasn't fallen... a public is necessary for recognition of action

others derive their significance from the fact that everybody sees and hears from a different position. . . . Only where things can be seen by many in a variety of aspects without changing their identity, so that those who are gathered around them know they see sameness in utter diversity, can worldly reality truly and reliably appear.[45]

Life as a Work of Art

While you can tell stories or write poems about life, you cannot make life poetic, live it as though it were a work of art.

Hannah Arendt, 1968

In 1900, the Viennese architect Adolf Loos published a thought-provoking fable, "The Story of a Poor Rich Man," in which a powerful and successful entrepreneur one day decided he wished to bring "Art" into his home.

> Whatever he started, he carried out energetically, so he went to a famous architect and proposed: "Bring me Art, let Art enter my four walls. Expense no object."

Wasting no time, the architect prepared and executed an elaborate proposal that transformed the rich man's house, and brought Art to every corner of his life there.

> Nothing, absolutely nothing had been omitted by the architect. Ashtrays, cutlery, light-switches, everything was designed by him. But they were not just the ordinary products of the architect's art, oh no, each ornament, each shape, each nail expressed the individuality of the owner (a psychological feat of great difficulty, as everybody will acknowledge).

> The rich man was exultant. Where ever he looked there was Art, Art in each and everything.

Moreover, "he was praised, he was envied: his rooms were illustrated, described and explained as models of their kind." Yet living in the house eventually became strained, the effort required to sustain the artistic coherence of the whole ensemble too taxing. "Once you held an object in your hand, there was no end to guessing and looking for its proper place, and sometimes the architect had to unroll his working drawings to rediscover the place for a match-box." Nevertheless, the rich man persevered, and "the celebrated art critics were full of praise for the man who had opened up a new field with his 'art in everyday use.'"[1]

As Loos had his fable unfold, the architect paid a visit to the house on the occasion of his client's birthday. The rich man proposed to consult him on how best to arrange the *objets d'art* he had been given. But before he was able to launch this discussion, the architect protested at the slippers he was wearing. The client pointed out they were slippers the architect himself had designed. But the architect insisted that they were meant to be worn only in the bedroom. His indignation rising, the architect then protested at the fact that the rich man had accepted any gifts at all, arguing that everything had been already taken care of. At this, a crisis was precipitated. Loos tells us: "A change took place in the rich man. He suddenly

1.1 Examples of cutlery designed by Josef Olbrich, from the period of Loos's critique of the cultural production of the Vienna Secession.

felt profoundly unhappy." The fable ends with the rich man's sad conclusion: "Now I have to learn to live with my own corpse. Yes, I am finished. I am complete."[2]

"The Story of a Poor Rich Man" has not loomed large in theoretical discussions about architecture since the time of its publication. Its influence has been slight by comparison with Loos's much more famous essay "Ornament and Crime," published in 1908, in which he argued that ornament, as such, constituted certain evidence of the primitiveness of a culture, and called for a stripping away of ornament from the artifacts of modern life as a necessary component of historical progress toward a higher level of civilization.[3] So great was the influence of this essay on a younger generation of architects and historians in Europe that for half a century the modern movement's leading polemicists continued to cite it as a key historical document.

More recently, the influence of "Ornament and Crime" has been in decline. But this does not seem to have resulted in any major reassessment of the potential theoretical import for our time of "The Story of a Poor Rich Man." The only contemporary text with which I am familiar that explicitly treats Loos's cautions as though they continued to be pertinent is Theodor Adorno's "Functionalism Today" of 1965.[4] For the most part, Loos's fateful warning tends to be regarded as a closed issue, having specifically to do with a historic European debate of the turn of the century.

Yet a clear pattern of subsequent episodes suggests strongly to me that this is an inappropriate reading. Indeed, it is my sense that the specter of "life as a work of art" continues to haunt architecture today, perhaps as much as it did in 1900. I am inclined, in fact, to speculate that the conception is really a fundamental one, perhaps only evident from time to time, but always lying hidden within the body of ideas and assumptions we commonly associate with modernity. Given that, it seems to me that a lucid grasp of the circumstances that provoked Loos to write "The Story of a Poor Rich Man" may well clarify for us the nature of that conception, and of its potentials and limitations.

In the first instance, Loos's fable is an attack on the Vienna Secession, the group of painters, architects, and designers that at the time played a prominent role in cultural debate in Vienna. Most of all, Loos's hostility can be see to be directed at J. M. Olbrich, leading Secessionist and (professionally speaking) Loos's key rival. In a text praising the forms of contemporary English design, Loos commended "cutlery for people who can eat, after the English fashion, and who cannot eat from designs by Olbrich." Beyond Olbrich, the critique extends to a more celebrated contemporary, Henry Van de Velde, the Belgian designer of furniture and applied art. "I tell

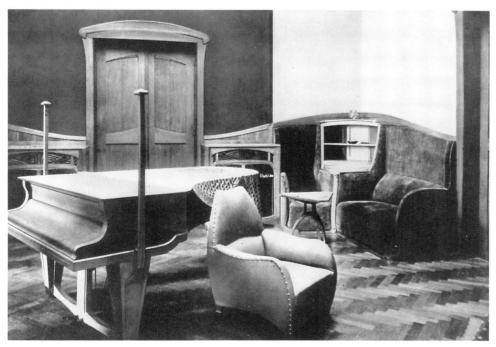

1.2   The comprehensively designed interior of a music room by Henry Van de Velde, also roughly contemporary with Loos's controversial critique. Note how the design integrates such typically architectural elements as wall moldings and wainscotting, together with both built-in and loose furniture.

you," Loos insisted, "the time will come, when the furnishings of a prison cell by Professor Van de Velde will be considered aggravation of the sentence."[5] And beyond that again, Loos's critique must be seen to extend even to the work of such admired architects of the turn of the century as the Belgian Victor Horta and the Scot Charles Rennie Mackintosh.

In short, Loos's critique challenged the entire corpus of work of the most significant group of innovative designers in Europe at that time. What is more, it did so in a fashion that can be seen to bring into focus the typical characteristics of the cultural conception known as the *Gesamtkunstwerk,* the total art work, as it was becoming manifest in architecture at that time.

The conception of the *Gesamtkunstwerk,* as it developed toward the end of the nineteenth century, is most familiar not in architecture but in the performing arts. Early productions of Wagner's operas were intended as hybrids of music, poetry, and drama, which would comprise a new, superior, and synthetic art form. Performances of new musical works by Scriabin were accompanied by dramatic odors pumped into the concert halls, so as to maximize the synaesthetic impact upon the audience. But by 1900, the characteristics of the *Gesamtkunstwerk* were clearly manifest in avant-garde architecture and applied arts as well. Following the argument of Loos's fable, we may outline those characteristics as follows:

Closed unity of conception
In Loos's words, "absolutely nothing was omitted by the architect." From the largest scale (the general configuration of the interior) to the smallest (ashtrays, cutlery), "everything was designed by him." This is the inclusive dimension of the unity of the *Gesamtkunstwerk.* As for the birthday gifts received, there "is no room for anything else." Conceptually speaking, the house is complete without them. From the architect's point of view, their insertion into it can only compromise that unity.

Uniqueness
Not only is the conception of the house complete, but it is unique. As Loos emphasizes, "they were not just the ordinary products of the archi-

1.3 A drawing of an interior alcove for a house by Josef Olbrich, showing the complete erosion of any boundary between architecture and furniture. Even the lighting fixtures have become part of the *Gesamtkunstwerk*.

tect's art, each ornament, each shape, each nail expressed the individuality of the owner." In effect, the unity of the conception requires that every element of the design (even technological ones such as light switches) must be uniquely custom-designed for the particular project, in order that the expression of the owner's individuality can be assured.

Assertiveness

Not only must the house's conceptual unity be complete and unique; it must be apparent that it is. According to Loos, upon completion of his house, the rich man "touched Art wherever he gripped a door handle, he sat on Art whenever he settled down in a chair . . . he indulged in Art with immense fervor."

In his own works, and in his writing, Loos advocated a quite different approach to architecture. Its characteristics were these:

Open unity of conception

By contrast with the contemporary works of the designers of the Secession, or of Van de Velde, Horta, or Mackintosh, Loos's works did not

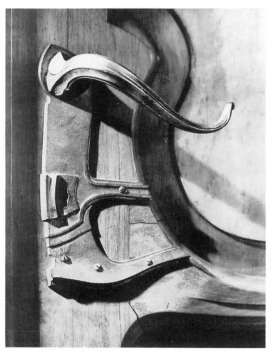

1.4   A detail of a door handle in the Solvay House in Brussels, designed by Victor Horta and built from 1895 to 1900.

1.5 A typical residential interior designed by Adolf Loos from the same period: the dining room of the Leopold Langer house, from 1901. (Graphische Sammlung Albertina, Vienna.)

require comprehensive design control by the architect. They were meant to accommodate a more heterogeneous combination of furniture and objects, without their conceptual unity thereby being called into question. Right down to the beginning of our century, argued Loos, "one bought furniture from the cabinet-maker, wallpapers from the upholsterer, light-fittings from the metal worker, etc. But then they did not match? Maybe. But no one was guided by such consideration."[6]

Typicality

As opposed to uniqueness, Loos cultivated typicality in his work. If it was in certain formal respects radical, it was in that respect only meant to be regarded as prototypical. He eschewed any effort to devise a unique character for each individual project designed. As for "the individuality of the owner," it was left to the owner to establish that—afterward—for himself.

which is not ∴ inherently anti-ornamental, but rather anti control.

Life as a Work of Art   **35**

1.6   A famous photograph of the interior of the Museum Cafe of Adolf Loos from 1899. Note the canonical employment of the bentwood chairs of Thonet. (Graphische Sammlung Albertina, Vienna.)

Moreover, to the extent that he assumed responsibility for detailed design, Loos endeavored to make use of precisely those "ordinary products" that the creator of the *Gesamtkunstwerk* would eschew. Thus he employed standard light fittings, hardware, and furniture, in situations where the Secession architects would have rejected or, failing that, have camouflaged them. His admiration for and recurring employment of the standard English leather club chair and the bentwood cafe furniture mass-produced by Thonet established such a clear precedent that both of these "ordinary products" became *objet-types* in the subsequent, fully developed vocabulary of the modern architectural interior.

Matter-of-factness

Rather than assertiveness, Loos ought to provide restrained backdrops for the activities his buildings were meant to accommodate. He used his "ordinary products" straightforwardly and matter-of-factly. His analogy here was with clothing. "When," he asked, "is a man dressed fashionably? When he is least noticed."[7]

Despite the force and clarity of Loos's critique of the *Gesamtkunstwerk,* the direction of design activity among his peers in Europe was not suddenly altered in its wake. Not until a decade and a half had passed did leading designers and polemicists espouse positions that were explicitly acknowledged to have been influenced by Loos. And that turn of events only occurred at a point when the leadership of the movement had begun to pass from Loos's generation to a younger one. In 1900, virtually the whole of the movement—Olbrich and Hoffmann in Austria, Behrens in Germany, Horta and Van de Velde in Belgium, and Mackintosh in Scotland—was still too committed to the conception of life as a work of art to be readily deflected.

Evidently, that commitment was a profoundly rooted one. Some measure of its depth and power may be seen in a characterization of Behrens, whom as late as 1908 critic Robert Breuer called "a forerunner of future religion of form, a man who knows how to grasp the sacred desire of our day, in the pathos of his lines and in the radiant tensions of his spaces."[8] In short, Loos faced what Adorno aptly characterized as the "religion" of the applied arts, which typified the European avant-garde of the turn of the century. Not all the members of the Secession, or of Jugendstil or of art nouveau, were equally explicit in their avowals, but all of them derived psychological strength and moral authority from the quasi-religious basis of their activity. It was this that imbued the devotees of the *Gesamtkunstwerk* with such "immense fervor," as Loos put it, and, for a time at least, legitimated its problematic characteristics.

ANTI
PLURALITY

For instance, the exclusive character of its conceptual unity was assumed to be morally necessary. The inclusion of incompatible elements in a total art ensemble was thought liable to sully the moral purity of the whole. Van de Velde, for instance, has told how his wife and he "felt duty bound to shield our children from the sight of ugly things by banishing anything liable to pervert a child's visual sensibility before they were born."[9] As for the uniqueness of the total art work, it was taken to be necessary if the work was to serve adequately to manifest the individuality of its possessor's personality. "With Van de Velde," according to Walter Benjamin, "there appeared the house as expression of the personality. Ornament was to such a house what the signature is to a painting."[10] Van de Velde himself called on the individual to "assert the consciousness of having an aesthetic conscience of his own, and bring some spontaneous echo of his inner being, some genuinely individual contribution to the furnishing of his own home."[11]

Between Benjamin's and Van de Velde's statements, the reader may discern some ambiguity as to whose "personality" is being expressed here, the possessor's or the designer's—unless, of course, they happened to be one and the same. But Van de Velde himself anticipated this question, expressing the concern he felt, very early in his career, about accepting a commission to design furniture to be sold anonymously in Paris:

> The very few pieces I had previously designed were for people I knew personally and could refer to at need, whose rooms were familiar to me. It was only slowly, and with aversion that I could reconcile myself to what was for me the unnatural handicap of having to design for the unknown homes of unknown persons.[12]

And it is a historical fact that the few masterpieces of art nouveau were almost all designed in circumstances of intimate rapport between designer and possessor.

Following these potent legitimations of exclusiveness and uniqueness, any vindication of the *Gesamtkunstwerk*'s assertiveness may seem redundant, merely a corollary of its highly didactic and demonstrative character. It is almost self-evident that as a creation of a "world-priest of beauty" (Breuer describing Behrens), a *Gesamtkunstwerk* would necessarily command extraordinary attentiveness on the part of society at large.

Viewed in the broadest sense, this effort of a whole generation of designers to configure life as a work of art constituted a quasi-religious mission to reform contemporary European society, which was seen as preoccupied with base and meretricious pursuits. Indeed, the whole generation is situated, historically speaking, in the center of the complex web of cultural movements commonly associated with aestheticism, or "art for art's sake," and with its intense nostalgia for the "aura," to use Walter Benjamin's word, that religious art had once had.

Indeed, so fervent was the turn-of-the-century resacralization that it even precipitated a discernible backlash within aestheticism itself. Bernard Shaw in *Candida* and Oscar Wilde in *The Importance of Being Earnest* both depicted the aestheticist revolt against society (in its various manifestations) to be as pompous as the society itself was meretricious. But notwithstanding internal differences, these various strands of late nineteenth-century cultural criticism are held together by a common opposition to the perceived philistinism of bourgeois society. Whatever their own differences, moralists such as Van de Velde, aesthetes such as Walter Pater, humorists such as Wilde, and even dandies such as Aubrey Beardsley can all be seen to have been late assentors to William Morris's apocalyptic speculation of 1874: "Perhaps the gods are preparing troubles and terrors for the world . . . again, that it may become beautiful and dramatic withal: for I do not believe that they will have it dull and ugly forever."[13]

Key representatives of the turn-of-the-century generation paid explicit homage to Morris. Van de Velde, for instance, expressed "the profound admiration [he] felt for Morris's magnificent designs and his notable faith in the advent of a free communal society."[14] But even as they were evident in the grand gestures of 1900, the ambitions of the generations of the Secession and of the Jugendstil to establish a new society had already become defensive. Commenting on the obsession of art nouveau with the new technique of iron construction, Benjamin observed that "through ornament, it strove to win back these forms for Art."[15] Following that, more defensive still, it found itself settling merely for a rescue of "Art" from bourgeois commercialization, for the cessation of "easel pictures" and "salon statuary" (in Van de Velde's words) "being executed . . . without the least regard to their eventual destination, like any other kind of consumer goods."[16] Ultimately, it is both historically and conceptually true for art nouveau that "the interior was the place of refuge of art."[17]

In the years immediately following 1900, the "immense fervor" of the turn-of-the-century generation did not forthwith abate, nor did the implicit commitment to a loftier configuration of life begin to falter. Yet it is as though some tentative realization, as Arendt would put it, that "life is

1.7 A view of the house at the Darmstadt Artists' Colony that Peter Behrens designed and built for himself in 1900, while he was still in what might be called his Jugendstil period. (Photograph by permission, from Leonardo Benevolo, *History of Modern Architecture*, MIT Press.)

neither essence nor elixir, and if you treat it as such it will only play its tricks on you,"[18] began to influence designers at that time. They tended to admit to a change of direction, but ascribed it to other influences. The biographer of Olbrich, Robert Clark, noting how "leading *Jugendstil* designers . . . seemed to feel that they had burned their fingers," suggests that they blamed it on "something too international or too undisciplined."[19] Peter Behrens, for one, began in his work after 1900 more and more deliberately to emulate the calm and serene character of the works of the German neoclassicist architect Karl Friedrich Schinkel. Olbrich, too, moved toward a more neoclassicist vocabulary of form.[20]

But of course this shift, although explained stylistically, also had the covert effect, conceptually speaking, of abandoning one of the constituent characteristics of the *Gesamtkunstwerk:* assertiveness. The neoclassical vocabulary of form is characteristically a restrained one. And whether influenced specifically by neoclassicism or not, most of the designers whose work has been under discussion in the years following 1900 modified their formal vocabularies in favor of greater restraint.

Following that, even the commitment to the exclusive character of the conceptual unity of the *Gesamtkunstwerk* began to dissolve. In 1907, for example, Peter Behrens was appointed artistic consultant to the large electric firm the AEG, shifting his professional attention even further away from the single private houses and interiors with which he had been involved, and toward what would now be called the "industrial design" of electrical appliances for mass production and the design of a series of large

1.8 A view of the well-known Exhibition Pavilion for the AEG, designed by Peter Behrens for the German Shipbuilding Exhibition in Berlin in 1908, after his turn to neoclassicism. (Photograph by permission, from Leonardo Benevolo, *History of Modern Architecture*, MIT Press.)

1.9 Examples of the industrially designed products for the AEG that marked Behrens's further turning away from the sensibility of the Jugendstil. (Photograph by permission, from Tilmann Buddensieg, *Industriekultur*, MIT Press.)

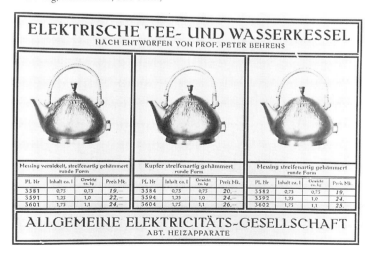

ELEKTRISCHE TEE- UND WASSERKESSEL
NACH ENTWÜRFEN VON PROF. PETER BEHRENS

Messing vernickelt, streifenartig gehämmert runde Form				Kupfer streifenartig gehämmert runde Form				Messing streifenartig gehämmert runde Form			
PL.Nr	Inhalt ca. l	Gewicht ca. kg	Preis Mk.	PL.Nr	Inhalt ca. l	Gewicht ca. kg	Preis Mk.	PL.Nr	Inhalt ca. l	Gewicht ca. kg	Preis Mk.
3581	0,75	0,75	19.—	3584	0,75	0,75	20.—	3582	0,75	0,75	19.
3591	1,25	1,0	22.—	3594	1,25	1,0	24.—	3592	1,25	1,0	24.
3601	1,75	1,1	24.—	3604	1,75	1,1	26.—	3602	1,75	1,1	25.

ALLGEMEINE ELEKTRICITÄTS-GESELLSCHAFT
ABT. HEIZAPPARATE

1.10 A relatively unfamiliar interior view of the famous Fagus Shoe Last Works, designed by Walter Gropius and Adolf Meyer and erected between 1911 and 1914.

industrial buildings to house those production processes.[21] By their very nature, these activities generated a more open and inclusive character in Behrens's works. In light of his continuing commitment to a loftier configuration of life, this change was described by Behrens's admirers as an attempt to "elevate technique into culture."[22]

There followed a major program of activity in the design of new industrial products and buildings. In 1911, Walter Gropius, who together with Le Corbusier and Ludwig Mies van der Rohe had been working in Behrens's office, erected the first major building of any of this trio who twenty years later would constitute the international leadership of the modern movement proper. This building was a factory building, the Fagus Shoe Last Works at Alfeld an der Leine.[23] Moreover, it was not only a building that housed an industrial process (like Behrens's work); it took a form that represented the industrialized character of its own fabrication. And this interest in industrial artifacts began to take on a historical dimension. In 1913, Gropius went so far as to publish—with guarded praises—illustrations of such vernacular industrial structures as North American grain elevators, notwithstanding the fact that these structures had been created utterly without intent to "elevate technique into culture."

This shift, in its turn, also called into question the last of the characteristics of the *Gesamtkunstwerk*, its uniqueness. The new interest in industrial products and industrial buildings necessarily limited the uniqueness of each individual design. Already in 1907, Behrens's foremost advocate, the critic and government advisor Hermann Muthesius, had launched the Deutscher Werkbund, an association of artists and designers that included most of the figures whose work has been discussed above. As early as that, Muthesius had felt able to describe the aim of the Werkbund to be "to ennoble craftsmanship, selecting the best representatives of arts, industry, crafts and trades, combining all existing efforts towards quality in industrial work."[24] In 1914, this tendency toward industrialization had moved to such a point as to precipitate a crisis amongst the members of the Werkbund, which by this time included Behrens and Gropius in addition to such senior figures as Muthesius and Van de Velde. The crisis in question has been seen, by almost all the earliest important histories of modern architecture, to have had a pivotal influence. During the annual congress of the Werkbund, Muthesius decisively and unequivocally rejected the ideas of the turn-of-the-century generation:

> Architecture and the entire sphere of activity of the *Werkbund* tend towards standardization. It is only by standardization that they can recover that universal importance which they possessed in ages of harmonious civilization. Only by standardization . . . as a salutary concentration of forces, can a generally accepted and reliable taste be introduced.[25]

With this statement, Muthesius closed the circle, conceptually speaking, begun in Loos's polemic of a decade and a half previously. Though the commitment to "elevate technique into culture" is still evident even here, Muthesius's abandonment of the *Gesamtkunstwerk* provoked Van de Velde's

1.11   A canonical view of the interior of Le Corbusier's 1925 Pavillon de l'Esprit Nouveau. Note the astonishing assurance with which Le Corbusier, at this pivotal moment in his career, has succeeded in condensing many of the emergent themes of modernity into a single, utterly potent ensemble.

equally famous rejoinder: "As long as there are artists in the *Werkbund* . . . they will protest against any proposed canon."[26] By 1914, the long evolution of thinking since 1900 had had its decisive effects, and Van de Velde's objection was seen in large measure as the last gasp of a generation whose ideas had been definitely abandoned; Muthesius was seen, by and large, to have been convincing in his call for a new matter-of-factness in architecture and design.[27]

I have noted already how current theory and criticism tend to treat the *Gesamtkunstwerk* as a distinctive historical phenomenon of its time, but not as more than that. How curious then to note its strange and insistent recurrence in architectural production in the years between Loos's daring commentary and the present. Even within the post-*Gesamtkunstwerk* era now commonly known as the "heroic period" of modern architecture, it is possible to trace a remarkable historical trajectory, and a significant bifurcation of sensibilities, that already evoke the Loosian dilemma anew.

In 1925 Le Corbusier announced to the world the creation of his Pavillon de l'Esprit Nouveau, which was to become one of the half-dozen most influential designs in the whole of modern architecture. Conceived as a definitive manifestation of what Le Corbusier called the New Spirit in design, the pavilion and its furnishings also show strong influence of the ideas of Adolf Loos. In order to convey an image of modern existence that was both profound and matter-of-fact at the same time, Le Corbusier had juxtaposed against the architectural setting he had created a carefully selected group of everyday objects, together with paintings by Fernand Léger, Juan Gris, and himself, as well as a sculpture by Jacques Lipchitz. Adroitly, Le Corbusier sought to elevate these everyday objects into culture, by their juxtaposition with the paintings, and simultaneously to situate the paintings in the everyday world, by their juxtaposition with the "ordinary" objects. Significantly, the paintings were not of "cultural" subjects but were culturally transformed representations of everyday objects and machinery. Conversely, the everyday objects selected included two key ones associated with the repertoire already established by Loos: the English leather club chair, and the molded wood dining chair by Thonet. In its careful cultural cross references, the interior of the Esprit Nouveau pavilion constituted—and still constitutes for us today—a definitive representation of cultural modernism, as it stood in 1925.

In 1927, Le Corbusier completed another of his major works of the period, the villa at Garches. Large and spatially complex, the Garches interior had cultural ambitions that went beyond those of the 1925 pavilion. Indeed, the canonic photographs of the interiors show them empty, save for a few strategically located pieces of *objet-type* furniture, as well as another sculpture of Lipchitz. Another series of photographs, however, taken by the visiting English photographer F. R. Yerbury, show the Garches interior as it looked shortly after its construction, when it was shared by the notable expatriate American family the Steins and Mme Gabrielle de Monzie; and these photographs enable us to press our conception of the cultural space of modernism as its existed in the late 1920s one key stage further. Famous for their art collection, including extensive examples of the work of Picasso and Matisse, the Steins moved into Garches a large collection of paintings, furniture, and other artifacts. Like Loos's clients of a quarter century before, the Steins furnished their domestic interior themselves. It cannot be said that the Garches interior as depicted by Yerbury projects the powerful image of cultural coherence and promise represented by the Esprit Nouveau pavilion. Still, it is interesting to note—even in this vernacular experiment in the creation of cultural ensembles—the degree of dialectical tension between housed object and setting. Unlikely though some of the Stein pieces of furniture are, it cannot

1.12   Another canonical view, this one of the interior of the main living space of the villa at Garches, as published in volume 1 of Le Corbusier's *Oeuvre complète*.

1.13   A noncanonical photograph taken by the English photographer Frank Yerbury, showing the same space shown in the previous figure, as actually inhabited by the Stein family and Mme de Monzie. (Photograph © Architectural Association, London.)

be said that they destroy the integrity of the architectural interior, or that they lacked cultural significance in their own right.[28]

By 1929, Le Corbusier, in association with Charlotte Perriand, had designed a range of furniture. Thus we find the iconic image of the modern architectural interior somewhat modified, as it was expressed by Le Corbusier in the set of interiors he designed for the Salon d'Automne of that year. Here were included the now celebrated series of leather and chrome chairs, as well as the famous chaise longue and a stool and table. Influenced by the *objets-type* of Loos, these pieces nevertheless had a more assertive, more sumptuous and more technological aura, supercharging the tone of matter-of-factness typical of the earlier Loosian quotations. Still, even these pieces were juxtaposed with a set of everyday objects, including typewriters and restaurant glassware as well as office accessories. Viewed generally, the Salon d'Automne interior conveyed a heightened sense of glamour without departing from the generally open unity of conception characteristic of the previous examples.

1.14 A 1929 illustration showing the range of furniture designed by Le Corbusier in collaboration with Charlotte Perriand. The image definitively portrays the delicate balance between luxury and openness of concept that characterized Le Corbusier's work at this time. (Fondation Le Corbusier, Paris.)

In 1930, two profoundly significant new architectural interiors were created that close the terms of the theoretical discussion of the cultural space of modernism for over half a century. These are the Maison de Verre in Paris, by Pierre Chareau and Bernard Bijvoet, and the Tugendhat house in Brno, Czechoslovakia, by Ludwig Mies van der Rohe. Both interiors grew relatively directly out of the evolution of design attitudes through the late 1920s that I have just traced. The Maison de Verre, for example, juxtaposed paintings and tapestries with industrial iconography in a manner reminiscent of the Esprit Nouveau pavilion. It incorporated antiques in a manner reminiscent of Garches. As for the Tugendhat house, it too was used as a setting for furniture (Mies van der Rohe, like Le Corbusier, had by this time entered into the design of furniture, in association with Lily Reich), as well as for certain experiments with materials and finishes that Mies had deployed in his project the previous year for the German pavilion at the 1929 world's fair in Barcelona.

But these interiors also mark a startling change in the evolution and diversification of ideas that we have traced so far. In the case of the Maison de Verre, for example, two key shifts can be discerned from the strategy we already know from the Esprit Nouveau pavilion. First, the ubiquitous

1.15   A view of the main living area of the Maison de Verre designed by Pierre Chareau and Bernard Bijvoet for the Dalsace family.

1.16 An exactly contemporary view of the main living area of the Tugendhat house, designed by Mies van der Rohe. (Museum of Modern Art, New York.)

everyday *objet-type* was deleted from the ensemble. In its stead, modernity was represented in a precocious array of technological virtuosities: Pirelli rubber tile flooring, glass block, manifold uses of innovative metal screens, and electrical apparatus. Second, the array of visible motifs was multiplied, layer upon layer, in a giddy collage of cross-cultural references: paintings of Lurçat, antique furniture already belonging to the clients, new furniture designed by Chareau and upholstered by Lurçat, a grand piano, as well as archaeological artifacts from the classical world. In short, the interior of the Maison de Verre took the modernist, Loosian open unity of conception to the very limit of its possibility. In its sheer heterogeneous virtuosity, and in the nonchalance of its spatial composition, it established—and in my view still sustains today—the possibility of future life, in an exhilarating cultural milieu at the edge of but still within the territory of modernism, as it might be conceived within a frame of reference deriving from the ideas of Loos.

THESIS –
plurality,
acceptance
of old & new

In the case of the last example of this series, this barely perceptible conceptual boundary must be seen to have been crossed. To be sure, the Tugendhat interior, like that of the Maison de Verre, can be seen in a quite broad formal and material sense to have moved onward from its predecessors of the late twenties. Like Chareau, Mies also here eschewed the ordinary *objet-type* as an element of the visual array of the interior. But unlike Chareau, Mies declined to significantly expand the range of cross references made by the elements of the interior. It is true, of course, that traces of the neoclassic can be read in his chairs and stools, and this is consistent with the interest he shared with Behrens and his contemporaries in the early nineteenth-century designs of Schinkel; but Mies's formal strategy in the Tugendhat interior was primarily one of reduction to essentials. Then too, if Chareau moved away from ordinariness in the direction of a certain luxuriousness, Mies must be seen to have moved much farther in this same direction. Instead of the bentwood and leather of the Esprit Nouveau pavilion, we now confront onyx, macassar paneling, and shimmering chrome. The disposition of elements has also changed. In the place of the casual composition of the Esprit Nouveau pavilion, or the nonchalant one of the Maison de Verre, we see at the Tugendhat house a highly controlled geometrical order. As often as not, the furniture was even drawn on the plan.

As a result of these subtle but strategic shifts in the vocabulary of modernism from the twenties, Mies accomplished an astonishing historical reversion, reconstituting, as it were, a new *Gesamtkunstwerk*. To be sure, the specific material and formal vocabulary of the Secession was left behind. Yet the repertoire of objects that we have come in this argument to associate with the Loos/Le Corbusier axis were here fundamentally changed. In a final closing of the circle from 1900, Mies re-presented us, inside the

1.17 A view of a typical reception corridor on the executive floor of the CBS Building in New York, designed by Eero Saarinen and Florence Knoll.

body of modern architecture as it had hitherto begun to be understood, with what we must now see as a renewed conception of life as a work of art.

To the best of my knowledge, no one in the thirties identified the Tugendhat house as such a phenomenon, nor am I aware of any commentary in the six intervening decades that has taken up this issue in a consequential way. Indeed, in the period of the dissemination of the supposed canonical ideas of modernism that stretched from the thirties through to the fifties, one can say that the conception played not even an implicit role. Only with the advent of the various revisionist modernisms of the late fifties and early sixties did this begin to change. At that time, public concern over what had come to be known, following the terminology of Walter Gropius, as "total design" dramatically and unexpectedly resurfaced. Perhaps the most notable instance was the controversy concerning Eero Saarinen's CBS Building in New York, in which the building's "total design" was attacked as a totalitarian imposition on the everyday lives of the CBS employees who inhabited it. In the April 1966 issue of *Life* magazine appeared an account of the occupants' attitude to the design of this building.[29] The "total design" extended from the architectural form of the building as a whole, designed by Eero Saarinen, through to the details of all furniture, fittings, and works of art, all designed, selected, or approved by Florence Knoll. The CBS staff were reported to appreciate its "uncluttered" appearance and "sensuous" fittings, yet an "underground of dissent" had reached the point where disgruntled employees began to plot furtive rearrangements of the various *objets d'art,* in order to test the alertness of the maintenance crew (called the Gestapo) whose task it was to patrol the offices and to ensure that each element of the Knoll interior was in its proper place (unrolling their sets of drawings, like Loos's architect, if need be, to make absolutely certain of the proper order). Astonishingly enough, none of the protagonists of such impassioned debates in the late sixties cited Loos's essay as a historical precedent. Perhaps this lack of any historical sense on their part should be seen as symptomatic, for the movement to which they belonged soon lost its momentum (as I indicate in chapter seven).

In the decade that followed their loss of influence, one might also have expected certain of the more theoretically minded of the formalist generation of designers, who subsequently came to the fore, to have paid some heed to the historical cautions of Loos. By the end of the seventies, for example, leading architects in Europe and in North America were enthusiastically participating in a revival of precisely the sort of *Kunstgewerbe* that had precipitated Loos's original dismay in 1900. Perhaps the most striking instance of this revival was the early 1980s work of Michael Graves, the American architect who came to great public prominence during those years. Having begun as a post-Corbusian member of the so-called New York Five, Graves began to move increasingly rapidly in the later seventies in a much more historically allusive direction. Then with quite startling suddenness, as he expanded his practice into the fields of furniture, fabric, and interior design, Graves began to exhibit an intense fascination with the turn-of-the-century work of the Viennese architect and designer Josef Hoffmann, one of the central members of the Vienna Secession that Loos's critique was directed against. Not only did Graves begin to emulate the scope of Hoffmann's design practice, he even began to reprise the formal motifs characteristic of Hoffmann's work at every scale, from tea services and table lamps right up to large-scale institutional buildings. In his Humana Headquarters Building in Louisville Kentucky of 1982, for example, Graves even employed Hoffmann fabrics as part of the corporate decor. And in his Sunar Hauserman furniture showrooms, in his own home in

1.18 A tea service designed by Josef Hoffmann in 1904.

1.19 A tea service designed by Michael Graves in 1982.

Princeton, and in his Diane von Furstenberg boutique (all of the period 1982–1986), Graves virtually reinvented the complete Hoffmannesque *Gesamtkunstwerk* in quintessential eighties terms.[30]

To be sure, in works of a later period Graves has moved away from the decorative intensity of his mid-eighties period, in the direction of a sobriety closer to that of the Italian rationalist architect Aldo Rossi. Still, it remains symptomatically intriguing that an architect of Graves's extraordinary formal inventiveness could have had his characteristic design vocabulary so colonized by a figure from history, albeit one as potent as Hoffmann. Some startling residual power must have survived in the idea of the *Gesamtkunstwerk* of 1900, with which Graves's personal sensibility happened to intersect in the revivalisms of half a century later.

And even this is not the most astonishing evidence of the enduring lure of the total art work. For it is possible also to discern evidence of it in the characteristic production of some young designers who see themselves as resolutely opposed to most of the tendencies associated with Michael Graves. Even the younger generation oriented so decisively to an architec-

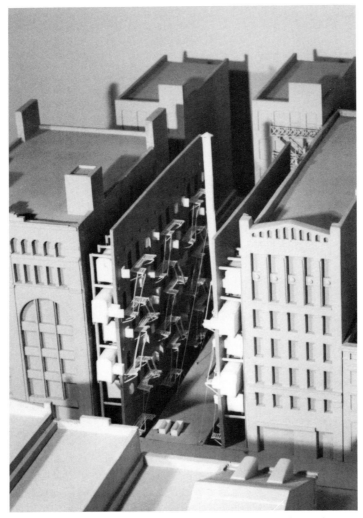

1.20   A view of Thomas Silva's student project from Cooper Union for a Men's Shelter on the Bowery, occupying a vacant lot in lower Manhattan. (Irwin S. Chanin School of Architecture Archive, The Cooper Union.)

ture of critique seems not entirely able to resist the tendency to radically fetishize the objects of its own creation. As an example, consider a provocative and highly declamatory student project from Cooper Union by Thomas Silva, a talented young designer who went on to win a Rome Prize in Architecture. Addressed to the plight of the homeless in Manhattan, Silva's project suspends a series of "pods" for inhabitation in the vertical void of a vacant lot in lower Manhattan. Well aware of its own sense of moral *frisson,* the project also has the disconcerting effect, it seems to me, of aestheticizing the social conditions it purports to challenge, and of rendering the individuals it proposes to accommodate curiously institutionalized objects of display.[31] Is it not possible to see such a project as evidence of a troubling fallibility on the part of this precocious young avant-gardist in respect to the risks in such rhetorically artistic praxes in architecture?

One is familiar, of course, with the moral imperative so strongly felt among young designers today to eschew any taking over of merely assumed social conventions. But perhaps full consideration has yet to be given to the fact that when design proposals following this premise reach a certain scale of intervention, it is a direct consequence of this escalation of scale that the individual designer in question is obliged—as an essential dimension of his or her praxis—to reinvent a larger territory of the world at large. And to do so, whilst at the same time sustaining the sought-after avant-gardist detachment, is an almost impossible task. No wonder, then, that Silva's project seems so fetishized. Is it surprising that the results of these contemporary efforts begin once again to evoke the memory of Loos's cautionary words? Is it possible that yet another ambitious young generation of architects is about to get its fingers burned?

Early Struggles in the Phenomenology of Modernism

It is highly unlikely that we, who can know, determine, and define the natural essences of all things surrounding us, which we are not, should ever be able to do the same for ourselves—this would be like jumping over our own shadows.

Hannah Arendt, 1958

The dispute between Muthesius and Van de Velde that took place at the 1914 Werkbund congress in Cologne was first portrayed as a key event in the formation of modern architecture in 1936, when Nikolaus Pevsner published *Pioneers of Modern Design.* Pevsner declared in his first chapter that the chief aim of his book was "to prove that the new style, the genuine and legitimate style of our century, was achieved by 1914." As he saw it, the "new" and "legitimate" style had been demonstrated in "the work of those German architects who agreed with Muthesius . . . especially Peter Behrens and Walter Gropius." Pevsner saw Muthesius as being so important in this context because he had for some time been "the acknowledged leader of a new tendency towards *Sachlichkeit,* which followed the short blossom-time of *Art Nouveau* in Germany." Of this highly influential German term, Pevsner remarked, "The untranslatable word *sachlich,* meaning at the same time pertinent, matter-of-fact, and objective, became the catch-word of the growing Modern Movement."[1]

To be sure, Pevsner was well aware of the fact that what we would nowadays call alternative "phenomenologies" of modernism—ones that could not very plausibly be characterized as "matter-of-fact, and objective"—had existed as real historical possibilities, in the years around 1914. He noted, for example, how the activities of the futurists, in the half-decade preceding the Werkbund congress of that year, had led that group to formulate a quite distinctive approach to modernism. Like the leaders of the Werkbund, the futurists were interested in the potential of technology—indeed, "interested" would have to be considered an understatement. Evidence enough can be found in the celebrated passage from *Le Futurisme* by Marinetti concerning engineers

> who live in high tension chambers where a hundred-thousand volts flicker through great bays of glass. They sit at control panels with meters, switches, rheostats and commutators to right and left, and everywhere the rich gleam of polished levers. These men enjoy, in short, a life of power between walls of iron and crystal; they have furniture of steel, twenty times lighter and cheaper than ours. They are free at last from the examples of fragility and softness offered by wood and fabrics with their rural ornaments. . . . Heat, humidity and ventilation regulated by a brief pass of the hand, they feel the fullness and solidity of their own will.[2]

Like Muthesius, Behrens, and Gropius, the futurists were interested in

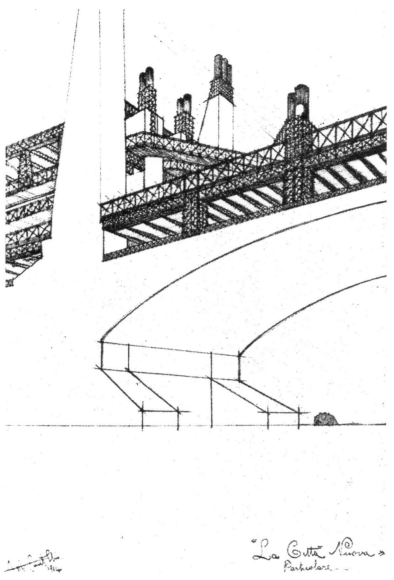

"La Città Nuova"
Particolare.

2.1   A typical drawing from the Città Nuova series of Antonio Sant'Elia, from 1914.

technology, but unlike the Germans they did not associate it with typicality and restraint. Instead, they sought a fervent redemption of what they saw as the inconsequentiality of modern existence, in a technological virtuosity that appeared to them a real historical possibility. Interestingly enough, their fervor in this regard must be seen as, among other things, a displacement of that of their Viennese predecessors, the artists of the Secession and of the Jugendstil, who had located theirs in the antitechnological individuality of the artistic gesture. Not for nothing, then, do the forms of the futurist designs of Sant'Elia remind us of those of the Secession from only a few years earlier.

But in the end, Pevsner dismissed the drawings of Sant'Elia as "sheer expressionism" and concluded that the architectural production of futurism as a whole could not be considered to have been a "solid achievement."[3] Only in a much later and revisionist historical text of 1960, *Theory and Design in the First Machine Age* by Pevsner's student Reyner Banham, did the futurist alternative to the hegemony of the Werkbund sensibility receive serious (if belated) historical scrutiny.[4]

2.2   A drawing of the Ferdinandsbrücke by Otto Wagner, from 1906.

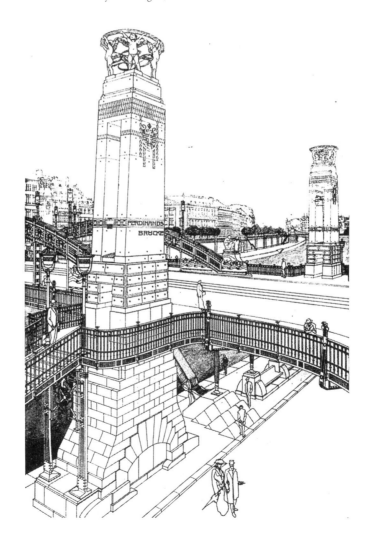

Still if the futurist alternative to *Sachlichkeit* had to wait until 1960 for such consideration, another important group of cultural dissenters may be seen still to be waiting for an adequate acknowledgment of the implicit challenge they made to the Werkbund in those years. The group in question here is the dadaists.

It was, after all, a year before the famous Werkbund congress was held in Cologne that Marcel Duchamp exhibited the first of his so-called readymades, the notorious *Bicycle Wheel* of 1913. And by this gesture, Duchamp challenged the premises of the Werkbund position in a different way. As Robert Lebel has pointed out, presaging a whole host of later, parallel assessments:

> Duchamp did not select a bicycle wheel as a beautiful modern object, as a Futurist might, he chose it just because it was commonplace. It was nothing but a wheel, like a hundred thousand others, and in fact if it were lost, it could soon be replaced by identical replicas. For the moment, resting upside down on a kitchen stool as a pedestal, it enjoyed an unexpected and derisive prestige, which depended entirely upon the act of choosing by which it was selected.[5]

Thus, where the futurists challenged the restraint of the Werkbund program, Duchamp put it into ironical question. For, as a commonplace product of contemporary technology, the bicycle wheel would surely suffice as an appropriate icon of the emerging *Sachlichkeit*. Yet by endowing it with such "derisive prestige," Duchamp both took the concept of typicality at face value and at the same time put its artistic status into acute doubt. To be sure, we are given to understand that Duchamp's aim was, in the first instance, to challenge the concept of the art object as it existed in museums and galleries at the time. But his bicycle wheel also had the unexpected reverse effect of challenging the typicality of the commonplace industrial object as the Werkbund saw it. And while it wasn't a rhetorical gesture such as a futurist would have made, Duchamp's had a deadpan irony that was far from the straightforwardly normative tone we associate with Muthesius and with the tendency toward *Sachlichkeit* that was to become the hallmark of Werkbund ascendancy.

It was, according to Pevsner, the studies of domestic architecture

2.3 Marcel Duchamp's *Bicycle Wheel,* from 1913.

Muthesius had carried out in England between 1896 and 1903 that brought the *sachlich* sensibility to the forefront of his thinking: "Reasonable *sachlichkeit* is what Muthesius praises in English architecture and crafts."[6] Indeed, the concept can quite prominently be discerned in the concluding argument of Part Two of the celebrated text that was the result of Muthesius's English sojourn: *The English House.* To capture the full tone

sammen in die Pfanne zu schütten und das Ganze dem Ofen zu übergeben. Für alle englischen Gerichte aber werden die besten Rohstoffe genommen. Nirgends gibt es ähnliche gute Hammelkeulen als in England, auch das Rindfleisch und die Gemüse sind vorzüglich. Diese guten Materialien entschädigen für die mangelnde Verfeinerung, ja man hat, nach einiger Gewöhnung an die urwüchsige englische Küche, die Empfindung, daß hier verschönernde Zutaten gar nicht erwünscht wären, und die raffinierte französische Kochkunst kommt einem nach Kennenlernen der englischen ziemlich rückgratlos, fast weichlich vor. Trotzdem besteht in vornehmen englischen Häusern die Sitte, französische Köche anzunehmen. Sie verdrängen nicht die guten Seiten der englischen Küche (das würden ihre Herren selbst nicht wünschen), sondern fügen diesen nur die Verfeinerung hinzu, die besonders bei festlichen Gelegenheiten nicht entbehrt werden kann. England ist mit diesen höheren Verfeinerungen stets von Frankreich abhängig gewesen. Die Kultur des Nachbarlandes deckt hier seit Jahrhunderten den geringen Bedarf, der bei den Spitzen der englischen Bevölkerung an höherer äußerer Kultur vorlag, ohne jedoch das englische Kulturbild, das im Grundzuge stets das eines ländlich-bäuerischen Volkes blieb, dauernd zu beeinflussen.

Ein weiterer bestimmender Einfluß auf die Gestalt des englischen Herdes liegt in dem Umstande, daß in jedem englischen Hause eine Warmwasserleitung mit dem Küchenherde verbunden ist, die alle Bäder und alle Becken in den Waschräumen mit warmem Wasser versorgt. Diese Warmwasserleitung tritt schon in den kleinsten Häusern von 5 Zimmern auf, und sie ist selbst im Hause von 20 bis 30 Zimmern noch mit dem Küchenherde verbunden. Ihre Einrichtung wird weiter hinten erörtert werden, hier sei nur vorweggenommen, daß diese Warmwasserversorgung den Herd in vielen Fällen ganz außergewöhnlich belastet und oft eine große Verschwendung an Brennmaterial zur Folge hat. Aber Sparsamkeit im Verbrauch von Brennmaterial ist ebensowenig beim englischen Küchenherd der leitende Gesichtspunkt wie beim englischen Kamin. Es werden zwar fortlaufend Verbesserungen auf den Markt gebracht, die diese Sparsamkeit zum Vorwand haben, allein die Verschwendung liegt in dem zusammengewürfelten Programm, das der englische Küchenherd in ein- und derselben Form erfüllen soll. Kann nach dem Vorgeführten der englische Herd keinen vorbildlichen Wert beanspruchen, so sollen hier doch einige seiner gebräuchlichsten Formen Erwähnung finden.

Man unterscheidet grundsätzlich zwischen range und kitchener in der Weise, daß ein range fest eingemauert, ein kitchener aber fertig in Eisen gebaut ist und nur an den Schornstein angeschlossen zu werden braucht. In der allgemeinen Anordnung beider Arten ist aber kein großer Unterschied zu finden. Die Abb. 20 und 21 stellen den gebräuchlichsten Kochherd dar. In der Mitte befindet sich die offene Feuerung, die durch Hervorziehen und Herunterklappen

Abb. 20. Gewöhnlicher englischer Küchenherd mit Bratofen und Warmwasserbehälter.

des hinter ihr sichtbaren Deckels zur geschlossenen umgewandelt werden kann, links von der Feuerung ist der Bratofen, rechts der Behälter für die Warmwasserversorgung des Hauses. Der obere Teil des Herdes ist auch dann von Seitenwänden und einer Decke umschlossen, wenn der Herd frei an der Wand steht, man hat also die alte, im range begründete Form ganz unnötiger Weise auch auf den kitchener übertragen. Kurz unter der Decke befindet sich stets ein eisernes Gittergestell zum Vorwärmen der Teller. Vor dem Herd liegt ein etwa 15 cm hohes eisernes

Abb. 21. Englische Küche mit eingebautem Herd.

Schutzgestell (fender), gerade wie vor jedem Kamin im Zimmer. An dem offenen Feuer wird das Brot in der Weise geröstet, daß man geschnittene Brotscheiben mit einer besonderen dafür vorhandenen sehr langstieligen Gabel (toast fork) vor die Feuerglut hält. Fleisch wird mittels besonderer Vorrichtungen ebenfalls vor der Feuerglut aufgehängt, wobei natürlich dafür Sorge getragen werden muß, daß alle Seiten dem Feuer gleichmäßig ausgesetzt werden. Dies geschieht in gewöhnlichen Haushaltungen manchmal nur durch fortgesetztes Wenden, meistens ist aber eine mechanische Drehvorrichtung dafür vorhanden. An den Küchenherden von der Art des in der Abbildung vorgeführten hängt man den Braten im letzteren Falle an dem allbekannten bottle-jack („Flaschenknecht") auf, in dessen flaschenartigem Teile ein Uhrwerk für die fortwährende Drehung sorgt (Abb. 22). Die Vorrichtung hängt entweder an einem herausragenden Trageisen oder sie befindet sich in einem besonderen, vor dem Herd stehenden Gestell, dem Bratenschirm (meat screen, Abb. 23), dessen nach dem Feuer gewendete Öffnung durch Rückstrahlung der Wärme zugleich für eine bessere Ausnutzung der Hitze sorgt. In früherer Zeit waren die Herdfeuer noch unmittelbarer für das Rösten am Spieß eingerichtet und in alten englischen Häusern finden sich jene fast monumental zu nennenden Einrichtungen noch in großer Anzahl, bei welchen vor einem mit Eisenstangen eingezäunten mächtigen Feuerbecken an beiderseits herausragenden Stangen sich drehte der fleischbeladene Spieß drehte. Die Drehung

2.4 A typical double-page spread from volume 2 of Hermann Muthesius's *Das englische Haus* of 1904.

of the term's usage, it is appropriate to quote the passage at length:

> The genuine and decisively valuable feature of the English house is its absolute practicality. Whatever it is, it is a house in which people want to live. There is nothing extravagant, no desire to impress about its conception, no flights of fancy in ornament and jumbles of forms; it does not give itself airs or try to be artistic, there is no pretentiousness, nor even any architecture. It stands there, not magnificent, unembellished, with that self-evident decency that, however obvious it may seem, has become so rare in our modern culture. And combined with it is a quality that constitutes a precious part of the English character: an unassuming naturalness. The English have long outgrown the cultural level of wanting to pretend to others, to impress them. Indeed (however pronounced the desire to do so may be in our own modern German culture), they are inclined rather to wish to be inconspicuous. To the Englishman, to parade whatever advantages of position or breeding he may have smacks immediately of the parvenu.
>
> Thus the richer a man is, the more restrained his behaviour, the more modest and inconspicuous he is. And this is expressed so clearly in the English houses of today, so unusually pleasantly for anyone who has recognized their character, that it is a delight to make their acquaintance. Fancifulness, originality (the self-conscious kind!), display, architectonic window-dressing, decorative forms—the English find them as little in place in the house as in the dress of the man who inhabits it. What serious-minded man today would think of wearing bizarre clothes? Even artists in England are careful to avoid making themselves look different from others by the way their hair is cut or their choice of tie.

And so, to an architect who presented him with a bizarre plan overladen with architectonic forms, an Englishman about to build a house would simply repeat the short sentence with which three-hundred years ago Bacon began his little essay on the building of houses: "Houses are built to live in, not to look at."[7]

Thus *Sachlichkeit* was associated not only with practicality and restraint; it had come virtually to stand for what Muthesius saw as an essential English characteristic: "Unassuming naturalness."

It will not be difficult for the reader to recognize here an echo of the views of Adolf Loos. Indeed, in his analogy of clothing with architecture, in his contempt for the parvenu, and in his scorn for the fanciful, Muthesius shared in the widespread cultural anglophilia that swept the German-speaking world at the turn of the century. What is more, in this relatively early appearance in architectural commentary, *Sachlichkeit* also formed part of the general body of ideas developed in Germany at the turn of the century that was supportive of a putative new "realism" in architecture and increasingly skeptical of the perceived excesses of art nouveau and the Jugendstil. From 1900 onward, *Sachlichkeit* was associated with concepts of the inclusive, the typical, and the restrained as they had been characterized by Loos, and with "the practical demands of purpose, comfort, and health" as they were being newly promulgated by such contemporaries as Richard Streiter.[8] It was these particular senses of the term that in large measure characterized it as it became the "catchword"—to use Pevsner's term—of the Werkbund from 1914 on.

Now it is true, of course, that notwithstanding Muthesius's and his colleagues' polemical victory in 1914, the new *Sachlichkeit* nevertheless suffered a cultural eclipse in the years during and immediately after the First World War. The war itself having had a profoundly traumatic effect on the morale of the European intelligentsia, its ending precipitated a dramatic new phase of utopian expressionism. It is this phase, especially in Germany, that we associate with the founding of the Bauhaus; with Gropius's own expressionist phase (including such works as the 1921 monument to the "March Heroes" in Weimar); and with the formation by Gropius and a number of his contemporaries of the Arbeitsrat für Kunst.[9] Yet notwith-

2.5 The *Monument to the March Heroes,* a tribute to participants in the 1848 revolution, designed by Walter Gropius and erected in Weimar in 1921. (Photograph by permission, from Hans Wingler, *The Bauhaus,* MIT Press.)

standing the renewed fervor of such groups in the early 1920s, the utopian expressionism it generated waned quite rapidly, as renewed doubts about it reemerged in architectural circles; as the practical possibilities for large-scale commissioned work began to emerge in the early years of the Weimar government; and as new architectural ideas from abroad—notably France and the Soviet Union—intersected with internal debates in Germany itself. For the rest of the decade, the precepts of *die neue Sachlichkeit* grew ever more widespread, to such a point that it was, by 1929, possible for Le Corbusier to describe it as representing the mainstream of progressive architectural thinking in Germany, Holland, and Czechoslovakia.

A figure well known and well connected in all of these countries, who was eventually to play a significant role in debate with Le Corbusier, was the Swiss architect Hannes Meyer. The evolution of his thinking, as evidenced in successive notes and designs from the twenties, will serve to illustrate for us the further evolution of the concept of *Sachlichkeit.*

A notable early text of Meyer's was a polemic entitled "The New World" from 1926. It was more or less contemporary with one of his most highly regarded design proposals, that for the Petersschule in Basel, done in collaboration with Hans Wittwer. Quotation *in extenso* will again convey the general tone:

> Motor cars dash along our streets. On a traffic island in the Champs Elysees from 6 to 8 p.m. there rages round one metropolitan dynamicism at its most strident. "Ford" and "Rolls Royce" have burst open the core of the town, obliterating distance and effacing the boundaries between town and country. Aircraft slip through the air: "Fokker" and "Farman" widen our range of movement and the distance between us and the earth; they disregard national frontiers and bring nation closer to nation. Illuminated signs twinkle, loud speakers screech, posters advertise, display windows shine forth. The simultaneity of events enormously extends our concept of "space and time", it enriches our life. We live faster and therefore longer. We have a keener sense of speed than ever before, and speed records are a direct gain for all. Gliding, parachute descents and music hall acrobatics refine our desire for balance. The precise division into hours of the time we spend working in office and factory and the split-minute timing of railway timetables make us live more consciously. . . . Radio, marconigram and phototelegraphy liberate us from our national seclusion and make us part of a world community.[10]

The reader will have no difficulty in recognizing the tone of this passage, since it echoes so strikingly that of the passage quoted earlier by Marinetti, from *Le Futurisme* of 1912. The same bold confidence in modern technology, the same breathless enthusiasm betray strong futurist sympathies. But one stops short of calling Meyer a futurist. For it is likelier that the tone of the passage is the result of the influence of Soviet Russian constructivism, of which curious German observers were hearing and seeing more and more during this period following Lissitzky's famous exhibition in Berlin in 1922. Indeed, in Meyer's juxtaposition of parachute descents and music hall acrobatics, we can detect a cultural sensibility we could almost call Eisensteinian. And a similar tone is evident in Meyer's notable Petersschule project. Designed to sit in an open space in the old section of Basel, the school comprises a simple vertical block, five stories high, off the side of which is slung a double-level cantilevered deck, suspended on cables from the top of the block, so that the ground space below is left entirely free. With its dramatic structural virtuosity and its astringent technological precision, the Petersschule project bears comparison with the most exciting proposals being put forward by Soviet designers at the same time.

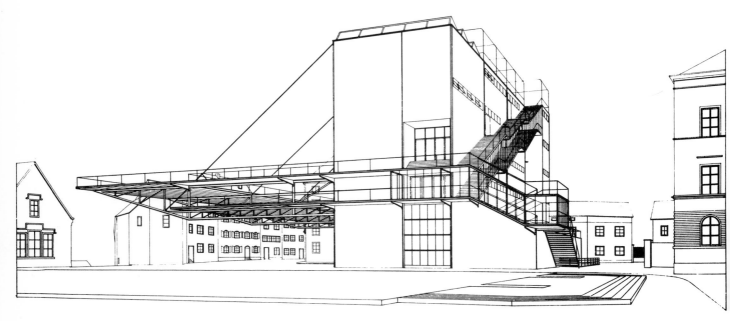

2.6   A drawing of Hannes Meyer and Hans Wittwer's Petersschule project for Basel, from 1926.
(Illustration by permission, from K. Michael Hays, *Modernism and the Posthumanist Subject*, MIT Press.)

But whether the influence was futurist, constructivist, or both, what is surely indisputable is that the cultural sensibility evident here is not one we can straightforwardly call *sachlich*. Interests in universality and typicality are clear enough, but the assertive tenor of both the text of "The New World" and the design of the Petersschule betray a posture that is more heroic than restrained.

By 1928, however, Meyer's position had noticeably shifted. Evidence of this may be seen in another pairing of text and building project from that year. The text is entitled simply "building"—significantly enough in lower-case type—and the building project is the Federal School of the German General Trade Unions Federation, at Bernau near Berlin. The text "building" begins with the best-known words Meyer ever wrote:

> all things in this world are a product of the formula: (function times economics) so none of these things are works of art: all art is composition and hence unsuited to a particular end. all life is function and therefore not artistic. the idea of the "composition of a dock" is enough to make a cat laugh! but how is a town plan designed? art or life????? building is a biological process. building is not an aesthetic process. in its basic design the new dwelling house becomes not only a piece of machinery for living in but also a biological apparatus serving the needs of body and mind.—the modern age provides new building materials for the new way of building houses. . . .
>
> architecture as an "embodiment of the artist's emotions" has no justification. architecture as "continuing the building tradition" means being carried on the tide of building history.[11]

recall Le Corbusier (but not against art)

Here we find a continued, perhaps even intensified interest in universality and the typical. And the preoccupation with technology has by now moved some significant way toward a rationalized, even scientific model of human existence. But gone altogether is the exuberant utopianism of "The New World." The studied restraint we have associated with Muthesius and with Loos reappears here, except that now even this can no longer be seen as a matter of discriminating bourgeois taste. Instead, we are faced with a militant, spartan and reductive critique of any form of "artistic" aspiration. Moreover, as "building" reads differently from "The New World," so the Trade Unions School looks different from the Petersschule. Gone are the structural virtuosity and spatial drama. Instead, we are presented with a highly restrained, meticulously configured low-rise group of buildings, jus-

2.7   An overall view of Meyer's Trade Unions School near Berlin, from 1928. (Illustration by permission, from K. Michael Hays, *Modernism and the Posthumanist Subject*, MIT Press.)

Early Struggles in the Phenomenology of Modernism

tified by carefully analytical sun diagrams and by an ambitious socioeconomic building program, both of which are reminiscent of the kinds of
pedagogical principles Meyer had by this time introduced into the architecture program of the Bauhaus, of which he had become director two years
before.

Now the shift of tone I have identified here forms only part of an entire
evolution of architectural opinions that took place in Europe between the
middle and late twenties. Meyer himself, for example, had been associated
since 1924 with a magazine called *ABC,* whose coeditors were the Swiss
architect Hans Schmidt and the Dutch Mart Stam. *ABC* was one locus of
evolving opinion that moved toward a radically matter-of-fact and materialist conception of architecture, thereby gaining both allies and critics. One
of the significant allies was the Czech architectural critic Karel Teige, one
of the editors of a Prague magazine called *Stavba,* which exchanged significant editorial material with *ABC.* By the time the first International Congress of Modern Architecture was held at La Sarraz, France, in 1928, the
Dutch, German, and Czechoslovakian representatives were (according to
Le Corbusier at least) recognizable as a group representing a particular and
distinct critical position, which he took to be too narrow a one. In this
view he was joined by such notable figures as Sigfried Giedion and Mies
van der Rohe.

Still, the 1928 meeting constituted a first major effort by the new generation of architects to assert the power of their general ideas against that of
the academies of various kinds, but especially the French Ecole des Beaux-
Arts, that had controlled the outcome of the 1927 competition for the
design of a new headquarters building for the League of Nations, with the
result that Le Corbusier's celebrated proposal had been rejected. Given the
academies' threat to all modern architecture, the various factions amongst
the moderns made efforts to reconcile their differences and present a
united front to their enemies.

By 1929, however, this fragile coalition was shattered, and the Czech critic
Teige took it upon himself to criticize Le Corbusier publicly, upon the

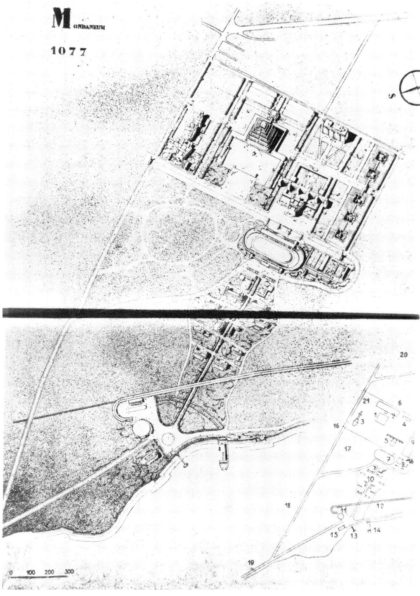

2.8   An overall image of Le Corbusier's 1929 project for the Mundaneum, on Lake Geneva.

occasion of the publication in *Stavba* of Le Corbusier's Mundaneum project. The Mundaneum was proposed to be built near Geneva at the instigation of the entrepreneur Paul Otlet. It was, in the first instance, to comprise five traditional institutions of intellectual creativity, a library, a museum, accommodation for scientific societies, a university, and an institute. Besides those, it was also intended to be a center for professional, scientific, philosophical, and artistic unions, social and artistic movements, and the headquarters for educational and hygienist groups, as well as archives.

Having concisely described the project as a whole, and having conceded the brilliance of Le Corbusier's design capabilities, Teige went on to criticize what he saw as historicist and formalist tendencies in the design of the Mundaneum. Moreover, he also deplored its being based on what he saw as abstract metaphysics.

> Modern architecture . . . was born not from abstract speculation, but from actual need, from the dictates of life, not the patronage of some academy or official group. Real need furnished programs: factories, bridges, railway stations, offices, housing for workers, schools, hospitals, hotels and apartments; from a fundamental understanding and shaping of these problems pure modern architecture was born. Today we have no architectural solutions for churches, palaces, or castles, which, in the purity and precision of their creative construction, can match the architecture of modern needs. . . .

> According to Le Corbusier, architecture as art believes that its mission begins where construction ends, namely with the rational solution and products of the engineer. It aspires to eternity, while the engineer responds to actuality. According to Poelzig, architecture as art begins where it does not submit to any practical purpose; buildings *für den lieben Gott.* In short, according to this argument, to become dignified as architecture, there must be some "plus" to the rational solution. Now this "plus" can either help purposefulness and strengthen function, in which case it is simply purpose and function and is not a "plus," or hinder it, in which case it is of course a minus. Further, it can neither help nor hinder, in which case it is superfluous and unnecessary, and that is a minus as well. The criterion of purposefulness; the only reliable criterion of quality in architectural production led modern architecture to discard "mammoth bodies of monumentality" and to cultivate its brain; instead of monuments, architecture creates instruments. . . . Only where no ideological-metaphysical-aesthetic intentions, but only the dictates of practical life direct the architect's work, does the affection for art stop.[12]

With this powerful charge, Teige laid down a profound challenge to Le Corbusier and put the supposed unity of the moderns into serious question. Le Corbusier for his part took the unaccustomed step of replying, and in doing so put the whole discussion of *die neue Sachlichkeit* into sharper perspective. According to Le Corbusier:

> *Sachlichkeit,* an opportune police measure perhaps, implies in the spirit of its inventors an incompleteness. If one wanted to be completely *sachlich,* one would say: this works; but I expect it to please me, to satisfy me, to quench my thirst, to interest me, to titillate me, to overwhelm me, etc. Because, poet, I ask you: what is the motive that restrains men from throwing themselves into revolution, from pillaging everything and then starving to death in their ruins? . . . And you will grant me that it is this capacity, to eat every day his spiritual food—as meagre as it may be—which helps him to tolerate the hard life of *Sachlichkeit* and which gives him hope of a release, a sense of creation, a motive, which enables him to create, to conceive an idea. . . .

> "Machine for living in" was the succinct terms with which, in 1921, I challenged the academies . . . setting aside the dispute with the academies and returning to our own, I immediately ask myself the question: "for living—how?" I pose here, simply, the question of quality. I can find it resolved only in composition, that is

2.9   Sketches by Le Corbusier of the wastebasket under discussion, before and after Alfred Roth's modifications to it.

to say, in the manner in which the creation of *sachlich* objects has been conceived; such objects constituting the whole of my problem, however small it may be.

Having thus defined architecture in this purely spiritual event of composition, I can see easily why the followers of *Sachlichkeit* are so inaccessible to my arguments. It is that, in general, they operate at levels where it is thought admissible to be a great architect of music or poetry but where, for some reason too complex to pursue in depth here, there is felt no imperative necessity of being "sachlich" in architecture, in respect to the objective conditions implied in plastic art.[13]

Or again:

Let's empty the back of *Sachlichkeit* completely. Its equivocal basis rests on the postulate that is as affirmative as it is doubtful: "that which is useful is beautiful"— that same old refrain. (You will not contradict me if I reveal to any uninformed readers that such is one of the supreme rules of the *neue Sachlichkeit*.)

Last year, upon completion of the drawings of the Mundaneum project . . . there was a minor revolt in our studio. The younger members of the group criticized the pyramid (which is one of the elements of the project). On other drawing boards, the drawings of the Centrosoyus for Moscow were just being finished and had received everyone's approval. They were reassuring because that scheme was clearly a rational problem of an office building. Nevertheless, the Mundaneum and the Centrosoyus both emerged from our heads during the same month of June.

All of a sudden the decisive argument popped out of a mouth "what is useful is beautiful!" At the same moment Alfred Roth (of such impetuous temperament) kicked in the side of a wire mesh wastebasket which couldn't hold the quantity of old drawings he was trying to stuff in. Under Roth's energetic pressure, this wastebasket, which had a technically *sachlich* curvature (a direct expression of the wire netting), deformed and took in the appearance in the sketch above. Everyone in the office roared. "It's awful," said Roth. "Ah, but this basket now contains much more," I replied; "it is more useful so we could say it is more beautiful! Be consistent with your principles!"

Early Struggles in the Phenomenology of Modernism   **73**

This example is amusing only because of the circumstances in which it arose so opportunely. I immediately re-established equitable balance by adding: "the function of beauty is independent of the function of utility; they are two different things. What is displeasing to the spirit is wasteful, because waste is foolish; that is why the useful pleases us. But the useful is not the beautiful."[14]

"Organization is the key," continued Le Corbusier, "virile substance that guides and corrects all that is *sachlich,* all that is muscle and bone. But what intention does this organization have? The *sachlich* I do not even discuss, conceding it to be evident, primary, inevitable, like the bricks with which one builds a wall."[15]

With this explicit exchange of opinions, we can assess the evolutionary status of the concept of *Sachlichkeit* as it stood in the eyes of divergent factions amongst the modernists circa 1929. For Teige, the principles of universality, typicality, and restraint were still fundamental ones. But two subtle new considerations had come into play. First, architectural merit was closely allied with correspondence with social program, to such a degree that the very idea of a nonprogrammatic architecture was excluded from consideration altogether. This in turn brought into play a key criterion of value that one might characterize as an absolute correspondence with perceived social reality. And not only was this new criterion given central prominence; the old criterion of restraint was given a newly restrictive coloration. For Teige, a narrowly defined purposefulness was the only reliable criterion of quality in architectural production.

As for Le Corbusier, it is first of all important to note that he was the one to introduce the terms *sachlich* and *Sachlichkeit* explicitly into the discussion. From Teige's noticeable avoidance of the terms, and from Le Corbusier's insistent and rhetorical usage of them, we can begin to surmise that certain polemical advantages and handicaps lurked between the lines of debate. Having assumed this rhetorically aggressive posture, Le Corbusier set up an opposition of *Sachlichkeit* to poetry (taking advantage of the fact that in addition to his work as an architectural critic, Karel Teige worked in Prague as a poet). Having done this, Le Corbusier both mocked and challenged the narrowly restrictive concept of architecture that—as he saw it—*Sachlichkeit* implied. In his emotional conclusion, he went so far as to cite the example of the Eiffel Tower:

> My dear Teige, would you also ponder your own enthusiasm for the Eiffel Tower—a constructive phenomenon which you deem exclusively *sachlich*? Remember that in 1889, the Eiffel Tower was used for nothing; it was a temple to calculation (a temple, a palace, a castle of calculation. It was an aesthetic manifestation of calculation.)[16]

By such an example, Le Corbusier managed even to put the boundaries of the definition of modern social programs, as it had been set out by Teige, into some question.

Comparing these two opposing positions, we can sense the scope of the cultural world view we have associated with the concept of *Sachlichkeit,* as it stood by 1929. First of all, we must note that what had previously been a concept had by this time taken on a number of the aspects of a polemic. *Die neue Sachlichkeit* was publicly recognized as a cultural tendency bearing considerable influence in a number of European countries. What is more, versions of the tendency by then also included literature, theater, painting, and photography.[17] In addition, the connotation of "objectivity" had gained greater prominence in comparison with the older usages connoting pertinence or matter-of-factness. In architecture, particularly from this period on, it became increasingly common to translate the term into English by the unequivocal and didactic word "functionalism." This is in itself an indication of the increased insistence on the primacy of social programs. In short, what we have hitherto understood as a cultural world view underpinning an attitude to the physical things of the world had become a polemical and divisive slogan. This is not to say that this shift makes *Sachlichkeit* any less a phenomenology of the world; it is just that the blatant and often partisan nature of the subsequent debate makes the philosophical assumptions more difficult to interpret clearly.

But of course, by virtue of their own polemical posture, the more militant advocates of *die neue Sachlichkeit* had invited such generalized and popular response. So it should not be entirely surprising that the form of that response was not always as they had anticipated. Barbara Miller Lane has pointed out how particularly true this had already become in Germany, in

Early Struggles in the Phenomenology of Modernism

the period from 1925 to 1928, when a number of architects associated with the group known as the Ring became more involved in public debate:

> The attention given to practical problems by the radical architects in their public utterances, combined with their interest in the social and cultural role of architecture, helped to influence the interpretations of the new architecture by professional commentators in a way which few of the Ring architects intended. Even friendly writers began to see the new style as merely engineering and planning and the Ring architects as seeking to subordinate art to the machine or to the practical needs of society. Through the writings of a new series of influential critics the new style came to be known as "functionalism," *Zweckmassigkeit,* or "the new practicality," *die neue Sachlichkeit.* [18]

This public perception also opened up unforeseen possibilities for criticism: "The wide acceptance of this interpretation allowed conservative writers to argue that the 'new society' which the new architecture claimed to express was a mechanistic and materialistic one, devoid of traditional 'German' spiritual values." A whole series of the leading commentators of the day contributed further to *Sachlichkeit*'s evolving public image: "The new style thus came to be considered by many of Germany's most influential critics as primarily a set of solutions to technical and sociological questions." [19]

By 1932, evidence of a certain new defensiveness in the manner in which the principles of *die neue Sachlichkeit* were being propounded can be found in the writings of a Dutch sympathizer of the movement, Johannes Duiker. Duiker was a partner of the distinguished designer Bernard Bijvoet and was also editor of a Dutch magazine, *8 en Opbouw.* In that magazine, in 1932, appeared a reprint of an interview that had been published in a leading Dutch newspaper by Henrik Berlage, by then the grand old man of Dutch architecture. In the interview Berlage addressed himself to the general state of Dutch architecture as well as more specifically to the Dutch version of the cultural tendency in question: The *Nieuwe Zakelijkheid.* In his introductory remarks, Duiker attempted to set Berlage's comments in context, by means of a series of observations on the inclinations of Dutch journalists in those days to disparage the *Nieuwe Zakelijkheid.*

> I have a few newspaper clippings in front of me; the press has been very preoccupied by the "nieuwe zakelijkheid" lately, and not only that; if anywhere in Amsterdam trees are needlessly cut down, the "nieuwe zakelijkheid" is supposed to be responsible for it. With their mounting interest, the press adds to the confusion of

existing thinking, and also enjoys promoting that typically pathological phenomenon; the anti-efficiency mania.[20]

Duiker evidently did not believe such complaints merited any serious sort of response. He continued:

> We may put aside these clippings, for they add nothing to the debate. The writers don't know any better than to make fun of the phenomenon, or to express their disgust. They never even seek to find the deeper meaning of what is, after all, an international phenomenon. There still remains however, a challenge of importance, an interview with Dr. H. P. Berlage in the *Voormt*, the Hague edition of *Het Voek*. Far be it from me to condemn the opinions expressed by Dr. Berlage. The need to devote a lead article in this magazine to his interview has grown out of a very real danger that others, ingenious journalists, will abuse Berlage's arguments—the arguments of a great and honest man—to their own base ends, and to execute the *Nieuwe Zakelijkheid* without benefit of trial.[21]

Concluding his very guarded introductory text, Duiker then turned to Berlage, who stated:

> I don't see the *Nieuwe Zakelijkheid* as a means, but as an end. It is the symbol of the end of bourgeois society; the *Nieuwe Zakelijkheid* fits in entirely with our own age of rationalization, as it leaves out all sentimental consideration and accepts exclusively technical merits. The *Nieuwe Zakelijkheid* with its capitalistic tendency is also governed, just like rationalized production, by one idea: as fast as possible, and as cheap as possible.

> Unions cannot accept a style as their own without sentimental considerations. They cannot do without emotions. I know that I am diametrically opposed to orthodox Marxists, but I must say too that I find a similarity between the *Nieuwe Zakelijkheid* and dogmatic Marxism. Dogmatic Marxism tracing all development to economic growth, is strongly attacked these days, because Marx in all his greatness, has neglected sentiment. There are many psychological factors which define the development of society. Psychologists are now trying to give Marxism its needed addition. Architecture, too, needs the addition of sentiment which is lacking in the *Nieuwe Zakelijkheid*. All architectural styles reach their pinnacle when they have achieved a complete harmony between rational and sentimental considerations. I see the *Nieuwe Zakelijkheid* as transitional, but it is really a symptom of the decadence of bourgeois society.[22]

Now these speculative observations of Berlage must be seen as decidedly problematic. What is more, the decision of such a thoughtful protagonist as Duiker to publish them in an architectural magazine known for its support of the tendency suggests some clearly emerging sense, on his part, of how threatened *Sachlichkeit* was by that time coming to be. For in a few

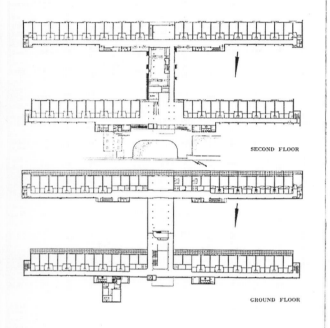

STAM & MOSER: BUDGE HOME FOR THE AGED, FRANKFORT, GERMANY, 1929–1930. Common rooms connect two wings of one-room apartments oriented to the south. Though built by architects who claim to be guided solely by considerations of economy and function, the building has real aesthetic merit as well.

SECOND FLOOR

GROUND FLOOR

2.10   A typical double-page spread from Hitchcock and Johnson's *The International Style* of 1932. The pages shown illustrate a home for the aged in Frankfurt, designed by Mart Stam and Karl Moser and built in 1929–1930.

short sentences, Berlage had managed to formulate a broad if admittedly impressionistic critique of it, which spanned from an expedient capitalism to a dogmatic Marxism. Most fatefully of all, the distinguished architectural commentator of the older Dutch generation, with the phrase "as fast as possible and as cheap as possible," had established a highly damaging correspondence of the avowed functionalism of the tendency with an "expediency" that had hitherto seemed quite alien to it.[23]

And as if this were not bad enough, in 1932 two visiting Americans, Henry-Russell Hitchcock and Philip Johnson, also entered the growing controversy, in a fashion that would prove to be profoundly significant. Hitchcock and Johnson's intervention took the form of a controversial exhibition and catalogue they prepared in that year for the new Museum of Modern Art in New York. While it covered recent architectural developments on both sides of the Atlantic, the exhibition, which eventually came to be known as "The International Style," was designed to introduce an English-speaking audience to the new architectural movements in Europe. Generally speaking, of course, Hitchcock and Johnson grouped together recent European and American buildings that they saw as significant. To have done so in the context of so dominant a discussion of "style" was to gravely offend almost all of the European architects who were included; but particularly dismayed were the advocates of *Sachlichkeit* with their by then well established antipathy to any consideration of aesthetics.

Of course, it is now possible to see that Hitchcock and Johnson were far from unaware of the tendentious nature of their generalizations. Indeed, it is possible to suppose that they even had some interest in stirring up the tensions between the various European factions. For example, a commentary by them on designs for the housing estates (*Siedlungen*) that had been erected for Social Democratic municipal administrations in Frankfurt and Berlin appears to have been deliberately framed so as to be as provocative as possible.

> The *Siedlung* implies preparation not for any given family but for a typical family. This statistical monster, the typical family, has no personal existence and cannot defend itself against the sociological theories of the architects. The European functionalists in their annual conferences set up standards for ideal minimal dwellings. These standards often have no relation to the actual way of living of those who are to inhabit them. Yet such theorizing has value as an instrument of social progress. Architects in private, as well as in public practice must suggest and provide for the amelioration and development of the functions of living. They are specialists who can translate vague desires into realities. But there should be a balance between evolving ideal houses for scientific living and providing comfortable houses for ordinary living.[24]

In a rather calculatedly patronizing tone, Hitchcock and Johnson summed up the work of the *sachlich* function as follows:

> The *Siedlungen* of the European functionalists generally reach the neutral aesthetic level of good building, while the work of those who apply more consciously the disciplines of the contemporary style often rises to the level of architecture. The

"Siedlungen" of the latter are not less practical. We must not be misled by the idealism of the European functionalists. Functionalism is absolute as an idea rather than as a reality. As an idea it must come to terms with other ideas such as that of aesthetic organization.[25]

Perhaps the most personally poignant incident of the troubled late years of *die neue Sachlichkeit* occurred in 1933, when the ever-conciliatory Duiker again found himself compelled to moderate argument in the pages of *8 en Opbouw*. The particular circumstances arose from the fact that his former partner Bernard Bijvoet had in recent years spent time in Paris, working with the French architect Pierre Chareau on a project for a house in the center of Paris. When the Dalsace house was published in *8 en Opbouw* in 1933, the visual presentation was accompanied by a severe criticism by one of Duiker's editorial colleagues, van Tijen. Above all else, van Tijen criticized the Maison de Verre for betraying the erroneous design quality of "preconception." Proceeding from a philosophical *parti pris* reminiscent of Karel Teige's attack on Le Corbusier, van Tijen evidently argued instead for a design method that, eschewing all precedent, would spring from "the data alone."[26]

This time, Duiker found himself in circumstances that were difficult for him personally as well as philosophically. His response was to mount a partial defense of his former partner's work, while still maintaining ranks with his colleagues of the Dutch *Nieuwe Zakelijkheid*. Thus we find him acknowledging that

> from the viewpoint of the principles studied to date for new building conventions—low-income housing, rational neighbourhood planning and functional city planning—the Maison de verre is a hopelessly uninteresting case.

Moreover, he conceded to the *sachlich* faction that

> what remains is a functional snobbishness much in demand in Paris and elsewhere: "nieuwe Zakelijkheid," steel, chrome and nickel, in soft fake spicy refinement where the author makes mistakes all the time and descends to a vulgar formalism.[27]

Still, having consented to such damaging criticism of the project, Duiker nevertheless made claims for its value as an experiment: "For even if this is a solution whose realization is closely connected with the fat wallet of a rich man, the principle contains a rational basis which doubtless could be put into economic reality." Following this line of thought, Duiker cited as an example the use of glass blocks for the exterior walls of the house, praising their utilization because of their transparency, which he saw as facilitating an innovative form of night illumination.

> A night illumination has been installed which appears to be snobbish, but which in reality fits perfectly into a rational building scheme, utilizing a number of flood-lights which connect the outside with the inside, even at night.
>
> We may only wonder how many congresses on the topic of new construction will be held before it is concluded that this particular idea will be universally adopted.[28]

Similarly, Duiker commended the open space planning of the house:

> An effort has been made to change the inner walls as much as possible into movable elements. Thus, one has succeeded in maintaining the size of the original space in its glass envelope. We may not yet have met this experiment as a standard element, however the road has been opened to make efforts in this direction, and to increase the apparent size of even a small dwelling through openness.[29]

In this seeking for social value in the experiment of Bijvoet and Chareau, in his eagerness to reconcile the positivist functionalism of van Tijen and the spatial intensity of the Maison de Verre, Duiker can in retrospect be seen to reflect the grave loss of momentum and of moral confidence that, by 1933, was inexorably coming to overwhelm the *sachlich* tendency altogether.

To be sure, any view of the fate of the tendency in a context larger than architecture can be seen by that date to have been ominous indeed. For a new concatenation of forces, intellectual and political as well as architectural, was coming into formation that would eclipse within a few years almost the entire cultural tendency that had become known under the rubric of *die neue Sachlichkeit*. Among the intellectual forces in question, the first to merit consideration was a by then quite developed stance shared by such prominent figures on the German cultural left as Walter Benjamin and Bertolt Brecht. It was in 1934 that Benjamin first delivered the address "The Author as Producer," with its startling attack on *die neue Sachlichkeit* and its arguments in favor of montage instead.[30]

2.11   A scene from Stanislavsky's production of *Armored Train*.

It is important to note that notwithstanding these generalizations among literature, photography, architecture, etc., the precise usages of the term *Sachlichkeit* were not always exactly parallel. Like that of his colleague Brecht, Benjamin's critique of *Sachlichkeit* had its origins in the theory of the cinema in the Soviet Union, particularly in the aesthetics of Sergei Eisenstein, who claimed to have invented montage:

> Don't forget it was a young engineer who was bent on finding a scientific approach to the secrets and mysteries of art. The disciplines he had studied had taught him one thing: in every scientific investigation there must be a unit of measurement. So he set out in search of the unit of impression produced by art! Science knows "ions," "electrons" and "neutrons." Let there be "attraction" in art. Everyday language borrowed from industry a word denoting the assembling of machinery, pipes, machine tools. This striking word is "montage" which means assembling, and though it is not yet in vogue, it has every qualification to become fashionable. Very well! Let units of impression combined into one whole be expressed through a dual term, half-industrial and half-music hall. Thus was the term "montage of attractions" coined.[31]

Eisenstein's interest in this concept, "half-industrial and half-music hall" as he put it, grew out of his early work with his contemporary Vsevolod Meyerhold. Peter Wollen has described Meyerhold's pioneering efforts to develop a theater combining "the fantastic, the marvellous, the popular, the folkloric," a theater, in short, of "biomechanics."[32] Such a conception of theater in the Soviet Union in the 1920s, was, of course, quite the opposite to that of Stanislavsky. Unlike those of Meyerhold, Stanislavsky's productions emphasized naturalism and psychologism. Indeed, in the eyes of Stanislavsky's constructivist detractors, his work even went so far as to embody a reprehensible mysticism. Thus we may see in this early opposition of two distinct and hostile conceptions of the theater how the concept of montage, from its inception, was conceived as antinaturalistic and antirealist, committed instead to radical juxtapositions of fragments of "reality" that, by the conscious action of an activist creator, had been removed from their normal contexts.

It was just such a technique of radical juxtaposition of fragments that so attracted Walter Benjamin to dada, and to which he attributed dada's "authenticity." "The revolutionary strength of dadaism," said Benjamin,

> lay in testing art for its authenticity. You made still-lifes out of tickets, spools of cotton, cigarette stubs, and mixed them with pictorial elements. You put a frame round the whole thing. And in this way you said to the public: look your picture frame destroys time; the smallest authentic fragment of everyday life says more than painting. Just as a murderer's bloody fingerprint on a page says more than the words printed on it. Much of this revolutionary attitude passed into photomontage. You need only think of the works of John Heartfield, whose technique made the book jacket into a political instrument.[33]

2.12   The set for Meyerhold's production of *Dawn*.

2.13 A photomontage by John Heartfield for *AIZ* magazine from 1932, entitled "The Meaning of the Hitler Salute."

But in the subsequent development of photography, Benjamin continued,

> What do we see? It has become more and more subtle, more and more modern, and the result is that it is now incapable of photographing a tenement or a rubbish-heap without transfiguring it. Not to mention a river dam or an electric cable factory: in front of these, photography can now only say, "How beautiful." *The World is Beautiful*—that is the title of the well-known picture book by Renger-Patzsch in which we see *neue Sachlichkeit* photography at its peak. It has succeeded in turning abject poverty itself, by handling it in a modish, technically perfect way, into an object of enjoyment. For if it is an economic function of photography to supply the masses, by modish processing, with matter which previously eluded mass consumption—Spring, famous people, foreign countries—then one of its political functions is to renovate the world as it is from the inside, i.e. by modish techniques.[34]

To be sure, this is a highly particular and highly polemical commentary, but we may note that Benjamin did not confine his criticism of *Sachlichkeit* to Renger-Patzsch's photography. In a related passage, he added: "Turning

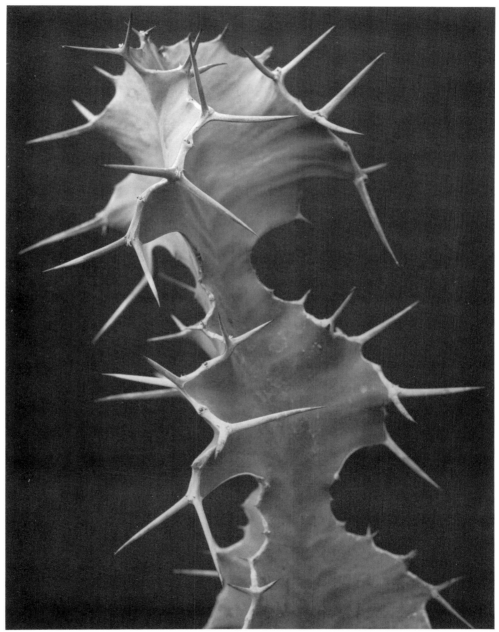

2.14 *Euphorbia grandicornis*; a photograph by Albert Renger-Patzsch, from 1922. (Photograph © Jürgen Wilde.)

to the *neue Sachlichkeit* as a literary movement, I must go a step further, an
say that it has turned the struggle against misery into an object of consumption."[35] As opposed to the "naturalistic" or "realist" mode of representing reality that Benjamin by then ascribed to *die neue Sachlichkeit,* he
argued for one that "disclosed" or "uncovered" aspects of reality inaccessible to everyday perception. A key example of the employment of this
mode, for Benjamin, was the "epic" theater that had been developed by
Brecht. According to Benjamin, Brecht declared that such theater

> must not develop actions but represent conditions. As we shall presently see, it
> obtains its "conditions" by allowing the actions to be interrupted. Let me remind
> you of the "songs," whose principal function consists in interrupting the action.
> Here, then—that is to say, with the principle of interruption—the epic theatre
> adopts a technique which has become familiar to you in recent years through film
> and radio, photography and the press. I speak of the technique of *montage,* for
> *montage* interrupts the context into which it is inserted. Allow me, however, to
> explain very briefly why it is here that this technique enjoys special, and perhaps
> supreme, rights. The interrupting of the action, the technique which entitles Brecht
> to describe his theatre as epic, always works against creating an illusion among the
> audience. Such illusion is of no use to a theatre which proposes to treat elements
> of reality as if they were elements of an experimental set-up. Yet the conditions
> stand at the end, not the beginning of the test. These conditions are, in one form
> or another, the conditions of our life. Yet they are not brought close to the specta-
> tor; they are distanced from him. He recognizes them as real—not, as in the
> theatre of naturalism, with complacency, but with astonishment. Epic theatre does
> not reproduce conditions; rather, it discloses, it uncovers them.[36]

Now this wide-ranging critique of *die neue Sachlichkeit* by Benjamin and
Brecht is of considerable historical importance. First of all, it occurred at a
key moment when, as we have already noted, the confident momentum of
the tendency was already faltering. Second, it was an attack on a cultural
tendency of the left, an attack that also came from the left and therefore
could not readily be dismissed as "merely" ideological. But third, and for
my purposes most important, it was a critique that once again invoked the
large and (as we now see) recurrent question of what would be an appropriate phenomenology of modernism.

Interestingly enough, Benjamin's and Brecht's attack on *Sachlichkeit* occurred only two years prior to the publication of Pevsner's *Pioneers of*

Modern Design, in which, as we have already seen, *Sachlichkeit* was pro-
nounced the catchword of what Pevsner saw as "the style of the century."
To be sure, the *Sachlichkeit* that Pevsner saw as such a consequential phenomenon was quite different from the one Benjamin and Brecht attacked
in the 1930s. What had been at the turn of the century for Muthesius and
his contemporaries a refined, bourgeois view of the possibilities of culture
in the modern world had been transformed in the hands of Hannes Meyer
and his allies in the twenties into a radically reductive materialism, the
imperatives of which were seen to be absolutely binding on any socially
responsible architect. Still, the fact remains that the one clearly evolved
from the other. As different as Muthesius's conception of *Sachlichkeit* is
from Meyer's, the lineage that connects them reveals certain significant
phenomenological commonalities. What is more, we have already noted
how, in his canonical text of 1936, Pevsner dismissed any claim of futurism
to play a significant role in the development of modern architecture and
ignored the potential contribution of dada altogether, pursuing instead his
unequivocal promotion of *Sachlichkeit* as it had been formulated in Werkbund circles around 1914. For Benjamin, on the other hand, dada was
obviously of profound value to the development of modernism, in that it
served as a key vehicle for the formation of the principles of montage at
the same time that it offered such an important means of "testing art for
its authenticity." In short, we may say that a review of disputes among the
leading protagonists of the European cultural left in the 1930s makes clear
how sharply demarcated the struggles in the phenomenology of modernism
had become in those years.

One might suppose that it had been the sheer force of the critique that
had been mounted by the Benjamin/Brecht group alone that resulted in
the eclipse of the *sachlich* tendency in the latter half of the thirties. But
that does not appear to have been the case. For it was the misfortune of
the protagonists of *Sachlichkeit,* in those same years when their confidence
was flagging, to face a parallel attack from another cultural quarter—a
quarter, in fact, from which they might even have expected support. While
Benjamin and Brecht were developing their arguments against *Sachlichkeit*
and in favor of montage, another leading figure within the cultural left in

*Pevsner's
selective
history*

Europe was elaborating a defense of "realism" as the only legitimate mode of modern cultural discourse. This was Georg Lukács, who had also vigorously opposed the ideas of *montage* supported by Benjamin and Brecht.

In a famous text published in 1932 and entitled "Reportage or Portrayal," Lukács criticized not just montage and "epic" theater but also any literary forms that emphasized the "documentary."[37] For him an appropriate mode of realism could not limit itself to the accurate reproduction of a surface reality; it had to go beyond that and "portray" the essence beneath. As a result of this conviction, Lukács offered no more support to the beleaguered tendency than Benjamin or Brecht had done. Effectively, it can be said that by the middle of the decade, *die neue Sachlichkeit* had been abandoned by both of the most compelling currents of left cultural criticism, at the same time as it was sustaining increasingly severe attacks from National Socialism in Germany and Stalinism in the Soviet Union. The extreme polarization of European politics in the 1930s, combined with an acute subsequent wariness on the part of such distanced observers of *Sachlichkeit*'s misfortunes as Giedion, Gropius, and Le Corbusier, led to its falling into the eclipse in which in large measure it remains to this day.

Still, it is possible in retrospect to see how, even in the absence of the cumulative crises that beset the tendency in the middle of the thirties, the internal doubt that was beginning to set in would surely have had its own consequences in any event. One thinks back to the innocent enough reservations expressed by Berlage, and to the inability of the protagonists of the tendency to articulate any sustainable distinction between the teleological functionalism it sought to promote and the "expediency" of which it was accused. Or, for that matter, to how defensive its phenomenology became, once the momentum of its ongoing efforts at a reduction to essentials had spent its initial force. By the time the critiques of Benjamin and Lukács had been formulated, *die neue Sachlichkeit* had forfeited any claim to a sufficiently efficacious subject to be able to fight back. In its increasingly positivist preoccupation with the reality of the world as a given, and with its demands for precise—even scientific—correspondence between architecture and the social reality it thought it perceived, *die neue Sachlichkeit*

eventually devolved into a condition we might characterize as a phenomenological impasse. Unable to countenance rhetoric or speculative exploration, insistent on proceeding from "the data alone," it found itself in
greater and greater difficulty in attempting to "interpret" reality, and
too passive any longer to attempt to transform it.

Objet-type; **Ideal Type;** *objet trouvé:* **Montage and Irony in the Alternative Phenomenology of Le Corbusier**

As we have already noted, the tradition of montage, which *die neue Sachlichkeit* in all its various phases consistently eschewed, can be seen to stretch
from dada as it was being practiced at the beginning of the First World
War, through much of the work of the Soviet avant-garde of the 1920s,
right on up to the theatrical productions of Brecht in the 1930s. What is
more, we have also noted how the tradition of montage departed so decisively from the characteristic self-effacement on the part of the perceiving
subject that proved so fateful to *die neue Sachlichkeit.* Instead the montage
tradition pursued a relationship of subject to object that was always restless and inquisitive, frequently aggressive, and sometimes even rhetorical.
As the preceding account of the early interventions of Marcel Duchamp
made clear, this very frequently involved the protagonists of montage in
postures of ironic detachment vis-à-vis their subject material. Indeed, I am
inclined to think that it would be possible, conceptually speaking, to draw
a clear line linking the studied irony of Duchamp, as represented in the
readymades of 1913 to 1915, right through to the "alienation effect" or
"estrangement" that Benjamin characterized as typical of Brecht's "epic"
theater of the 1930s. This close conceptual relationship of an active subject
to montage, and to irony, is important to all the cultural modes of modernism. As a postscript to the general account of the various struggles in
the phenomenology of modernism between 1900 and the mid-1930s, I will
examine more closely a particular architectural trajectory within that period. The trajectory in question is that of Le Corbusier, and the particular
sequence of projects under consideration stretches from the Pavillon de
l'Esprit Nouveau of 1925 through to the de Beistegui penthouse of
1929–1930.

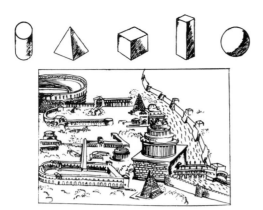

2.15   A sketch from Le Corbusier's *Vers une architecture* of 1922, illustrating what he saw as the timeless architectonic qualities of the typical Phileban solids.

In my earlier discussion of the Pavillon de l'Esprit Nouveau, I noted how the Loosian *objets-type* of its interior—the English leather club chairs and Thonet chairs—contributed in large measure to its restrained sobriety. Indeed, they could be said to lie quite definitively within the tradition of *Sachlichkeit* as it was still understood by Loos as well as by Muthesius. It is in this profound sense that Le Corbusier must be seen to have situated himself so centrally within the tradition of modernism that had stretched from turn-of-the-century Vienna to the Paris of the 1920s.

But at the same time that they speak the *Sachlichkeit* of this particular tradition of modernity, the *objets-type* of the pavilion interior also hint at another level of meaning. For in their spartan purity they also bespeak a certain Platonism, and if we move forward from the Esprit Nouveau pavilion to the exhibition at the Salon d'Automne of 1929, this streak of Platonic idealism becomes even more evident. First, the latter interior prominently displayed pieces of Le Corbusier's own furniture, and while these were still conceived in the form of types, they exuded both a technological precocity and a material luxuriousness that went well beyond the matter-of-factness of the club chair and the Thonet chair so often employed by Loos. Then too, these qualities cause us to see the other elements of the interior of the Salon d'Automne, the restaurant glassware and office equipment, in a more exotic light as well. Like Le Corbusier's own pieces, these took on an ideal geometrical purity that we must associate with the illustrations of Phileban solids and ancient Roman monuments he used to illustrate his arguments in *Towards a New Architecture,* back in 1922.

In short, Le Corbusier managed in 1929 to orchestrate a cultural ensemble in which the *objets-type* that had been so characteristic of his oeuvre in the period from 1922 to 1925 became at the same time Platonic ideal types. A

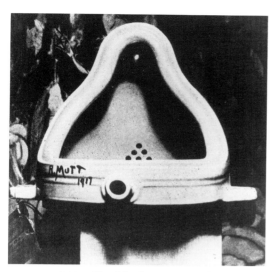

2.16 Marcel Duchamp's *Fountain,* from 1917.

Maison Pirsoul.

AUTRES ICONES
LES MUSÉES

Il y a les bons musées, puis les mauvais. Puis ceux qui ont pêle-mêle du bon et du mauvais. Mais le musée est une entité consacrée qui circonvient le jugement.

2.17 The opening page of chapter 2 of Le Corbusier's *L'Art décoratif d'aujourd'hui,* from 1924.

phenomenal world of things was created possessing the astonishing quality of being typical and ideal at the same time. This was at the time a cultural accomplishment of considerable significance, and it remains a high point of modernism.

But even this was not the end of Le Corbusier's ambition. I have already noted the latent significance for the concept of *Sachlichkeit,* circa 1914, of Marcel Duchamp's readymade the *Bicycle Wheel.* Following the *Bicycle Wheel,* Duchamp presented two more readymades that are significant for my argument, the *Bottle Dryer* of 1914 and the *Fountain* (urinal) of 1917. It is not coincidental that Le Corbusier, in 1924, opened the second chapter of his

La religion des belles matières n'est encore que spasme dernier d'une agonie.

*
* *

En ces années écoulées, nous avons assisté aux étapes successives de l'événement : avec la construction métallique, la *dissociation du décor et de la structure*. Puis la mode d'*accuser la construction*, indice d'une formation nouvelle. Puis l'éblouissement devant la *nature*, révélant le désir de retrouver (par quel bizarre détour d'application!) les lois d'un *organisme*. Puis la toquade du *simple*, première prise de contact avec les vérités de la mécanique nous ramenant au bon sens et instinctive manifestation d'une esthétique d'époque.

On peut nouer la gerbe : un déclic dans l'esprit, un classement, et viendra l'expression libérée d'un sentiment normal des choses de notre existence qui discrimine celles intensivement pratiques du travail, de celles intensément libres, vivantes et idéales de l'esprit.

N° 37
Fauteuil fond feuillard dossier à lyre

2.18   The typical French garden chair, illustrated in *L'Art décoratif d'aujourd'hui*.

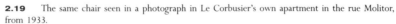

2.19   The same chair seen in a photograph in Le Corbusier's own apartment in the rue Molitor, from 1933.

L'Art décoratif d'aujourd'hui with an illustration of a bidet that powerfully echoed Duchamp's gestures of a decade previously. Of course, Le Corbusier had a keen knowledge of and interest in the work of the surrealists, and this interest indicates yet a third level of meaning in his corpus of works from the twenties, the level of the *objet trouvé.*

Now it is true, of course, that a hint of the irony of the readymades could be considered to have been associated with the *objet-type* from an early stage. For it is surely significant that the Thonet chair projects a somewhat whimsical visual aspect, especially in its more elaborately curvilinear models. And one supposes that this whimsy was intended to introduce a slight *frisson* to the image of typicality otherwise so straightforwardly propounded. Still, it might be argued that this is merely coincidental. It is certainly true that in his canonic interiors, Le Corbusier did usually select from amongst the most restrained of the full range of Thonet's designs. But it seems to me nevertheless that the disposition toward *frisson* remains undeniable, in that it recurs so strikingly in another of Le Corbusier's classic *objets-type,* the metal garden chair. This interesting and somewhat inscrutable object, with a generally *sachlich* construction but possessing a highly decorative spiral arm motif, appears in classic Corbusian interiors from the Esprit Nouveau pavilion in 1925 through many of the major works of the 1920s. Indeed, one such chair is prominently situated in one of the canonic images of Le Corbusier's own apartment in the rue Molitor from 1933.

Le Corbusier's penchant for irony is elaborated most strikingly in a project of the late twenties and early thirties, the penthouse for Charles de Beistegui. Beistegui was not a typical Corbusian client. A restless, highly mobile, and opinionated socialite, with strong tastes of his own, he brought to the commission demands for a particular decor, which even the legendarily obstinate Le Corbusier could not entirely resist. Thus, even in the canonic photos of the project in the *Oeuvre complète,* we find evidence of Le Corbusier working with such (up to that point uncustomary) elements as crystal chandeliers and candelabras, glass-lensed doors, and topiary—among the very ones he had disparaged in *Towards a New Architecture* and *L'Art décoratif*

2.20   A canonical view of the interior of the Beistegui penthouse by Le Corbusier, from 1930–1931, illustrated in volume 2 of the *Oeuvre complète*.

d'aujourd'hui. Yet in those photographs, they form part, albeit a discreet part, of the spatial ensemble of the penthouse.

That this cannot be inadvertent is conclusively demonstrated in the brilliantly rhetorical outdoor "room with the sky for a roof" at the very peak of the spatial composition. Here, in one of the most surrealist of all Le Corbusier's images, we find a grouping of *objet-type* park chairs around a preposterous rococo chimney piece, all on a grass carpet, with the top of the Arc de Triomphe peeking over the wall beyond. In that ensemble, Corbusier succeeded in employing the ironic techniques of montage to create a complex cultural image encompassing an extraordinarily wide range of the phenomena of the domestic milieu, at the same time causing us to see the whole as a dialectical and newly modernist unity.

2.21 A view of the Beistegui penthouse showing the interior as actually furnished by the client, as documented in the French magazine *Architecture/Mouvement/Continuité,* no. 49, from 1979.

2.22 Another canonical view from the same source, this one depicting the famous "outdoor room with the sky for a roof." (Fondation Le Corbusier, Paris.)

Now it is true, of course, that the brilliant cultural image Le Corbusier had created was a highly vulnerable one. Sad proof of that vulnerability can be found in a series of images that have subsequently been published, illustrating the apartment as it appeared while actually inhabited by the client. Here we can perceive no complex cultural space such as was created by the Stein family's belongings occupying the villa at Garches. Instead, we sense only the willful vulgarity of an assertive individual, pushing Le Corbusier's fragile irony past any possible limits and collapsing the interiors back into a realm of kitsch. Where Le Corbusier's canonic images show a view of the reception room before the furniture, we now see the same space furnished by the client with grotesque flounces and ottomans, overstuffed chairs, and meretricious statuary. Where Le Corbusier's image depicts the room under the sky as a deft surrealist joke, we now see added to the grouping a parakeet on a stand, a mirror (bisected by the top of the enclosing wall) and a rococo clock and candlestick on the mantle. Here too the image is shattered, and the limits of Le Corbusier's brilliantly delicate interlayering of the typical, the ideal, and the ironic are revealed in its poignant vulnerability.

2.23 A view showing the outdoor room, similarly modified.

"The Labour of Our Body and the Work of Our Hands"

Though the earth and all inferior creatures be common to all men, yet every man has a property in his own person; this nobody has any right to but himself. The labour of his body and the work of his hands, we may say, are properly his.

John Locke, 1690

In 1922, in Germany, the architectural theorist and critic Adolf Behne published in *Die neue Rundschau* an essay entitled "Kunst, Handwerk, Technik."[1] This provocative text was little discussed in the annals of modern architectural theory until Francesco Dal Co made it a centerpiece of his history of the period, *Abitare nel moderno*.[2] Behne's essay laid down a challenge to many of his contemporaries in Germany. In the first instance, it distanced him from his colleagues in the Arbeitsrat für Kunst and in the Bauhaus, where mystical, expressionist, and craft-oriented architectural ideologies were quite intense in the period following the end of the First World War. At the same time, it reflected the growing interest among younger German architects in the formal and expressive potential they saw in the work of the Russian constructivists, which was exhibited for the first time in Berlin in that same year.

Behne began by polarizing the concepts of "craft" and "technique," noting how in the polemics of "naturalist" commentators, the former always had positive connotations and the latter negative ones. Having briefly outlined what he believed to be at stake in this distinction, Behne declared his *parti pris*—notwithstanding leading opinion in the German avant-garde at the time—and made a case in favor of "technique" and against "handicraft." He recognized the clear connection of technique to technology, and beyond that, the logical dependence of technology on the fundamental principle of the "division of labor."

> General opinion distinguishes technology from craftsmanship at the point where the formerly unified work process is made subject to the principle of the division of labor. In craft the unity of invention and execution is in one person; in technology, it is split between the one who invents here, and the one who executes there.[3]

Behne elaborated an extended defense of a technological orientation to architectural design, and at the same time mounted a bold attack on the pieties of craftsmanship, which he held to be reactionary, hypocritical and, in a word, "naturalistic." He contended that the era of naturalism had by his day been irretrievably lost, and that efforts to resurrect it could only result in disingenuousness. He insisted that the "natural correctness" of things associated with craft in history must be given up in favor of a new

"The Labour of Our Body and the Work of Our Hands"

and modern "estrangement," which, he argued, could become "the point of departure of a much stronger bond."

"The natural state," he conceded, "is one of connectedness. Very few men progress beyond its enjoyment." However, he continued,

> for passionate spirits, organic and material connection do not suffice. The strength of their love destroys the natural, intimate connection, tears it apart, introduces a radical, contrary element: in contrast to the shifting data of sensations, the impersonally hard, cold mechanism, which forces a new and higher unity created by the intellect, by human consciousness. The more mechanically perfect the one element, the more passionate, intellectual the other—assuming that the man in question is adequate to the demands of his intellectual consciousness.[4]

Behne went on to mock the fetishistic admiration of the devotees of craft for "imperfections in the work." Seeing the phenomenon of the *Gesamtkunstwerk* as inherently "naturalistic," he contrasted it with the "separated" art that he advocated instead.

> On the one side is the total work of art, erected out of architecture, sculpture, and painting, all permeating each other like elements of a single organism, grown according to the example of nature; on the other is the conscious separation of the disciplines in order to make unity possible at all. There intertwining labor, here division of labor.[5]

As against the emotional claims of the *Gesamtkunstwerk,* Behne argued as follows:

> The more strictly, the more strongly, the more purely architecture becomes architecture, sculpture becomes sculpture, and painting becomes painting, the sooner will it be possible for them to work cooperatively and for each of the arts to become a pillar of the whole. Until each discipline has returned to its own unique basic law, there can be no unity. Each must follow its own thoughts through to their conclusion, and the farther this contemplation of their own being seems to lead them apart, the more surely it will lead them to each other in reality.[6]

Having thus dispatched the principal arguments of the advocates of naturalism, Behne turned to the known objections to "the division of labor," on which his commitment to technology rested. First, he dealt with objections to specialization:

> In the days of handicrafts, material was distributed and each craftsman worked on all stages of development. Today, the work is distributed. In each stage of the work, the material passes at a determined point along one of its pathways. In this way the work becomes dematerialized and functional.

It would be myopic to complain that work is thus made dull and loveless. It has so often become so because of the difficulties and contradictions in every transition, not because of the process itself. To be sure, in modern labor the "natural, material connection" is removed. The unity is no longer concrete, but abstract, if one will, intellectually constructed. To see this requires an effort of imagination. In handicrafts, the unity in the development from crude material to shining bowl, etc., is present and visible; in technology this unity must be created intellectually by the individual, and I believe that this presupposes a greater, not lesser, measure of involvement and love.[7]

Far from conceding even a political point to his critics, Behne went so far as to argue that "the means of getting working men to relate to one another is the machine." Conversely, he disparaged "folk art":

Does this folk art not bear a fatal resemblance to kitsch? Does anyone long for it other than a few fanatics? Should we not be glad that the machine can provide these useful objects much, much more practically and in a much better and more pleasing form? Folk art can only gain a completely new meaning with and through the machine, technology, and the division of labor. Folk art in the old sense, the art of those not touched by the great stream of consciousness of a time, the groping, naive, heavy art of "the people" in a limited, limiting sense, will come to an end. In replacement, the entire activity of a whole people will become a conscious, light, lucid form-making—art![8]

In conclusion, Behne pointed to what he saw as an emerging new form of art that accepted depersonalization.

This depersonalization, which is logically an objectivization, will not bring the artistic renewal of handicrafts and folk art, but only the new, technological concept of labor. A glance at the new and decisive European art—at Léger, Malevich, Archipenko, Schlemmer, Baumeister, Tatlin, Mondrian, Doesburg—is sufficient. Does this art still have any inner connection with craft? It is anti-craft, intellectual-constructive, technological.[9]

And with such a list of names, he made his new allegiance clear. Here we find figures of constructivism linked to those of De Stijl—even to that of van Doesburg, who at this time was sowing controversy in the Bauhaus with his notorious attacks on Johannes Itten. Indeed, we must read "Art, Handicraft, Technology" even as an attack on Behne's close colleague Gropius, who had just completed the Sommerfeld house in Berlin-Dahlem, the late German expressionist extravaganza of "craftsmanship" that marked the conclusion of Gropius's own forays in this area.

Such observations serve to locate Behne's dramatic theoretical gesture in its immediate cultural context of debate among young German architects in the early twenties. But his challenge also had—and arguably still has—a significance in a much larger historical context. First of all, Behne's text constitutes a key historical critique of the phenomenon of the *Gesamtkunstwerk,* one that echoes that of Adolf Loos from two decades previously in his "Story of a Poor Rich Man." No doubt Behne saw in the activities and ideology of the Weimar Bauhaus a resurgence of the drive toward the creation of the "total art work" that had been so characteristic of architects of the Vienna Secession. To be sure, the thrust of Behne's critique is not parallel to that of Loos; nor for that matter is it altogether correspondent with that of Walter Benjamin from a decade later. Still, we can certainly see in Behne's advocacy of "estrangement"—as opposed to "natural connectedness"—a precursor of the stance later taken up so assertively by Benjamin's colleague of the thirties, Brecht. Indeed, in setting out the concept of estrangement so forthrightly, it seems to me that Behne made a contribution to the debate on the supposed imperatives of cultural modernity that remains relevant to the present day.

Then there is Behne's similarly forthright advocacy of the division of labor, a concept close to the heart of modernity insofar as it is seen as encompassing technology. One prime cause of estrangement as we have come to know it in the modern era, the division of labor has been central to discussion of the processes of fabrication from the period of the early work of Karl Marx, and relevant to such discussion for at least a century before that. As if these two bold gestures were not enough, Behne also chose to make a highly rhetorical juxtaposition of "quality" and "kitsch," echoing—and inverting—the familiar arguments of William Morris from half a century before. Where Morris had extolled the virtues of "handicraft" and disparaged machine production as "dull and ugly," Behne shockingly reversed this valuation, dismissing the contemporary production of craft products as "kitsch." Such a dramatic step marks a strategic turning point in modernist cultural debate.

Dal Co himself has made part of this larger historical context clear, point-

3.1 A view of the intensely "crafted" foyer of the Somerfeld house in Berlin-Dahlem, by Walter Gropius and Adolf Meyer, from 1921. (Photograph by permission, from Hans Wingler, *The Bauhaus*, MIT Press.)

ing out how Behne's radical gesture challenged a cultural tradition that had been associated for over a decade with Hermann Muthesius and with the Deutscher Werkbund.[10] For Dal Co, Behne was a force that significantly shifted the concentration of his generation of architects toward technology and industrial production. While he sees Muthesius and his colleagues in the Werkbund as the failing advocates of what were by then anachronisms, Behne, for Dal Co, points the way forward, to the full-fledged conception of architectural modernity that was later to be promulgated by such figures as Nikolaus Pevsner and Sigfried Giedion.

I wish to sketch out a still broader historical framework, in which the polemical victory of Behne over Muthesius will be seen from two distinct perspectives. First of all, the victory had its own consequential historical precedents, forming part of a historical pattern stretching from the middle of the nineteenth to the middle of the twentieth century. Secondly, this victory was at the same time a more contingent historical event than might be supposed, commanding authority only as long as cultural modernity also did.

To begin with the pattern of recurrence, the first precedent I should like to cite is one involving Muthesius himself—except that in this case he is

and so, if today "cultural" modernity is in question, so would the authority of the polemic

3.2   An archival photograph of the Crystal Palace, shortly after its completion. (Victoria and Albert Museum.)

cast in the role of the advocate of change rather than the defender of established values. This is the well-known argument that broke out at the 1913 conference of the Werkbund in Cologne, already discussed in chapter one, between Muthesius and certain others such as Henry Van de Velde. In broad terms, we may say that the results of the 1913 argument had similarities to those of 1922. The advocates of change by and large held sway, and experiments with industry formed an increasingly important part of the work of Werkbund members, save for the brief postwar resurgence of craft-oriented expressionism against which Behne's 1922 text argued. But in a still earlier instance, the results had not been so clear-cut. Half a century before, another debate along these lines had ensued between John Ruskin and the group of reformers around Henry Cole's *Journal of Design and Manufactures.* The dispute in this case was more general in its nature, having to do with the strong desire of Cole's group to improve contemporary English product design, as well as with cultural response to Ruskin's recently published *Seven Lamps of Architecture* and with Ruskin's own critical opposition to such manifestations of technological modernity as the Crystal Palace—that great technological enterprise of midcentury that had been designed both to symbolize and to house the promise of industrialization. For Ruskin, the great structure was nothing but a "magnified conservatory," and a "cucumber frame"; "not," in his worlds, "architecture at all."[11] To no avail did Digby Wyatt challenge him in Cole's *Journal*:

> Instead of boldly recognising the tendencies of the age, which are inevitable . . . instead of considering the means of improving these tendencies . . . he either puts up his back against their further development, or would attempt to bring back the world of art to what its course of action was four centuries ago.[12]

great moral critique

Rather, Ruskin persisted in his hostility to industrialization. Indeed he saw it as central to his hatred of modern civilization:

> The great cry that rises from all our manufacturing cities, louder than their furnace blast, is all in very deed for this—that we manufacture everything except men; we blanch cotton, and strengthen steel, and refine sugar, and shape pottery; but to brighten, to strengthen, to refine or to form a single living spirit, never enters our estimate of advantages.[13]

As I have already hinted, the great English debate of midcentury, unlike the disputes of 1922 and 1913, failed to result in a clear-cut victory for the advocates of modernity. Indeed, the *Journal* in which Cole made his famous case for improvements to industrial product designs ceased publication after only four issues, and Ruskin continued his critique of industrialization right up until his death. It took the later efforts of Behne's successors as historians of modernism, figures such as Pevsner and Giedion, to resurrect the reputation of Henry Cole as a precursor of the cultural modernity that they saw triumph in the 1920s and 1930s.

chronology

1852, 1913, 1922. Viewed in the perspective of the familiar history of modernism, this pattern of recurrence is one in which the inevitability of the incorporation of industrialization into the corpus of the theory of modernity grows ever more evident. A failure in 1852, a partial success in 1913, and a triumph in 1922. Certainly it is possible in this historical perspective to see what a raw nerve Behne touched with his rhetorical polemic. For the turning of the European design avant-garde away from craft and toward the technological, in the years following 1922, could hardly have been more decisive or more thoroughgoing. For example, between 1922 and 1924, at Walter Gropius's behest, the educational philosophy of the Bauhaus was fundamentally rethought. Johannes Itten, the advocate of mystical methods and of the revival of craft, was dismissed, to be replaced by László Moholy-Nagy, who developed a new curriculum more oriented to technology and to mass production. More or less simultaneously, Le Corbusier, in his *Vers une architecture,* launched the strong pleas for the industrialization of architecture that constituted a hallmark of the entire first phase of his career. By 1927, most of Gropius's colleagues in the Ring, including Mies van der Rohe and Max and Bruno Taut, had turned more resolutely to industrialization as a vehicle for the expression of modern architectural ideas. Then too, the various movements in the Soviet Union grouped loosely under the rubric of constructivism also pressed the vocabulary of modern architectural form in the direction of a dramatic iconography of technological optimism. In Holland, Germany, and Czechoslovakia a slightly younger generation of designers pressed even further. In the ABC group, for example, there emerged an even more technologically rigorous approach to modern design, an approach that led, in its turn, to such important production in the 1930s and 1940s as that of Buckminster Fuller. By 1939, the date of publication of the first comprehensive history of modernism in architecture, Sigfried Giedion's *Space, Time and Architecture,* industrialization had been more or less entirely accepted as an integral component of the body of theoretical ideas associated with the movement. And the promotion of industrialized building as a key to the solution of urban housing problems became one of the principal activities of CIAM from the 1930s right through to the 1950s.

Thus far in my account, the overall pattern of recurring historical debate falls clearly within the generally accepted discourse of mainstream modern architectural theory. At this point I wish to bring into view a series of still more widespread and problematic debates, debates that show, in my view, how Behne's 1922 polemical victory has turned out, historically, to have been a highly contingent one. Contingent upon the supposition that the forging of the "much stronger bond" than "natural connectedness," as Behne advocated, was in fact ultimately achievable within modern fabrication processes; contingent upon the supposition that the division of labor, and the concomitant processes of mass production, would on the one hand preclude "kitsch" and on the other successfully elude a recurrent condition of worker alienation.

author intent.

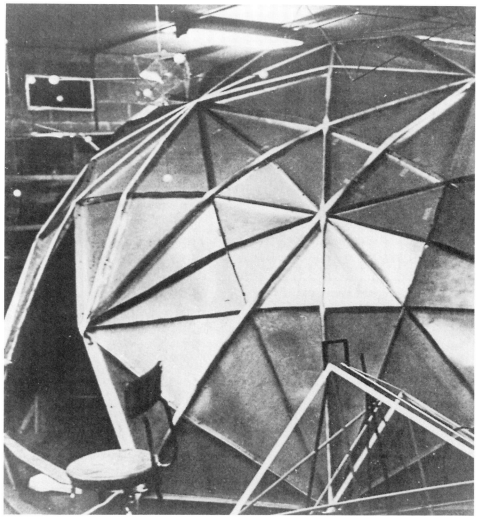

3.3   A "pentahexaedron" designed by Buckminster Fuller and constructed in cooperation with the Institute of Design in Chicago in 1948. (Photograph by permission, from Hans Wingler, *The Bauhaus*, MIT Press.)

From the vantage point of the late twentieth century, it is now evident that neither of these suppositions can be considered unquestionable. If we recollect for a moment the 1968 events that so shook the equanimity of conventional architectural praxis, we can readily see how doubtful both suppositions had already become. For the great revolt of the young embodied a profound reconsideration of the very precepts of contemporary fabrication that Behne had so resolutely advocated. Young architects and architecture students, who played so pivotal a role in the events of that year, turned especially strongly against modes of architectural praxis that depended on the division of labor. Some turned against it so totally as to seek to abandon any dependence on contemporary technology altogether, retreating to establish new communities in the wilderness that focused on a revival of craftsmanship. Others, less extreme in their rejection of modern technologies, nevertheless sought by the employment of what they called "alternative technologies" to establish "autonomous communities" that would minimize the degree of specialization of social roles which Behne had seen as so desirable within modern fabrication processes.

Some two and a half decades later, the great youth revolt of the late sixties in large measure forgotten; yet the social issues it brought to the fore are still with us. An innovative concept in recent labor relations has been the "team concept," which in the automobile industry in particular has been put forward as a means of reducing the high degree of specialization involved in assembly line production, and of reuniting, in significant measure, the labour that, according to theorists from Adam Smith to Henry Ford, had been so advantageously divided. It is true, of course, that the fabrication of buildings in the modern world has never been as industrialized as that of such products as automobiles. But this does not mean that the question of the so-called industrialization of building should not be considered in light of the renewed debate on the division of labor.

Given the great reconsideration of Enlightenment rationality now under way on so many fronts, it should not be surprising that debate about the moral and tectonic appropriateness of the division of labor is nowadays reemerging. For Marx himself, surely the most thoughtful and original of all labor theorists, was profoundly reserved on this very point. Realistic as he wished to be, and well aware of the centrality of the division of labor to the nineteenth-century triumph of capitalism, Marx also saw it as a key cause of the worker alienation he lamented. In *Capital,* he cited with decisive approbation the teacher of Adam Smith, Adam Ferguson, "who had pointed out the harmful effects of the division of labor" a century before Marx's own work.[14] It is only in the subsequent theories of such followers as Lenin that the division of labor is unequivocally accepted as a necessary concomitant of modernization, and it is from such followers, we may suppose, that Behne derived his own enthusiasm for it.

Marx's ambivalence regarding the division of labor being what it is, we should perhaps not be surprised to find parallel ambiguity within the ongoing arguments for architectural modernism. Certain premonitions of it can even be seen in an important theoretical text of the 1940s, Giedion's *Mechanization Takes Command,* which appeared until recently to have been the culmination of modernism's engagement with technology and mass production.[15] In a magisterial survey of the history of mechanization from the Middle Ages until the present, Giedion documented the impact of the phenomenon on agriculture and on human surroundings, including furniture, appliances, and plumbing equipment. Necessarily, his argument led him to return to the controversial question of the division of labor. In Part III of his text, Giedion depicted in considerable detail the evolution of the assembly line and of scientific management, the two great concepts of industrialization in the nineteenth century that resulted from implementing the previous century's idea of dividing labor. Giedion traced the development of the assembly line out of the concepts of "continuous production," first in the food industry at the beginning of the nineteenth century and then in clothing manufacturing and in meat packing. This led him in turn to a brief review of the appearance of "scientific management" late in the nineteenth century, at the initiative of the controversial figure Frederick Taylor. Eventually, Taylor's thinking was to arrive at the concept of the assembly line, as it became most familiar after 1900 in the new automobile factories of Henry Ford.

Interestingly enough, given the overall orientation of his text, Giedion did not give any account in his overview of the polemic launched by Behne in 1922, to which I have devoted such detailed discussion. Perhaps this is because, from the perspective of 1948, the conversion to industrialization had begun to appear historically inevitable. Certainly it is noteworthy that Giedion did offer brief comments on the earlier polemics against mechanization of Ruskin and Morris, offering belated support to Henry Cole and his group of reformers in the great English controversy of the middle of the nineteenth century.

Giedion traced the influence of Ruskin and Morris, which he saw as negative, on an American movement of the turn of the century led by the influential figure Gustave Stickley. Stickley was the—for a time—highly successful publisher and editor of a journal called simply *The Craftsman,* which

> advocated "the simplification of daily life and a more reasonable way of living." It advocated country houses, often sound in detail. It advocates self-sufficiency: "a pleasant comfortable dwelling situated on a piece of ground large enough to yield a great part of the food for the family." . . . This movement as against the English arts and crafts, was simply called Craftsman: Craftsman houses, craftsman furniture, craftsman farms. It did not seek individuality in furniture.[16]

The great historian of mechanization argued that this movement, like that of Ruskin and Morris, represented a historical dead end. Employing arguments almost exactly parallel to those of Behne, Giedion ruled out any long-term potential for Stickley's admitted grass roots success.

> From the start it had no chance of survival. Even if seconded by real genius, such attempts must have been abortive in an environment growing ever closer to full mechanization.

He even came close to a characterization of craftsmanship as "kitsch": "From time to time, *The Craftsman* would carry designs of benches, bookshelves, tables or chests, solely for the purpose of the home-worker. One 25-cent booklet of the Popular Mechanics series addresses the amateur on 'Mission Furniture, How to Make It.'"[17] Giedion concluded his account with a sharp observation that uncannily prefigures a later view of Hannah Arendt on the limitations of craftsmanship in the contemporary world. "The movement," said Giedion, "was to end in a hobby."[18] Only in the very conclusion of Giedion's historical overview, and only in the broadest possible terms, does he betray any hint of doubt as to the ultimate value of the impact of the division of labor on the quality of modern life:

> In a Chicago packing house, hogs, hanging head downwards, moved uninterruptedly past a staunch Negro woman at the curve of the conveyor system. Her task was to stamp, with a rubber stamp, the carcasses examined by the inspectors. With a sweeping movement she smacked the rubber stamp on each skin.

3.4 "Suggestions for Dining Room," an illustration from Stickley's *The Craftsman,* volume 2, no. 1 (1902).

> Perhaps we start from false premises; but in an outside observer a strange feeling was aroused: a creature of the human race trained to do nothing else but, day after day, stamp thousand after thousand of carcasses in four places.[19]

A decade after the publication of Giedion's seminal work, the whole matter of the role of the division of labor in the fabrication of the "things of the world" was, philosophically speaking, fundamentally reopened. For 1958 saw the first publication of Hannah Arendt's provocative text *The Human Condition.* Developing an argument whose sole intellectual precedent is Marx, Arendt launched a fundamental reconsideration not only of the concept of the division of labor, but also of the ongoing disputes concerning quality and kitsch that had located Behne and Morris in opposing camps. Moreover Arendt sought structurally to link contemporary manifestations of worker alienation to "worldliness," offering the possibility of situating the Behne/Morris opposition in a new and suggestive light.

Arendt presented John Locke's distinction between "the labour of [our] body" and "the work of [our] hands" as basic to her own consideration of the fabrication of "the things of the world." Indeed, Arendt argued that Adam Smith's seminal formulation of the division of labor must be seen as a mutant of earlier ideas formulated by Locke. Following Locke's distinction and terminology, Arendt argued that labor must be seen primarily to have to do with

> all those "good things" which are "really useful to the life of man," to the "necessity of subsisting," [and which] are "generally of short duration, such as—if they are not consumed by use—will decay and perish by themselves." After a brief stay in the world, they return into the natural process which yielded them either through absorption into the life process of the human animal or through decay; in their man-made shape, through which they acquired their ephemeral place in the world of man-made things, they disappear more quickly than any other part of the world. Considered in their worldliness, they are the least worldly and at the same time the most natural of all things. Although they are man-made, they come and go, are produced and consumed, in accordance with the ever-recurrent cyclical movement of nature.[20]

As for the products of "work," Arendt saw them in a quite different light:

> The work of our hands, as distinguished from the labor of our bodies—*homo faber* who makes and literally "works upon" as distinguished from the *animal laborans* which labors and "mixes with"—fabricates the sheer unending variety of things whose sum total constitutes the human artifice. They are mostly, but not exclusively, objects for use and they possess the durability Locke needed for the establishment of property, the "value" Adam Smith needed for the exchange market, and they bear testimony to productivity, which Marx believed to be the test of human nature. Their proper use does not cause them to disappear and they give the human artifice the stability and solidity without which it could not be relied upon to house the unstable and mortal creature which is man.

> The durability of the human artifice is not absolute; the use we make of it, even though we do not consume it, uses it up. The life process which permeates our whole being invades it, too, and if we do not use the things of the world, they also will eventually decay, return into the over-all natural process from which they were drawn and against which they were erected. If left to itself or discarded from the human world, the chair will again become wood, and the wood will decay and return to the soil from which the tree sprang before it was cut off to become the material upon which to work and with which to build. But though this may be the unavoidable end of all single things in the world, the sign of their being products of a mortal maker, it is not so certainly the eventual fate of the human artifice itself, where all single things can be constantly replaced with the change of generations which come and inhabit the man-made world and go away.[21]

Now Arendt has argued that in the evolution of ideas in the age of the Enlightenment, the status of the activity of "work" was eventually superseded by that of "labor," that in turn becoming eventually "divided."

> The sudden, spectacular rise of labor from the lowest, most despised position to

the highest rank, as the most esteemed of all human activities, began when Locke discovered that labor is the source of all property. It followed its course when Adam Smith asserted that labor was the source of all wealth and found its climax in Marx's "system of labor," where labor became the source of all productivity and the expression of the very humanity of man.[22]

Then too, according to Arendt,

the elevation of laboring was preceded by certain deviations and variations from the traditional mentality of *homo faber* which were highly characteristic of the modern age and which, indeed, arose almost automatically from the very nature of the events that ushered it in. What changed the mentality of *homo faber* was the central position of the concept of process in modernity.[23]

At this point the next step, the division of labor was quite straightforward. "Division of labor indeed grows directly out of the laboring process." According to Arendt, it

is based on the fact that two men can put their labor power together and "behave toward each other as though they were one." This one-ness is the exact opposite of co-operation, it indicates the unity of the species with regard to which every single member is the same and exchangeable. . . . Since none of the activities into which the process is divided has an end in itself, their "natural" end is exactly the same as in the case of "undivided" labor: either the simple reproduction of the means of subsistence, that is, the capacity for consumption of the laborers, or the exhaustion of human labor power.[24]

The best-known argument for and illustration of the process of the division of labor is that of Adam Smith himself, in the first chapter of *The Wealth of Nations:*

This great increase in the quantity of work, which, in consequence of the division of labour, the same number of people are capable of performing, is owing to three different circumstances; first to the increase of dexterity in every particular workman; secondly, to the saving of the time which is commonly lost in passing from one species of work to another; and lastly, to the invention of a great number of machines which facilitate and abridge labour, and enable one man to do the work of many.[25]

And with this, the transforming evolution, according to Arendt, is complete.

The ideals of *homo faber,* the fabricator of the world, which are permanence, stability, and durability, have been sacrificed to abundance, the ideal of the *animal laborans.* We live today in a laborers' society because only laboring, with its inherent fertility, is likely to bring about abundance; and we have changed work into labor-

3.5 A view of the Waite house, one of a group designed and built "do-it-yourself style" by friends of the architect Sim van der Ryn, from the University of California at Berkeley, in the wake of the 1968 events.

ing, broken it up into its minute particles until it has lent itself to division where the common denominator of the simplest performance is reached.[26]

author hedges his bets.

Now it is true, of course, that such fundamental objections to the division of labor as Arendt has put forward are far from having been absorbed in contemporary labor theory, let alone in contemporary architecture. Indeed, one supposes that contentious discussion on this complex and divisive question will continue for some time to come. Yet in the years following 1968, consequential efforts have been made by architects of various persuasions to come to grips with the issue, and these efforts merit critical scrutiny.

We may begin by returning to the effort, which was both early and extreme, by a number of groups of post-1968 rebels to reject technological society altogether. As noted above, they abandoned metropolitan centers and moved to remote rural destinations, where they created a whole series of notable alternative communities of the early 1970s, communities in which so-called high technologies were eschewed in favor of low, self-sufficient ones, and in which the social concept of "do-it-yourself" was raised to a new level of moral prestige. One particular offshoot of the retreat from modernity took its commitment to do-it-yourself craftsmanship so far as to acquire for the results of its efforts the name "the wood-butcher's art." Viewing its results, one is strangely reminded of earlier contributions to the ongoing debate. Think of the parallel of William

Morris on the medieval methods that preceded the division of labor:

> Consider, I pray you what these wonderful works are, and how they were made.
> . . . They were common things . . . no rarities. . . . They were made by common
> fellows . . . in the course of their daily labour. . . . And . . . many a grin of
> pleasure . . . went to the carrying through of their jobs.[27]

The pertinence of this to my argument is not exhausted in the analogy
it evokes between the cultural revolts of the late nineteenth century and
those of the mid-twentieth. For it is surely not irrelevant, in the larger
context of the relationship of handicraft to technology, that the revival of
craftsmanship of the 1970s proved as marginal to the ongoing evolution of
fabrication processes in our own time as Morris's own had done a century
before. For we have seen the same fate befall the countercultural experiments of the early seventies as Giedion portrayed for the efforts of Gustave
Stickley at the turn of the century. Once again, a brave effort to revive
craftsmanship saw its influence gradually devolve into nothing more than
a "hobby." Indeed, the successive failures of Morris, Stickley, and the early
seventies counterculture to accomplish a definitive revival of craft would
seem rather powerfully to suggest that whatever the difficulties of the
division of labor in our time, a simple revival of craftsmanship has by now
been historically precluded. In fact, certain of Arendt's observations on
fabrication may even give some indication as to the cause of these successive failures. For while she never referred specifically to Morris's efforts at
reform, she left no doubt of her scorn for any praxis that presumed to
employ one's "pleasure" while engaged in it as any appropriate measure of
"worldliness." Indeed, it would appear to be a logical consequence of her
arguments in this regard that though the "pain" of alienated labor is palpably real, "pleasurable" craft does not of itself constitute a world. On the
contrary, the employment of "pleasure" as any such measure would seem
consistently and inexorably to have led to the sad inconsequentiality of
craftsmanship becoming merely a hobby, a curious historical *cul-de-sac*
within the ongoing evolution of the processes of fabrication in the modern
era.

Since the fateful loss of momentum of the efforts of the architectural
counterculture in the late 1970s, there have been a series of more main-

stream and in some ways more consequential responses to the crisis of fabrication in our time. Indeed, much of the work of serious practitioners today can be seen to constitute diverse efforts to meet the challenge of the historic loss of confidence in technology. At one extreme, we may cite the efforts of the notable polemicist of postmodernism Robert Stern. As his own professional practice matured, and as his dismay with orthodox modernism prompted him to move progressively farther from its techniques as he had learned them as a student, he became interested in certain issues of fabrication from his own philosophical position. In the process of designing a series of rather substantial residences in the mid to late 1970s, Stern was quite struck to discover the extent to which, within the northeastern United States, it remained possible to obtain the services of such traditional craftsmen as decorative plasterers and stone carvers. Stern's admiration for such early twentieth-century American architects as George Howe and McKim, Mead and White, together with his increasing disaffection from the conventional wisdom of modernist practice, inclined him to see this availability of traditional crafts as theoretically significant. For it seemed to disprove the deterministically modernist proposition that such crafts could play no role in an architecture in our own time—indeed, that they were socioeconomically obsolete. As a result, Stern chose to expand the scope of his postmodern polemics of those years, and using the availability of the plasters and the carvers as yet further proof of the fallacy of conventional modernist rhetoric, in this case in respect to fabrication.

It is true, of course, in an era of such extensive restoration of historical monuments as the past three decades have been, that any reasonable observer would be compelled to acknowledge the truth of Stern's claim, at the level of historical fact. We know now that such skills remain in our time relatively widely available. Yet it does not seem possible to proceed from this toward a larger theoretical claim that a revival of craftsmanship, such as was promoted by Morris in the late nineteenth century or by the Werkbund in the early twentieth, is once again possible in our own time. While the contemporary socioeconomic circumstances of construction have indeed not eliminated such skills from the realm of current architectural production, they have nevertheless radically circumscribed their availability.

and yet, all bldg. is typically financed by wealthy developers & institutions.

In fact, they remain limited to building projects of a relatively luxurious kind, whether private projects for the well-to-do or major public edifices (unless, of course, they are do-it-yourself undertakings, which will also, alas, fall into the category of "hobbies"). In short, they will remain the exception rather than the rule, and therefore cannot be employed as exemplars, in the fashion intended by both Morris and the Werkbund, to illustrate a revival of craftsmanship relevant to architectural theory in our time.

It may even be possible to discern, in the evolution of Stern's approach to design in subsequent years as well as in the popular influence of his work, some tacit acknowledgment of this limited relevance. To take the case of his own work first, I don't think it is coincidental that in the years following his rediscovery of traditional craftsmanship, Stern's architectural vocabulary has itself become progressively less ironic in a postmodern sense and more conventionally revivalist. It is almost as though the rediscovery of the traditional crafts had carried with it some broader obligation to "tradition" in a more generally conventional sense. If we turn to Stern's influence, along with that of his various postmodern colleagues, on the evolving architectural vernacular of our time, then an opposite but no less troubling tendency is evident. For in the everyday world of commercial postmodernism, the motifs of the vocabulary are deployed in various ways that pay almost no heed at all to the imperatives of craftsmanship, and rely on a "scenographic" *modus operandi* that embodies no ironic intention at all. Indeed, even in the relativized terms of contemporary discourse, it seems to me that this particular realm of design activity cannot escape characterization as a revival of the kitsch already deplored by Behne in 1922.

the Hyper-Moderns.

Among current approaches to architecture, few could be thought to be farther from Robert Stern than that of the movement represented by such figures as Norman Foster, Renzo Piano, and Richard Rogers. This group must be seen as attempting to defy the ongoing contemporary crisis of technology and, by sheer heroic resolution, to reconstitute the original brave confidence of technological modernity circa 1922. In the case of such important projects as the Centre Pompidou in Paris, by Piano and Rogers,

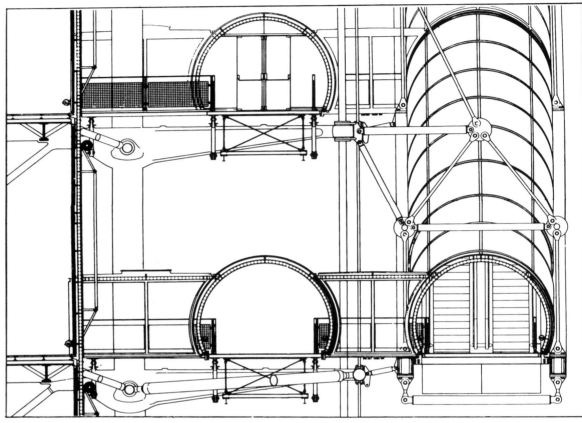

3.6   A cross section of the cantilevered set of escalator enclosures slung off the side of Piano and Rogers's Pompidou Center in Paris, from 1971–1977.

a strategy has been employed that makes the entire edifice into a represen-tation primarily of the process of fabrication through which it came into beginning. What is more, in a manner evoking certain projects from the 1960s by members of the Archigram group—from whom Rogers drew early sustenance—the revelatory configuration of this array of fabricated components even succeeds in conveying a certain impression of liberation, and of a possible image of buildings as instruments for pleasure.

But to date, it seems to me, the architectural products of this tendency have generally not succeeded in eluding the contingent consequences of so strong a reliance on the symbolism of the fabrication process alone, or of their prospective absorption into the cycle of consumption. For one thing, the sheer blatancy of the technological array often obscures any reading of built form above and beyond that as process of fabrication. As a result, notwithstanding the resounding affirmation of the technological array, little broader sense of symbolic decorum, whether urban, programmatic, or transcendent, is readily available to the tendency's most militant protagonists. In this sense, one feels let down by a curiously self-constrained symbolic discourse, and the buildings thereby fail to contribute adequately to the condition of worldliness that I, following Arendt, would argue remains the fundamental *raison d'être* of work.

One may point also to another contemporary architectural effort, one more poignant than either the postmodernism of Stern and his colleagues or the opposed technological fetishism of Rogers and his. This was the profoundly thought-provoking experience of Leon Krier in connection with

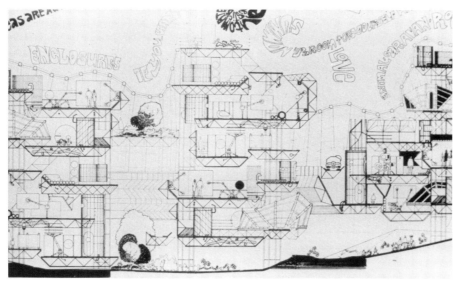

3.7   The would-be architecture of liberatory hedonism: Archigram's "Control and Choice" project, in which inhabitants would have the option to modify at will the form of enclosure provided by their dwelling, by means of technologies emergent at the time.

a project (1977–1979) for a school proposed to be built in the French community of St. Quentin-en-Yvelines. In this case, Krier proposed a system of fabrication that was certainly not of a high order of technological sophistication, though it was not so historicist as the systems recently being employed by Stern either. Rather, it combined bearing wall masonry with a system of columns and beams, relying for its tectonic integrity on a high-quality series of connections of materials that I would associate with the rationalist methods of construction of French public buildings of the late nineteenth century. As Krier's design work on the project proceeded, it turned out that even such a moderately reformist proposition in respect to fabrication would be unfeasible within the extant socioeconomics of French public building construction. Krier was faced with the prospect of drastically revising the design to comply with the more customary techniques of contemporary French building construction, and by this means with contemporary construction budgets. Rather than compromise the integrity of his architectonic vision, the obdurate architect chose not to attempt to pursue the realization of the project at all, preferring to allow it to attain the purer but more limited cultural reality of a utopian project.[28]

Such a series of examples must begin to give one pause, insofar as one looks to them for any resolution of the great questions of the division of labor and its influence on possible future modes of architectural praxis. On the one hand, we see efforts at a revival of craftsmanship prove inapplicable to building in an exemplary sense, leading instead to a further proliferation of kitsch. On the other, we see a radical commitment to the representation of fabrication in architecture fail adequately to address the imperative of worldliness. Worst of all, one sees in the mass vernacular commercial architecture of our time a sort of convergence of the most troubling aspects of both these tendencies. In the shopping malls, fast food outlets, and motels of contemporary suburbia, a system of construction has now been devised that takes over the efficacy of the position represented by Foster, Piano, and Rogers but eschews its technical iconography, relying instead, for its symbolic expression, on a vocabulary of kitsch that has been borrowed—without permission—from the "tradition of quality" sought by such distinct contemporary opponents of technological fetishism as Stern and Krier.

[handwritten margin note:] very clear general critique of the failure of both camps: tradition & hypermodern

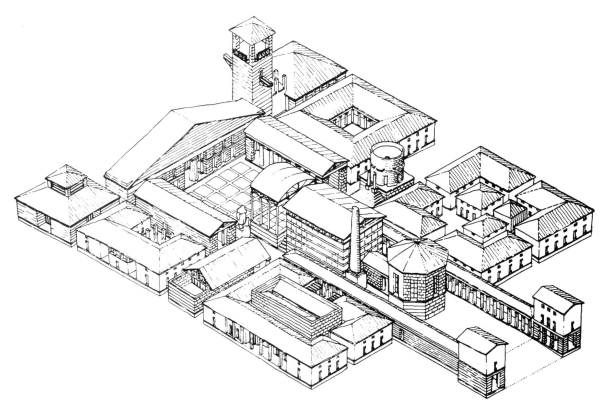

3.8 Leon Krier's project for a school at St. Quentin-en-Yvelines, France, from 1977–1979. (Illustration: Leon Krier.)

From the results of these varied, valiant efforts to address the relationship of craftsmanship and technology in our time, it seems to me that a definitive historical resolution of the painful questions of kitsch and of alienation is not near at hand. Indeed, my commentary suggests the need, before such a large philosophical question could even be faced, to formulate what we might call a "political economy of construction," wherein the characteristic evolution of building technologies, construction economics, and development industry practices would be carefully correlated within local social situations. Were such an economy eventually to become available as an operative tool in architectural discourse, it might be possible for us to discuss intelligently the claims made, and the dilemmas confronted by, such figures as Stern, Krier, Rogers, and their colleagues. We might even be offered more ample analytical techniques than those available to date with which to discuss the characteristic and provocative use of "profane" materials, such as chain link fencing that marked for a time the work of such designers as Robert Venturi and Frank Gehry.

Specifically, I am thinking of their use by Venturi at Guild House in Philadelphia from 1961, and by Gehry in his house for himself from 1978 as well as at the subsequent Santa Monica Place Shopping Center. To be sure,

3.9   Chain link fencing ceremonially inflected to form the entrance to Venturi, Rauch, and Scott Brown's Guild House in Philadelphia, from 1961. (Photograph: William Watkins.)

I don't suggest that the two utilizations are entirely parallel—Venturi's seems to me to constitute a sort of ironic homage to brutalism, such as typified his pop art phase at its best, while Gehry's is more likely a sort of anarchic salutation of constructivism. These differences notwithstanding, it is true that prior to such seminal uses, chain link fencing played no discernible formal or iconographic role in the architectural production of the

3.10 Chain link fencing extravagantly deployed in the configuration of Frank Gehry's house for himself in Santa Monica, California, from 1978.

past few decades. In this series of precedent-setting works, first Venturi and then Gehry achieved what I would call a socioeconomic shift in architectural fabrication.

In the case of Venturi, we may say that by his deft deployment of the material in a virtually baroque plan form for the entrance at Guild House, he accomplished a provocative material redemption of the product's customary ordinariness. In the case of Gehry, the extravagant redundancies in its use force us to consider possible wider readings of its iconic significance, a reading pressed still further in its use as a complex collage of moiré patterns on the entire south facade of Santa Monica Place. And, of course, both uses were achieved quite economically, on account of the relatively low material cost of the product in relation to typical construction budgets for such projects. Indeed, it can be said that it was the

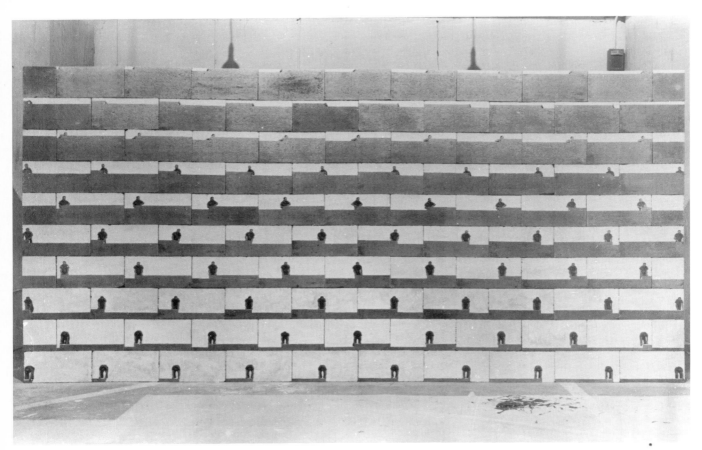

3.11 "Recording Wall": a project by Dan Hoffman from 1991, consisting of a concrete wall on each block of which is mounted a photograph of the incremental process of the laying up of the wall itself. (Photograph courtesy Dan Hoffman.)

relatively modest cost of the material per square foot, in the first instance, that opened the way for these innovative designers to redeem its previously characteristic social meaning by deploying it both so extensively and so unexpectedly.

More recently, efforts by a younger generation of designers have had the effect not only of redeeming the significances of "profane" materials, but also of putting further into question the division of labor according to which they have, in orthodox modern architecture, been customarily assembled. I am thinking here of examples such as those explored at the Cranbrook Academy of Art, where Dan Hoffman and his students have for some years now been engaged in the execution of a series of in situ projects that have been both designed and fabricated without any conceptual or sociological division of labor between the two procedures. Hoffman and his students, in effect, have reversed the set of assumptions that have been made by most modern architects since Behne's contentious polemic of 1922. It seems clear today that the formulation of a new mode of analysis adequate to the challenges now being made to the historic position of orthodox modernism—as much by the reluctance of a young generation to accept specialization as by the onset of full computerization of the relationship of design to fabrication—will be a hallmark of advanced thinking in regard to the fabrication of "the things of the world" in the future. Indeed, it may even be possible to begin to discern how certain emergent uses of the computer that bridge from design to fabrication—without the familiar intervening step of shop drawings—may in themselves contribute to a process of despecializing architects.

At any event it would seem certain that, in the absence of some such new method of analysis, we will not soon see in the architecture of our time any attainment of that "much stronger bond" that Behne looked forward to as the result of the "new and higher unity" he expected "estrangement," in due course, to produce.

Instruments and Monuments

Only a very small part of architecture belongs to art: the tomb and the monument. Everything else, everything which serves a purpose should be excluded from the realms of art.

Adolf Loos, 1910

Instead of monuments, architecture creates instruments.

Karel Teige, 1929

Adolf Loos's and Karel Teige's epigrams are among the more thought-provoking comments on architecture made in the twentieth century. Though there is no direct connection between the two, they are by no means entirely unrelated. Partly allied and partly opposed to one another, both comments posit sociocultural distinctions about architecture that are fundamental in nature; and both imply a morally directive view of design activity.

Loos, of course, can be seen here pursuing the historic effort he made with his colleague Karl Kraus to maintain fundamental distinctions amongst the heterogeneous "things of the world" that make up daily existence. In Kraus's own words:

> Adolf Loos and I—he literally and I grammatically—have done nothing more than show that there is a distinction between an urn and a chamberpot and that it is this distinction above all that provides culture with elbow room. The others, those who fail to make this distinction, are divided into those who use the urn as a chamberpot and those who use the chamberpot as an urn.[1]

In this striking image, Kraus encapsulated their effort simultaneously to resist the manifold degradations of the processes of fabrication that had characterized nineteenth-century industry—and which by their time were familiar to all knowledgeable cultural critics—at the same time as they also dissented from the reforming efforts of contemporary architects, artists, and craftsmen in the Vienna Secession, seeing such efforts as naive and counterproductive.

If Loos and Kraus, at the turn of the century, were looking for "elbow room" for "culture," the same cannot be said of Karel Teige in his polemic of 1929. For he, through what we now think of as a "positivist" moral conviction, was seeking to expunge from architecture all aspirations to higher values, in favor of a pure instrumentality. His ambition in this respect is clearly evident in the criticism he published in *Stavba* of Le Corbusier's project for the Mundaneum, the proposed center of world thought that was to be erected on the shore of Lake Geneva. Teige extolled the virtues of a rigorous functionalism, an exclusive respect for material reality, and a precise correspondence of building form to known

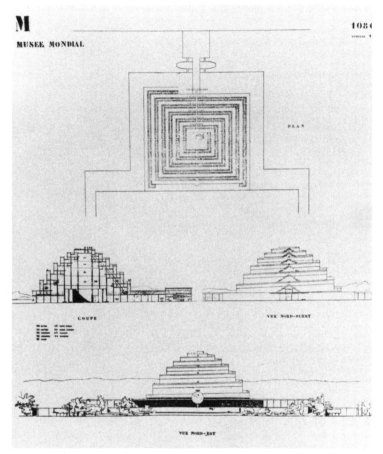

4.1   The Mundaneum project of Le Corbusier, from 1929, showing a detail of the museum and an early version of the spiral that would recur so frequently in museum designs later in Le Corbusier's career.

social program. By contrast, he opposed what he saw as "archaism"—what we would nowadays probably call "historicism"—abstract metaphysics, and formalism.[2] In both respects Teige found Le Corbusier's project problematic. In his view, it lacked a convincing social program; it betrayed historicist—in this case Mayan and Aztec—stylistic precedents; and it was overly preoccupied both by composition and by a geometry that he saw as metaphysical—the evidence for this last being Le Corbusier's interest in regulating lines. It is in the context of such objections that Teige made the radically instrumentalist statement quoted above.

Pure instrumentality, of course, is hardly a new concept in modern intellectual discourse. Indeed, it is the quintessential praxis of *homo faber,* as Arendt named him, the work of whose hands, on her view, constitutes "the world" that mortal men inhabit. In her words:

> The implements and tools of *homo faber,* from which the most fundamental experience of instrumentality arises, determine all work and fabrication. Here it is indeed true that the end justifies the means; it does more, it produces and organizes them. . . . During the work process, everything is judged in terms of suitability and usefulness for the desired end, and for nothing else.[3]

Moreover, she continued,

> The same standards of means and end apply to the product itself. Though it is an end with respect to the means by which it is produced and is the end of the fabrication process, it never becomes, so to speak, an end in itself, at least not as long as it remains an object for use. The chair which is the end of carpentering can show its usefulness only by again becoming a means, either as a thing whose durability permits its use as a means for comfortable living or as a means of exchange.[4]

It is Arendt's view that among the hallmarks of the early stages of the long process of technological modernization that began in the sixteenth and seventeenth centuries—and particularly of the scientific revolution of Galileo and Newton that formed part of it—was the exalted new prestige acquired by the activities of *homo faber:* "This was natural enough, since it had been an instrument" (Arendt is thinking here of the epochal invention of the telescope) "and therefore man insofar as he is a toolmaker that led to the modern revolution."[5] The consequences of that new prestige, in her view, have been profound:

> Among the outstanding characteristics of the modern age from its beginning to our own time we find the typical attitudes of *homo faber:* his instrumentalization of the world, his confidence in tools and in the productivity of the maker of artificial objects; his trust in the all-comprehensive range of the means-end category, his conviction that every issue can be solved and every human motivation reduced to the principle of utility.[6]

It is, of course, precisely such an all-encompassing "instrumentalization" that lies in the background of Teige's attack on Le Corbusier.

While the philosophical backdrop of Teige's attack is quite evident, that of Le Corbusier's reply is less clear. For example, he declined to take up

Teige's schema of "instruments" and "monuments," relying instead on a highly rhetorical usage of the terms *sachlich* and *Sachlichkeit* to keep his opponents at bay. And he took great polemical advantage of the fact that his critic was a poet as well as an architectural critic, to put Teige's putative materialism into question.

Notwithstanding the lack of a philosophical backdrop as clear as Teige's, Le Corbusier's implicit opposition to a purely instrumental architecture is evident. His summary makes it so:

> The matter of *Sachlichkeit,* the present theme being proposed to contemporary architects, is obviously this: to equip a country with what is necessary and sufficient. A timely and urgent theme for which an immediate solution is indispensable: this is the socializing theme of the present age. But is architecture to be subsumed in this theme entirely? No![7]

Indeed, he went on to point out, "there is no known way to avoid architecture altogether, since it is the quality brought to a solution containing precisely those potentials of architecture: order, composition, and so on."[8] Then, too, he made a profound plea for an architecture that transcended techniques of problem solving.

> There can be no architecture until problems are posed; but there is architecture the instant a human begins to pursue a creative end, that is to say, to order, to compose the elements of a problem to create an organism. At this point, there opens before us the unlimited field of quality. You, poet, and I, architect, we are both only interested in the means that lead to the purest quality. Because—let's not play hide-and-seek again—we know perfectly well, looking at ten solutions, the one which is elegant, and we will applaud it![9]

We should probably not be too surprised that Le Corbusier stopped at elegance, eschewing consideration of "monumentality" itself. For he was still, at this time, anxious not to become associated with the Beaux-Arts enemies who had successfully lobbied against his much-admired entry to the 1927 competition for a new headquarters for the League of Nations. Indeed, it is part of his reply that the reproaches Teige directed at him really belong to the academy, and should have been directed there.

If Le Corbusier was disinclined at the end of the twenties to embrace monumentality unequivocally, no such inhibition affected the behavior of the two recent American visitors to the European architectural milieu,

a different side to the canon of Corb. as presented by UMCP

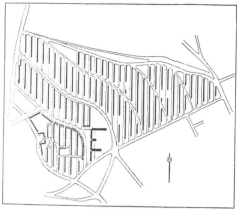

PLAN OF SIEDLUNG

TYPICAL PLANS

152

OTTO HAESLER: SIEDLUNG ROTHENBERG, KASSEL, GERMANY. 1930
The long bands of windows are made possible by steel construction. The inset balconies and the thick capping of the stairwells break the regular fenestration disagreeably. The stepping of the roof line, on the other hand, gives an interesting variety to the general system of regularity.

153

4.2   Two pages from Hitchcock and Johnson's *The International Style,* illustrating one of the controversially doctrinaire German *Siedlungen*—this one by Otto Haesler in Kassel.

Henry-Russell Hitchcock and Philip Johnson, who mounted a major exhibition of the new architecture at the Museum of Modern Art in 1932. In the notorious book that followed, they addressed the matter of architecture and building quite directly, and in conventionally academic terms:

> We still have architecture: that is, edifices consciously raised above the level of mere building. Architecture is seldom merely neutral aesthetically. It is good architecture or it is bad. When it is bad, the extreme contentions of the functionalist seem justified. But when it is good, such negative contentions appear an essential denial of the important spiritual function which all art serves. Good modern architecture may be as richly and coherently imbued with the style of our days as were the great edifices of the past with that of theirs.[10]

Not only that; in their conclusions, they advocated monumentality with neither reservation nor polemical anxiety: "The application of aesthetic principles of order, the formal simplification of complexity, will raise a good work of building to a fine monument of architecture."[11]

For these particular American observers, the dense, engaged, and guarded quarrels that had been proceeding between the different factions within

135
Instruments and Monuments

the International Congress of Modern Architecture lacked the intensity they had for those who had initiated them. In fact, it is difficult, in retrospect, not to suppose that Hitchcock and Johnson were aware of the controversy their observations were causing in those circles, and that they supported the growing pressures on architects in many European countries to monumentalize and to particularize architecture, in a manner quite distinct from the *sachlich* universality that had been sought in so much of the work of the twenties.

Still, the American unanimity represented by Hitchcock and Johnson's unequivocal embrace of monumentality was not to continue unchallenged for very long. In 1937, their American colleague Lewis Mumford, who had contributed to but was not central to the 1932 exhibition, published in the English magazine *Circle* a highly polemical excerpt from his about-to-be-published magnum opus *The Culture of Cities.* Mumford's essay "The Death of the Monument" was a most unusual piece of architectural commentary. To be sure, it must be seen to arise, at least in part, out of the basic concept of "bio-technicism" that eventually became central to his thinking, and to which I shall return in chapter six below. Indeed, Mumford's "organicist" leanings, growing out of his long-standing interests in nineteenth-century trancendentalism, surely led him to the militant opposition to monumentality that he put forward in 1937. And mounting it in the way he did, he introduced a provocatively American dimension to the arguments against monumentality. But in making a highly polemical entrée to a bitter European debate, Mumford oddly made no reference to that debate, or for that matter to Hitchcock and Johnson's tendentious commentaries either, choosing only to disparage certain then familiar examples of monuments such as the Lincoln Memorial in Washington and the Victor Emmanuel monument in Rome.

If it is true that "The Death of the Monument" failed to acknowledge any role in an ongoing intellectual debate either in America or in Europe, it nevertheless made its author's position unequivocally clear. Indeed, it may be considered to constitute one of the most extreme statements on architecture in its author's extensive body of writings. On the central point, for example, Mumford declared: "The very notion of a modern monument is a contradiction in terms. If it is a monument, it is not modern, and if it is modern, it cannot be a monument." In a related argument he elaborated a model of city growth that eschewed "fixities and permanence of function":

> The protective function of the city, tendencies toward fixities and permanence of function, have been overdone: for a living creature the only real protection and permanence comes through growth and renewal and reproduction: processes which are precisely the opposite of petrification.[12]

And this led Mumford to enquire:

> Does this mean that the modern city is to be renewed every generation"? Does this mean that the city is no longer to be an accretion of the memorials of the past, in which the needs of the living are narrowly filled in between ancient landmarks, whose value no longer lies in direct service, but in sentiments and piety?
>
> Yes to the first question and no to the second.[13]

In turn, this line of argument led him to propound an extraordinary model of urban evolution for our times. He began by allowing to some degree for the the survival of the fabric of the historical city: "The accretion of the past, the very mark of the historic city, with its successive stratifications of spirit, may well remain."[14] But he argued strenuously for severe constraints in contemporary reuse of the fabric in question. Indeed, he hypothesized a new mode of preservation of historic monuments in which they would under no circumstances be subject to technological modernization. In his words, "the surviving memorial itself [will not] be endangered and diminished by being made over—now with a system of gas lighting, now with a toilet, now with a 'restoration' in the barbarous manner of the Victorian restorers."[15] Objecting to both modernization and restoration, Mumford insisted: "If the city is to escape being a museum, what belongs to the past must either be put into a museum or be transformed as a whole into a museum—set aside; put to the special uses of education, but no longer lived in."[16]

Whether or not it was in any way in response to Mumford's extraordinary intervention we do not know, but in 1944, during the closing months of World War II, a symposium was convened in the United States by the historian Paul Zucker, with one entire session devoted to the topic "The Problem of a New Monumentality." Sigfried Giedion took up the contentious topic once again, this time from a viewpoint opposing that of Mumford.[17] So controversial was Giedion's 1944 argument that he was invited to deliver it again at the Royal Institute of British Architects in 1946. And in 1948, the magazine *Architectural Review* republished Giedion's text together with comments by the Swedish historian and critic Gregor Paulsson, Henry-Russell Hitchcock, the English architect and planner William Holford, Walter Gropius, the Brazilian architect Lucio Costa, and the Swiss Alfred Roth.[18]

Giedion began by arguing that modern architecture had to take three steps.

> The first was the single cell. . . . Modern architecture had to begin from scratch; it had to begin with the single cell, the smallest unit, the low cost dwelling, which to the last century seemed not worth the attention of the architect. . . . From the single cell, to the neighbourhood unit, to the city and the organization of the whole region, is one direct sequence. Thus it can be said that the second step of modern architecture was concentrated on urbanism. . . .

> The third step lies ahead. . . . This is the reconquest of monumental expression. The people want buildings representing their social, ceremonial and community life. They want their buildings to be more than a functional fulfillment. . . . This demand for monumentality cannot, in the long run, be suppressed. It tries to find an outlet at all costs.[19]

Notwithstanding his circumspect tone, Giedion was well aware of the tendentious nature of his argument. Indeed, his fellow symposiasts took widely divergent views in the matter. As one might expect, given his role in the creation of the International Style exhibition from 1932, Henry-Russell Hitchcock had no difficulty with the concept, and rather nonchalantly argued in favor.

> If some modern architects are beginning to feel today the desirability of monumentality, it might be explained by cynics as due to the fact that they have grown older, and are less satisfied that their entire production should be in the realm of the evanescent. But the feeling is undoubtedly more broadly based than that. There is evidence—for example in Russia—that the public likes in public architecture at least the simulacra of monumentality, as in other arts the public continues to demand various qualities abjured by the leading practitioners of the older genera-

tion. A psychosomatic functionalism itself might even suggest that the human purposes of architecture cannot be completely solved by a purely material calculus.[20]

Gregor Paulsson, on the other hand, while not as hard-line a materialist as Teige had been, continued to maintain what we might call a classically "social democratic" position, and resolutely opposed monumentality:

> The quality of monumentality is possible in contemporary buildings. The new materials and the new techniques do not exclude it. Functionalism itself need not necessarily exclude it, as even functionalism can very well be used to express pomp, dominance and mass appeal.

> But monumentality is not desirable. . . . The totalitarian society has always taken monumentality into its service to strengthen its power over people, the democratic society in conformity with its nature is anti-monumental. . . . Intimacy not monumentality should be the emotional goal, even in cities, as far as this is possible.[21]

remember, this is on immediately post war debate.

Between these opposing positions, Giedion attempted to develop an argument in favor of monumentality with considerable care. We can detect between the lines of his prose an acute recollection of the difficulties the moderns had faced in the late twenties, when modernism had been attacked as "mechanistic" and "soulless." (This issue will be discussed in greater detail in chapter seven.) Not only that, Giedion had obviously recognized, more painfully than had Hitchcock, how the political regimes of both Stalin and Hitler had rejected modernism in favor of a more monumental style. Indeed, despite Paulsson's claims for the supposed aversion of democratic society to monumentality, Giedion did not fail to note how even the New Deal of President Roosevelt had not proven uninterested in monumentality:

> There is no special political or economic system which is to blame for this. As different as they may be in their political and economic orientations, whether the most progressive or the most reactionary, there is one point where the governments of all countries will meet. And that is in their conception of "monumentality".[22]

Having conceded this, Giedion did go on to criticize the conception such governments had of it (at least to some degree) and struggled to raise the debate to a higher plane. Specifically, he charged that what had been produced in these varied cases was a parvenu style he called "pseudo-monumentality," citing such now familiar examples as Paul Troost's House of German Art in Munich and the Mellon Institute in Pittsburgh.

J. N. L. Durand
1760-1834

Munich 1937   Adolf Hitler's "Das Haus der Deutschen Kunst"

PSEUDO-MONUMENTALITY

Pseudo-Monumentality has nothing to do with Roman, Greek or any other style or tradition. It comes into being within the sphere of the Napoleonic society, imitating the manner of a former ruling class. Napoleon represents the type that gave to the nineteenth century its form: the self-made man, who became inwardly uncertain.

The origin of pseudo-monumentality buildings can be found in paper architecture, in lifeless schemes, that later became reality everywhere.

The model is the scheme for a museum by J. N. L. Durand (1760-1834), as it is represented in his lectures "Précis de leçons d'architecture" (1801-05) which were frequently translated and reprinted and were used by architects of every country. They are forgotten today, but the buildings which came out of their studios are still standing and new ones are added in a continuous stream since 140 years. The recipe is always the same: take some curtains of columns and put them in front of any building, whatever its purpose and to whatever consequences it may lead.

Pittsburgh 1937   The Mellon Institute

4.3 "Pseudo-monumentality," illustrated by Sigfried Giedion in his 1944 text "The Need for a New Monumentality."

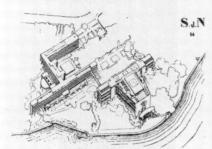

Is the artist estranged from life? There are several reasons to believe that he is not. But the artist has not been able to do anything about it because he has been artificially expelled from direct contact with the community.

Le Corbusier and Pierre Jeanneret:
Scheme for the Palace of the League of Nations at Geneva. 1927.

What will live in history of the Palace of the League of Nations is not the executed building which, when it finally was finished in 1937, proved to be—what it was from the beginning—an enormous tombstone. What will live in history is the project for this palace by Le Corbusier and P. Jeanneret, [1927]. It was the stroke of genius among 377 projects. The whole development of modern architecture towards a new monumentality would have been advanced for decades, if the officials could have understood its quality.

There are reasons to believe that the modern artists are right. We remember that throughout the whole nineteenth century, the masses, poor and rich under the domination of the press, academy, and governments, were always wrong in their taste and judgment, and that all the official art of that period appears so ridiculous

558

today, that the museums no longer show it to the public. *Those artists*, on the other hand, who had been *driven into seclusion, reveal today the creative spirit* which permeated the nineteenth century.

The same situation persists today. Nothing has changed in this

Le Corbusier and Pierre Jeanneret:
Palace of the League of Nations at Geneva, 1927.
The front of the office building (Secrétariat).

respect. I have seen in painting, sculpture, architecture, and poetry, a long row of artistic leaders (and I mean those who shape our emotional life) living their isolated existence, far from the public and the understanding of those who could have brought them in touch with the community. How is it possible to develop an art "satisfying" the people, when those who embody the creative forces are not allowed to work on the living body of our period?

Not the second-hand man, but *only the imagination of the real creators is suited* to build the lacking civic centers, again to instil the

559

4.4   Giedion's view of promising future possibilities: Le Corbusier's entry in the 1927 competition for a new headquarters building for the League of Nations of Geneva.

But, Giedion concluded, the explanation had to be in the uneducated taste of the governmental leaders who commission such projects. He saw some promise of future possibilities, however, and cited examples. First among these, interestingly enough, was Le Corbusier's 1927 project for the League of Nations. "Had [this proposal] not been killed by the leading politicians of the League," lamented Giedion, "the development of monumentality in contemporary architecture would probably be today on another level."[23] He also saw buildings such as Le Corbusier's and Oscar Niemeyer's Ministry of Education in Rio de Janeiro of 1942 as moving in the right direction.[24] A last instance of Giedion's caution in this delicate debate may

4.5 Le Corbusier and Oscar Niemeyer's 1942 building for the Ministry of Education in Rio de Janeiro—more evidence of Giedion's hope for a modern monumentality.

perhaps be seen as late as 1951, in his citation of the work of Giuseppe Terragni in the CIAM publication *A Decade of New Architecture*. For there we find inscrutably listed under "Row Houses and Apartment Blocks" Terragni's politically contentious local headquarters for the Italian Fascist Party, here titled innocuously a "political club."[25]

But by and large, by 1951 this generation's contribution to the debate must be seen already to have ended. As evidence, we may note that in 1949 Lewis Mumford had taken it upon himself to reply to Giedion's proposals, in a text entitled "Monumentalism, Symbolism and Style," in

The ferro concrete building forms a quadrangle of 33×33 metres. The main feature of the whole structure is the 16×14 metres glass-brick covered, two storeys high, assembly room. Offices, committee-rooms, library are built around this "inner court". A four storeys loggia opens on the large Piazza Castello and gave occasion for a keen and artistic use of the pure ferroconcrete skeletons. Elements of the Renaissance palaces (inner court and loggia) form here also essential parts; yet perforated and opened, they express a completely different conception of space.

Bâtiment en béton armé à la forme carrée de 33 m de côté. La partie principale est la salle de réunion de 16×14 m à deux étages et couverte de briques de verre. Les bureaux, les salles des comités, la librairie sont disposés autour de cette cour intérieure. Une loggia à quatre étages s'ouvre sur la Piazza Castello montrant une élégante ossature de béton armé aux formes très pures. Ces éléments des palais de la Renaissance (cour intérieure et loggia) ont ici une importance essentielle, mais, ajourés et ouverts, ils expriment une conception de l'espace absolument différente.

116   G. **Terragni**, 1904—1943 Casa del Popolo, **Como** 1936 **ITALY**

4.6   Giuseppe Terragni's Casa del Fascio, as published in Giedion's 1951 *A Decade of New Architecture.*

which he employed a tone as surprising as that of "The Death of the Monument" from twelve years before—except that this time the surprise is blandness rather than extremism. Here Mumford declined to answer Giedion's claims for monumentality directly, choosing instead to shift the frame of reference. For he indicated he was prepared to concede that there existed a broad social need, not for monumentality but for symbolism. Even then, Mumford insisted on delineating two ways in which one might consider modern architecture. The first of these, the "sound way," he saw as deriving from the organic principles of biotechnicism. As in 1937, he was prepared to characterize a lineage of architects who, in his view, followed it: "from Frank Lloyd Wright to van der Rohe, from Baillie Scott and MacIntosh, to Aalto and Mendelsohn."[26] Interestingly enough, this is a lineage that emphasizes the linkage of the very early work of Mies van der Rohe to that of Frank Lloyd Wright, while failing to take note of the significant neoclassicizing tendencies in Mies's later work—tendencies a careful eye would already have discerned by 1949.[27] Still, his proposed lineage can be seen to constitute a coherent constellation of architectural positions, especially when it is set explicitly against the second way of viewing modern architecture, which he disparaged as "mechanocentric." This he blamed first on an undue architectural influence of cubist theories of painting, second on Le Corbusier, and then on his erstwhile critical colleagues Hitchcock and Johnson, as well as on the Museum of Modern Art. According to Mumford, their "narrow canon of modernity gives an arbitrary starting point for the movement and produces a new kind of academicism, in which a very limited system of architectural forms takes the place of the classic five orders."[28]

Yet having made these disparaging remarks, and having redefined the tendency toward monumentality as a need for symbolism, Mumford nevertheless concluded his text with a reference to one of the German housing estates from the late twenties, a reference that remains to this day inexplicable. The project was Römerstadt in Frankfurt-am-Main, one that might well have been included in the International Style exhibition. One of its siting elements was a long semicircular retaining wall separating the housing blocks proper from a lower range of allotment gardens. This wall,

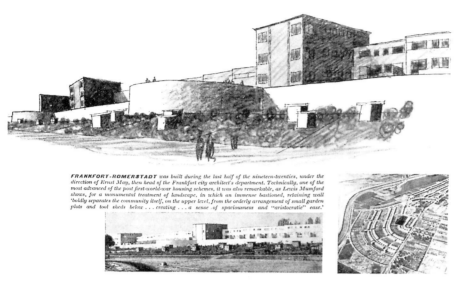

4.7   Lewis Mumford's 1948 characterization of "true monumentality": the retaining wall forming part of the landscaping of the German *Siedlung* Frankfurt-Römerstadt, as illustrated in the April 1949 issue of the *Architectural Review*.

Mumford claimed, was "one of the high points in the architectural expression of our time," and he indicated, despite all his previous argument, that he was prepared to let it pass as an example of "true monumentality."[29] With this somewhat startling shift of ground, Mumford concluded his American foray into this (hitherto) largely European controversy, attempting to rescue his palpably weakened critical position with a citation of an indisputably "social" and supposedly "unintentional" formal episode in a modern architectural project that, despite his characteristically American orientation to the argument, would have to be seen as quintessentially European. Still, if this last riposte of Mumford's failed to meet the challenge that had been mounted by Giedion, it is also true that the momentum of the overall theoretical debate had by this time already passed into the hands of two younger architectural critics. Both, as it happens, were English: Colin Rowe and Reyner Banham.

Once again, the terms of debate underwent a subtle shift. Rowe's entry into the debate launched his critical career in 1947: a now famous essay in the *Architectural Review* entitled "The Mathematics of the Ideal Villa." Rowe did not take up a defense of monumentality per se; indeed, his ironic and elliptical intelligence would disincline him to any such normative critical posture. Yet he did put a radical challenge to the view of Le Corbusier as a rationalist, technologically oriented originator of a new vocabulary of form based on industrial buildings.[30] In its place Rowe offered a vision of Le Corbusier that compared him to Palladio in his profound range of

Colin Rowe: new views on Corb.

free arrangement; there must be, at least partly, the personal exigencies of high style, for asymmetrical buildings in the traditional manner in fact remain standing, and frame buildings of conventional plan continue to give aesthetic satisfaction.

In both houses the principal rooms are on the first floor, linked to the garden by an external feature and flight of steps. The main floor of the Malcontenta shows a cruciform hall, and symmetrically disposed about it are two suites of three rooms each, two staircases and a portico. At Garches the central hall remains, one of the two staircases occupies a similar position, but the other has been turned through an angle of ninety degrees, the entrance hall has been revealed from this level by an asymmetrical well, and the external feature corresponding to the portico becomes partly a re-entrant volume, obliterating a line of support and placed in a less perceptible relationship to the main room. The cruciform shape has disappeared, and a Z-shaped balance is achieved by throwing the small library into the main apartment. There is a subsidiary cross axis at Malcontenta, which is suggested at Garches by the central voids of the end walls. These convey a certain careful character to the plan, but there is no through vista.

The wall at the Malcontenta forms the traditional solid pierced by vertical openings, with the central emphasis in the pediment; and the outer ones have the windows placed towards the extremities of the façade, a device which seems to reinforce the cubic quality of the block. The double bay in the middle is expressed by a single door, or in the rear elevation by a "Roman baths" motif, and carries the upper pediments of the roof. Horizontally the wall falls into three main divisions: base; piano nobile, corresponding to the Ionic order of the portico, terminated by a flattened entablature; and a superposed attic with cornice. The base plays the part of a projecting, consistently supporting solid, upon which the house rests; but while the attic and piano nobile are rusticated, the base is treated as a plain surface. A feeling of even greater weight carried here is achieved by this highly emotional inversion of the usual order.

In the Villa at Garches the exploitation of the structural system has led to the conception of the wall as a series of horizontal strips, alternating void and solid, a system which places equal interest in both centre and extremity of the façade, and is maintained in elevation of the wider spans of the double bays, which are arranged to read as two separate bays. Any system of central vertical accent, and inflection of the wall leading up to it, is profoundly modified. The immediate result in the garden elevation at Garches shows itself in the displacing of portico and roof pavilion from the central position which they occupy in the Malcontenta. They are separated, the one occupying the three bays to the left of the façade, and the other a central position in the solid; but an asymmetrical one in the whole elevation. The diagonal of the staircase forms the balance.

The entrance elevation retains the central feature in the upper storey, but it is noticeable that the further development of this feature within itself is asymmetrical. The downward indication of weights in this sort of façade is impossible; and to use the central feature, interrupted by the horizontal voids, centrally repeated in the base, would be grotesque. Displacement and breaking up of the feature are again compensated by diagonal relationships; and in the ground floor entrance marquise and service door fulfil these purposes.

The other chief point of difference lies in the idea of the roof. In the Malcontenta it forms a pyramidal superstructure dominated by the temple fronts of the upper pediments, which occur above, and augment the central features of the main wall. Interest and silhouette are provided by the highly romantic chimneys, which possess a medieval existing quality, recalling the complicated machicolations of the now disappeared courtyard walls. Garches has a flat roof on two levels, treated partly as enclosure cut out of the block, and scattered with the irregular incident of gazebo, perforation and pavilion. The main

plastic elements, the framed terrace of the entrance elevation and the pavilion of the garden front, are placed respectively in symmetrical and asymmetrical relation to the façades below. As at the Malcontenta, they are dominant features in the composition, but in neither case are they placed in direct vertical relationship with the principal features of the lower wall.

Corbusier's treatment of the base is not continuous. In the cantilevered façade it is affirmed by set-backs or horizontal voids, elsewhere it is not expressed.

Mathematics and musical concord as the basis of ideal proportion was a common belief in Palladio's North Italian circle, where there was felt to be a correspondence between the perfect numbers, the proportions of the human figure and the elements of musical harmony. Sir Henry Wotton, as Ambassador at Venice, reflects some part of this attitude when he writes:—

"The two principal Consonances that most ravish the Ear are, by the consent of all Nature, the Fifth and the Octave, whereof the first riseth radically from the Proportion between two and three, the other from the double Interval between one and two, or between two and four, etc. Now if we shall transport these Proportions, from audible to visual Objects, and apply them as shall fall fittest . . . , there will inevitably result from either, a graceful and harmonious Contentment to the Eye."

It was not in fact suggested that architectural proportions derived from musical harmonies, but rather that the laws of proportion were established mathematically and universally diffused. The Platonic and Pythagorean universe was compounded of the simpler relationships of numbers, and such a world was formed within the triangle made by the square and cube of the numbers 1, 2, 3. Its qualities, rhythms and relationships were established within this framework of numbers up to 27; and if such numbers governed the works of God, it was fitting that the works of man should be similarly constructed, and that a building should be a representative in microcosm, of the same process exhibited to a larger scale in the workings of the world. In Alberti's words "Nature is sure to act consistently and with a constant analogy in all her operations," what is patent in music must also be so in architecture, proportions are a reflection of the harmony of the universe, their basis, scientific and religious, was quite unassailable. Palladio had the satisfaction of an entirely objective aesthetic.

Corbusier has expressed similar convictions about proportion. Mathematics bring "des verités réconfortantes," and "on ne quitte pas son ouvrage qu' avec la certitude d'être arrivé à la chose exacte." It is, indeed, exactness, precision, neatness that he seeks, the overall controlling shape; and within, not the unchallengeable clearness of Palladio's volumes, but a sort of planned obscurity. Consequently, while in the Malcontenta geometry is diffused through the internal volumes of the building, at Garches it resides only in the total block and the disposition of its supports.

The theoretical basis on which Palladio rested broke down in the eighteenth century, when proportion became a matter of individual sensibility and inspiration; and Corbusier, in spite of the comforts which mathematics afford him, occupies no such unassailable position. The functionalist theory was, perhaps, an attempt to re-assert a scientific aesthetic with the objective value of the old. Its interpretation was crude. Results can be measured in terms of the solution of a particular process; proportions are apparently accidental and gratuitous. It is in contradiction of this theory that Corbusier imposes mathematical patterns upon his buildings; these are the universal "verités réconfortantes."

Thus, either because, or in spite of theory, both architects share a common standard, a mathematical one, defined by Wren as "natural beauty"; and within the limitations of a particular programme, it is not surprising that the blocks should be of corresponding volume—8:5½:5. Corbusier has carefully indicated his relationships by regulating lines, dimensions and figures, and over all he places the ratio of the golden section,

Villa Malcontenta

The modular grid, plan and section of Palladio's Villa Malcontenta below provide a revealing comparison with those of the villa by Le Corbusier opposite. For all their differences of style and construction, in the mathematical basis of their design these two buildings have an important factor in common.

modular grid

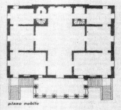

piano nobile

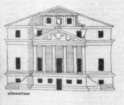

elevation

interests in geometry, history, and myth. It will be worthwhile to quote Rowe's provocative conclusion at length:

> Geometrically, both architects may be said to have approached something of the Platonic archetype of the ideal villa to which the fantasy of the Virgilian drama might be supposed to relate; and the realization of an idea which is represented by the house as a cube could also be presumed to lend itself very readily to the purposes of Virgilian dreaming. For here is set up the conflict between the absolute and the contingent, the abstract and the natural; and the gap between the ideal world and the too human exigencies of realization here receives its most pathetic presentation. The bridging must be as competent and compelling as the construction of a well-executed fugue; and, if it may be charged, as at the Malcontenta with almost religious seriousness, or, as at Garches, imbued with sophisticated and witty allusion, its successful organization is an intellectual feat which reconciles the mind to what may be some fundamental discrepancies in the program.

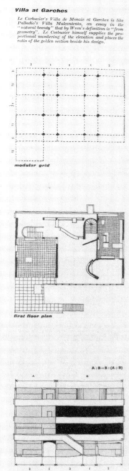

Villa at Garches

Le Corbusier's Villa de Monzie at Garches is like Palladio's Villa Malcontenta, an essay in the "natural beauty" that by Wren's definition is "from geometry". Le Corbusier himself supplies the proportional numbering of the elevation and places the ratio of the golden section beside his design.

modular grid

first floor plan

$A : B = B : (A + B)$

elevation

4.8   Colin Rowe's precedent-shattering "The Mathematics of the Ideal Villa," in the *Architectural Review,* March 1947.

As a constructor of architectural figures, Palladio is the convinced classicist with a sixteenth century repertory of well-humanized forms; and he translates his received material with a passion and a high seriousness fitting to the continued validity that he finds it to possess. . . .

By contrast Le Corbusier is, in some ways, the most catholic and ingenious of eclectics. The orders, the Roman references, were the traditional architectural clothing of authority; and, if it is hard for the modern architect to be quite so emphatic about any particular civilization as was Palladio about the Roman, with Le Corbusier there is always an element of wit suggesting that the historical (or contemporary) reference has remained a quotation between inverted commas, possessing always the double value of the quotation, the associations of both old and new context. In spite of his admiration for the Acropolis and Michelangelo, the world of high classical Mediterranean culture on which Palladio drew so expressively is

4.9   Neo-Palladianism and the new American monumentality, 1: Philip Johnson's Oneto house at Irvington on Hudson, from 1950. (Photograph by Ezra Stoller, © Esto.)

largely closed for Le Corbusier . . . as a result, while allusion at the Malcontenta is concentrated and direct, as Garches it is dissipated and inferential. Within the one cube the performance attempts the Roman; but, within the other, no such exclusive cultural ideal is entertained. Instead, as the sponsors of his virtuosity, Le Corbusier largely selects a variety of hitherto undiscriminated phenomena. He selects the casual incidents of Paris, or Istanbul, or wherever it may be; aspects of the fortuitously picturesque, of the mechanical, of whatever might seem to represent the present and the usable past; and all those items, while transformed by their new context, retain their original implications which signify maybe Platonic ideality, maybe Rococo intimacy, maybe mechanical precision, maybe a process of natural selection.[31]

With this virtuoso interpretation of the methodological sensibilities of the two architects, Rowe forced on his contemporaries a dramatic expansion of the realm of discourse within which modern architecture had hitherto been discussed. Moreover, two years after its publication, Rowe's mentor the architectural historian Rudolf Wittkower published *Architectural Principles in the Age of Humanism,* a text that added in its turn to the growing body of argument in favor of a highly charged iconographic reading of architecture. Wittkower began his text with a general historical argument against a view he called "Ruskinian," according to which "Renaissance architecture is an architecture of pure form." Wittkower argued instead that "the forms of the Renaissance church have symbolical value, or at least that they are charged with a particular meaning which the pure forms as such do not contain."[32] This claim also had the effect of reinforcing arguments for a contemporary concept of architecture that transcended instrumentality. Indeed, Rowe's and Wittkower's publications can be seen in retrospect as a starting point of the phenomenon that became known, both in Europe and North America, as neo-Palladianism. With the advent of the new interest in symmetry, centrality, and elementary volume, which was increasingly evident in the American work of Mies van der Rohe from that period, neo-Palladianism quickly became linked with a putative neo-classicism. As Rowe put it:

> Neo-Palladianism . . . has inherited—particularly from Mies—a sense of propriety. It has adopted particularly from him an ordinance of the building envelope. It has been led by him to accept as sufficient the statement of elementary volume. Its preferred textures, its taste for big scale and immaculate finish are largely Miesian, while it has enjoyed the same sanction for its symmetrical solutions. And to a not so extreme degree the same statements are also true of the less formulated neo-"classical" manner.[33]

Once neo-Palladianism and neoclassicism were placed on the table, new ideas about architecture, especially in the United States, began to evolve very rapidly indeed. Vincent Scully has pointed out just how rapidly in an engaging reminiscence:

> By 1950, following Dr. Wittkower's lead, we had the *Architectural Forum* putting together this picture of Vignola's urban facades with one of Mies' constructions at I.I.T. and indicating concordance between them. Now it seems to me again that

4.10 Mies van der Rohe's plan for the Illinois Institute of Technology juxtaposed with Vignola's facades, as illustrated in Vincent Scully's essay in *Perspecta* in 1965.

> 1949 is the critical date here. It is the date when Philip Johnson began to give his splendid talks, which those of us who first heard them regarded as pronouncements of the Devil. He stood up on the platform at Yale University, and he said to a shocked hush across the room, "I would rather sleep in the nave of Chartres Cathedral with the nearest john two blocks down the street than I would in a Harvard house with back-to-back bathrooms!" This sacrilegious and rather frightening pronouncement was the one after which, for the first time, I remember students saying to me, "He's talking about architecture as art!"[34]

Such powerful sentiments and such keen interests in the formal and historical aspects of architecture led to a renewed enthusiasm, on the part of a significant group of American architects around Johnson, for the idea of a "new monumentality." The evidence of this could soon be seen not only in the work of Johnson himself but in that of other American architects as well, probably most consequentially in that of Louis Kahn.

Colin Rowe's contemporary Reyner Banham had, from the beginning of his career as a critic, distinguished himself from his countryman by his keen interest in technology. Having undertaken a doctoral thesis under Pevsner (in parallel with Rowe's work under Wittkower), Banham in his 1960 book *Theory and Design in the First Machine Age* reasserted claims for architectural instrumentality with great polemical force. In his concluding chapter entitled "Functionalism and Technology," by now a historical subject of considerable controversy, Banham returned to the very Corbusian masterpieces that Rowe had discussed in 1947 and mounted an aggressive counterattack, using as a weapon the ideas of Buckminster Fuller.

> We are entitled to enquire, at the very highest level, whether the aims of the International Style were worth entertaining, and whether its estimate of a Machine Age was a viable one. Something like a flat rebuttal of both aims and estimates can be found in the writings of Buckminster Fuller.[35]

Banham continued, quoting from Fuller himself:

> It was apparent that the going design-blindness of the lay level . . . afforded European designers an opportunity . . . to develop their preview discernment of the more appealing simplicities of the industrial structures that had inadvertently earned their architectural freedom [Fuller is referring here to the discovery by the European architectural avant-garde in the earlier part of the century, of such industrial structures as the—by now well known—grain elevators of North America], not by conscious aesthetic innovation, but through profit-inspired discard of eco-

4.11   Neo-Palladianism and the new American monumentality, 2: Louis Kahn's Jewish Community Center in Ewing Township, New Jersey, from 1954–1959.

nomic irrelevancies. . . . This surprise discovery, as the European designers well knew, could soon be made universally appealing as a fad, for had they not themselves been so faddishly inspired. The "International Style" brought to America by the Bauhaus innovators, demonstrated fashion-inoculation without necessity of knowledge of the scientific fundamentals of structural mechanics and chemistry. . . .

The International Style "simplification" then was but superficial. It peeled off yesterday's exterior embellishment and put on instead formalised novelties of quasi-simplicity, permitted by the same hidden structural elements of modern alloys that had permitted the discarded Beaux-Arts garmentation.[36]

Following Fuller's mode of argument, Banham continued:

> In cutting themselves off from the philosophical aspects of Futurism, though hoping to retain its prestige as Machine Age art, theorists and designers of the waning Twenties cut themselves off not only from their own historical beginnings, but also from their foothold in the world of technology, whose character Fuller defined, and rightly, as an "unhaltable trend to constantly accelerating change," a trend that the Futurists had fully appreciated before him.

> But the mainstream of the Modern Movement had begun to lose sight of this aspect of technology very early in the Twenties. . . .[37]

This led him to the conclusion with which he laid down his challenge to the new advocates of formal and historical interests in architecture:

> In the upshot, the historian must find [that the architects of the twenties] produced a Machine Age architecture only in the sense that its monuments were built in a Machine Age, and expressed an attitude to machinery—in the sense that one might stand on French soil and discuss French politics, and still be speaking English. It may well be that what we have hitherto understood as architecture, and what we are beginning to understand of technology are incompatible disciplines. The architect who proposes to run with technology knows now that he will be in fast company, and that, in order to keep up, he may have to emulate the Futurists and discard his whole cultural load, including the professional garments by which he is recognised as an architect. If, on the other hand, he decides not to do this, he may find that a technological culture has decided to go on without him.[38]

With this passage, Banham set in motion a chain of events in which a renewed concept of instrumentality rapidly gained credibility, particularly in certain architectural circles in Britain and the United States. He was soon to go on to argue that not only the architects of the twenties but also many more recent ones failed to meet his stringent criteria of instrumental modernity. In 1966, for example, he published a historical account of an architectural movement in which he had himself been a participant during the 1950s and 1960s. This was *The New Brutalism,* which Banham concluded with a text entitled "Memoirs of a Survivor" in which he disparaged the bulk of the work whose history he had just recounted, on account of its failure, on his view, to keep up with technological advance. "For a short period, around 1953–55," wrote Banham, "it looked as if an 'other architecture'"—one Banham hoped would parallel the *art autre* being promulgated during those same years on the Continent by artists

4.12   A view of the Jewett Arts Center at Wellesley College, by Paul Rudolph, from 1955–1958.

such as Jean Dubuffet—

> might indeed emerge, entirely free of the professional preconceptions and preju-
> dices that have encrusted architecture since it became "an art." It looked for a
> moment as if we might be on the threshold of an utterly uninhibited functionalism,
> free, even, of the machine aesthetic that had trapped the white architecture of the
> thirties and made it impossible for Gropius to reach through to the native Ameri-
> can machine ethic that might have broken the back of the Beaux-Arts tradition
> that still cripples architectural thinking in America.[39]

Dismissing not only the "neo-Palladian" Philip Johnson but also such occa-
sional technological innovators in America as Paul Rudolph, Banham came
to the conclusion that all these notable Americans were "quicker than I
was to see that the Brutalists were really their allies and not mine; committed in the last resort to the classical tradition, not the technological."[40]

By the time *The New Brutalism* had been published, Banham had taken up
with a younger group of architects who seemed to him more likely than
the brutalists to fulfil his radical technological hopes. This group included
the English designer of the controversial 1966 Thinkbelt project, Cedric

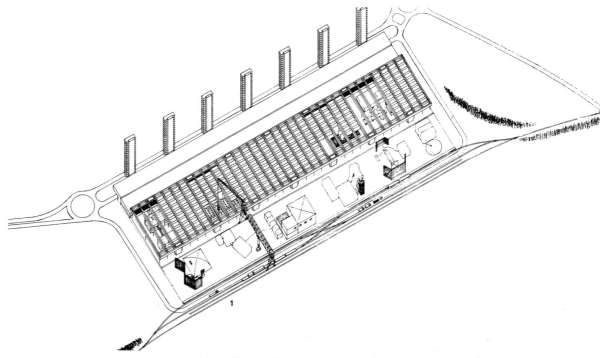

4.13   An axonometric of the Madeley Transfer Area, a component of Cedric Price's Think-belt project of 1966.

Price, as well as the members of the Archigram group who were then just beginning to receive widespread international publicity.[41] Price's Thinkbelt, a radically minimalist and austere instrumentalist analogue of a university, was proposed by him as an economic-cum-academic catalyst to development in the economically depressed English Midlands. So thorough was Price in his rigorous efforts to conceive a "value-free" architecture that its austere instrumentality generated instead a wildly labile social imagery, conjuring up, for this observer at least, a possible reading of the complex as "concentration camp."[42] With the Archigram group, on the other hand, the resultant imagery was quite different. Less puritanically averse to a sensuous reading of their architecture—indeed, more authentically Benthamite in their modern psychology of pain and pleasure—the Archigram group conjured up an architecture of radically individualist and hedonist gratification. Not only did they not eschew symbolic readings of their projects, they deliberately orchestrated arrays of sensuous color and of infinitely, individually manipulable configurations of a possible inhabited world, a world that would be almost entirely consumed in the immediate future as the result of its occupants' exercise of their ongoing libertarian hedonism.

For his own part, Banham reached what might be called a "degree zero" of architectural instrumentality in a revealing 1965 text entitled "A Home is not a House," a sweeping attack on American architects in the name of a mythical American layman. "Architects," insisted Banham,

> especially American architects, sense that [the invasion of mechanical equipment in contemporary architecture] is a cultural threat to their position in the world. They are certainly right to feel this, because their professional specialty, the art of creating monumental spaces, has never been securely established on [their] continent.[43]

Turning from American architects to the mythical American layman, Banham depicted a different vision: "Left to their own devices, Americans do not monumentalize or make architecture."[44] And this line of thinking, Banham indicated, led him to the conclusion that

> if dirty old Nature could be kept under the proper degree of control . . . by other means, the United States would be happy to dispense with architecture and buildings altogether. Buckminster Fuller is of course very big on this proposition. His famous non-rhetorical question, "Madam, do you know what your house weighs?", articulates a subversive suspicion of the monumental. This suspicion is inarticulately shared by the untold thousands of Americans who have already shed the deadweight of domestic architecture and live in mobile homes which, though they may never actually be moved, still deliver rather better performance as shelter than do ground-anchored structures costing at least three times as much and weighing ten times more.[45]

For Banham, the logical result of this line of argument was a mylar airdome equipped only with a technologically sophisticated kit providing environmental control and complete sound and video systems, inside of which the inhabitants could lounge without the need even of clothing.[46]

4.14   The Environment-Bubble of 1968, conceived by Reyner Banham and illustrated by François Dallegret.

With this project, radical instrumentality had led Banham to the paradoxical point—in principle—of achieving his objective of abolishing architecture altogether.

Interestingly enough, two other movements parallel to this one concerned themselves during those same years with an attempt at radical instrumentalization of the design process. A canonical text of one of them, also at that time based in England, was a book called *Notes on the Synthesis of Form,* published in 1964, by Christopher Alexander.[47] This book was greeted in instrumentalist circles as epochal, and it opened the way to a decade of research focused on what came to be known as "design methodology." Like Banham's radical instrumentality, like the more militant of the versions of *Sachlichkeit* discussed in chapter two, design methodology sought to establish the primacy of a supposedly discoverable direct relationship of "life" to "building" that was unmediated by any known or even assumed condition of symbol, myth, or history. Through an intellectual process of radical reductivism, which relied in the first instance on the elementary principles of logic and, following that, on the so-called operations research that had largely succeeded the Taylorization of the turn of the century, Alexander and the various apostles of design methodology progressively came to find wanting, one by one, all the traditional precepts of architectural design, until eventually, with a logically rigorous positivist consistency, they satisfied themselves that they had abolished the theoretical premises of the existence of architectural design, as successfully as Banham had just abolished the phenomenon of architecture itself.

In Ulm, Germany, from the late fifties through the late sixties, another radical experiment in the methodology of design was essayed at the Hochschule für Gestaltung. The Ulm experiment was inspired by a number of factors, including, of course, the same disenchantment with the reclaimed knowledge of modernism that was shared by most thoughtful observers in that era. But Ulm in the 1950s hybridized this disenchantment with an almost mystical loyalty to the *sachlich* traditions of the materialist European left of the twenties, and with a discovery of the more sophisticated techniques of operations research such as became widespread outside architecture after the Second World War. But the Ulm experiment eventually came to as problematic an end as did the parallel Anglo-American ones, especially when its interest in graphics, and in early versions of the emergent discipline of semiotics, enmeshed it in the utterly unassimilable realm of advertising.[48]

In retrospect, it is remarkable to note with what consistency both the Anglo-American and the German episodes of extreme instrumentality in the 1960s played out, in a miniature reprise, the long chain of consequences of European culture's initial abandonment of any reasonable relationship of means and ends in the seventeenth and eighteenth centuries, which Arendt had so dramatically portrayed a decade before. To be sure, for her the issue had not been instrumentality, the use of means to achieve an end, as such,

> but rather the generalization of the fabrication experience in which usefulness and utility are established as the ultimate standards for life and the world of men. . . . Only in so far as fabrication chiefly fabricates use objects does the finished product again become a means, and only in so far as the life process takes hold of things and uses them for its purposes does the productive and limited instrumentality of fabrication change into the limitless instrumentalization of everything that exists.[49]

But of course, it was precisely such a "limitless instrumentalization" that underlay the ambition of the committed design methodologists in architecture, and of Reyner Banham and his colleagues in design, in the 1960s episode under discussion here. Small wonder, then, that the result of their efforts was a "perplexity" that Arendt has characterized as "inherent in all consistent utilitarianism." That is to say, it "gets caught in the unending chain of means and ends without ever arriving at some principle which could justify the category of means and end, that is, of utility itself."[50]

The problematic consequences of such thoroughgoing utilitarianism had already led Arendt to reiterate an old proposition of Plato's in respect to the appropriate criteria that might be applied to the "things of the world." Interestingly enough, even though the criteria to which Arendt appealed were concerned with the formulation of some appropriately fixed and interrelated hierarchy of "means and ends," they are strikingly reminiscent of the effort of Kraus and Loos to sustain some credible hierarchy of phe-

Instruments and Monuments

nomenological decorum within which both the chamber pot and the urn might find their appropriate place. As Arendt saw it, the ancient Greek philosophers were astute enough to recognize

> the sheer vulgarity of all consistent utilitarianism. To what extent they were aware of the consequences of seeing in *homo faber* the highest human possibility is perhaps best illustrated by Plato's famous argument against Protagoras and his apparently self-evident statement that "man is the measure of all use things."[51]

In Arendt's opinion, it was

> because of these consequences that Plato, who at the end of his life recalls once more in the *Laws* the saying of Protagoras, replies with an almost paradoxical formula: not man—who because of his wants and talents wishes to use everything and therefore ends by depriving all things of their intrinsic worth—but "the god is the measure [even] of mere use objects."[52]

"Elbow Room for Culture": A Seventies Postscript

While the progressive campaign on the part of the radical instrumentalists proceeded into the 1970s (prior to its ironically appropriate self-extinction in the middle of that decade), a group of "formalist" followers of Colin Rowe in the United States proceeded to develop a position from which to challenge it again, not only in the radical form in which it had been put forward by Banham and his allies but even in the milder and more generally accepted form in which it had been simply part and parcel of the received view of modernism from the 1920s, prior to such theoretical and historical interventions as those of Rowe and Wittkower. This challenge eventually came to focus on the quite anti-instrumental conception of the "autonomy of architecture."

Already in the 1972 publication *Five Architects,* illustrating the work of a group of young American architects who had been associated with Rowe, an implicit new defense of architecture's autonomy was discernible.[53] For a period in the mid-seventies, one of the Five, Michael Graves, became well known on the North American architecture school lecture circuit for his attacks on the milder version of modern instrumentality, which Graves saw as typical of the mainstream modern architecture of the fifties and sixties. In such presentations, Graves would systematically mock such typical ele-

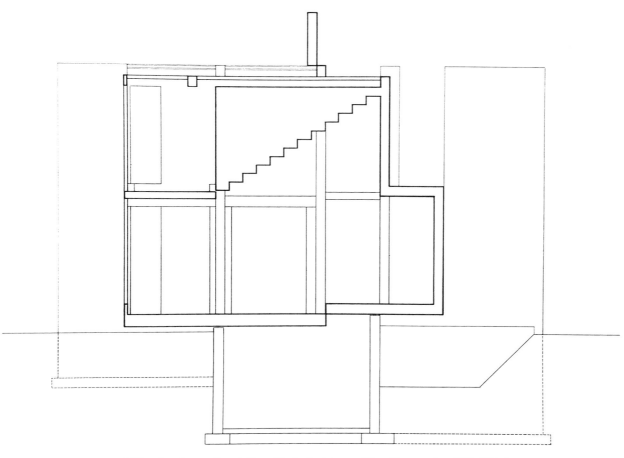

4.15   A section cut through House VI, the Frank house of Peter Eisenman, from 1972–1976, show-ing the profile of the notorious upside-down staircase. (Illustration courtesy Oxford University Press.)

ments of the mainstream architecture of the period as the automated glass doors to airport concourses, seeing in such devices a capitulation to a contemporary technological rationality and a loss of all sense of any older, more humane, more phenomenological sense of entry.

However severe they might have seemed at the time, Graves's attacks on the "inhumanity" of mainstream modernism were soon superseded by the more radical stance of his colleague among the Five, Peter Eisenman. Eisenman found himself compelled, by both moral conviction and intellec-tual consistency, to go so far as to deny the legitimacy not just of radical instrumentality but of any form of social program in architecture whatso-ever. Using a series of houses he designed in the early seventies as test cases, he argued that even such apparently pragmatic buildings as one might suppose houses to be should be seen instead as merely comprising sets of formal relationships of solid and void, positive and negative interval, and spatial modulation, these relationships only incidentally accommodating the customary activities of eating, sleeping, etc.[54]

For all the rhetorical scandal of his own theoretical *parti pris,* Eisenman nevertheless chose in 1976 to yield the floor in the debate to a European architect for whom he expressed profound admiration: Aldo Rossi. In that year, Eisenman and his fellow editors published in their magazine *Oppositions* Rossi's now famous project for the Modena cemetery, together with a commentary on his concept of the autonomy of architecture by the Spanish architect and critic Rafael Moneo. How remarkable that a project so profoundly challenging instrumentality in contemporary architecture should be one for a cemetery, reminding us yet again of the thought-provoking words of Adolf Loos from 1910 with which I began.

Eisenman commenced his editor's introduction to the material by stating, "There is no question for the editors of *Oppositions* but that the face of

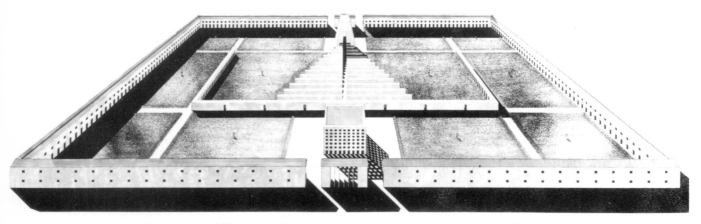

4.16 An image of Aldo Rossi's 1971 competition-winning scheme for the Modena cemetery. (Illustration © Aldo Rossi.)

architecture of 1975 is radically altered from that of 1965. Equally, there can be little argument that a significant contribution to that difference is the concept of autonomous architecture."[55] In his own introduction to Rossi's ideas, Moneo began by explaining the context of revisionist thinking about modern architecture itself and about the extant form of the historical city, thinking that had developed in the late fifties and sixties around the magazine *Casabella*.

> A fundamental principle developed slowly in the work of Rossi and in the entire group: the idea that there was a specificity or a particular aspect of architecture which could allow it to be considered as an autonomous discipline. It was Rossi's idea that through a study of the city, seen as the finest and most complete expression of architecture, a knowledge of these principles could be found.[56]

For Rossi, autonomy was not simply a matter of the transcendence of instrumentality. As Moneo pointed out, Rossi's ambition was to reconstitute architecture as "a category of reality," as it had been for certain architects of the early European Enlightenment. Moneo continued:

> It is necessary to recall the architectonic category of permanence which Rossi associates with memory. There are, in the city, urban facts which are permanent, that withstand the passage of time; these urban facts are the monuments that, in one way or another, constitute or make up and configure the city. The monument therefore has more than an intelligible and atmospheric value, it is not only architecture as anecdote, as the picturesque, but it gives meaning to the life of the city which, through these monuments, both remembers the past, and uses "its memory."

> The monument . . . is restored by Rossi who understands the role [it] has played in giving structure to the city. Faced with such a conservative view of the past, Rossi also achieves a vindication of the presence of monuments insofar as they also embody the current moment—the city's present.

> The recovery of monuments then is far from a merely archaeological devotion to the past. Monuments from the perspective proposed by Rossi acquire a real dimension and an immediacy that disturbs any conservative vision of the city described in terms of immobility and inalterability.[57]

As Rossi himself put it:

> the monument is something permanent because it is already in a dialectic position within urban development, permitting an understanding of the city as something that is created through points (primary elements) and areas (neighborhoods); and while it acquires value as such through the former, it disappears in the latter from which the value of use comes forth.[58]

Rossi's subtle argument constituted a most compelling new rationale for
monumentality in architecture. Indeed, one can even go so far as to say
that in positing a dialectic between monuments as "primary elements" and
residential neighbourhoods as "areas," he succeeded—on an urban level, at
least—in reestablishing that "elbow room for culture" so eloquently advocated by Kraus and Loos. One might, given the magnitude of this intellectual achievement, have supposed that one of the great debates respecting
modernism in our time had been definitively settled. Yet in the various and
widespread interpretations of Rossi's ideas that have been made in recent
years, this has not quite proved to be the case. With astute prescience,
Moneo in his introductory text (written in 1973, published in English in
1975) already flagged a concern that has proven a consequential one.

> It is . . . necessary to indicate some objections, not so much with the theory, but
> rather with the results of Rossi's projects and proposals. The reference to surreal-
> ism, to certain Renaissance and metaphysical perspectives, puts us on the track of
> one of Rossi's characteristics that is both greatly disputed and consciously pro-
> posed: this is his estrangement from the real, understood as the everyday occur-
> rence. Certainly one could speak of the recovery of an authentic dimension of
> reality as happened in the architecture of the Enlightenment. But Rossi's imposition
> of a deliberate distance between the image of reality, trivialized and banalized
> through use, and the perspective that proposes what an architecture of the city
> might be, also points out a certain attitude which says something about the possible
> future of architecture in our present society.[59]

"One more step," warned Moneo, and a more extreme form of autonomy
might arise. According to this worrisome scenario, he argued that such
autonomy might be construed

> as merely allowing the architect to carry out his work through inoperative parame-
> ters, as a pure game. . . . This architecture may be seen as capable of assuming its
> architectural condition, its specific reality, because it is only interested in the prob-
> lems that concern it, without necessarily reaching a level of objectivity, however
> desirable, because in doing so, it would intrude into other aspects of social life.
> From the architect's personal or individual condition this autonomous position
> would have value since it does not trust the social transcendence of its work.[60]

Perhaps more remarkable still, Peter Eisenman, in his editor's introduction,
also took up the question of the variable and even doubtful interpretations
of autonomy that might be anticipated. "What remains in question," speculated Eisenman, "is whether 'architettura autonoma' is merely another

4.17   The model of Peter Eisenman's design for the proposed Max Reinhardt Haus in Berlin. Note how startlingly this so-called Moebius strip skyscraper sits in the urban context the model so faithfully depicts. It seems to me that this project probably represents the zenith of Eisenman's ongoing quest to leave behind all of architecture's normative conventions. (Photograph: Jöchen Littkemann.)

architect's smokescreen as Functionalism was, for 'aesthetic free-play.'"[61] The years since 1976 would seem to have proven Moneo's—and to some extent even Eisenman's—fears well taken. Ironically enough, we may even see Eisenman's own work in that period as bearing out the concerns that had been expressed by Moneo.

To be sure, Eisenman had held a position of radical anti-instrumentality before he developed his interest in the conception of autonomy propounded by Rossi. And that anti-instrumental stance was so passionate that it had led him to deny the relevance of social program in architecture altogether. Even so, Eisenman's further theorizing after 1975 has moved progressively, and systematically, away from the quotidian norms of social life. Indeed, it would be possible to characterize the recent trajectory of his work as a progressive effort to escape any and all identifiable, normative conventions of what has hitherto been thought of as architecture. One recognizes, of course, that Eisenman has seen his effort at such an escape as a libertarian one, and this dimension of his activities might be thought to offer the possibility of some long-term future social relevance. But this is to employ the precept of architecture's autonomy in such a way as to fly in the face of Rossi's profoundly "conservative" view of architecture's possible "reality," and thereby to confirm Moneo's fears. It is in this sense that it is possible, in retrospect, to read Moneo's caveat of 1973 as applying to Eisenman's own more recent architectural production: "This architecture may be seen as capable of assuming its architectural condition, its specific reality, because it is only interested in the problems that concern it."[62]

Indisputably noninstrumental, the production of this particular avant-garde is consciously antimonumental as well. Ironically enough, in its sedulous efforts to escape quotidian reality it may be seen to have thwarted the important European lessons of the last quarter of a century, and to have collapsed once again that essential elbow room for culture so perceptively identified at the turn of the century by Kraus and Loos.

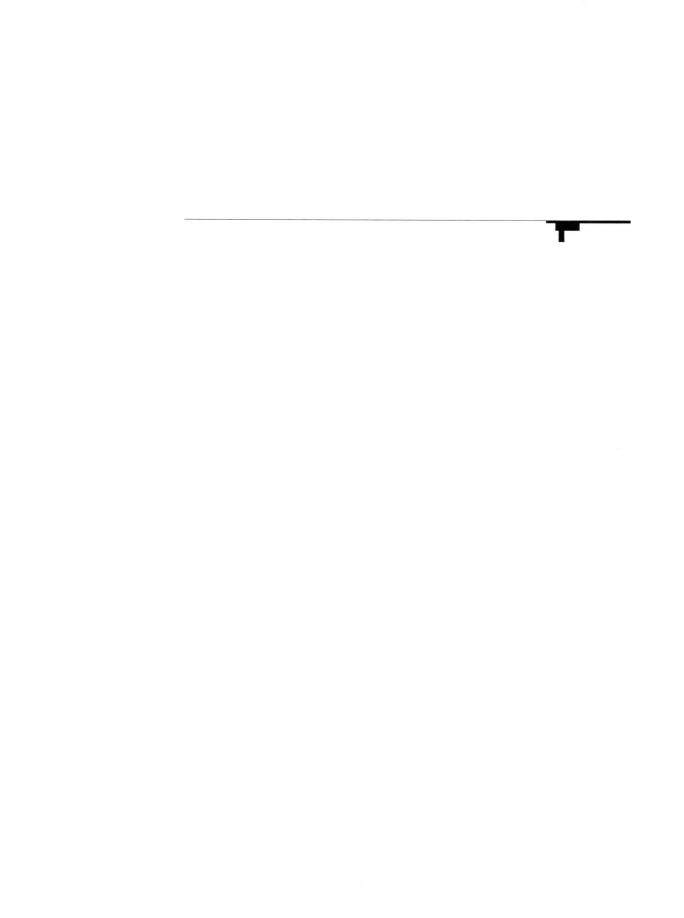

Panopticism

Chapter Five

Morals reformed—health preserved—industry invigorated—instruction
diffused—public burthens lightened—economy seated, as it were,
upon a rock—the gordian knot of the Poor Laws not cut,
but untied—all by a simple idea in Architecture!

Jeremy Bentham, 1791

During the period of consolidation of the Bolshevik revolution in the mid-1920s, the Soviet Union became an especially intense locus of activity for many of the more radical modern architects. Barbara Kreis has noted how the Russian avant-garde in particular

> saw themselves as serving the new social situation, and used the instruments which symbolized the advancement of the new society. In order to create new forms for the new contents, they proclaimed in their projects a scientific rational organization, construction and building materials that were functionally and technically highly developed, and a collectivized system of living.[1]

An example of their commitment to "a collectivized system of living" that has already become well known in modern architectural history is the Narkomfin project for a collective housing building dating from 1929, designed by the leading constructivist Moisei Ginzburg in collaboration with I. Milinis. The Narkomfin was based on an entry by Ginzburg for a 1927 competition dedicated to the theme of the "New Living"; the project comprised a series of quite standardized, compact dwelling cells with only minimal internal cooking facilities. Instead, provision was made for meals to be taken collectively in dining facilities forming a part of the extensive communal facilities of the complex, including a gymnasium and a child care center. In short, the Narkomfin constituted, in the terminology of the time, a *dom-kommuna*.[2]

The ambition of the Russian avant-garde of the era to use architecture as a mechanism of social transformation, of which the Narkomfin is only one well-known example, was almost without limit.

> The technical aspects of collectivization and industrialization influenced architecture so greatly that many architects began to consider themselves as designing instructions for the entire operation of life, and their architectural designs resembled industrial operational plans; particularly in their use of time and motion studies, as these were influenced by Taylor's principles of scientific management and by the methodology of the conveyor belt.[3]

As designs for "the entire operation of life," such proposals did not stop with individuals' waking hours. Kreis went on to describe one typical example:

> In Konstantin Melnikov's "Green City" plan, even sleep was to be regarded as socialistic. He was to project huge communal sleep pavilions, where the workers' sleep would be accompanied by orchestral music throughout the night. The goal,

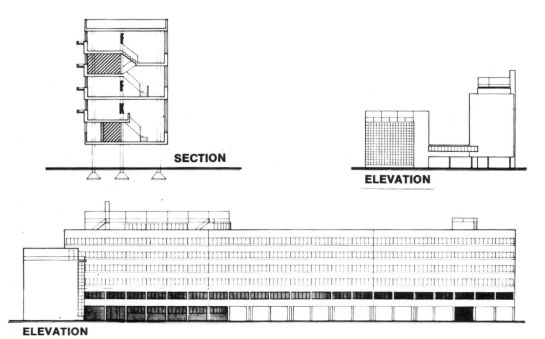

SECTION

ELEVATION

ELEVATION

5.1 Elevations and a section of the well-known Narkomfin building from 1929, by Moisei Ginzburg and I. Milinis. The section in the upper left of the illustration shows the very shallow depth of the individual living spaces provided; the two elevations show the separate communal dining area provided to the inhabitants in lieu of more generous individual living space.

again, was a scientifically ordered life and the model being used corresponded to Taylorized management, with its functional and rational division of labor.[4]

A particular group of constructivists took such ideas so far as to become known as supercollectivists. One of the most notable supercollectivists was Ivan Kuzmin, who

> interpreted all life functions as forms of work, and [who] wrote in 1930 in regard to the scientific organization of life that emotion was a consequence of intensive labor, since man "works" even while sleeping. As far as he was concerned, there was no absolute recreation. He demanded a clear differentiation of the working process as a prerequisite for the planning of housing since the present chaos of individual households did not allow any single human function to be satisfactorily fulfilled. . . . Kuzmin proposed instead the strict division of the daytime routine into precise minute-by-minute "time frames" according to which workers would lead their daily lives.[5]

It is this "division of the day-time routine" of the typical worker that has secured for Kuzmin his now somewhat notorious place in the history of architecture in the twentieth century. His daily plan for the workers' lives was as follows:

1.	Lights out.	10:00 pm
2.	8 hours of sleep. Reveille.	6:00 am
3.	Calisthenics—5 min.	6:05 am
4.	Toilet—10 min.	6:15 am
5.	Shower (optional—5 min.)	6:20 am
6.	Dress—5 min.	6:25 am
7.	To the dining room—3 min.	6:28 am
8.	Breakfast—15 min.	6:43 am
9.	To the cloakrooms—2 min.	6:45 am
10.	Put on outdoor clothing—5 min.	6:50 am
11.	To the mine—10 min.	7:00 am
12.	Work in the mine—8 hours.	3:00 pm
13.	To the commune—10 min.	3:10 pm
14.	Take off outdoor clothing—7 min.	3:17 pm
15.	Wash—8 min.	3:25 pm
16.	Dinner—30 min.	3:55 pm
17.	To the hall of rest for free hour—3 min.	3:58 pm
18.	Free hour for naps and so on. Those who wish may retire to the bedrooms.	4:58 pm
19.	Toilet and change—10 min.	5:08 pm
20.	To the dining room—2 min.	5:10 pm
21.	Tea—15 minutes	5:25 pm
22.	To the club. Recreation. Cultural development. Gymnastics. Perhaps a bath or swim. Here it is life itself that will determine how time is spent, that will draw up the plan. Allotted time, 4 hours.	9:25 pm
23.	To the dining room, supper, and to the bedrooms—25 min.	9:50 pm
24.	Prepare to retire (a shower may be taken)—10 min.	10:00 pm[6]

With this often-cited program of daily routine, the constructivists' presumption in regard to the "scientific management" of life can be seen to have reached a sort of apogee, insofar as that presumption formed a part of the ongoing development of modern architectural theory. What is more, the utter absence of any inhibition in the commitment of the Soviet avant-garde to "scientific management" compels the contemporary reader to acknowledge the extent to which that commitment constitutes an "instrumentalization," one that went well beyond that of "the world," such as was discussed in chapter four. In fact, the radical and unqualified efforts made by so many of the architects among the Soviet avant-garde constitute as unequivocal evidence as exists within modern architectural theory of an ambition toward the instrumentalization not just of things, but of men themselves. In this regard, one is again reminded of Arendt's lament in respect to the "typical attitudes of *homo faber*," in particular "his conviction that every issue can be solved and every human motivation reduced to the principle of utility; [and] his sovereignty, which regards everything given as material"[7]—except, of course, that in the case of the ambitions now under consideration, the "material" in question is man himself.

The commitments of the radical Soviet architects of the twenties to the scientific management of life did not arise in a social and political vacuum. They had significant precedent in the ideas of the leading figures of the Bolshevik revolution itself. We may quote one famous slogan of the time: "Let us take the storm of Revolution in Soviet Russia, unite it to the pulse of American life and do our work like a chronometer!"[8] What is more, the recurrent references by the Russian theorists to Taylor and to "Taylorizing," which link them to the late nineteenth-century work of the controversial American inventor of scientific management, also reflect the thinking of the Bolshevik leadership. Lenin himself urged the adoption in the Soviet Union of Taylorization:

> The Soviet Republic must at all costs adopt all that is valuable in the achievements of science and technology in this field. The possibility of building socialism depends exactly upon our success in combining the Soviet power and the Soviet organization of administration with the up-to-date achievements of capitalism. We must organize in Russia the study and teaching of the Taylor system and systematically try it out and adapt it to our ends.[9]

Frederick Taylor was a pivotal figure in the development of the methods of mass production, and subsequently of the assembly line. Beginning his studies in the mines of Andrew Carnegie, Taylor went on to examine various other forms of industrial labor, always rationalizing and systematizing the physical efforts of individual workers so as to progressively maximize the precise division of labor in those efforts, and thereby to maximize the productivity of the work force as a whole.

An extensive and detailed account of Taylor's efforts was prepared by Harry Braverman, in his *Labor and Monopoly Capital* of 1974. The first principle of Taylor's method, according to Braverman, was the "dissociation of the labor process from the skills of the workers." Taylor himself enunciated the principle as follows:

> The managers assume . . . the burden of gathering together all of the traditional knowledge which in the past has been possessed by the workmen and then of classifying, tabulating, and reducing this knowledge to rules, laws, and formulae.

The second principle, Braverman continued, is that "all possible brain work should be removed from the shop and centered in the planning or laying-out department."[10] This Braverman calls the "separation of conception from execution." Finally:

> Perhaps the most prominent single element in modern scientific management is the task idea. The work of every workman is fully planned out by the management at least one day in advance, and each man receives in most cases complete written instructions, describing in detail the task which he is to accomplish, as well as the means to be used in doing the work. . . . This task specifies . . . what is to be done and the exact time allowed for doing it. . . . Scientific management consists very largely in preparing for and carrying out these tasks.

> Thus, if the first principle is the gathering and development of knowledge of labor processes, and the second is the concentration of this knowledge as the exclusive province of management—together with its essential converse, the absence of such knowledge among the workers—then the third is the use of this monopoly over knowledge to control each step of the labor process and its mode of execution.[11]

Such a radically instrumentalist conception of the labor process as Taylor's—a conception, interestingly enough, that was welcomed equally enthusiastically by capitalists such as Carnegie and by the Bolshevik leadership in the Soviet Union—would have been inconceivable, even in the later nineteenth century, had not the philosophical groundwork been laid a century before in utilitarianism. Among the philosophers and economists in Great Britain and in France who had developed the utilitarian position, Jeremy Bentham is particularly relevant to the present argument, for it was he who conceived the notorious "calculus of pain and pleasure" that, according to Arendt, enabled him to turn Adam Smith's economy into a psychology and thus opened the way to the great process of the instrumentalization of men that followed.

Architecture and its specific role in that historic process being the focus of our discussion, we may take as a particularly clear expression of Bentham's utilitarian psychology his famous proposal for a Panopticon or Inspection House. This was the seminal design in the instrumentalizing of labor, having been conceived for the explicit purpose of what we now know as "behavior modification." The design was for a generic circular edifice, which ranged a series of cubicles or rooms or cells around the circumference of a large interior void, the center of which was to be occupied by a viewing position from which a central inspector could survey the behavior of the occupants at all times. Of course it wasn't necessary that an inspector be on duty at all times, since Bentham intended that the central inspection point be screened in such a way that the occupants of the Panopticon could not tell whether the inspection point was manned or not. The purpose, as Bentham put it, was to "see without being seen." It was this constancy of surveillance, on Bentham's view, that would assure that the sought-after modification of the behavior of the occupants would indeed occur. The Panopticon was conceived to deal with a wide range of social concerns; its premise was the tabula rasa psychology that utilitarianism had adopted from certain of Bentham's eighteenth-century mentors, who took the persona of any individual to be infinitely modifiable.

The full scope of its social potential, as seen by Bentham, can best be assessed by quoting the famous words from the beginning of the preface of the book in which he introduced the concept, and with which I have headed this chapter. We may take his points in order. "Morals reformed": this refers to the capacity he claimed for the Panopticon to alter the behavior of criminals. "Health preserved:" this refers to the therapeutic potential of the Panopticon as against the unhealthy traditional jail as a vehicle for the incarceration of social miscreants. "Industry invigorated": this indicates Bentham's belief that the occupants of the Panopticon should be involved in productive activity, forming a part of the industrial machine

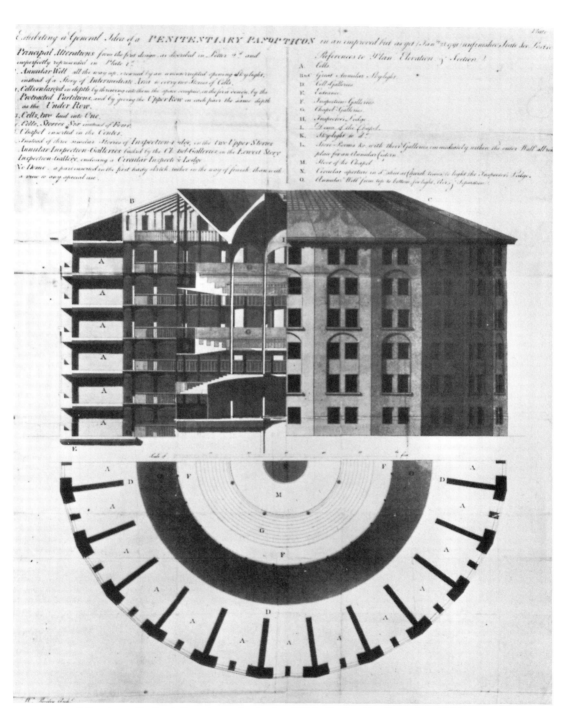

5.2   Jeremy Bentham's Panopticon; a drawing from 1791 by Bentham himself, together with his brother Samuel and Willey Reverley. (Illustration courtesy Cambridge University Press.)

of the larger society outside. "Instruction diffused:" this refers to the capacity of the Panopticon to serve as the architectural vehicle for the instruction of children or young people. "Public burthens lightened:" this interesting claim follows from Bentham's intention that the Panopticon should be a private, not a public, enterprise. According to Gertrude Himmelfarb, he expected to operate the Panopticon himself, as a private entrepreneur, generating sufficient revenue from the sale of the products of the occupants to pay the Panopticon's operating costs and to make a profit for himself as well. No other simple idea in architecture, before or since, has ever made such large claims!

The brazen tone of these statements of Taylor and of Bentham has been a considerable embarrassment to the sensibility of the contemporary modernist for some time now. Even before the great reconsideration of instrumentalist modernity that has been proceeding in our own time got under way, earlier protagonists of modernism (such as Giedion, already cited in chapter four) sought to downplay the presumptuous manipulation of men that was embodied in the thinking of the two pioneers of modernist labor theory. But notwithstanding such embarrassment, the historical fact is that the instrumentalization conceived by Bentham and Taylor, and so strikingly embodied in such examples of modern architectural theory as those from the twenties in the Soviet Union cited above, has continued to play a profoundly influential role, even in mainstream modern architectural thinking, right up to our own time. Only now, when instrumentalist rationality has begun to come under criticism in such varied aspects of modern life, has it become possible to begin to challenge that long-lasting influence directly. Indeed, it has even become possible, in the perspective opened up by this line of discussion, to look again at that whole series of nineteenth-century critiques of technological modernity that, during the century-long period of instrumentality's unchallenged hegemony, always seemed to be a historical embarrassment of an opposite kind to that we nowadays tend to see in Taylor and in Bentham.

Let us look, for example, at a sad statement of William Morris toward the end of his career, at a time when the influence of Frederick Taylor on the forms of modern life had not yet occurred but when that of Bentham was already quite well known indeed, especially to a dissenter such as Morris.

> Apart from the desire to produce beautiful things the leading passion of my life had been and is hatred of modern civilization. . . . What shall I say concerning its mastery of and its waste of mechanical power, its enemies of the commonwealth so rich, its stupendous organization—for the misery of life! Its contempt of simple pleasures which everyone could enjoy but for its folly? Its eyeless vulgarity which has destroyed art, the one certain solace of labour? . . . The struggles of mankind for many ages had produced nothing but this sordid, aimless, ugly confusion; the immediate future seemed to me likely to intensify all the present evils by sweeping away the last survivals of the days before the dull squalor of civilization had settled down on the world. . . . Think of it! Was it all to end in a counting-house on top of a cinder-heap, with Podsnap's drawing-room in the offing, and a Whig committee dealing out champagne to the rich, and margarine to the poor, in such convenient proportions as would make all men contented together, though the pleasure of the eyes was gone from the world, and the place of Homer was to be taken by Huxley.[12]

A close examination of the conclusion of this text yields further contextual significances: "Was it all to end in a counting-house on top of a cinder-heap?" Clearly a summary image of capital accumulation based on resource exploitation, of exactly the sort to which Taylor's techniques of manipulation particularly applied. "With Podsnap's drawing room in the offing." A reference to a character in Dickens whom we are told was modeled in some ways on Bentham. "And a Whig committee dealing out champagne to the rich, and margarine to the poor, in such convenient proportions as would make all men contended together." A sardonic observation on the model of an ideal liberal society in which the "greatest happiness of the greatest number"—itself a by-product of Bentham's "calculus of pain and pleasure"—could be regarded as an accomplished fact. "Though the pleasure of the eyes was gone from the world, and the place of Homer was to be taken by Huxley": the disappearance of myth from the realms of human experience in the modern world, and its replacement by a new and, in Morris's view, much more pedestrian ideal of scientific exactitude. As a summary critique of the tendencies of nineteenth-century British thought deriving from the utilitarian tradition, this could hardly be more comprehensive.

But it is the Dickensian reference in Morris's statement that I particularly wish to pursue, turning to a major piece of evidence in this argument by Dickens himself, his fascinating novel of 1854, *Hard Times*. *Hard Times* has yielded the quintessential name of an industrial town, Coketown, which has become a standard part of the vocabulary of any discussion of nineteenth-century architecture and planning. Coketown, you may recall, Dickens describes as "a triumph of fact."

> It was a town of red brick, or of brick that would have been red if the smoke and ashes had allowed it; but as matters stood, it was a town of unnatural red and black, like the painted face of a savage. It was a town of machinery and tall chimneys, out of which interminable serpents of smoke trailed themselves for ever and ever, and never got uncoiled. It had a black canal in it, and a river that ran purple with ill-smelling dye, and vast piles of building full of windows where there was a rattling and trembling all day long, and where the piston of the steam-engine worked monotonously up and down, like the head of an elephant in a state of melancholy madness. It contained several large streets all very like one another, and many small streets still more like one another inhabited by people equally like one another, who all went in and out at the same hours, with the same sound upon the same pavements, to do the same work, and to whom everyday was the same as yesterday and tomorrow, and every year the counterpart of the last and next.[13]

More interesting still, Coketown is the preeminent domain of two major Dickensian characters, Josian Bounderby and Thomas Gradgrind. Bounderby is a newly rich capitalist entrepreneur who has risen from humble origins. As Dickens puts it:

> He was a rich man, banker, merchant, manufacturer and what not. A big loud man, made out of a coarse material, which seemed to have been stretched to make so much of him. . . . A man who was always proclaiming, through that brassy speaking trumpet of a voice of his, his old ignorance and his old poverty. A man who was the bully of humility.[14]

Gradgrind, on the other hand, is a social philosopher, educationalist, and politician. Dickens describes him as follows:

> Thomas Gradgrind Sir. A man of realities. A man of facts and calculations. A man who proceeds upon the principle that two and two are four, and nothing over. . . . With a rule and a pair of scales, and the multiplication table always ready in his pocket . . . ready to weigh and measure any parcel of human nature, and tell you exactly what it comes to. It is a mere question of figures, a case of simple arithmetic.[15]

Needless to say, the coarse, exploitative capitalist Bounderby merits very little approbation in Dickens's eyes. But what has made *Hard Times* so famous—and so illuminating—is that Gradgrind, the utilitarian activist, fares little better. As Raymond Williams has pointed out:

> The case against him is so good, and his refutation by experience so masterly, that it is easy for the modern reader to forget exactly what Gradgrind is. It is surprising how common is the mistake of using the remembered name, Gradgrind, as a class-name for the hard Victorian employer. The valuation which Dickens actually asks us to make is more difficult. Gradgrind is a Utilitarian: seen by Dickens as one of the feeloosofer intellects described by Carlyle. This line is easy enough, but one could easily draw another: say, Thomas Gradgrind, Edwin Chadwick, John Stuart Mill. Chadwick, we are told, was "the most hated man in England", and he worked by methods, and was blamed for "meddling", in terms that are hardly any distance from Dickens' Gradgrind.[16]

Williams has thus taken us as close to architecture as Edwin Chadwick, the great reformer who was responsible for the country-wide programs of installation of water supply and sewers, and for other aspects of the general improvement of facilities for the protection of public health in Great Britain. In broadening the scope of implied critique to this degree, Williams has shown how Dickens, even in the middle of the nineteenth century, had already managed to put into question the whole tradition of modernist thought as manifested in utilitarian terms. And that question extended not just to the laissez-faire economics associated with liberalism, but also to the ostensibly beneficent reform movements associated with it as well.

Of course, it is also now possible to recognize the historical fact that Bentham's ideas sustained very harsh criticism soon after they had first been promulgated. We may take as cases in point both Augustus Pugin and Samuel Coleridge. Pugin is famous for the polemically paired series of images entitled *Contrasts* that he published in 1838.[17] In the single most famous of these pairs of images, Pugin juxtaposes a view of a "Catholic Town in 1440" with a second one of "the same town in 1840." In the former, we survey an idyllic scene of medieval urbanity, looking across a river to a town surmounted by a host of church spires, all surrounding that focus of medieval workmanship, the Guild Hall. In the latter image, we see the fate that has befallen the same town in the nineteenth century. The series of churches that dominate the fifteenth-century scene has now

THE SAME TOWN IN 1840

1. St Michaels Tower, rebuilt in 1750. 2. New Parsonage House & Pleasure Grounds. 3. The New Jail. 4. Gas Works. 5. Lunatic Asylum. 6. Iron Works & Ruins of St Maries Abbey. 7. St Evans Chapel. 8. Baptist Chapel. 9. Unitarian Chapel. 10. New Church. 11 New Town Hall & Concert Room. 12. Wesleyan Centenary Chapel. 13. New Christian Society. 14. Quakers Meeting. 15. Socialist Hall of Science.

Catholic town in 1440.

1. St Michaels on the Hill. 2. Queens Cross. 3. St Thomas's Chapel. 4. St Maries Abbey. 5. All Saints. 6. St Johns. 7. St Peters. 8. St Albourale. 9. St Maries. 10. St Edmunds. 11. Grey Friars. 12. St Cuthberts. 13. Guild hall. 14. Trinity. 15. St Olaves. 16. St Botolphs.

5.3   Pugin's most famous contrast: a "Catholic town" in 1440 and in 1840. (Illustration: Leicester University Press.)

been largely superseded by a new group of buildings, including the Baptist Chapel, the Unitarian Chapel, the "new Church," the Wesleyan Centenary Chapel and the Quaker's Meeting Hall. What is worse, the fifteenth-century abbey has been replaced by an iron works, and the whole foreground of the scene is occupied by a new jail built on Bentham's Panopticon principle. In this image, Pugin has managed to encapsulate a critique of virtually the whole of what, in the eyes both of his own contemporaries and of ourselves, stands as the legacy of Enlightenment rationality—not just utilitarianism itself, but even such constituent components of modernity as secularization and industrialization.

In another pair of images from the same volume, less well known but for our purposes more significant, Pugin contrasted a view of a "modern" and

an "ancient" poorhouse. In this pair, the attack on Bentham is made quite
explicit. In the medieval example, we see "one of the poor men" standing
erect before the doors of the chapel, his dignity intact; we see "the master" distributing coins, we see evidence of a diet of roast beef, wine, and
cheese, and in the strongest image of the series a deceased member of the
"poor house" receiving the last rites of the Church. In the corresponding
image from the modern period, we see the same "one of the poor men"
huddled in a barred cell. Here "the master" is depicted carrying a whip
and handcuffs, surrounded by other pieces of the apparatus of incarceration. The modern diet is shown to consist of bread, gruel, and potatoes,
and finally, in place of the last rites, we see a series of coffins labeled "for
vivisections" being loaded onto a cart, in front of a sign reading "a variety
of subjects always ready for medical students."

5.4   A second contrast, in which an ancient poorhouse is savagely juxtaposed to a modern institution
clearly recognizable as a Panopticon. (Illustration: Leicester University Press.)

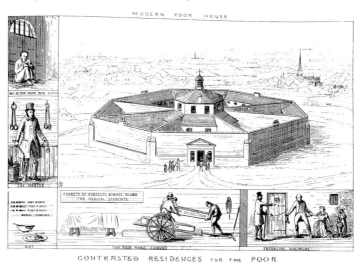

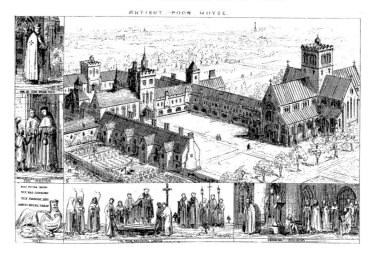

If Pugin most dramatically symbolized the opposition to Bentham of the critics of modernity, Coleridge charged that Bentham's utilitarian political economy amounted to nothing more than a moral expediency.

> It is this accursed practise of ever considering only what seems expedient for the occasion, disjointed from all principle, or enlarged systems of action, of never listening to the true and unerring impulses of our better nature, which has led the cold-hearted men to the study of political economy![18]

It is one of the more remarkable historical facts of the nineteenth century that this series of critiques of the implications of Benthamite utilitarianism had so little contemporary effect. Evidently the instrumentalist world view—especially once it had been further energized by theories of evolution and of progress that were derived from the epochal midcentury studies of Darwin—proved unchallengeable. Notwithstanding the dissent of Bentham's critics, the instrumentalization, both of things and of men, that had been so powerfully launched in the late years of the eighteenth century continued to hold sway over the dominant evolution of ideas in the western world well into the middle of the twentieth. The unguarded enthusiasm in respect to the instrumentalization of men that was demonstrated by the Russian constructivists must be seen as an extreme example of a tendency that extended throughout all the known branches of mainstream modern architecture.

To be sure, with his customary prescience, Le Corbusier early on began to distance himself from the most intense of the instrumentalist enthusiasms in question. We have already noted the guarded stance he assumed in response to the attack made on him by Karel Teige in 1929. Interestingly enough, in that same reply he also chose explicitly to disavow Taylorism itself. Chiding Teige and his Czech colleagues of the *sachlich* tendency for what he saw as hypocrisy, he noted how they all came to Paris "looking for the especially tender caress of the Parisian sky." By contrast, and despite their supposed "functionalist" convictions, Le Corbusier noted: "Not one of you will go to see the cruel places of hard work, of ruthless Taylorism, out in St. Denis, at St. Ouen."[19] So for Le Corbusier, as early as 1933, the great principles of scientific management that had been invented by Taylor and taken up so enthusiastically by the architectural left in Europe already seemed "ruthless." Still, this must be seen only as one quite partial reservation in respect to an aspect of modernist instrumentality, and that by one architect, albeit a profoundly influential one. By and large, few such reservations can be detected, by him or by any other important modernist, in the two decades that followed. Indeed, not until the major crisis of confidence of the mid-sixties did architectural modernism's profound complicity with the processes of instrumentality come into serious, broad-based question.

Outside architectural circles, fundamental doubts had begun to set in much earlier. Recent scholarship is beginning to see the publication, in 1944, of the *Dialectic of Enlightenment* by Max Horkheimer and Theodor Adorno as a very early example of a reconsideration of certain aspects of modernity, by a pair of thinkers who form an indisputable part of the tradition of modernity itself. Written in the dark years of World War II by the two German exiles in the United States, this ground-breaking text reveals very clearly the beginning of a profoundly pessimistic view of the consequences in the modern world of the untrammeled hegemony of instrumentality, as well as a reconsideration of the prerogatives and the ostensible legitimacies of "reason" as these had been promulgated in earlier texts. In their introduction, the two authors reflected:

> If it were only a question of the obstacles resulting from the self-oblivious instrumentalization of science, then a critique of social problems could at least attach itself to trends opposed to the accepted scientific mode; yet even these are affected by the total process of production. They have changed no less than the ideology to which they referred.[20]

The reconsideration of the philosophical grounding of modernity has grown ever more evident in the years since 1944. In 1958, Horkheimer and Adorno's effort was joined by another that derived from a quite different philosophical perspective but concurred almost entirely with their reservations in respect to instrumentality. This was Hannah Arendt's *The Human Condition,* whose view of modernism derived in significant measure from that of Martin Heidegger, whose student Arendt had been in the mid-nineteen-twenties. Only three years later, it was joined in turn by a parallel critique from yet another perspective. In Michel Foucault's *Madness and Civilization,* the long-unchallenged rationality of the European Enlightenment was attacked yet again—this time for what Foucault saw as its presumptuous categorizations of "madness" and "sanity," and for the whole series of social transformations across the eighteenth and nineteenth centuries that resulted from them.[21] Aptly for my present purposes, Michel Foucault followed *Madness and Civilization* with a successor text in 1975, *Discipline and Punish,* in which he specifically characterized Bentham's Panopticon as symptomatic of a particular mode of instrumentalist thinking in the nineteenth century. As he put it:

> On the whole, one can speak of the formation of a disciplinary society in this movement that stretches from the enclosed disciplines, a sort of social "quarantine," to an indefinitely generalizable mechanism of "panopticism." Not because the disciplinary modality of power has replaced all the others; but because it has infiltrated the others, sometimes undermining them, but serving as an intermediary between them, linking them together, extending them and above all making it possible to bring the effects of power to the most minute and distant element.

Moreover, Foucault continued,

> In a society in which the principal elements are no longer the community and public life, but, on the one hand, private individuals and, on the other, the state, relations can be regulated only in a form that is the exact reverse of the spectacle: It was to the modern age, to the ever-growing influence of the state, to its ever more profound intervention in all the details and all the relations of social life, that was reserved the task of increasing and perfecting its guarantees, by using and directing towards that great aim the building and distribution of buildings intended to observe a great multitude of men at the same time.[22]

If this was the conceptual method of panopticism, then according to Foucault it also entailed

> a tactics of power that fulfills three criteria: firstly, to obtain the exercise of power at the lowest possible cost (economically, by the low expenditure it involves; politically, by its discretion, its low exteriorization, its relative invisibility, the little resistance it arouses); secondly, to bring the effects of this social power to their maximum intensity and to extend them as far as possible, without either failure or interval; thirdly, to link this "economic" growth of power with the output of the apparatuses (educational, military, industrial or medical) within which it is exercised; in short, to increase both the docility and the utility of all the elements of the system.[23]

Given this, it is hardly surprising to discover that "the technological muta-
tions of the apparatus of production, the division of labor and the elabora-
tion of the disciplinary techniques sustained an ensemble of very close
relations."[24]

With this observation, we are once again returned precisely to that nexus
of instrumentality in the nineteenth century that joins Bentham through
Taylor directly to the core of modernist architectural theory. Except that
in the perspective of the various critiques that have recently been made,
both of it and of its devastating consequences for the forms of life in the
modern world, we can now see that large sections of that entire body of
theory have been shown to be indefensible.

key insight to author's p.o.v.

Take, for example, the entire body of ideas that modernism has long subsumed under the name of functionalism. If the thoroughgoing complicity
of architectural functionalism in the "limitless instrumentalization of everything that exists" had not become evident enough in chapter four, the
most cursory examination of the reach of panopticism in our time would
indisputably show this to be the case. To take one instance, one need only
extend the arguments of Harry Braverman to trace the historical lineage
from Taylorism at the turn of the century directly to the time-motion
studies of the 1920s and 1930s, and then to the operations research of the
1940s and 1950s.[25] Following this, it is only one step further to the enterprise of the mid-to-late 1960s that proceeded under the name of "design
methodology." And should that step by taken, there will then appear ripe
for reexamination recent architecture's increasing absorption within the
processes of cost-benefit analysis and proformas, so fundamental to the
work of what we now know as the development industry. *and construction mgt./value engineering*

very true

To be sure, all this suggests that the reconsideration of so many of the
central tenets of the familiar theory of modernism in architecture will
necessarily occur only in the context of a broad reassessment of the role of
those tenets within the whole of contemporary society. Given this, we may
suppose not only that the reconsideration of functionalism I am calling for

will be protracted and painful for current architectural praxis, but also that its specific historical consequences will be both wide-ranging and in many respects unpredictable.

My speculation so far has only covered functionalism per se. In the same critical perspective delineated above, it would appear that the whole body of professional practices that currently constitute "institutional programming" will come under similarly skeptical scrutiny. The particular intellectual methods employed by Foucault have already focused on institutional "deconstruction" in an intermediate historical range. It can only be a matter of time before shorter-range investigations now being formulated bring the architectural programs of contemporary institutions under critical scrutiny. Indeed, it can be said that one phase of such criticism has already occurred. In the immediate aftermath of architecture's cultural and political controversies associated with the 1968 events, both Europe and North America saw a series of efforts to formulate a newly deinstitutionalized architecture intended to honor the quasi-anarchist aspirations of 1968. the efforts of such groups as the situationists in Europe and "advocacy planners" in North America were important symbolic precedents for those ambitious formulations.[26] Yet such efforts soon faltered and were abandoned. The reasons for this are not yet clear, but one can surmise that they have to do, among other things, with the eventual realization by the wisest of the '68 architectural rebels that architecture is inescapably institutional; that instrumentalization and institutionalization are two distinct legacies of the Enlightenment, which require historical disentangling; and that the challenge now before us is to formulate a conception of architecture for our time that is indeed deinstrumentalized, yet is also appropriately reinstituted.

It is my impression that this is not a task that will be easily accomplished. Architecture being situated so centrally within the larger systems of signification of society, the task will necessarily be strongly structured by current discourses on the degree to which current information technologies necessarily manifest propensities to a Foucaultian domination that should be

"the web" etc.

resisted. And on this critical question, contemporary cultural theory is profoundly ambivalent.

We may take as a particularly pertinent case in point the later writings of Jean Baudrillard, already cited in the introduction to this book. Endlessly fascinated by the current modalities of information technology, apocalyptic in the tenor of his descriptions of their possible social effects, Baudrillard nevertheless finds himself unable to assess them critically, save by the archest and most self-reflexive possible modes of defensive irony. Yet in this problematic, paralytic ambiguity, Baudrillard can appropriately be placed at the center of a range of current intellectual positions. To the decisively pessimistic side of him can be seen a group of more or less neo-Marxist commentators such as Guy Debord, Fredric Jameson, and Tomás Maldonado.[27] All these figures, whatever their intellectual differences one from another, would be far readier than Baudrillard is to condemn the domination of which these characteristic technologies are capable, and to do so from a more or less normative perspective. To the other side of Baudrillard—the optimistic side—can be ranged such influential figures as Jean-François Lyotard and Bruce Sterling.[28] For them, the liberating potentials of the new technologies are so overwhelmingly strong as to incline them to support them, despite the admitted risks of doing so. "Give the public free access to the memory and data banks," declares Lyotard, "the stakes would be knowledge . . . , and the reserve of knowledge—language's reserve of possible utterances—is inexhaustible."[29] Given this startling range of orientations, it is hardly surprising that practitioners in architecture have great difficulty taking their lead in this matter from cultural theorists.

My own sense of the situation is as follows. First of all, I am inclined to think that the disconcerting range of opinions currently held amongst cultural theorists in this matter is itself an indication of the magnitude of the dilemma Foucaultian deconstruction has caused for us all. Second, I would suggest that in stepping back from a full confrontation with the problematic ethical status of information technology per se, architects could gain insight from certain specific methodological analyses of one of its historic aspects already cited in chapter three, that of the division of labor, as this was originally formulated by Adam Smith in the eighteenth century and as it evolved into scientific management at the instigation of Frederick Taylor a century later.

As I have already stated, nothing is more fundamental to the concept of the division of labor than the mandatory specialization of the tasks of the individual worker. It was due to precisely this specialization, in Smith's view, that the new division of labor was able to realize the "saving of time which is commonly lost in passing from one species of work to another." Similarly, for Taylor, "the most prominent single element in modern scientific management" was "the task idea." Moreover, it was the historic adoption of this principle by Henry Ford that led directly to his brilliant invention of the idea of an assembly line. How interesting, then, that among the most revolutionary developments in recent manufacturing and labor theory should be the definitive reconsideration—and even in many cases the abandonment—of this fundamental tenet. In the advanced manufacturing plants of today, workers no longer assume such minutely specialized roles. A few years back, radical innovations on the assembly line in automobile manufacturing resulted in the implementation of the concept of the "work team," according to which groups of workers took responsibility for related sets of tasks, amongst which they individually rotated during the work day. It became the responsibility of the group as a whole to decide how to optimize the relationships of their individual work roles and the efficiency of their component of the overall production process. During the original flowering of the "work team" concept, the relentless assembly line familiar to the public at large from films such as Chaplin's *Modern Times* was quite fundamentally altered. It is true, of course, that more recent developments in automobile production, especially those of the Japanese manufacturers, have shifted emphasis from the worker on the line to the system of delivery of components to the line. As a result, the most recent form of automobile plant design has seen some revival of the basic characteristics of the traditional assembly line (this set of operational moves now being named "lean production"). But even here the workers are expected to work in pairs at a minimum, as well as to assume responsibility for the conceptual efficiency of their respective parts of the process.

Looking back to the thrust of the arguments of chapter three, it is easy enough to recall that almost as fundamental as "the task idea" to the historical division of labor has been what Braverman called the "dissociation of the labor process from the skills of the workers." To quote Taylor again, "the managers assume . . . the traditional burden of gathering together all of the traditional knowledge which in the past has been possessed by the workmen." The recent developments just described in manufacturing and in labor theory have laid down a startling challenge to this basic precept of the traditional division of labor. Once the workers have again been asked to think, and to reconceptualize their own role in the overall production process, this fundamental premise of Taylorization has been abandoned. What is more, no management can presume to anticipate—or even decisively to shape—the thrust of the revived processes of thinking on the part of the workers, once they have been set in motion. In a recent and highly provocative study entitled *In the Age of the Smart Machine,* the American labor theorist Shoshana Zuboff has documented how the advent of computerization in many of the traditional tasks of both industrial and clerical work has begun to make the traditionally hierarchical control of all management functions unexpectedly irrelevant.[30] In a case study of banking, for example, she has documented how the administration of one organization came reluctantly to accept that the traditional withholding of confidential data from on-line lower-echelon employees no longer made any operational sense. A secondary consequence of the same realization was a decision to radically restructure the administrative hierarchy of the entire bank. In many such unforeseen ways is the whole concept of the division of labor in our time coming under radical reconsideration, within the very processes of work themselves.

It seems to me that it is in examining such detailed aspects of the role of information technology today, rather than in such generalized ethical observations as those of Baudrillard, Jameson, et al., that architects will find helpful strategies with which to attempt to formulate a deinstrumentalized and reinstituted architecture appropriate to our time. In this effort they may even wish to take encouragement, as I do myself, from the recent thoughtful and constructive observations of Constance Penley and Andrew Ross.

In their introduction to a recent collection of texts on the relationship of contemporary communication technologies to social and cultural change, which parallel to some degree the kinds of changes that can be expected in architecture, Penley and Ross describe themselves as "wary, on the one hand, of the disempowering habit of deionizing technology as a satanic mill of domination, and weary, on the other, of postmodernist celebrations of the technological sublime." Attempting to position themselves both realistically and optimistically, they continue: "We fully recognize that cultural technologies are far from neutral, and that they are the result of social processes and power relations. Like all technologies, they are ultimately developed in the interests of industrial and corporate profits and seldom in the name of greater community participation or creative autonomy." At the same time the two authors

> recognize that the kinds of liberatory fantasies that surround new technologies are a powerful and persuasive means of social agency, and that their source to some extent lies in real popular needs and desires. Technoculture, as we conceive it, is located as much in the work of everyday fantasies and actions as at the level of corporate or military decision making. It is a mistake to dismiss such fantasies as false consciousness and such actions as compensatory bait, or to see their subjects as witless dupes of a smooth confidence trick. To deny the capacity of ordinary women and men to think of themselves as somehow in charge of even their most highly mediated environments is to cede any opportunity of making popular appeals for a more democratic kind of technoculture.[31]

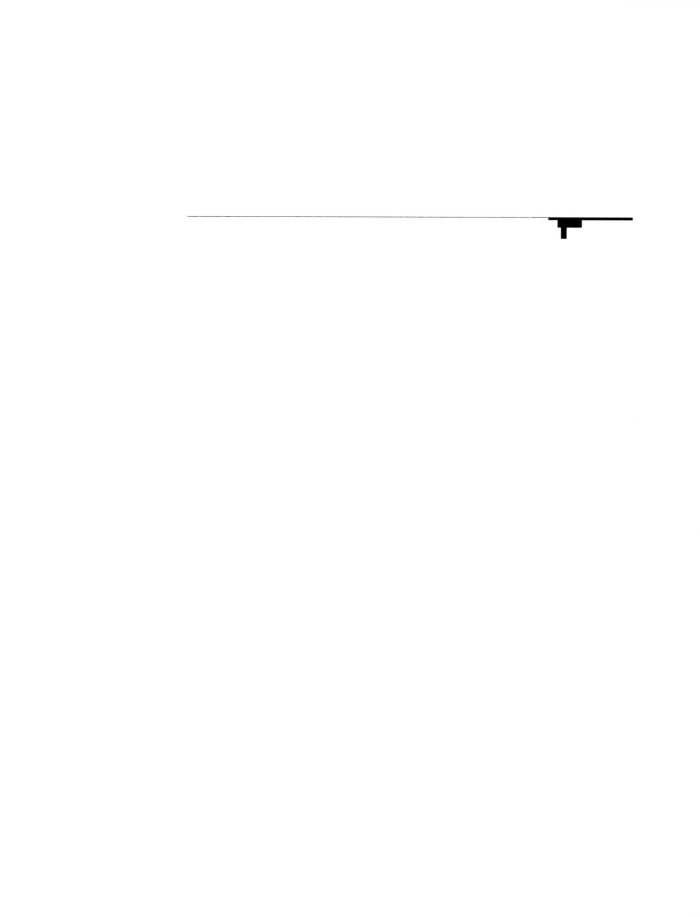

Organicist Yearnings and Their Consequences

The reader will recall Lewis Mumford's claim, cited in chapter four, that "the very notion of a modern monument is a contradiction in terms." The statement formed part of Mumford's polemic of 1937, "The Death of the Monument," in which he stated his strong objections to the revival of monumentality in architecture that had been promoted in certain circles in both Europe and North America since the beginning of the 1930s. Whether or not it was the intensity of his aversion to such a revival that was the cause we do not know, but Mumford allowed the logic of the argument of that short text to drive him to embrace quite a surprising position on architecture and on the city. Indeed, to the best of my knowledge, it is a position more extreme than any other he propounded either before the date of the 1937 text or during the long period of his career afterward.[1]

The position Mumford took also went well beyond the straightforward opposition of "instruments" and "monuments" that first prompted me to quote him. As I noted in chapter four, he went on in the same text to argue:

> The protective function of the city, tendencies toward fixities and permanence of function, have been overdone: for a living creature the only real protection and permanence comes through growth and renewal and reproduction: processes which are precisely the opposite of petrification.[2]

Mumford's opposition between "fixities and permanence of function" on the one hand and "growth and renewal and reproduction" on the other gives an indication of the direction his argument was about to take. Having declared his belief that historical monuments in the modern city should "no longer be lived in," he continued:

> Our distrust for the monumental does not merely apply to actual tombs and memorials; it must apply even more to the physical apparatus of city life, in particular, to its mechanical equipment. These, too, are capable of taking on a monumental character; indeed the Roman roads and aqueducts and sewers have survived at least as well as the Tomb of Hadrian and the Arch of Constantine. The more the energies of a community become immobilized in such material structures, the less ready is it to adjust itself to new emergencies. A two-storey building, with small foundations, may be easily torn down, if a different type of structure or the widening of a street to accommodate a new type of traffic proves necessary. But a twenty-storey building has a deeper foundation and a more elaborate superstruc-

ture; it is served by a greater variety of expensive mechanical utilities, such as elevators: it is not easily removed: moreover the water mains and sewers and wired connections that serve such a building are all correspondingly large and expensive: one does not readily tear such a structure down; and above all, one does not tear it down when it is to be replaced by a smaller building, or no building at all.[3]

It is this extraordinary conclusion of Mumford's that requires extended analysis and commentary. First of all, we may note that it took him to the brink of endorsing the same "limitless instrumentalization of everything" that was to be promulgated with such enthusiasm by Reyner Banham and by the Archigram Group in England some thirty years later. To be sure, in Mumford's case it was not a celebration of instrumentality per se that led him to such an unexpected conclusion; rather it was his effort to oppose the tendencies he saw in the architecture of the late thirties toward monumentalization or, to use his term, petrification.

But the fact that this is true does not alter the consequence of Mumford's declaration. His commendation of "flexibility" and of "adaptation" in the same text makes this incontrovertibly clear. In short, we may conclude that his aversion to "monumentality" in architecture led the author of *The City in History,* at a point in his career well before the writing of that famous work, to launch a polemic in which he allowed himself to come to the conclusion that the overall durability of the urban artifact was a bad thing; that selected historical buildings might well be retained within the overall urban fabric but not lived in; and that the need for flexibility and adaptation made a deliberate condition of impermanence a desirable characteristic of both the fabric and the infrastructure of the contemporary city. How could the same critic who was to become famous for his long-standing objection to the supposed "mechanocentric" characteristics of the work of Le Corbusier have entertained a mode of instrumentalization of urban form far more radical than any ever considered by Le Corbusier himself? To answer that large and complex question, it will be necessary to undertake an extended review of the fateful theme of "organicism," first as it played a role in the development of Mumford's own thinking, and then in the larger context of contemporary architectural theory generally.

To begin with the case of Mumford's own intellectual development, the basic historical facts are by now well enough known. For much of the earlier part of his career, he was, by his own admission, under the profound intellectual influence of the Scottish botanist, sociologist, and planner Patrick Geddes. Indeed, the first decade or so of Mumford's career can be seen to constitute an effort on his part to establish an independent intellectual position for himself, notwithstanding both his own avowed debt to Geddes and the older mans' persistent efforts to turn Mumford into his amanuensis. For his part, Geddes had been principally influenced by ideas that had been developed by two French thinkers, the botanist Chevalier de Lamarck and the sociologist Frédéric Le Play, earlier in the nineteenth century. Indeed, Geddes has been referred to a "neo-Lamarckian" on account of the centrality within his own body of thought of a vitalist evolutionism deriving from the work of the earlier botanist. Geddes took the teleology implicit in Lamarck's work and applied it to the form of the city, the result being the body of organicist ideas of "growth and renewal and reproduction" (to use Mumford's words) that formed the basis of Geddes's influential book of 1915, *Cities in Evolution.* To be sure, Mumford's intellectual curiosity ranged widely, from the transcendental philosophy of Ralph Waldo Emerson to the reformism of the English author of *Garden Cities of Tomorrow,* Ebenezer Howard. Yet insofar as ideas of the organic were always central to his thinking, they derived in largest measure from the mentor Mumford referred to as "master": Patrick Geddes.

Mumford and Geddes were far from alone in their deep engagement with the powerful metaphor of the organic. It has had a broad influence across the entire history of ideas in the past two centuries, not least in the interrelated realms of society and art. We have already noted, for example, how Geddes derived his organicism from the late eighteenth- and early nineteenth-century ideas of evolution developed by Lamarck. The English social historian Raymond Williams has argued that the idea of an "organic society" can be foreseen even earlier than that, in Edmund Burke's well-known characterization of a "nation":

> A nation is not an idea only of local extent, and individual momentary aggregation; but it is an idea of continuity, which extends in time as well as in numbers and in

space. And this is a choice not of one day, or one set of people, not a tumultuary and giddy choice; it is a deliberate election of the ages and of generations; it is a constitution made by what is ten thousand times better than choice, it is made by the peculiar circumstances, occasions, tempers, dispositions, and moral, civil, and social habitudes of the people, which disclose themselves only in a long space of time.[4]

Burke's familiar conjunction of "circumstances, occasions, tempers, dispositions . . . and habitudes" was succeeded early in the nineteenth century by more explicitly organic intellectual formulations. A full-fledged appearance of the metaphor in aesthetic theory occurred when Samuel Coleridge employed it to characterize the work of Shakespeare. The literary critic's now famous usage must also be seen to have been a seminal one, in that it set the "organic" explicitly against the "mechanic," presaging the form of a whole later stream of architectural criticism of which Mumford himself would form part.

The form is mechanic, when on any given material we impress a predetermined form, not necessarily arising out of the properties of the material; as when to a mass of wet clay we give whatever shape we wish it to retain when hardened. The organic form, on the other hand, is innate; it shapes, as it develops, itself from within, and the fullness of its development is one and the same with the perfection of its outward form.[5]

From the middle of the nineteenth century onward, organicism grew ever more pervasive in aesthetic and in social theory. Consider, for instance, the historic episode in which John Ruskin took up residence on site during the construction of the new Natural History Museum, designed for Oxford by the firm of Deane and Woodward. With Ruskin's assistance, the architects had arranged to bring a family of Irish stone carvers to the site to work for an extended period on the decorative stonework for the building. For his part, Ruskin spent his mornings during his stay on the site taking the carvers on nature walks and instructing them about the local flora and fauna, so as to equip them with sufficient creative inspiration for the upcoming afternoon's program of stone carving.

In 1887, the evolution of the idea of the organic in society took another major turn with the publication of Ferdinand Tonnies's *Gemeinschaft und*

Gesellschaft.[6] What makes Tonnies's text important in the present context is the fact that its author proceeded from a different set of influences than those of Ruskin and the other English social critics who preceded him. Rather, the innovative father of modern German sociology began from a reinterpretation of the work of Hobbes and Marx, arriving in the end at a conceptual model of society now well known for the invidious contrast between what it depicted as the authentic, organic harmony of community and the materialistic fragmentation of business society.

In Tonnies's work the concepts of "the organic" and of "community" were explicitly conjoined, beginning a new tradition that has stretched right to our own time. Tonnies's influence was profound, for example, in the development of the Chicago school of sociology in the United States. One of its leading figures was the late nineteenth-century Chicago reformer Jane Addams, the founder of the famous hostel Hull House. Addams pressed the naturalistic metaphor far indeed: "All higher aims live only by communion and fellowship [and] are cultivated most easily in the fostering soil of community life." According to Morton and Lucia White, "Jane Addams' idea of the city as an organism even extended to the point where she said that the aim of the residents of Hull House was 'to be swallowed and digested, to disappear into the bulk of the people.'"[7] By the time of Robert Park, one of Addams's successors in the Chicago School, the idea of organicism had moved from the "city" to encompass the whole of society.

Of course, the best-known use of the metaphor of the "organic" in architecture itself also began in Chicago, in the work of a young man who had at one time been associated with Hull House and who was also later to become a tempestuous sometime ally of Mumford's. This was Frank Lloyd Wright, who argued in a 1935 text that even as a young man he had been drawn to the idea of the organic:

> A growing idea of simplicity as organic, as I had been born into it and trained in it, was anew as a quality of thought, able to strengthen and refresh the spirit in any circumstances. Organic simplicity might everywhere be seen producing significant character in the ruthless but harmonious order I was taught to call nature.[8]

Later in the same essay, Wright linked the idea of the organic directly to building.

> Continuity . . . appeared to me as the natural means to achieve truly organic architecture by machine technique or by any other natural technique. Here was direct means, the only means I could then see or can now see to express, objectify and again bring natural form to architecture. Here by instinct at first (all ideas germinate) principle had entered into building as the new aesthetic, "continuity."
> . . . But were the full import of continuity in architecture to be grasped, aesthetic and structure become completely one, it would continue to revolutionize the use and wont of our machine age architecture, making it superior in harmony and beauty to any architecture, Gothic or Greek. This ideal at working upon materials by nature of the process or tools used means a living architecture in a new age, organic architecture, the only architecture that can live and let live because it never can become a mere style.[9]

We have already noted how Coleridge opposed his literary conception of the organic to an alternative he labeled mechanic. We are aware also, that Mumford employed a parallel opposition a century later on to commend the work of Wright and of certain other modern architects he admired, and to disparage that of Le Corbusier and others grouped by Hitchcock and Johnson under the rubric of "the International Style." It turns out, in long historical retrospect, that the opposition of the organic to the mechanic—or mechanocentric, to use Mumford's term—has been a structural element within the organicist tradition. Coleridge, for example, generalized his opposition to the mechanic to encompass his broad antipathy to the whole philosophy of utilitarianism (discussed in chapter five), which he associated with Jeremy Bentham. In a letter to the poet Wordsworth, he lamented the whole

> philosophy of mechanism, which in everything that is most worthy of the human intellect, strikes Death, and cheats itself by mistaking clear images for distinct conceptions, and which idly demands conceptions where intuitions alone are possible or adequate to the majesty of the Truth.[10]

For all the differences in their respective critical approaches to nineteenth-century society, neither Pugin nor Ruskin would have demurred at William Morris's lament of 1884 that "the Revival of Architecture" in which he had participated had in the end been a failure. Morris thought that the failure was due to the fact that the group of revivalists to which he had belonged was

> part of a society which will not and cannot have a living style, because it is an economical necessity for its existence that the ordinary everyday work of its popu-

lation shall be mechanical drudgery; and because it is the harmony of the ordinary everyday work of the population which produces Gothic, that is living architectural art, and mechanical drudgery cannot be harmonized into art.[11]

Following Hobbes and Marx, Tonnies generalized the organic/mechanical opposition in more specific economic terms. Leiberson has reported that "Tonnies' image of *Gemeinschaft* contained an idealized version of medieval Germany. . . . Bonds of blood relation, place and friendship tied individuals to one another, and drew houses into the larger units of clan, ethnic group, and people, of village, county and province." Following this, "Tonnies made an abrupt transition from this theory of *Gemeinschaft* as stable collective organism to a theory of *Gesellschaft* strongly colored by Marx." For him, as for Marx himself, "Modern society was constituted by commodity exchange."[12] Thus when Mumford employed the term mechanocentric in 1948 to disparage the so-called second way in modern architecture, his usage might even by then be thought to have been anachronistic.

But this is still to anticipate the thrust of my argument. Before we can come to terms with the paradox represented in Mumford's 1937 polemic—conjoining, as it does, an opposition to mechanism with an evident acquiescence in instrumentalization—we must consider two further, closely related themes within the tradition of organicism in architecture during the period under discussion. The first of these is the fascinating assumption, deep within the body of most organicist theory in architecture, of the condition of abundance, that problematic ideal of the *animal laborans* to which Hannah Arendt has so provocatively referred. As a fully developed concept, abundance evidently manifested itself in the history of ideas well before the nineteenth century. In his remarkable *The Great Chain of Being,* Arthur Lovejoy characterized an earlier version of it—plenitude—as having been implicit in western thought since Plato. "This strange and pregnant theorem of the 'fullness' of the realization of conceptual possibility in actuality" Lovejoy thought required greater exposition and consideration than it had hitherto received:

> It has, so far as I know, never been distinguished by an appropriate name; and for want of this, its identity in varying contexts and in different phrasings seems often to have escaped recognition by historians. I shall call it the principle of plenitude, but shall use the term to cover a wider range of inferences from premises identical

with Plato's than he himself draws; i.e., not only the thesis that the universe is a *plenum formarum* in which the range of conceivably diversity of *kinds* of living things is exhaustively exemplified, but also any other deductions from the assumption that no genuine potentiality of being can remain unfulfilled, that the extent and abundance of the creation must be as great as the possibility of existence and commensurate with the productive capacity of a "perfect" and inexhaustible Source, and that the world is better, the more things it contains.[13]

But by the middle of the nineteenth century, the implicit association of plenitude, or abundance, with the laboring process had already been made a central part of Marx's theory of labor. As Arendt has pointed out,

the true meaning of labor's newly discovered productivity becomes manifest only in Marx's work, where it rests on the equation of productivity with fertility, so that the famous development of mankind's "productive forces" into a society of an abundance of "good things" actually obeys no other law and is subject to no other necessity than the aboriginal command, "Be ye fruitful and multiply," in which it is as though the voice of nature herself speaks to us.[14]

A naturalist and organic image of abundance is central to the later nineteenth-century philosophical writings of American transcendentalists such as Emerson and Thoreau. And it was precisely from such figures as these that Frank Lloyd Wright derived his own concepts of the organic, so thoroughly embodying a central assumption of a condition of abundance. It is true, of course, that Mumford's own concepts of organicism eschew the full-blooded nineteenth-century romanticism that we associate with the Emerson-Thoreau-Wright lineage. In light of the more scientific approaches Mumford had learned from the work of such later nineteenth-century biologists as Mendel and Weisman, he eventually proposed for public consideration the concept of biotechnicism as the appropriate basis for urban life in our time. From Mumford's biotechnicism, it is only one short step further to a concept put forward some years later by Mumford's protégé Ian McHarg.

In his introduction to McHarg's highly influential book of 1969, *Design with Nature,* Mumford saluted what he called McHarg's effort

to determine what constitutes a self-renewing environment, containing all the ingredients necessary for man's biological prosperity, social cooperation and spiritual stimulation. The name of this effort, in so far as it draws upon science, is "ecology," a body of knowledge that brings together so many aspects of nature that it necessarily came late upon the scene. Ian McHarg, while trained professionally as a town planner and a landscape architect, might better be described as an inspired ecologist.[15]

Now it might be thought that "ecology," as the successor to Mumford's own biotechnicism, would have left the somewhat romanticist notion of organicist abundance behind. But this is not so. McHarg's first sentence in his own text makes his allegiance irrefutably clear: "The world is a glorious bounty."[16] In short, from the earliest architectural appropriations of ideas from American transcendentalism right through to major environmental polemics of the very recent past, the main tradition of organicist thought has made "abundance" both a basic assumption and a primary value.

We turn now to the second of the two related themes to which I referred above, one the tenacious advocates of organicism in architecture and urbanism have, during this entire period, consistently managed to ignore. In organicism's root discipline of biology, the converse concept of scarcity has been as important in the evolution of biological theory as abundance has been. An adequate understanding of the impact of the organic in the modern world requires an account of this concept as well.

Perhaps the most notorious early appearance of the concept of scarcity in a social context was Thomas Malthus's controversial *Essay on Population* of 1830. There he set out the hypothesis that human populations manifested a structural tendency to continue to increase until such time as available food supplies ceased to be sufficient to support them, following which a condition of starvation could be expected to set in until such time as the size of the dependent population had restabilized. Malthus characterized this process, which he portrayed as cyclical, as "the principle of population," and his startling principle had quite widespread influence throughout the remainder of the nineteenth century. Not the least important was on the natural scientist Charles Darwin, who by midcentury had reworked the concept to formulate the "principle of natural selection" on which his epoch-making *Origin of Species* was largely based. With the publication of that work, Darwin became even more controversial than Malthus had been, and the direction of innovative thinking in numerous fields began to bear his influence. In his fascinating history of ideas of the period, Richard Hofstadter observed: "Almost everywhere in western civilization, though in varying degrees according to intellectual traditions and personal temperaments, thinkers of the Darwinian era seized upon the new theory and attempted to sound its meaning for the several social disciplines."[17]

In turn, one of the key intellectual influences resulting from Darwin's work was on the English sociologist and popularizing philosopher Herbert Spencer, who took certain of Darwin's ideas derived from natural history and in his *Synthetic Philosophy* of 1864 applied them to society at large. The influential result of this application was the celebrated phrase "the survival of the fittest." Together with its companion "the struggle for existence," this slogan in its turn became the basis of Spencer's great appeal in North America in the latter part of the nineteenth century, both to a sector of the intelligentsia and to the newly ascendant forces of large-scale industrial capital. Hofstadter has cited social views promulgated by Spencer that led to his popularity in such circles.

> His categorical repudiation of state inference with the "natural" unimpeded growth of society led him to oppose all state aid to the poor. They were unfit, he said, and should be eliminated. "The whole effort of nature is to get rid of such, to clear the world of them, and make room for better."[18]

Spencer's profound influence in the United States extended to the work of the sociologist William Graham Sumner. In his turn, Sumner broadened the usage of the Spencerian concept of the survival of the fittest further still, giving rise to the whole sociopolitical movement of the late nineteenth century that became known as social Darwinism. In this guise, the concept of scarcity became a key component of the intellectual arguments formulated to legitimate laissez-faire capitalism in its most militant mode. In a notorious and often-quoted address to a Sunday School class, for example, John D. Rockefeller observed:

> The growth of a large business is merely a survival of the fittest. . . . The American Beauty rose can be produced in the splendor and fragrance which bring cheer to its beholder only by sacrificing the early buds which grow up around it. This is not an evil tendency in business. It is merely the working-out of a law of nature and a law of God.[19]

The appeal of Spencer's interpretation of Darwin was not limited to the political right:

> Karl Marx himself, with his belief in universal "dialectical" principles, had been as much a monist as . . . Spencer. Reading *The Origin of Species* in 1860, he reported to Friedrich Engels, and later declared to Ferdinand Lassalle, that "Darwin's book is very important and serves me as a basis in natural science for the class struggle in history."[20]

Before the end of the nineteenth century, the scarcity model of organicism, which was fundamental to the ideas of natural selection and of the survival of the fittest, had assumed a very broad role within the mainstream of western European social thought. And while it is true that a whole later generation of thinkers, including William James, John Dewey, and Geddes and Mumford themselves, took great pains to refute the seeming "inevitability" of the Spencerian system, it did not then—and in my view still has not now—lost all of its persuasive power.

It is significant that in tracing the parallel lines of the concepts of abundance and scarcity, I have cited the name of only one thinker in connection with both. This is Marx, who saw abundance as a logical concomitant of his labor theory, at the same time that he appropriated the social Darwinist "struggle for existence" as a component of his own concept of the "class struggle." We may see it as a key aspect of Marx's dialectic, for our present purposes, that he is one of the surprisingly small number of thinkers deeply engaged by organicism within whose intellectual systems both abundance and scarcity were incorporated with equivalent weight.

Scarcity, as the above line of argument has suggested, has principally been emphasized in the fields of sociology and politics, and mainly right-wing politics at that. As Hofstadter has remarked:

> If Spencer's abiding impact on American thought seems impalpable to later generations, it is perhaps only because it has been so thoroughly absorbed. His language has become a standard feature of the folklore of individualism. "You can't make the world all planned and soft," says the businessman of Middletown. "The strongest and best survive—that's the law of nature after all—always has been and always will be."[21]

Abundance, on the other hand, has tended to a much greater degree to remain the preferred mode of "organicism" for thinkers in culture and the arts. The intellectual lineage that has been traced from Wright through Mumford to McHarg makes this amply clear. This consistent bifurcation (save for exceptions such as Marx), within the broad stream of organicist thought since the eighteenth century, and the fact that organicists within the field of architecture have so consistently emphasized abundance over scarcity, now, in long historical retrospect, begins to seem problematic.

We have already noted Arendt's account of the pivotal stages of development in western European thinking during the seventeenth and eighteenth centuries, which resulted in "the generalization of the fabrication experience in which usefulness and utility are established as the ultimate standards for life and the world of men."[22] This was the result that she named "the victory of *homo faber.*" Yet it was also her view that his "victory" was, in broad historical terms, astonishingly short-lived.

> Nothing perhaps indicates clearer the ultimate failure of *homo faber* to assert himself than the rapidity with which the principle of utility, the very quintessence of his world view, was found wanting and was superseded by the principle of "the greatest happiness of the greatest number." When this happened it was manifest that the conviction of the age that man can know only what he makes himself—which seemingly was so eminently propitious to a full victory of *homo faber*—would be overruled and eventually destroyed by the even more modern principle of process, whose concepts and categories are altogether alien to the needs and ideals of *homo faber.* . . . If worldly things are no longer primarily considered in their usefulness but as more or less incidental results of the production process which brought them into being, so that the end product of the production process is no longer a true end and the produced thing is valued not for the sake of its predetermined usage but "for its production of something else," then, obviously, the objection can be "raised that . . . its value is secondary only." . . . If one applies the principle of utility in this context at all, then it refers primarily not to use objects and not to usage but to the production process. . . . In other words, the ultimate standard of measurement is not utility and usage at all, but "happiness," that is, the amount of pain and pleasure experienced in the production or in the consumption of things.[23]

And of course, a world in which "happiness" is the ultimate standard is a world that has seen the victory of the *animal laborans.* As has already been discussed in chapter three, in such a world virtually all the "things of the world" "come and go, are produced and consumed, in accordance with the ever-recurrent cyclical movement of nature."[24]

This is a conclusion with the profoundest consequences for the historical advocacy of the values of organicism in the modern world. For it suggests that during the very period in which the early protagonists of the organic were rehearsing their critiques of mechanism, mechanism as an ascendant world view had in fact already been superseded. Also, it would appear, in the long historical retrospect of the present day, that the specific form of that supersession was one whereby instrumentality—the hallmark of *homo faber*—was subsumed within the biological cycle of production and consumption—the hallmark of *animal laborans*—and the defining characteristic of what we have in our own time learned to call "consumer society." Of all the great protagonists of organicism from the nineteenth century and from our own, only a few, among whom we have already cited Marx, were sufficiently astute to recognize the two sides of the organicist coin: abundance and scarcity. We can now see that even such historical phenomena from the nineteenth century as the industrial revolution, and the great machine of capitalism that fascinated Marx and Spencer alike, are both dialectical products of the victory of the *animal laborans,* and of the dual nature of organicism that went so largely unrecognized until the time of Arendt's pioneering critique in the late 1950s. In short, in would seem that organicism has in fact already achieved the ascendancy that its many advocates have sought so assiduously for it over the years, albeit in a form that most of them, at least in architecture, would wish to eschew.

Needless to say, this is a historical reinterpretation that places the activities of the advocates of organicism in our own time in a disconcerting new light. It would certainly surprise Lewis Mumford's many admirers to characterize him as complicit in the onset of consumer society, given his lifelong efforts to reassert the individualist values that he saw as preeminently American, and which he associated with the lives and works of Emerson, Thoreau, Whitman, and Melville from the middle of the nineteenth century, not to mention his assiduous campaign to create a form of urban life in America other than that of the ever more ubiquitous suburbia. My seemingly paradoxical charge requires further elucidation.

Mumford came on the stage of American intellectual life just after a generation that had struggled to refute what it saw as the oversimplified ideas of the body politic that had been promoted by Spencer and Sumner in the late nineteenth century. Thus, by the time of his own first arguments in respect to modern urban life, the once so shocking schemas of "the survival of the fittest" and of the "struggle for existence" had been significantly moderated. Then too, Mumford himself held a distinctly qualified view of the cycle of production and consumption, and argued from a very early point in his career for the "controlled growth" of urban areas and eventually for what he called a "normalized standard of consumption" for society generally. So we may say that by Mumford's time, the consequences of the unchecked ascendancy of the *animal laborans* were beginning to be evident, even if the historic complicity of organicism in them was not yet so. Yet it still seems to me that these qualifications only succeed in qualifying, not in justifying, the problematic nature of Mumford's position. We may note, for example, that modern organicist theory never succeeded in articulating a coherent or compelling measure of control of growth, such as Mumford advocated—at least not until the era of the great energy crisis of the mid-1970s.[25]

A more sympathetic commentator than myself would probably ascribe such limitations to a certain ultimate fallibility, even of such a comprehensive mind as Mumford's. But given the larger intellectual context of the tradition of organicist thought, it is my view that these failures of Mumford's thinking can be characterized as structural rather than as contingent. And this may be demonstrated by returning to the text of the untypical polemic of Mumford's with which I began this chapter, "The Death of the Monument."

The reader will recall how, in that revelatory text, Mumford allowed his aversion to monumentality in architecture to lead him to defend an uncharacteristically extreme position, one that argued against the overall durability of the urban fabric, opposed the reuse of historical buildings other than as museums, and argued for a deliberate condition of impermanence of urban infrastructure. "Growth and renewal and reproduction," "flexibility," and "adaptation" he advocated, instead of "petrification." What is so interesting, in the context of the preceding commentary, is the extent to which all of these seeming aberrations of the otherwise moderate Mumford can be seen to be quite consistent with the organicism of the nineteenth century, as promulgated by its partisans from that earlier time. Like Spencer and Sumner, Mumford had come to see urban life teleologically. Evolutionary transformation, in his argument, is imbued with the imprimatur of virtue, and the effort to stay it is opposed as "petrification." Ironically enough, in his indiscreet 1937 text the great American theorist of urban life aligned himself unequivocally with the forces of unceasing cyclical change, and assumed a position against what Arendt called "the ideals of *homo faber,* the fabricator of the world, which are permanence, stability, and durability."[26]

If the confusions that have reigned in the realm of organicist thought in the past two centuries have been sufficiently sweeping as to engulf even an intellect as acute as Mumford's, then it should not come as any surprise that those same confusions have led to organicism's utterly unknowing complicity in almost all the characteristic manifestations of consumer society, at least as they were extant from the 1920s through almost to our own time. It was not by chance that Arendt thought to observe in 1958: "We live in a laborers' society because only laboring, with its inherent fertility, is likely to bring about abundance."[27] It is true, of course, that a significant change, intellectually speaking, has occurred since the date of Arendt's sad observation. In the context of any discussion of organicist ideas, one would cite the change as having principally to do with the fateful energy crisis of 1974, and with its complex and as yet unconcluded aftermath. One might think of that event as having justified, after the fact, positions that organicists had previously taken. But I do not think that is the case. Insofar as one applies an organicist schema to the events of 1974, one can only realistically do so in the context of a consideration of scarcity rather than of abundance. Yet within the theory of architecture and urbanism prior to 1974, the principal thrust of organicist polemic always revolved around the concept of abundance. To be sure, in the great sea change that has occurred since that fateful year, one has become accustomed to hearing the devotees of the organic return time and again to the

209
Organicist Yearnings and Their Consequences

theme of scarcity. But these appeals are of the nature of closing the barn door after the horse has been stolen. For the great ascendancy of consumerism, in which organicism can now be seen to have been so complicit, had by then long since become a fundamental characteristic of the form of modern life in advanced societies.

Thus even the events of 1974 must be seen as further evidence of the sad consequences of organicist yearnings, rather than as any harbinger of redemptive possibility. Indeed, in retrospect, those events must also be seen as another part of the great loss of confidence in Enlightenment rationality that has been the consistent intellectual theme of the last two decades. It is now apparent that organicism has been as much a part of Enlightenment rationality as instrumentality, panopticism, and the division of labor have been. It would thus seem that whatever world view is presently in formation, vis-à-vis the urgent matter of the preservation of the environment itself, it will have to derive its principles from ones other than those of organicism as we have known it since the nineteenth century.

In addition to its own confused relationship to the phenomena of abundance and scarcity, the tradition of organicist thought has had one other distinctly discernible and problematic result. This is its emergent skepticism, if not outright hostility, to the idea of the city and to the possibility of a public realm within it. An early step in this process can be seen in the polemics of A. W. N. Pugin discussed in chapter five. For Pugin, already by 1838, the nineteenth-century industrial city constituted a historical catastrophe, and the famous series of *Contrasts* he published in that year conclusively demonstrate his own alienation from contemporary urban life. William Morris took this aspect of Pugin's opposition a step further and applied it much more broadly. His famous *News from Nowhere* of 1888 made a deliberate polemical example of London itself, imagining it a century hence as having ceased to be a metropolis at all and reverted to a linked series of semiautonomous villages, evocative of the Middle Ages. With that image, Morris joined a cultural tradition opposed to the metropolis that would stretch forward through William Dean Howells's *A Traveller from Altruria* of 1894 and Frank Borsodi's *Flight from the City* of 1933 to Frank

Lloyd Wright's astonishing proposal for Broadacre City of 1935. Then too, *News from Nowhere* also already embodied the scorn for the public realm of his time that Morris shared with Karl Marx, a scorn that would become so sadly typical of organicist polemics against the modern city. It surfaces, for example, in the account of a boat ride down the Thames of the future given to the protagonist of the tale by his guide Dick:

> I looked to the right . . . and said, in a rather doubtful tone of voice, "Why there are the Houses of Parliament! Do you still use them?" He burst out laughing, and was some time before he could control himself; then he clapped me on the back and said: "I take you neighbor; you may well wonder at our keeping them standing, and I know something about that, and my old kinsman has given me books to read about the strange game they played there. Use them! Well, yes, they are used for a sort of subsidiary market, and a storage place for manure, and they are handy for that, being on the waterside."**28**

By the turn of the century, feeding off Tonnies's distinction between *Gemeinschaft* and *Gesellschaft,* organicist thought had even begun to see community and metropolis as opposed conceptions of society. And this, in its turn, set loose a highly problematic tension between commitment to the idea of community and the political phenomenon of "plurality" (the subject of a more detailed discussion in chapter eight). The longer historical trajectory of these developments, from 1900 through to the political storms of the 1930s, is well enough known, especially in the context of Germany, where extremists on both the left and the right sought to exalt the former over the latter, even to the point of xenophobia and racism. The linkage to architectural and urban thinking, however, is less clear that it might be. If a commitment to the idea of community has impelled certain branches of the tradition of organicist thought to mistrust the city, the metropolis, and plurality itself, this would explain why so many organicist efforts at the reform of modern urban life during the period in question have involved a disposition toward a distinctly apolitical social homogeneity. This characteristic disposition I shall return to, but first it will be useful to give a brief account of the by now century-old tradition of efforts at organicist reform of modern urban life.

It is a tradition Francesco Dal Co has described as a trajectory "from parks

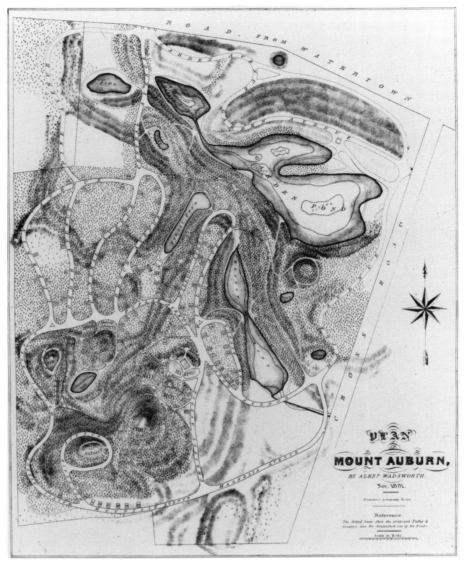

6.1 An 1831 plan for Mount Auburn Cemetery in Cambridge, Massachusetts. The precedent-breaking ideological preference for a naturalistic construction of gently rolling hills, picturesque ponds, and winding paths and roadways is quite clear.

to region," beginning with the innovative design of rural cemeteries such as Mount Auburn, outside of Boston, in the 1820s, and then leading to a full-fledged "rediscovery of nature" on the part of the nascent American intelligentsia.[29] Following that rediscovery, but before the great project of attempted organicist reform got significantly under way, a distinct bifurcation can already be seen to have occurred. Organicist urban reform consti-tutes two distinct streams, each characterized by its respective orientation toward the city and the metropolis. These two streams I would name "exclusivist" and "inclusivist," the former tending to mistrust the city so acutely as to consistently attempt to escape from it altogether, while the latter has attempted instead an ambitious series of efforts at transforming the metropolis on the basis of organicist principles.

Generally speaking, the exclusivist stream was responsible for the ongoing nineteenth-century programs for establishing utterly new communities unsullied by the vices of the city. One important historical group of such communities are those now known as utopian, of which recent history has made such nineteenth-century American examples as Oneida, Amana, and Salt Lake City famous, not least on account of their remarkable longevity as utopian social experiments. Indeed, it is now recognized that such religiously based communities as these have consistently proved far more likely to endure for a significant period of time than such secular utopias as those proposed by the British industrialist-reformer Robert Owen. The exclusivity such communities exhibit is made up of a series of features that

6.2 A view of one of the buildings from the Perfectionist utopian community at Oneida in upstate New York: the Second Mansion House from 1861–1862. (Photograph by permission, from Dolores Hayden, *Seven American Utopias*, MIT Press.)

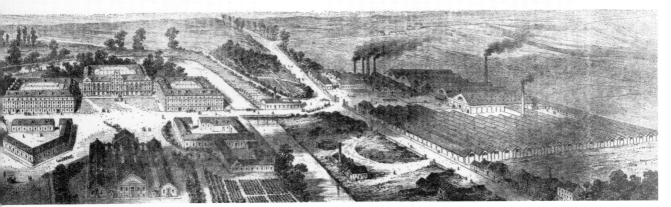

6.3 A panoramic view of the remarkably durable phalanstery at Guise, France, published in Jean-Baptiste-André Godin's *Solutions sociales,* from 1871. (Archives d'Architecture Moderne, Brussels.)

sharply distinguish them from the metropolis, such as aspirations to economic self-sufficiency, physical discreteness from the metropolis (possibly including sheer physical distance), and in some cases, a highly legible unity of architectural form. Significantly enough, the durability of the religiously based utopian communities has tended to have as a concomitant a social homogeneity that carries with it a deep mistrust of plurality.

A second important group of nineteenth-century communities includes those we now know as "company towns": Guise in France; Bourneville and Port Sunlight in England; Lowell and Pullman in the United States. All of these came into being through the initiatives and reformist instincts of industrialist entrepreneurs who had their own views of the undesirable characteristics of the metropolis, and the of the advantages to be gained, socially and economically, from the establishment of new communities outside it. Less rigorously exclusivist in their orientation than the utopian communities, company towns have also as a rule proven less durable, unless, of course, they have simply been absorbed physically into a nearby metropolis as a suburb. Still, during their effective operational periods as company towns these communities have also been notable for their (at least putative) social homogeneity, as well as for the clear absence of plurality within them.

A third group of such communities, an interesting and more recent one, comprises a series of artists' colonies created in Europe and in North America from 1900 onward. The most famous of these was established outside of Darmstadt in southern Germany, just at the turn of the century, by the Grand Duke of Hesse; among its residents, at least for a time, were such major cultural figures as the architects Peter Behrens and Josef Olbrich. Not without interest, however, is an American example from 1909 that was proposed to be built for a group of academics from the University of Chicago by Frank Lloyd Wright. This was the Como Orchards summer colony at Darby, Montana, for which Wright prepared

6.4 A drawing by Josef Olbrich of a part of the site plan of the Artists' Colony at Darmstadt from 1900—the same colony in which Peter Behrens had built a house for himself. Note how the hierarchy of the plan shows Olbrich's own house located right next to the Ernst Ludwigs Haus, the art school and central social institution in the community.

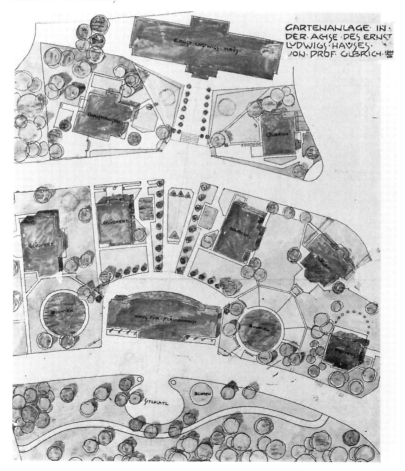

6.5   An illustration of the Como Orchards summer colony in Darby, Montana, prepared by Frank Lloyd Wright's studio in 1909 and included in the famous 1913 Wasmuth edition of his works. (Illustration by permission, Ernst Wasmuth Verlag.)

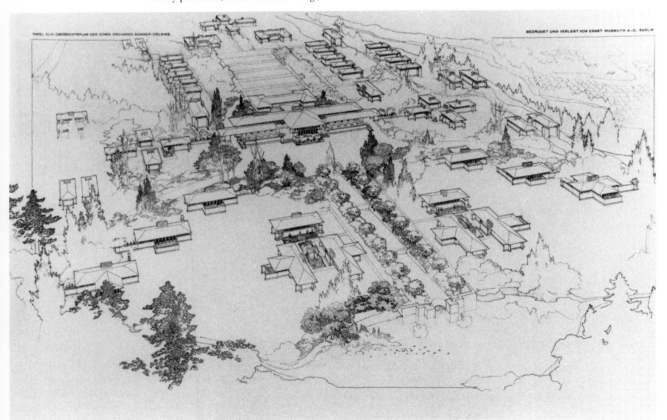

early designs and which was partly implemented by two of his collaborators, Marion Mahony and Walter Burley Griffin.

As a product of the bohemian *haute bourgeoisie*—unlike either the utopian community or the company town—the artists' colony was more symbolic in its exclusivity than either of its historic counterparts. Not really economically self-sufficient—in the case of Darmstadt not even all that physically remote from the larger and established city with which it participated in a denied reciprocity—the artists' colony set especially great store by its architectural design. The Darmstadt colony compensated for its metropolitan dependency by a number of highly symbolic design devices. These included the intensity of its putative communitarian focus, the distinct intensity of its Secessionist architectural language, and the explicitness of the demarcation of its physical boundaries against the world outside. In the case of the Como Orchards project, which possessed a site that truly was remote, the design emphasized instead the unitary formal coherence and centrality of its ground plan. In an account of the evolution of Wright's urban—and eventually antiurban—thinking, Giorgio Ciucci, to whom my argument here is in significant debt, sees the Como Orchards project as important enough for Wright to have included it, even in its then incomplete form, in the 1910 Wasmuth edition of his works. According to Ciucci, its urgent importance for Wright at that time lay precisely in its aspiration to an image of community transcending the simple house/city polarity that had characterized his previous work, and which he had just concluded was so inadequate: "It is an idealization of communal life, inspired by a bygone type of existence, possible only far from the city in the midst of nature."[30]

While the exclusivist stream of organicism has always attempted to separate itself from the "problematic" metropolis—if not by sheer physical distance, then by socially compelling symbolic techniques—the inclusivist stream has attempted to deal with the phenomenon by opposite means. If the exclusivists have tried to leave the metropolis behind, the inclusivists have consistently attempted, one way or another, to dissolve it.

Organicist Yearnings and Their Consequences

Effectively summarizing much of this stream of thought, though without employing my rubric of inclusivism, Francesco Dal Co has characterized the evolution of this thinking as leading toward a body of ideas that by the 1930s could be seen to constitute "regionalism." Having noted the importance of the new tendencies in rural cemetery design, Dal Co went on to outline a range of technological and scientific breakthroughs that were eventually to form part of a major new intellectual enterprise. Following Mumford, for example, he noted the importance of the conservation movement of the mid-nineteenth century, which contributed so fundamentally, as he saw it, to the development of organic conceptions of planning.[31] But the pivotal step came with the innovations of Frederick Law Olmsted and his collaborators, as exemplified in their work on plans for Central Park in New York City, Prospect Park in Brooklyn, and communities such as Riverside. Olmsted's designs reversed the tendency of the rural cemeteries, which were programmatically located outside the city, and followed instead a model in which the park was proposed to take over the city itself: "The park was no longer an 'addition,' no longer an exceptional undertaking in the city. As the typical expression of American democracy, it was the fundamental structure of the urban environment."[32] Soon after the turn of the century, two further impetuses enabled the inclusivist stream of thought to expand its horizons of influence further still. The first of these was the European innovation of the garden city, a conception that, while not unrelated to the utopian community of the exclusivists, nevertheless was seen by its protagonists as performing its envisioned role by transforming the metropolis rather than simply opposing it. And during the period immediately prior to the First World War, this innovation was joined by the compelling new idea of the region as it had been conceived by Patrick Geddes.

Through his intellectual influence on Lewis Mumford, Geddes made a seminal contribution to the entire conception of regional planning as it evolved in the United States in the 1920s and 1930s. By this stage, organicism had developed a set of tools with which it was finally in a position to attempt to control the configuration of the metropolis at every scale, from the neighborhood, which was now seen as its basic constituent element, right

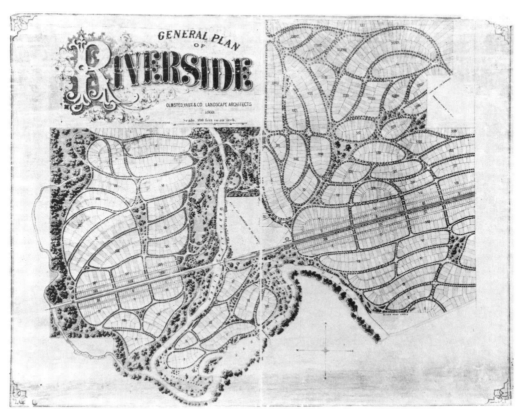

6.6 A plan from 1869 by F. L. Olmsted and Calvert Vaux for the Chicago suburb of Riverside. Note how the plan weaves open space throughout most of the residential area proposed to be developed.

up to the region itself. As neighborhood, the principal model of the newly ascendant organicism was definitively demonstrated in the new Garden City of Radburn, New Jersey, designed by Clarence S. Stein and Henry Wright and built from 1928 to 1933. Appropriately enough for an organicist model, Radburn was in no way conditioned by preexisting settlements. Thus Stein and Wright had a free hand in its creation. It was based on

> a strict separation of the road systems through the creation of through-roads that do not interfere with the life of the residential complexes, which are served by a secondary road system, further articulated by the culs-de-sac of each of the residential complexes, or superblocks, as their architects termed them. This scheme made it possible for each superblock, composed of diverse building types, to enclose a continuous interior park, the greenery of which forms the core of each complex.[33]

An equivalent example of the same principles, this time at the scale of the region, was set out in the plan for New York State prepared from 1923 to

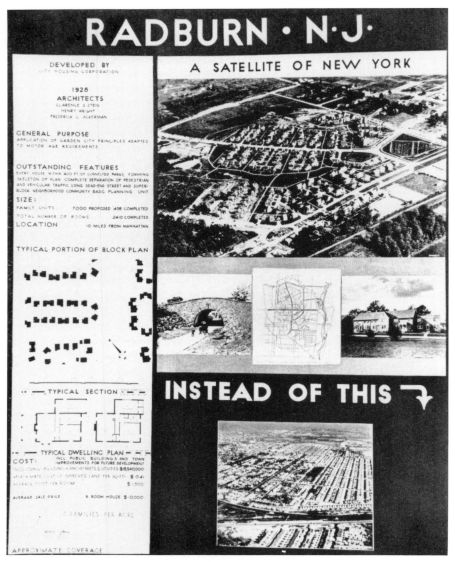

RADBURN · N·J·

A SATELLITE OF NEW YORK

DEVELOPED BY
CITY HOUSING CORPORATION

1928
ARCHITECTS
CLARENCE S. STEIN
HENRY WRIGHT
FREDERICK L. ACKERMAN

GENERAL PURPOSE
APPLICATION OF GARDEN CITY PRINCIPLES ADAPTED
TO MOTOR AGE REQUIREMENTS

OUTSTANDING FEATURES
EVERY HOUSE WITHIN 400 FT OF CONNECTED PARKS, FORMING
SKELETON OF PLAN. COMPLETE SEPARATION OF PEDESTRIAN
AND VEHICULAR TRAFFIC USING DEAD-END STREET AND SUPER-
BLOCK. NEIGHBORHOOD COMMUNITY BASIC PLANNING UNIT

SIZE:
FAMILY UNITS   7000 PROPOSED 458 COMPLETED
TOTAL NUMBER OF ROOMS   2410 COMPLETED
LOCATION   10 MILES FROM MANHATTAN

TYPICAL PORTION OF BLOCK PLAN

INSTEAD OF THIS

TYPICAL SECTION

TYPICAL DWELLING PLAN

COST: INCL PUBLIC BUILDINGS AND TOWN
            IMPROVEMENTS FOR FUTURE DEVELOPMENT
INCLUDING BUILDINGS AND STREETS & UTILITIES $8,540,000
APPROXIMATE COST OF IMPROVED LAND PER SQ FT- $ 0.41
AVERAGE COST PER ROOM $ 1,500

AVERAGE SALE PRICE   6 ROOM HOUSE $ 10,000

7 FAMILIES PER ACRE

APPROXIMATE COVERAGE

6.7 A polemical document contrasting the advantages of Stein and Wright's Radburn with the disadvantages of the more traditional form of residential planning then common in the United States, published in the *Architectural Forum* in April 1933.

1926 by the Regional Planning Association of America. As one might by now expect, that plan entailed a conclusive rejection of the metropolis. Where others had apotheosized "the great city" as "the sum of all our possible aspirations," Stein disparaged it as a "dinosaur." Instead, summing up two decades of previous thinking by RPAA thinkers, the plan incorporated such new orthodoxies of organicism as "the theory of the community of controlled size" as well as "the hypothesis of the garden city as a regional urban entity." While it is true that the RPAA's great plan was not adopted, its principles were to have a pervasive influence within a whole series of programs of the New Deal. In this indirect way, the plan can be seen as representing a peak in the inclusivist organicist ambition to take the metropolis over altogether and to dissolve it, decisively, into a vast, natural landscape.

With McHarg's *Design with Nature* of 1969, the planning methodologies of organicism were taken a stage further still, to a level of determinism that remains unsurpassed to the present day. As might be expected, McHarg incorporated in his polemic a broad critique of the modern metropolis, including in his text a number of images of its characteristic form intended to demonstrate a series of tendencies he saw as both lamentable and innate, which he summarized under the general rubric of "economic determinism." Yet such opposition did not incline him to turn away from deterministic models per se. Following quite consistently the principles of organicism as they have been outlined in my argument thus far, he chose to supplant the determinism he deplored by another one, this time called "physiographic."

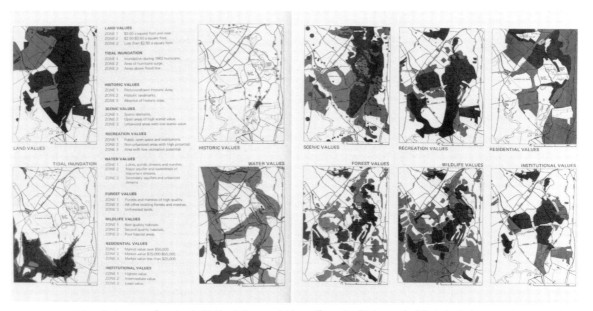

6.8 Facing pages from Ian L. McHarg's *Design with Nature,* illustrating his key methodological principle of ecological planning: overlaid transparencies generating a result that can be described as having "minimum impact" on the as-found condition.

The basic methodological technique that McHarg employed—and which I would identify as deterministic—consisted of an extensive series of analytical overlays of categories of characteristics of a given environment. These were identified by him in advance by meriting conceptual consideration and probable retention. A typical enumeration of such characteristics includes "land values, tidal inundation, historic values, scenic values, recreation values, water values, forest values, wildlife values, residential values, and institutional values." Or another: "historic features, existing forest quality, marsh quality, beach quality, stream quality, water wildlife quality, intertidal habitat value, geological features quality, physiographic features quality, scenic value (land), scenic value (water), and ecological associations value."[34] It is clear that any such enumeration of characteristics would necessarily bring into play a host of social, political, and scientific considerations of a highly diverse and consequential kind. Nevertheless, according to the methodology of physiographic determinism, each of these categories is deemed susceptible to ranking on a numerical scale of priority, following which a certain ecologically appropriate design configuration can be discerned. In one of the above cases, the result was the recommended alignment for a proposed highway (that is to say, the "recommended minimum-social-cost alignment"); in the other, it was the identification of possible areas of appropriate urbanization within an as yet undeveloped agricultural territory. By such means, hitherto incommensurable aspects of contemporary life have been brought within the purview of a unified conceptual methodology, and the now two-century-old tradition of the organic has been represented in our own era, this time anointing proposals for vast regions with the deterministic inevitability of "science" and the moral irreproachability of nature. With McHarg's *Design with Nature* the organicist program of reform reached the zenith of its historic ambition.

In light of the historic misunderstanding, on the part of the advocates of organicism, of the startling historic reality of its relationship to instrumentality, of its related mistrust of the public realm, and of its profound ambition to transform modern urban life nonetheless, a concluding assessment of its efforts to reconstitute community must be attempted. Such an assessment, it seems to me, can most effectively be launched with a short theoretical consideration of the concept of community in relation to the "intentionality" of inhabitants. It seems to me that we can identify three distinct types of community in this respect, which I would call "intentional," "unintentional," and "nonintentional."

Intentional community, according to my parlance, is the result of a broad social agreement amongst inhabitants concerning the desirable form of collective life, an agreement that usually even precedes any such physically realized entity as a town. The religiously based nineteenth-century utopian communities of North America constitute classic examples of intentional communities. In almost all such cases, it is a fact that the physical configuration of the community is a relatively pragmatic result of the social commitment the members of the group have already made to one another; it rarely assumes any geometrical, material, or iconographic form designed to influence the behavior of the members of the group. Indeed, given the overriding prearchitectural commitment its members have already made to one another, any such influence could be thought redundant.

Unintentional community, more problematically, involves an explicitly symbolic physical representation of the idea of community without any such prior agreement between the members of the community in question, a representation designed to influence the behavior of the members of the group. Indeed, it can be said that in this case the physical configuration is designed to bring into being, ex post facto, the very basis of broad social agreement among the members of the group that did not previously exist. Some utopian communities of the nineteenth century also fall into this category; one thinks in particular of those promoted by Robert Owen. However, the organically planned communities of the twentieth century constitute some of the most problematic instances of unintentional community. Clearly Radburn falls into this category, but even more commonly do residential precincts planned to accommodate significant populations that lack the financial means to acquire market housing for themselves. In these cases, the arriving residents encounter the explicit symbols of community intended by the designers to engender community life, and must make of them what they can, irrespective of the fact that the communitarian intentions in question have not been their own.

The last of the three modes of community I have characterized, the nonintentional, entails neither the explicit prior commitment associated with intentional community nor the explicit built-in symbolism associated with unintentional community. Instead, it relies for its potency on its dialectical rapport with the existing public realm of the larger urban entity in relation to which the new community is proposed. Many of the so-called infill residential projects of recent years fall into this last category. It is true, given the traditional preference of organicism either to escape the metropolis or fundamentally to dissolve it—not to mention its long-standing mistrust of any extant form of the public realm—that the nonintentional mode of community has held almost no historical appeal for it. Indeed, just as Lewis Mumford and his colleagues in the RPAA scorned the alternative plan for New York State prepared more or less at the same time as their own by a different sponsor (the Russell Sage Foundation) because it was in their eyes excessively accommodating of extant metropolitan tendencies in the region, so also have rigorous recent organicists tended to view infill projects as conceptually compromised.[35] Even when they have countenanced infill proposals, organicist planners have consistently attempted to influence plans for them in such a way as to emphasize introverted community foci and clearly demarcated perimeter buffers, and to minimize the extent of their public linkages to the existing urban territory beyond.

I have noted how the religiously based utopian communities of the nineteenth century manifested a high degree of social homogeneity. Historically, this has been one of the ways in which the tradition of the organic has been impelled to give priority to community over plurality. In the long term, I believe it has become apparent that intentional community and social plurality are effectively incompatible political concepts. For unintentional community the consequences are no less troubling. First of all, we must note how low the survival rate has been among the unintentional utopias of the nineteenth century. Without the binding element of prior agreement on the desirable form of social life, such utopias have characteristically tended to dissolve after one or two generations of existence. As for the contemporary instances of unintentional community that have been designed by organicist planners for the socially disadvantaged, they have all too typically been perceived, both by their inhabitants and by residents of the larger urban world outside, as ghettoes as much as if not more than as communities. Indeed, the very symbols of community that planners have designed in often come to be perceived as the collective badges of ghetto-ization. As for nonintentional community, its lack of appeal for the protagonists of organicism has given it insufficient influence on the course of organicist efforts at urban reform to warrant further discussion here.

Of all modern architecture's efforts at such reform, the most consistent and the most heroic was of course that of Frank Lloyd Wright. Giorgio Ciucci has delineated the historical course of that effort, from the early projects in Oak Park before the First World War through to the preparation of the ambitious scheme for Broadacre City of 1935. As Ciucci saw it, the early period of Wright's professional career did not yet involve any preoccupation with either a model of organic community or the constitution of a public realm. Instead, Wright remained closed in the local realm of Oak Park, in which he attempted only a personal synthesis of city and country. For Ciucci, Wright established his initial reputation as "an architect who worked within the 'community' to give new form to the house, not . . . one who intervened in the form of the city."[36] From this perspective, Ciucci developed a unique interpretation of the crisis that overwhelmed Wright in 1909, leading him to abandon his wife, children, and career and flee to Europe.

> Wright had sought a synthesis between the life of the city and that of the suburbs, but he could not accept a compromise, and he realized that his existential equilibrium was about to collapse. Living between the boundless prairie of the West, mythical territory of the American pioneer, and the city, still far from the suburbs but rapidly expanding, Wright decided deliberately to overturn this balance before the city crushed his individuality. On what might appear a sudden impulse, but was actually the logical consequence of his determination to renounce completely the choice he had made twenty years earlier under very different conditions, Wright fled not only from Oak Park but also from his family.[37]

Following his two-year self-imposed exile, Wright took the next step in the philosophical evolution that was to lead him eventually to Broadacre City, taking refuge in his new home Taliesin. With its creation, he defini-

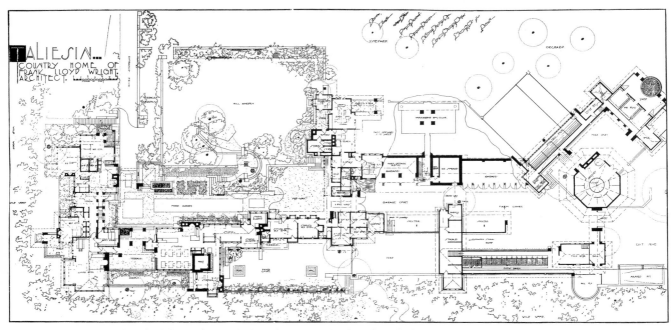

6.9   A particularly detailed plan of Frank Lloyd Wright's long-standing home base of Taliesin. Close examination of the plan will reveal the extent to which it had been conceived as an autonomous world. To the far left are the conventional domestic spaces of the complex; to the right of those can be seen the studio and drafting room; to the right of those, various service spaces of the complex; and then at the far right, the farm buildings, stables, grain storage, etc., within which the same apprentices who worked in the studio were expected to look after the animals.

tively joined the larger historical trajectory of the organicist effort at the reform of urban life. More specifically, we must see the creation of Taliesin as a radical social innovation within the stream of organicist reform that I have characterized as exclusivist. Taking Ciucci's own striking description of Taliesin as our point of departure, we can read the rambling complex in the hills outside Spring Green as a classic instance of exclusivist organicism.

> It was to be not only a home but also "an architect's workshop, a dwelling as well, for the young workers who would come to assist. And . . . a farm cottage for the farm help. The place was to be self-sustaining if not self-sufficient, and with its domain of two hundred acres was to be shelter, food, clothes and even entertainment within itself. It had to be its own light-plant, fuel yard, transportation and

water system." Taliesin was the still personal model of an autonomous settlement situated within nature and an agrarian world: a place outside the world, far from the city he had so clamorously rejected but which, in fact, still existed and in which he continued to build.[38]

Ciucci also traced two further strands of thought pertinent to the eventual conceptualization of Broadacres. On the one hand, there was the development in the 1920s, particularly in the American South, of the body of antiurban and decentralist ideas that have come to be known as "agrarian." Wright himself grew increasingly interested in agrarian ideas during the late twenties and early thirties—so much so, in fact, that he himself saw fit to make yet another great gesture at once personal and ideological, based on his own interpretation of the values of the American frontier, which he rebaptized Usonia. For him, this new world would combine "nature" and "technology" in a quintessentially American construct. And following a decade's search, he found what he thought was the ideal location for it: the desert. As a result, he set up in 1927 a new outpost of his Taliesin community, this time in Arizona. The outpost was the Ocotillo Camp, an encampment on the model of the old western forts but, like Taliesin, composed of living quarters, a work area, and a variety of related communal spaces.

But Ocotillo did not serve just as an outpost of Taliesin. It was the seed from which Wright would go on to formulate the idea of Broadacres, the new city that will be "nowhere, yet everywhere." The great vision was

6.10 A view of Ocotillo Camp, from 1927, Wright's second effort to establish an American utopia that would leave the known urban world behind.

6.11   An aerial view of a part of the model of Wright's 1935 proposal for Broadacre City.

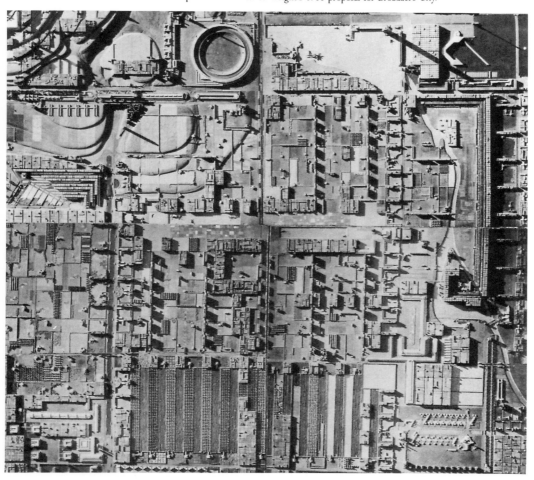

finally exhibited in 1935, ironically enough—given Wright's scorn for New York City—at Rockefeller Center.

A typical countryside development that summarized all his proposals for a new social organization, Broadacres was conceived for some 1,400 families comprising 7,000 inhabitants. It included services, civic installations, parks, and dwellings, which themselves included laboratories and workshops. In the manner of both Taliesin and Ocotillo, industry was directly connected with the home. As might be expected, the scheme was also based on a principal road axis, to which all automobile services as well as the industries were connected, and from which a secondary road network accommodated the dwellings, services, and civic functions. Parallel to the principal artery was a strip of vineyards and orchards, bounded at one end by a large parking lot and at the other by a commercial complex. This strip not only embodied the merging of city and country—and in ways that eerily foretell the suburbia of our own era—but also separated the more active part of Broadacres from the residential area. The sparsely distributed dwellings were focused on the school, in the manner also to become typical of later suburbia, even if the scale of distribution of dwellings was much vaster than what would later become common. Beyond, and parallel to the residential area, were the county offices, sporting clubs, offices, and a stadium. Adjacent to them were located an aquarium, a zoo, an arboretum, and a building for scientific and agricultural research. All these, in their turn, were at the foot of a hill on which were located the more elaborate dwellings for those at the apex of the "broad-based Pyramid" that for Wright represented the "true capitalist system."

> In Broadacres, houses are no longer classified according to the number of rooms but according to the number of cars the family owns, so that the dwellings are distinguished as one-car, two-car, three-car, or five-car houses. The automobile becomes the measure of individual liberty and indicates the make up of the family unit.[39]

Such then, was the form of the utopian community with which the greatest American architect of the twentieth century attempted a definitive, organicist dissolution of the modern urban metropolis.

> Broadacres was, in fact, a proposal for a place in which man could live a life based on the Jeffersonian concept of self-government. . . . Uncontaminated, wild nature, which for Thoreau could be understood and enjoyed only by isolating oneself from the world in a hut in the midst of the woods, was now to be recaptured by means of the most advanced technology. It was no longer the inhabitant of the city who would seek the reason for his own existence in nature, as Thoreau had advocated or as Wright had done in first taking refuge at Taliesin in 1911; now it was the inhabitant of the country, the man who lived in nature, who would extract from the city the undeniable advantages it offered.[40]

Looking back from the vantage point of the present, we can say that it is the heroism of the idea of Broadacres that makes its historical fate so tragic. It is not just that the great vision as a whole was never implemented in any form that Wright would have wished to see. Far, far worse: such were the far-reaching consequences of the great organicist misunderstanding of its own role in the coming into being of the metropolis that certain of Broadacres's innovative components, as Wright had conceived them, were simply taken over, incorporated into the metropolis's own ongoing growth and evolution—such propensity for growth, evolution, and absorption being, of course, part of the metropolis's own unacknowledged organicist legacy. Thus the motels, service stations, and commercial centers so strikingly visible in the published images of Broadacres, and which seem to us now so poignantly innovative, have their aberrant offspring in the everyday suburbia of the actual contemporary metropolis that Wright had fought so hard to prevent from coming into being. Far from manifesting the spirit of "anarchic individualism" that had been Broadacres's author's intention, the suburbia that has been the result of the great metropolitan mutation of the past half-century is now seen instead as the definitive social territory of acquiescent consumerism.

As for the Jefferson *res publica* that was supposed to be manifested in "the new city that will be nowhere, yet everywhere," it didn't even survive in mutated form. Indeed, so faintly is it manifested within the vast territory of the contemporary megalopolis that history seems to have proven the anarchist architect—Wright—wrong, and the political philosopher—Marx—right. This is a double irony in that both historical proofs have manifested themselves in spite of their confounded protagonists.

In a rueful observation, Hannah Arendt remarked of Marx that he "predicted correctly, though with an unjustified glee, 'the withering away' of the public realm under conditions of unhampered development of the 'productive forces of society.'" She went on (and this is the part of her historical speculation that would seem, sadly, to apply as much to Wright as to Marx himself): "he was equally right, that is, consistent with his conception of man as an *animal laborans,* when he foresaw that 'socialized

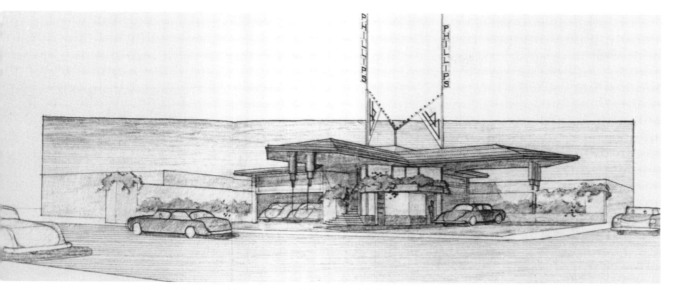

6.12 An image by Wright of one of his innovative and all-too-powerful adaptations at Broadacres of an already emergent suburban building type, the service station.

men' would spend their freedom from laboring in those strictly private and essentially worldless activities we call 'hobbies.'"[41]

Organicism versus the *res publica*: A European Postscript

It is true, of course, that the historical consequences of instrumentality's defeat by organicism have been especially evident in the evolution of urban forms in North America during the past half-century. It is this fact that makes the episode of Frank Lloyd Wright and Broadacres so poignant. But it will offer a significant comparison to the defeat of Wright in North America, and will also yield a sense of the larger fate of the *res publica* in our time, if we conclude this account of the organicist yearning for community with a brief and parallel consideration of two European projects for new communities, both of which are more or less contemporary with Wright's Broadacres, and both of which also manifest high ambitions in respect of the possible transformation of modern urban life. The first of the two, Alvar Aalto's "ideal" company town at Sunila, in Finland, was implemented in its entirety, more or less as planned. The other, Le Corbusier's project for a cooperative agricultural village to be located at Piace in the department of Sarthe, remained unimplemented.

In the case of Sunila, we are faced with an important project of the great Finnish architect, who, at that point in his career, was in the midst of a

6.13   A view of the main plant at the Sunila Cellulose Factory in Finland, by Alvar Aalto, from 1936–1939.

transition from the rationalism he had learned from his modernist mentors from the 1920s to the more personal and more plastic style that was to characterize his mature period. What is more, in assessing Sunila we are obliged to acknowledge that notwithstanding the very large scale of the project (it included an entire pulp and paper plant, as well as housing and other facilities for senior staff and workers), Aalto was significantly constrained in its overall site planning by engineering and operational considerations. Still, having said that, we can also note that within the relative scope of symbolic expression that was open to him, Aalto saw fit to establish a very particular and highly interpretable form of community plan for Sunila.

Sitting high on a rock face looking toward the open sea is the plant itself. Exploiting the volumetric complexities of the functional program for his own formal purposes, Aalto managed quite brilliantly to make out of it a dense collage of planes and transparencies that still stands, despite certain subsequent functional modifications, as a major icon of European modern architecture.

Inland from the great rock island, and on a more gently sloping terrain, is located the residential component of the complex. It comprises a series of linear *Siedlungen* three stories high, ranged in a gentle fan shape along the slopes of the forested site, looking out toward playing fields, to a series of allotment gardens, and to the principal access road to the plant. Between the residential sector and the beginning of the causeway to the plant, the road passes by what clearly performs as the social "pivot" of the entire complex, a sort of depot and post office, from which point a secondary road also leads back into the woods, to the more elaborate residences occupied by supervisory personnel, and to the villa of the plant manager.

To date, most discussion of Sunila has been devoted to the evolution of the design of the successive housing blocks for the workers, as a result of which Aalto was led gradually away from the characteristic forms of the typical German *Siedlungen* of the twenties, to a terraced form that would become quite typical of his own later work. And the complex of dwellings for the supervisory personnel has a particular formal interest, in that it is one of the earliest of his distinctive splayed plan forms.

But what is of central importance to my discussion here is the overall plan form of Sunila, and its possible symbolic readings in respect to the *res publica* and to the political phenomenon of plurality. First of all, we note how the general organization of the buildings is strongly influenced by Aalto's view of the topography. As Goran Schildt put it, "one of his guiding principles was to blend the buildings with the natural surroundings."[42] Thus the project eschews any effort at a symbolic focus of community that might be generated by the architecture itself. Rather, the disposition of

Organicist Yearnings and Their Consequences

elements is such as to suggest that the human occupation of the site is a merely incidental modification to its "natural" state, which should in all possible other respects remain undisturbed. Thus we see here the rationalist planning principles of housing blocks, which Aalto inherited from his 1920s modernist predecessors, modified by a naturalist site planning idea that bears strong marks of the general organicist metaphor discussed above. As a result, what community focus the complex does manifest is not derived from an architectural intention; rather, it is a mere by-product of the principal functional component of the plan: its road system. But this has its own unforeseen implications. The principal road intersection of the complex occurs at the point where the route from the workers' housing blocks, the route across the causeway to the main plant, and the route to the residences of the supervisory personnel and of the plant manager all intersect. Thus, the result of the superimposition of the organicist pastoral

6.14 A range of typical workers' housing from Sunila, following the by now familiar German model of the *Siedlung*, here modified through the picturesqueness of the site-planning strategy.

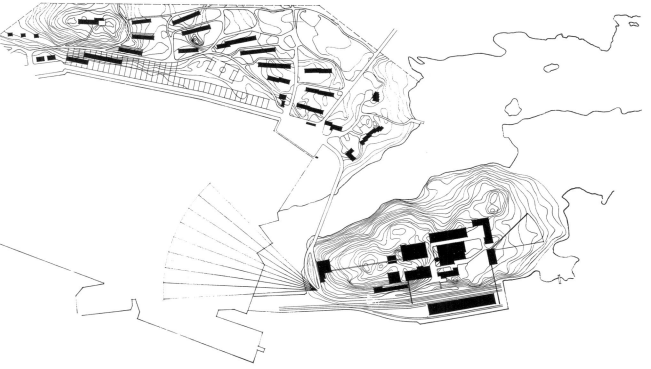

6.15 An overall site plan of the Sunila community. On the outcrop of rock at lower right are located the industrial components of the complex. To the far left are the *Siedlungen* occupied by the workers. In between the two, at the center of the plan, are located the depot and the post office, behind which are the buildings housing the supervisory personnel and the villa of the plant manager. Thus is the "naturalized" panopticism of Aalto's plan for Sunila made manifest.

image atop the functional logistics of the site plan is a sort of disguised panopticism. No one who finds himself at any particular point within the territory of the complex can readily move to any other consequential destination within it without passing by the social pivot of the principal intersection. The inherent conditions of surveillance thereby created void any possible condition of political plurality that might be thought possible within such a community. Thus it would appear that even the radical European social experiment of Sunila proves yet another modern example of an unintentional community, with all the problematic connotations of assumed social homogeneity—or, failing that, of required social control—that such a community entails.

The almost exactly contemporary project of Le Corbusier for a cooperative agricultural village took a quite different form. Here no effort was made to

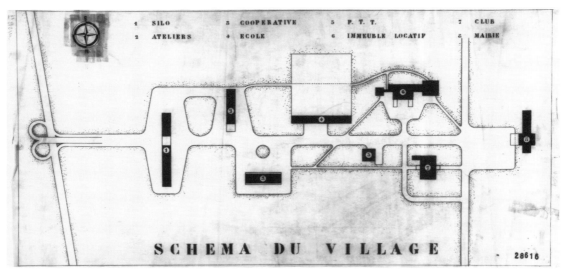

1 SILO   3 COOPERATIVE   5 P. T. T.   7 CLUB
2 ATELIERS   4 ECOLE   6 IMMEUBLE LOCATIF   8 MAIRIE

SCHEMA DU VILLAGE

28616

6.16 An overall plan of Le Corbusier's proposal for a cooperative agricultural village. (Fondation Le Corbusier, Paris.)

6.17 A view of the model of Le Corbusier's proposal for the agricultural village. The view has been taken from the main road outside the village, looking through the gateway formed by the silos, to the town hall located on axis at the opposite end of the entry spine.

blend in, and even the somewhat domesticated agricultural landscape of the surrounding territory was conceived in a dialectical relationship with the explicitly set out order of human settlement on the site. Its plan begins from a long axial approach road, which leads in turn to a spine of circulation accommodating all the program components that make up the co-op: a group of silos, workshops, a store, a post office, a school, an apartment block (one of the predecessors of the *unité d'habitation* proposed by the designer a few years later), a town hall, and a club. As contrasted with Sunila, the co-op village disposes its constituent elements so as to render their possible symbolic interrelationship as clear as possible. First of all, most of the constituent elements of the plan are public rather than domestic ones. Secondly, the elements are set out in clearly formal relations to one another. The silos, for example, form a symbolic gate to the complex as a whole, at the opposite end of whose spine is situated the town hall. All the other components of the plan—components that in social and political terms can be seen to be intermediary compared with the first two, which represent respectively production and the *res publica*—are organized along one or the other side of the spine. To be sure, there is about the project a strong sense of the corporatist political stance that so engaged Le Corbusier at this stage of his career. We now know that such corporatism is hardly compatible with any vigorous conception of plurality. Still, the declamatory explicitness with which the co-op village project sets out its social and political agenda separates it decisively from the disguised panopticism of Sunila, and distinguishes it also from any evident influence of the organicist metaphor to which even Aalto's ambitious European initiative fell victim.

Architecture and Politics

Chapter Seven

Architecture or Revolution? Revolution can be avoided.

Le Corbusier, 1922

Architecture is not political; it is only an instrument of politics.

Leon Krier, 1976

Le Corbusier's and Krier's neatly symmetrical observations, half a century apart, aptly bracket a painfully contentious ongoing debate within the history of architectural modernism. Le Corbusier's rhetorical declaration can in many ways be seen to represent the high tide of belief in architecture's capacity for large-scale social and political transformation.[1] The statement of Leon Krier, like many other of his polemics, is a striking mirror opposite of Le Corbusier's. At the beginning of his career as an architectural polemicist, Krier militantly declared his opposition to modern industrial capitalism. Indeed, his lectures to students of architecture during visits to North America in the mid-1970s characteristically began with a political prologue, which explicitly dissociated him from the politics of the society within which those lectures were to be given. Only later in his career did Krier make the controversial statement cited above, and he did so in aid of an effort to rescue an architecture he had decided he held in considerable regard—that of Albert Speer—from widespread critical opprobrium.

Whatever historical nuances may color our ultimate views of the politics of Le Corbusier's and Krier's careers, the two statements themselves serve not only to bracket the historical period during which the ongoing dispute has proceeded, but also to establish the outer boundaries of opposing opinion in the difficult matter of what possible relationship, if any, may be thought to hold between architecture and politics in our era, a dispute in which legions of rhetorically less adept figures than Le Corbusier and Krier have over the years found themselves, often involuntarily, caught up. Moreover, even when arguments supporting explicitly political commitments by architects have been set aside—as they often enough have been in the course of the twentieth century—arguments concerning the subtler question of the implicit or circumstantial politics that a given architecture may be thought to represent have proceeded. Even when charges of architecture's explicit politicization have been defeated, the subtler allegations of this latter kind have never been conclusively dismissed.

Two prominent historical episodes in the twentieth century constitute explicit politicizations of architecture. The first of these commenced in the mid-1920s and came to crisis a decade or so later. Then, following what might be called an apolitical interlude of some thirty years, a second phase of apparent politicization began in the early 1960s, coming to its own crisis in 1968. Each of these phases had its own set of causes and effects, but a striking series of both parallels and contradictions between the two can be outlined. In several important respects, the events of 1968 can be seen as a reprise of the early 1930s; certainly it is indisputable that the shadow of the earlier controversy looms over the later one. As if that were not significant enough, the events of 1968 have themselves become a part of unconsidered history, casting their own thought-provoking shadow over the controversies of the present.

By the mid 1920s a certain concatenation of ideas had already begun to take on an overall cultural formation that would eventually come to be known as modern architecture. By both its advocates and its critics, modernism was coming to be seen as a project of (largely) utopian instrumentality that was universalist, reformist (if not revolutionary), technological, and reductivist. It was utopian, and instrumentalist, in its echoes and invocations of the dreams of the Enlightenment; universalist in its claims for widespread geographic applicability; reformist, when not revolutionary, in its sweeping ambitions for the transformation of modern social life; technological in its enthusiastic acceptance of recently devised methods of construction, and in its efforts to employ them; the reductivist in its opposition to the eclecticism and the elaborate iconography of the formal languages of the architecture of the preceding century.

However, this concatenation of ideas did not form a seamless philosophical web. This is evident in the fact that considerable dispute continued within the camp of the moderns in regard to a range of important issues. In particular, intense debate occurred during the pivotal years of 1927 and 1928 in connection with the founding of CIAM. What is more, the dispute in question revealed significant divergences of opinion that must be seen, already at this early date, to have been politically based. If we focus on the German, Dutch, and Swiss modernists, for example, we may note how such figures as Giedion and Gropius, while supporting a generally reformist politics of modernism, resisted the formation of any explicit political alignments within the movement. During his term as director of the Bauhaus, Gropius went so far as to discourage any direct political activity by staff or students within the institution. Other modernists, such as Johannes Duiker and Hannes Meyer, chose instead to insist upon what they saw as the obvious, explicit socialist program of modernism, and saw efforts to deny it as compromised equivocation. Notwithstanding these differences of opinion, feelings of modernist solidarity were sufficiently strong that such important events as the 1928 founding meeting of CIAM concluded without explicit political battle lines being drawn. Concluding statements on that occasion took the form of generalized arguments for the socially transforming power of architecture. Evidently most if not all delegates found this strategy acceptable. And the expanding practice of modernist principles in many European countries proceeded on that basis until the early 1930s.

Yet as the twenties drew to a close, the political formation of western European society became increasingly polarized. The eventual results for the practice of modern architecture, at least according to the set of principles that had characterized it during the twenties, were catastrophic. Indeed, the internal politics of the modern architectural debate of the late 1920s and early 1930s gradually came to be first subsumed and then consumed in the larger political controversy that engaged all of Europe in the years following.

Recent accounts of the political fate of modern architecture in various European countries indicate how important are certain distinctions in the general social and political circumstances in which modernism was being promoted and practiced in such countries as Germany, the Soviet Union, and Italy.[2] To take the case of Germany, for example, it is of great importance for our understanding of the eventual course of history that the evolving institution of modern architecture, as well as the regime that was its principal political sponsor—the Weimar Republic—both prospered during the early to middle twenties. And when the republic, in the latter part of the decade, began to founder, so too did architectural modernism as it had hitherto been known. In the Soviet Union, the architectural avant-garde that had supported the 1917 October Revolution found itself, throughout the twenties, in a rather tenuous relationship with the new Bolshevik regime. To be sure, as long as he held the position of Commissar of Culture, Anatoly Lunacharsky offered a certain degree of political protection for the experiments of the cultural avant-garde. Still, both Lenin and Trotsky expressed great skepticism if not hostility to its work at a very early stage. By the time the Soviet architectural avant-garde attempted to establish a broad social and political rationale for its cultural program it was already too late: larger political circumstances had overtaken events. In the case of Italy, the course of events was more complex still. There, the political regime from which modernist architects sought support—the Fascist regime of Mussolini—was already established by the time these architects began their proselytism. As Diane Ghirardo has pointed out:

> Fascism preceded the birth of the Modern Movement in Italy as Nazism did not in Germany. By the time the Rationalists were constructing their first buildings, Fascism was well entrenched. The social pretensions that characterized the Modern Movement in Germany and Holland, where critics and architects alike seized on the new architecture as a solution for social and political problems, had already been pre-empted in Italy by Fascism.[3]

Rather than reject modernism outright, as Hitler and Stalin both eventually did, Mussolini retained a curiosity about it, admittedly a complex and contentious one, for the duration of his regime. As a result, the ultimate political fate of modern architecture in Italy can only be discussed in the context of the fate of the regime itself. Or, to put it another way, it is the specially complex case of Italy that requires the resolving of an overall account of the relationship of architecture to politics in a broader historical and philosophical perspective than has traditionally been invoked.

Brief accounts of the vicissitudes of architectural modernism in these three countries follow.

Germany

In her 1968 book *Architecture and Politics in Germany, 1918–1945*, Barbara Miller Lane outlined what she saw as the particularly German form "the new architecture and the vision of a new society" took in the first half of the 1920s. The precepts of modernism were received largely favorably by

7.1 The famous Hufeisen Siedlung in Berlin, designed by prominent Ring members Martin Wagner and Bruno Taut and built from 1925 onward.

the German public at large during the middle years of the decade, although a significant and persistent critique of modernism had been evident in German cultural circles as early as 1920, when conservatives had opposed the ideas and practices of Walter Gropius's original Bauhaus at Weimar. In consequence, a dramatic backlash confronted modernism once a substantial number of buildings embodying its principles had been erected in major German cities such as Stuttgart, Frankfurt, and Berlin. Lane notes how somewhat technical criticisms of the work of the group of architects who called themselves the Ring eventually gave way to broader and more insidious cultural and social allegations by conservative critics such as Emil Hogg and Paul Schultze-Naumburg.

> Criticism of the building methods of the Ring architects, attractive as it was to disaffected architects and craftsmen, never in itself aroused much interest outside the building trades and the architectural profession. It was only by adopting the terminology of the Weimar controversy that the opponents of the new style found a wider audience. . . . Hogg and Schultze-Naumburg incorporated sociological and cultural criticisms of "industrialized" buildings into a nationalist and racist theory of architecture which was intended to serve as a theoretical defense of historicist architecture. . . . Hogg attacked the new methods of building construction, but not merely on the grounds that they represented poor technique. Instead, he declared that the use of standard parts and plans in "mass apartment buildings and warehouses for families" would produce "nomadic architecture," leading to "uprootedness, spiritual impoverishment and proletarianization." . . . And as some of the opponents of the Bauhaus had done earlier, he concluded that the break with the past and the adoption of a totally new aesthetic meant the creating of a "Bolshevist" architecture.[4]

7.2 By contrast, this illustration shows housing erected in Aachen after 1933, when new Nazi policies had come into effect.

Between 1928 and 1932, the polarization of opinion became much more intense. Within the camp of the modernists, grave splits had now begun to occur. Having succeeded Walter Gropius as director of the Bauhaus at Dessau, Hannes Meyer reorganized the curriculum in a fashion that relied much more heavily on mathematics and science, at the same time introducing more explicit sociological concepts into the school. As part of this general turning toward a more scientific approach to design, Meyer and his colleagues began a systematic disparagement of the production of the institution during the previous, Gropius era, dismissing it as a "Bauhaus style" (in an institution that, they argued, was supposed to be pedagogically opposed to the very idea of style) and criticizing Gropius's and his colleagues design methods as "formalist." In the increasingly tense atmosphere of German cultural politics of the late twenties, Meyer's experiments with "scientific building research" and with the "precedence of the people's needs" grew progressively more controversial until 1930, when he was fired from his position as director by the mayor of Dessau. At Gropius's suggestion, Mies van der Rohe was appointed director to succeed Meyer, but by this time the solidarity of the modernist camp had been severely shaken.

While this severing of links had been occurring within the circles of modern architecture, a conservative cultural reaction was overtaking a large part of the German population. By 1932 National Socialist cultural propaganda had sought to turn this sensibility directly against modern architecture and its practitioners and advocates in Germany. A series of articles on architecture published in that year in the Nazi party newspaper, the *Völkischer Beobachter,* for example, combined cultural attack and racism:

> The Bauhaus—that was "the cathedral of Marxism," a cathedral, however, which damned well looked like a Synagogue. To the "inspiration" of this "model school" we owe . . . those oriental boxes . . . which are repugnant to good taste. . . .

> After just a few years these buildings, prized as today's highest accomplishments, began to develop great cracks at every edge and corner. Yes, whole blocks of dwellings were so full of damp that the health authorities had to intervene. . . .

> The protests of good German architects have remained unheard for a long time, because certain industries had financial interests in the experiments of the Bauhaus—we speak of the Bauhaus here always as a concept—and the international [political] parties expected a lot from the cultural bolshevism which they carried on openly. . . . And they were right, for this architecture came to be the spiritual expression of their spirit. . . . They believed that "the house is an instrument like an automobile." . . . Thus these men reveal their character as typical nomads of the metropolis, who no longer understand blood and soil. . . . Now their secret is known! The new dwelling is an instrument for the destruction of the family and the race. Now we understand the deeper sense of that architectural nonsense which built housing developments in the style of prison cells, and perpetrated an asiatic interlude on German soil. . . . Bolshevism, the arch-enemy of all mature culture, works towards the victory of this (architectural) desolation and horror![5]

By 1933, even under Mies's less contentious leadership, the Bauhaus remained in difficulty and was closed. From this date commenced a dramatic series of exoduses of modern architects from Germany, some to other European countries, some to the Soviet Union, and some to North America. By the mid-1930s the great cultural experiment of modern architecture in Germany was largely ended.

The Soviet Union
In the early stages of modern architectural developments following the 1917 revolution, important activities focused on the Vkhutemas schools. Figures central to this period included the artists Kazimir Malevich, Naum

Gabo, and Antoine Pevsner, the artist-architect El Lissitzky, and the architect Konstantin Melnikov. However, as the formation of modernism took on more specific shape, particular lines of discussion within the camp of the moderns began to emerge in the Soviet Union as in Germany. A more socially and politically militant group was formed in 1925 that simultaneously opposed the old architecture of the academies and dismissed many of the interests of the older generation of Gabo and Pevsner as formalism. OSA (the Association of Contemporary Architects), founded by Moisei Ginzburg, the three Vesnin brothers, and others, argued instead for "constructivism and functionalism." The biases of OSA can readily enough be discerned in a statement on architectural ideology released at its 1928 conference.

7.3 Lissitzky's well-known design for a speaking rostrum for Lenin, completed in 1924, just prior to the attack of the younger generation of OSA on Lissitzky and his contemporaries. (Stedelijk Van Abbemuseum, Eindhoven.)

7.4 A perspective drawing of the proposed project for the offices of *Leningradskaya Pravda*, by Aleksandr and Viktor Vesnin, two of the leading members of OSA, in 1924.

The first conference of the Association of Contemporary Architects stresses its complete unity, and adopts the ideological position and the working program of constructivism in architecture. . . .

We are opposed to such prerevolutionary building types as the speculative apartment house, the private residence, the "noblemen's club," etc., all products of prerevolutionary social, technical, and economic circumstances, but still serving as a model for buildings now being erected in the U.S.S.R.: new types of communal housing, new types of clubs, palaces of labour, new factories, etc., which in fact should be the conductors and condensers of socialist culture. . . .

To all this we oppose the organic growth of Soviet architecture as it develops out of the specific characteristics of a new social order and technically advanced methods of construction and production.

The statement concluded:

DOWN WITH THE SPECULATIVE ART OF THE RIGHTISTS AND LEFTISTS!

DOWN WITH DILETTANTISM AND AMATEURISM IN SOCIETY AND ART!

LONG LIVE THE MATERIALIST SCHOOL OF ARTISTIC CREATION—CONSTRUCTIVISM![6]

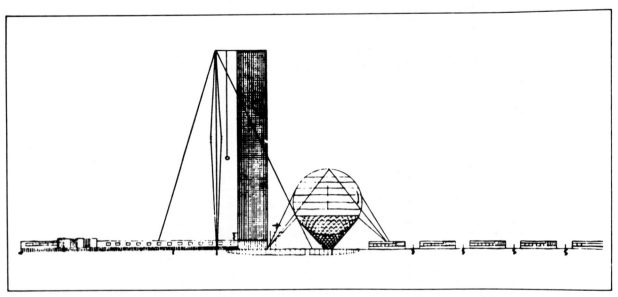

7.5 Arguably the most celebrated project by the young Ivan Leonidov, the Lenin Institute of 1929, the same year as his attack on the Vesnin brothers.

The split between OSA and its predecessors bears certain affinities with the intergenerational arguments already outlined in western Europe. A younger generation of designers had developed keener interests in scientific methods and in technology than its elders, and, in pressing forward, resorted to the epithet "formalist" to criticize their work. At the same time there was a clear implication, in the new critique being mounted by the young, that a commitment to science and to praxis in the real world entailed a more engaged and militant form of politics than characterized the positions of the older generation. A few years later, one of the more ironical turns of events in the history of constructivism saw a bright star of a younger generation still, Ivan Leonidov, attack the Vesnins on similar grounds. Leonidov, whose career as a designer effectively began only in 1927, launched his attack in late 1929, accusing the Vesnins of a lack of commitment to the principles of functionalism and of being too preoccupied by constructivism.

But this series of intergenerational challenges was soon to come to an end. In hindsight, the conclusion to the Soviet modernist episode can already be seen to have commenced with the creation in 1925 of VOPRA, a Prolet-kult organization devoted to an explicit interpretation of party directives on architecture, an ominous occurrence that eventually opened the way for the Stalinist power structure to propound "socialist realism as the basic method of Soviet architecture," and for the discredited representatives of the prerevolutionary academies such as Shchusev to regain their former eminence as architects to the new Soviet state.

The momentum of the modern movement in the Soviet Union had clearly disintegrated by the 1931 International Competition for the Palace of the Soviets, a contemporary account of which was given by a western observer, Hans Schmidt.

> The outcome of the competition for the Palace of the Soviets has filled all radical architects in the West with indignation and disbelief. We have no intention of using this occasion to mollify their outrage; on the contrary, it is incumbent upon us to inform the reader in the same breath that this decision was neither accidental nor an isolated occurrence.[7]

7.6 A photograph of the model of the entry to the 1931 competition for a new Palace of the Soviets in Moscow by Le Corbusier, perhaps only the most notable of the many modernist projects submitted, all of which were rejected in favor of a design by Yofan, Gel'freikh, and Shchuko, who had lain low since the revolution of 1917 and were in a convenient position, politically speaking, to appeal to the antimodernist tastes of the by then all-powerful regime of Stalin.

Putting the recent Soviet decision into a somewhat broader historical context, Schmidt continued:

> The victory of the October Revolution brought to the forefront a number of young architects who identified with the aims of the Revolution. Taking up the cudgel in the fight with the older generation of architects they apparently were bringing about the triumph of modern architecture. At a time when relatively very little construction could actually be realized in the Soviet Union, this young and technically inexperienced generation devoted all of its energies to utopian projects, in many cases outstripping the real situation of revolutionary development by decades. . . . In the Soviet Union of today elaborate utopias have consequently lost much of their attraction. First say goes to the well-trained architect and the experienced technician. In the meantime, a great number of old architects have offered their services to the Soviets. It is clear that these people have filled the vacuum created by modern architecture, which was characterized by a lack of both technical and cultural preparation. . . . As things stand now, modern architecture has gambled away its chance, at least for the time being. Even the broad masses and youth have joined the ranks of the general opposition. What is even worse, though, is the fact that the modern movement in architecture has presently run into a closed ideological front ranged against it.[8]

Schmidt's summary of the situation in the Soviet Union as it stood in 1932 has, to the best of my knowledge, not been superseded by any later interpretation:

> On ideological grounds, the following objections have been raised in the Soviet Union against modern architecture:
>
> 1. The ideas of modern architecture, known in the West under the label of "constructivism," "functionalism," and "mechanism," are an outgrowth of contemporary capitalism and its rationalized and standardized technology.
>
> 2. Modern architecture's renunciation of monumentality and symbolic expression, its disavowal of absolute beauty, and its inability to carry out the artistic and ideological mission of architecture, are an expression of the decline of bourgeois culture.
>
> 3. The idealistic-utopian direction of modern architecture (Le Corbusier), together with the ideas of "left utopians" in politics represent an attempt to bypass the natural stages leading toward Socialism, and thus are counter-revolutionary in the political sense.
>
> 4. It is not the goal of Socialism to destroy the cultural values of the past; quite to the contrary Socialism, in contrast to disintegrating contemporary capitalism, tries to preserve these values and give them continuity.[9]

This text may be taken to epitomize the conclusion of the epoch of modernism in the Soviet Union. After that date, certain efforts by modernists in the planning area continued to achieve political support, but full-fledged building projects were no longer possible for them. The exodus of modernists from the Soviet Union did not match that precipitated by the Nazis in Germany; indeed, a number of leftist Germans, including Hannes Meyer, Martin Wagner, and Ernst May, had all just emigrated from Germany to Russia. But most modernists' careers in both countries were severely damaged, if not destroyed. Figures such as Melnikov from the generation of ASNOVA shared with younger men like Leonidov the sad fate of becoming cultural exiles within their own societies.

Italy

Notwithstanding considerable ongoing controversy regarding the political trajectory of modern architecture in Italy in the period between the two world wars, most observers agree that two factors significantly marked the early stages of development in the 1920s. The first of these has to do with the fact that its protagonists inside Italy saw modern architecture as already having reached a significantly advanced level of development in other European countries. As the members of the Milan Group 7 put it in a 1926 manifesto:

> A group of famous European architects—Behrens, Mies van der Rohe, Mendelsohn, Gropius, Le Corbusier—create architecture tightly connected to the necessities of our time, and from these necessities extract a new aesthetic. Therefore there *exists,* particularly in architecture, a new spirit. . . . It remains for Italy to give maximum development to the new spirit, to carry it to its logical conclusion, until it dictates a *style* to other nations, as it has done in the great periods of the past.[10]

Secondly, despite their unquestionable enthusiasm for the adoption of the "new spirit" in Italy, they nevertheless qualified to some extent the general commitment to radical innovation that was clearly integral to the "new architecture" elsewhere in Europe. This was the result of a major historical reservation they held about the cultural legacy of futurism. Their 1926 manifesto put it as follows:

> How far away [futurism] already seem[s] to us, . . . with its attitude of the systematic destruction of the past—still a very romantic concept.

7.7 A view of the concourse of the Santa Maria Novella railway station in Florence, the result of a 1932 competition won by a team led by Giovanni Michelucci. The broad openness of the building's spatial concept and the "floating" quality of the concourse's hovering ceiling still mark the project as indisputably "modern," in conventional political terms. (Photograph by permission, from Leonardo Benevolo, *History of Modern Architecture*, MIT Press.)

> The youth of today follows a completely different road. We all feel a great necessity for clarity, revision, and *order*. . . .
>
> The legacy of the avant-garde that preceded us was an artificial impulse—an empty, destructive fury that confused good and bad. The natural right of youth today is a desire for *lucidity,* for *wisdom.*[11]

Bringing the benefits of modernity to Italy, while tempering the antitraditionalist excesses of futurism, was the posture with which modernism's protagonists there began their campaign. In 1928, a Roman member of Group 7, Adalberto Libera, founded the Movimento Italiano per l'Architettura Razionale and launched it with a major exhibition in Rome. In 1931 and in 1932 the MIAR group mounted two further exhibitions, designed to establish rationalism—the term the young selected to define their modernity in the Italian context—as the official architecture of the Fascist regime. From that point on, an ongoing series of disputes proceeded between three factions within the Italian architectural profession.

> To the far right were the *accademici* [who] could be found on the faculties of most of the universities, and typically adhered to 19th-century eclecticism, or to a faithful, unaltered, and often uninspired replication of neo-classical architecture. They were united in their opposition to the two other groups of architects, the moderates and the Rationalists, reserving most of their contempt for the latter.[12]

According to Diane Ghirardo, the intergenerational figure Marcello Piacentini "mediated disputes between the moderates and the academics, just as he did between these two groups and the Rationalists, thereby achieving a central position in the architectural culture of the time."[13]

Against the backdrop of such disputes, one can trace a sequence of building projects representative of the course of events from 1932 until 1942. The sequence begins with an early set of three, all designed and erected between 1932 and 1936. The first of these can be viewed as a relatively straightforward example of rationalist design principles: the Santa Maria Novella railway station in Florence, erected as the result of a design competition won by a team led by Giovanni Michelucci. I say relatively straightforward because it has become a factor of some historical significance in recent discussions that even this modernist design was selected with the support of the ubiquitous Piacentini. The second of the three is the local Fascist party headquarters building in Como, designed by Giuseppe Terragni. The political orthodoxy of this building's modernity has been more contentious than that of the Florence railway station. On the one hand, Sigfried Giedion was prepared to include it in his worldwide postwar review *A Decade of New Architecture,* on account of certain formal characteristics it indisputably shared with other major projects in this 1950 compendium. On the other hand, its very function as the local party headquarters has made it difficult historically to dissociate in any decisive way from what might be thought of as the characteristic cultural production of Italian Fascism. Ghirardo has taken particular pains to refute the possibility of any such dissociation: "For [Terragni], the ideals of Fascism as he understood them were embodied in perfect harmony in his building."[14] The case of the third project in question, that of the University of Rome, is still more problematic. Not only was the project undertaken under the general direction of Piacentini, but one of the major individual buildings within the complex, the Institute of Physics, was designed by a major rationalist, Giuseppe Pagano, who saw fit to employ for it an architectural language that shifted more conclusively toward the monumental and the

7.8   The building for the Institute of Physics at the University of Rome from 1932, designed by Giuseppe Pagano but also forming a part of the overall project directed by Marcello Piacentini: modernist volumetrics refracted through the insidiously monumentalizing sensibility of Fascism. (Photograph by permission, from Leonardo Benevolo, *History of Modern Architecture,* MIT Press.)

7.9   A detail of the room in the Danteum dedicated by Terragni to the New Roman Empire which it was expected would be established by Mussolini: modernism now definitively monumentalized.

classical, as advocated by Piacentini, than did Terragni's contemporary Casa del Fascio in Como. An observer inclined to view Michelucci's railway station as still belonging to the realm of modernism—as it was originally characterized in the 1920s—would encounter considerable difficulty in seeing the project for the University of Rome as belonging, straightforwardly, to the same realm.

With projects from the late thirties and early forties, difficulties with orthodox interpretations become more problematic still. We may focus on two characteristically contentious examples: first, the 1938 project by Terragni and Lingeri for a major monument and museum dedicated to Dante; and second, the project for a world exposition proposed to be held in 1942, for which a number of thought-provoking competition schemes were prepared by various architects. In the case of the Danteum, we are faced with a project of astonishing formal and iconographic brilliance, which for two years Terragni attempted to persuade Mussolini to build. It would seem that had it not been for the onset of World War II, he would have succeeded. Thomas Schumacher has shown how the Danteum's general organizational scheme derives directly from Corbusian plan motifs that were of keen interest to Terragni at that stage of his career.[15] In the final project, these motifs were transmuted into an intensely material and monumental image that could indeed he thought to offer Italy a chance to "dictate a style to other nations," just as Group 7 in 1926 had hoped. Among the languages of architecture in Italy in the late 1930s, the Danteum stands as the clearest extant reinterpretation of the principles of modernism in the service of Fascism.

The competition schemes for the proposed 1942 exposition are another matter. We may take as an extreme but symptomatic case the competition entry for the Piazza Imperiale by Luigi Moretti together with the Quaroni/Fariello/Muratori group. Their proposal for the exposition shifted ground much farther even than did Pagano's for the University of Rome. Bombastic in both its plan form and its materialization, the proposal for the Piazza Imperiale moved the discourse of Italian rationalism to an utterly decorative hieraticism that can hardly be thought of as modern at all.[16] But of

7.10 A perspective forming part of the submission by Luigi Moretti and the Quaroni/Fariello/Muratori group to the competition for a Piazza Imperiale, at the 1942 exposition then being planned. The final stage in Italian modernism's passage to a completely politicized rhetoric.

course, by the time 1942 arrived, not only had it become apparent that the projected exposition was not going to be held, but both modern Italian architecture with all its ambiguities and the Fascist regime itself were being swept into the whirlwind of World War II.

At this point, we may essay a provisional summary of the political fate of modernism in the three countries under discussion, as it unfolded in the years from the late 1930s to the early 1940s. In Germany, as a result of a shift in political attitudes in society at large from the late twenties onward, modern architecture lost the political constituency that had lent it key support in the early part of that decade. Then, after a period of some policy ambiguity, the ascendancy of National Socialism in the 1930s led to modernism's rejection as "cultural bolshevism." In the Soviet Union, a gradually evolving Stalinist *Realpolitik* led in the late twenties and early thirties to modernism losing its political constituency within the Soviet leadership. The movement was accused of cultural decadence, its building proposals were judged technically impracticable, and these together led to a quite decisive rejection of modern architecture in favor of a coarse classicism that was thought capable of reincarnating a popular sense of cultural tradition. Finally, in Italy, where the modernist architects themselves had from the beginning had the strongest interest in tradition, and where the regime in power maintained the greatest degree of cultural plurality vis-à-vis architecture, modernism was never rejected outright but saw its distinctive modes of linguistic expression obscured and eventually compromised by their particular form of implementation within the Fascist state.

By the onset of World War II, thoughtful observers had not failed to notice that all three totalitarian regimes, after varying degrees of exploration of modernist options, had manifested a clear preference for some mode of classicism as the preferred vehicle of symbolic political expression. To be sure, the Italian mode was the most culturally significant, in that the accommodations of the rationalists had led to the creation of a Mediterranean style that looked "metaphysical," and whose iconographic opacity has made it the focus of considerable recent fascination. The German one was a sort of austere and unsupple stripped classicism that, through its ubiquitous cinematographic usages, probably stands to this day in the western popular imagination as the generic architectural imagery of totalitarianism. Least ambiguous, and most blatant, was the Stalinist Soviet reaction, which led to an architecture of a formal vulgarity barely distinguishable from the "pompier style" of kitsch of the late nineteenth century that had contributed significantly to the early modernist crisis of authenticity in the first place.[17]

The de facto political eclipse of modernism in these three countries had a number important historical consequences, both within and without the small world of European architectural culture. First of all, it confirmed the convictions of the moderate and/or apolitical modernists that explicit political commitments by architects had been an imprudent idea from the beginning. It is of great interest in this regard to note that the key early histories of modern architecture published in the 1930s—Nikolaus Pevsner's *Pioneers of Modern Design* of 1936 and Sigfried Giedion's *Space, Time and Architecture*" of 1941–both eschewed any explicit political interpretation of modernism, arguing instead the more general relevance of modernism's commitments to technological efficacy, mass production, and healthfulness, all within the frame of a general endorsement of liberal democracy.

To be sure, as early as 1928 Giedion had already published a popular little booklet, *Befreites Wohnen,* the thrust of which was to associate the precepts of modernism with sunshine, good ventilation, and other principles of good health—even with a campaign against tuberculosis.[18] So it cannot be said that the apolitical version of modernism only came into existence in the thirties. Moreover, in his epochal 1941 publication he undertook to marry these concepts to a more cultural conception of space and time that linked cubist painting theory to Einsteinian physics. Still, Giedion was so successful in portraying a relatively depoliticized modernism in this canonical text that it was a full two and a half decades before a younger generation of architectural commentators began to criticize it, alleging among other things that he had systematically excluded from his history such important and openly politicized figures as Hannes Meyer.

4

5

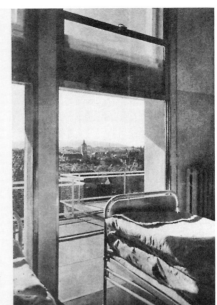

Schlafzelle
in einem
1928
erbauten
Zuchthaus

Foto „I.A.Z.‟

R. DÖCKER

Krankenhaus
Waiblingen

1926/28

Foto R. Döcker

Nicht nur Zuchthauszellen sperren wir von Luft und Licht ab. Eisen und Eisen-
beton gestatten dem Licht freiesten Einlaß. Aber Behörden und „aesthetische‟
Paragraphen sorgen dafür, daß unsere Wohnhäuser und öffentlichen
Bauten, Kranken- und Schulhäuser, Postgebäude, Banken, zwecks
Erhöhung ihrer „Monumentalität‟ ihre freien Öffnungen durch steinerne
Attrappen wieder verhängen. Künstlich umgeben wir uns mit Kerkermauern.

Ausblick von einem Zimmer auf die Terrassen und die Landschaft (vgl. Abb. 57, 58).
Der Skelettbau gestattet, die Wand in Glas aufzulösen. Nur die Konstruktion
bleibt stehen. Die Landschaft strömt herein. Der Kranke fühlt sich nicht mehr
von der Welt isoliert. Der Kranke braucht Licht und psychische Erheiterung
ebenso notwendig wie Antisepsis. Wir aber bauen im allgemeinen unsere
Krankenhäuser wie Zuchthäuser und Kasernen.

7.11 Facing pages from Sigfried Giedion's small propaganda volume of 1928, *Befreites Wohnen,* in which the "healthiness" of modern architecture is vigorously advocated.

But this is to anticipate the events of a later period. In the wake of the political defeat of modernism in Europe, the cultural and political refugees from Germany and Russia began to arrive in Britain, Israel, and the United States. And by and large, the view of modernism and its meanings that they brought with them was the view portrayed in *Space, Time and Architecture.* For the younger generation of architects who learned the lessons of modernism from Giedion and his colleagues after the Second World War, the earlier political controversy that had engulfed modernism only surfaced in discussions of the appropriate usages of monumentality (on which, see chapter four). As we have seen, the general thrust of such discussions was that formal precepts such as symmetry were inherently totalitarian, while asymmetry could be considered democratic. When, in 1951, Giedion included Terragni's Casa del Fascio in his compilation *A Decade of New Architecture,* he carefully labeled it, anonymously, a "political club."[19] After the war, CIAM itself became the moderate liberal advocate of modern architecture and town planning, commanding broad authority throughout much of the world for a decade and a half of postwar reconstruction.

The dramatic repoliticization of modern architecture that forms the second episode here under discussion did not manifest itself with significant force until the mid 1960s, after which debate grew gradually more intense, culminating in the dramatic May events of 1968 that engulfed architecture schools throughout Europe and North America. But the seeds of the critique of the mainstream modernism that was the legacy of CIAM can already be seen in the immediate postwar critiques launched by such important innovators as Colin Rowe. Not, of course, that Rowe's celebrated essays of 1947 ("The Mathematics of the Ideal Villa") and 1950 ("Mannerism and Modern Architecture") were intended as political commentaries.[20] Rowe has always avowed an apolitical stance vis-à-vis modernism, even to the point of disappointing and frustrating a number of his younger admirers. Nevertheless, his two essays were among the key challenges to the monolithic authority of the received view of modernism propounded by CIAM. Rowe argued that despite the received view, modernism could be seen to have been historically charged (it was in this sense that he represented Le Corbusier as a new Palladio), and ambitious in formal terms that far transcended program (here he portrayed Le Corbusier as a full-fledged mannerist).

Another important precursor of modern architecture's late sixties repoliticization was Robert Venturi's *Complexity and Contradiction in Architecture* of 1966.[21] Where Rowe's positing of historic and mannerist precedents for Le Corbusier's canonical modernist works of the 1920s had challenged Giedion, Venturi's arguments a decade and a half later challenged the pedagogical principles of design activity that mainstream modernism had institutionalized in architecture schools throughout Europe and North America. Indeed, it was Venturi who employed the term "orthodox modern architecture" with such recurrent ironical intent that it soon came to be seen as an epithet of abuse. In the mid-sixties, when opposition to American participation in the Vietnam War was joined, in the minds of the young, to critiques of urban renewal and to the increasing scale of corporate redevelopment of city cores around the world, the position of "orthodox modernism," both as praxis and as pedagogy, became exceedingly precarious. Consequently, when the newly politicized students saw fit to challenge the pedagogy of their schools, their teachers made the shocking discovery that the formal precepts to which they attempted to revert had in fact already been discredited. As a result, between 1968 and 1970 architecture schools in France, Germany, Italy, Great Britain, the United States, and Canada were all fundamentally transformed by a powerful wave of student revolt against a modernism that by then was seen as the handmaiden, implement, and symbol of an unthinking, monolithic, and exploitative "military-industrial complex."

By 1971 two topical texts had been published that still exemplify the new hostility toward modernism, and the depth and breadth of the newly formulated political critique of it. One was Robert Goodman's *After the Planners,* the author of which had found himself profoundly disillusioned by the practice of mainstream architecture in his time, concluding that architecture in the end constituted little more than a "cultural coating" for repression.[22] But he went far beyond this in his attacks on his professional colleagues. Insofar as mainstream modernism still retained any ambitions toward utopianism, Goodman saw it as manipulatively autocratic; insofar as it was reformist, he saw it as patronizing and maladroit; insofar as it was technologically advanced he saw it as fatally allied with the same military-industrial complex that was prosecuting the Vietnam War. Goodman even dismissed such a critic of orthodoxy as Robert Venturi, complaining that his interests in an "inclusive" architecture were misleading and inadequate. Despite its promise, [Complexity and Contradiction in Architecture] was for Goodman a great disappointment:

> In reality, Venturi seems to have little concern with "the experience of life." I searched the entire book for any description of how people used architecture; there was hardly a word about it—instead the same aesthetic jargon. A series of building plans, elevations and photos show how certain architectural qualities make a building seem more complex and contradictory. There is almost no analysis of whether the buildings used as examples really accommodate the complexity and contradiction of human activities they were intended to serve. The important thing is simply the appearance of architectural forms.[23]

As for *Learning from Las Vegas,* the later work by Venturi and his new collaborators Denise Scott Brown and Steven Izenour, it confirmed Goodman's gravest suspicions. Noting that orthodox modernists had consistently

7.12   The cover of the notorious book *Learning from Las Vegas* by Robert Venturi, Denise Scott Brown, and Steven Izenour, from 1972. (Illustration by permission, MIT Press.)

opposed the sort of commercial strip development that was becoming ever more ubiquitous along American highways, Goodman remarked:

> Along comes Venturi and says all that stuff they've been calling ugly really is beautiful! He tells us we're looking at the highway strip through the wrong set of theoretical glasses. Wouldn't it be revolutionary if we suddenly saw as beautiful all that stuff we've been calling ugly? That's obviously true, but what does such a distortion of our perception do to our larger view of the world? To be revolutionary for the architect should mean something more than promoting a perversion of taste. It should involve a revolution in the way people live; it means using architecture as a way of breaking down the established social order. In this sense Venturi's architecture is in fact the epitome of a counter revolutionary one. The real revolu-

tionary architects are people like the squatters in Latin America. Faced with the problem of society where they own no land and need homes, they make the act of designing and building their own homes a political act of defiance against their social system.[24]

In short, for Goodman the entire formal apparatus of architecture had become at best irrelevant, and at worse oppressive. He concluded by calling for architects to reject what he saw as their traditional roles:

> Instead of remaining the "outside expert" trying to resolve the conflicting needs of the low-middle-high income metropolis, or simply "helping the poor," we can become participants in our own community's search for new family structures or other changing patterns of association, and participants in the process of creating physical settings which would foster these ways of life—in effect, we become a part of, rather than an expert for, cultural change.[25]

Beyond this, Goodman commended to his fellow professionals another new operational concept:

> In what might be called guerilla architecture, I've found that the style of action, in fact, plays a crucial role in determining the effectiveness of a demand. This is more clearly the case with squatters' housing in South America and also increasingly so in the United States.

He welcomed this process by which the disenfranchised "become aware of their potential power when they are willing to act together." Goodman took pains to point out that he did not see himself as altogether antitechnology: "My emphasis on people's ability to make environmental decisions should not be confused with a vision of a pre-industrial, crafts-producing society with everybody building his own little house." Rather, he looked forward, in a vague way, to the possibility of modern technology being employed for new social purposes.

> A country which has the capacity to produce sophisticated instruments of mass destruction and containers carrying men to explore space, which must adapt to subtle variations in temperature, wind stress and the movement of the universe, should indeed have the ability to produce building products for humane living which are flexible enough to allow human changes in fixed positions here on earth.[26]

A British contemporary of Goodman's, Martin Pawley, had an even keener interest in technological issues in architecture. He also explored more systematically the antecedents, developed principles, and implementation strategies of modernist housing practices, in a devastating text entitled _Architecture versus Housing_. Pawley began by noting how the phenomenon of mass housing gradually came into being between the seventeenth and the nineteenth centuries, with a public responsibility for housing gradually coming to be recognized in all the major European countries. As he summarized the limited accomplishments of housing programs—including those of the modernists—up until the Second World War, certain provocative themes emerged. The first was a contention, hard for the protagonists of CIAM to accept, that in the provision of housing the private sector consistently outperformed the public sector. The second was that the production of housing has lagged behind need, or at least behind demand, for virtually the entire twentieth century. He took an even dimmer view of the activities of the CIAM generation in the areas of housing and planning during and after the Second World War. In an inflammatory chapter entitled "Bombers are a Plan's Best Friend," for example, he charged that the benevolent utopians of modernism saw the damage caused by the aerial bombardments of the war as creating the sort of opportunity for the implementation of modernist housing programs that had hitherto been politically impossible.[27]

In his most damaging accusation of all, Pawley outlined the catastrophic consequences of a set of planning and housing theories, already judged inappropriate and inadequate in Europe and North America, when they were applied to such third world countries as Venezuela and Nigeria. Of the former, Pawley reported:

> At a cost of $200 million, ninety-seven fifteen-storey high-rise superbloques were built in Caracas and the neighbouring port city of La Guaria. 180,000 slum dwellers were rehoused in these buildings whose emphasis on hygiene and public health echoed that of the Victorians in England, but whose form and architectural ethos derived from Le Corbusier and the prophets of the modern movement. This unique combination was not successful; in fact the United Nations Evaluation Report on the whole enterprise claimed that "the accompanying social, economic and administrative difficulties proved to be so serious, that in effect a civil anarchy prevailed.[28]

In Lagos, Nigeria, according to Pawley, the results were no more successful:

The government of Nigeria launched a similarly magnificent slum clearance of seventy acres in the centre of the city. Unfortunately, by 1962, only twenty-five acres had been cleared and the cost of maintaining the displaced 11,000 occupants at subsidized rents was rising alarmingly. Worse still the original owners were failing to repurchase the cleared areas for a number of unforeseen reasons: Firstly, because replanning had reduced the available area by one third, secondly, because zoning had restricted the possible uses of the remainder, and thirdly, because many of the former owners had sold their right to repurchase to outside entrepreneurs. Of the few who did repurchase most failed to rise to the occasion by building splendid new quarters: instead they constructed makeshift stalls and shops similar to those originally demolished.[29]

Pawley's conclusions, as harsh as Goodman's had been in regard to the reformist ambitions of modernism, were perhaps even more devastating on a theoretical plane. For Pawley focused on what he saw as a central theoretical problem of method, based on a concept he borrowed from the sociologist Alan Lipman:

These two spectacular failures in housing policy are also nails in the coffin of what Alan Lipman has called "the architectural belief system": the idea that a manipulable relationship exists between spaces, volumes, textures, micro-environment and lay-out and social behaviour. This is not to say that the architects of the Venezuelan superblocks were solely to blame for the mayhem which succeeded their completion; nor that British trained planners were responsible for the dismal failure of the Lagos slum clearance programme to the exclusion of everyone else involved. Nonetheless, there can be little doubt that the presence of architectural drawings and models played an important part in launching both these grandiloquent projects, and that an image of the social behaviour of the occupants existed in the minds of those who authorized the schemes.[30]

Goodman's and Pawley's conclusions were more than sufficient to confirm the emerging loss of confidence in modernism's reformist social mission. But a less inflammatory yet ultimately more influential contribution to the post-1968 debate was made by another English architect, John F. C. Turner. Unlike polemicists such as Goodman and Pawley, Turner had already devoted himself to detailed study of the creation of housing in the third world. His profoundly thought-provoking conclusions were published in two key texts of the period, *Freedom to Build* of 1971 and *Housing by People* of 1976.[31] Turner, too, had become profoundly disillusioned with modern architecture's ambitions in the field of housing—ambitions he had

[handwritten margin note: loss of faith ✳ in arch. as a method of social change]

concluded were megalomaniac—and with the lack of participation in the political decision-making process by residents. Like Goodman and Pawley, he found himself horrified at the inappropriateness of the architectural proposals to the social situations they were supposed to accommodate. But Turner's sensibility was a more reflective one than Goodman's, and he was more sympathetic to modernism's original philosophical and social ambitions than Pawley was. Moreover, his firsthand experiences of experiments in housing, which he found far more promising than the centralist solutions of mainstream modernism, gave his arguments both a moderation of tone and a philosophical potentiality of considerable force. Indeed, Turner's early interest in anarchist political theory and his later encounters with the social philosopher Ivan Illich had provided him a conceptual apparatus for the consideration of issues in modern housing that is almost unique.

In a preface to *Housing by People,* the English commentator Colin Ward summarized what he saw as Turner's overall approach:

> Out of his past writings and speeches, I have, without any authorization from him, distilled Turner's three laws of housing. Turner's Second Law says that the important thing about housing is not what it is, but what it does in people's lives, in other words, that dweller satisfaction is not necessarily related to the imposition of standards. Turner's Third Law says that deficiencies and imperfections in your housing are infinitely more tolerable if they are your responsibility than if they are somebody else's. But, beyond the psychological truths of the second and third laws, are the social and economic truths of Turner's First Law, which I take from the book *Freedom to Build:*

> "When dwellers control the major decisions and are free to make their own contribution to the design, construction or management of their housing, both the process and the environment produced stimulate individual and social well-being. When people have no control over, nor responsibility for key decisions in the housing process, on the other hand, dwelling environments may instead become a barrier to personal fulfillment and a burden on the economy."[32]

In *Housing by People,* Turner elaborated the arguments in favor of dweller autonomy and decentralized decision making in the provision of housing. Reviewing the housing policies of a series of major first and third world countries through the past century, Turner asked why "so many houses over 400 years old are in good condition, while so many less than 40 years old, and built at a far greater scarce-resource cost, are already in such

very much the Pyatok office approach.

poor condition that they have to be demolished." His explanation is the revealed fact that "the life of dwelling structures has more to do with human institutions than building technologies." Turner also noted previous observers' views

> that the energy used in modern building is three times that used in traditional hand-hewn stone construction—and the latter, of course is vastly longer lived, even with low levels of maintenance. Moreover, indigenous buildings offer enormous energy savings over conventional modern buildings. And those who suppose that indigenous houses are inflexible should see how well most traditional structures have responded to the changing needs of generations of users. And as a measure of their desirability, they should note the high prices they fetch.[33]

Turner proposed as a new concept "the value of housing." To illustrate it he used two revealing case studies, which he called, respectively, "the supportive shack" and "the oppressive house" (terms derived from the research of his colleague Tomasz Sudra). As an example of the former, he cited the dwelling outside Mexico City of a car painter and his family, who occupied a shack rent-free in the backyard of their godmother. Its supportive nature was not a function of its physical quality. Indeed, Turner argued,

> The physical quality of the shelter is secondary and almost anything will do as long as the health of the family is not unduly threatened, especially by contaminated water or exposure to damp and cold. As the family is on the look-out for new job opportunities, which may be in any part of the city or even in other cities, it must be free to move at short notice. Meanwhile, of course, continuity of tenure is important.

> All these conditions are met by the car painter's shack. While the family would undoubtedly enjoy a higher standard of dwelling, this is relatively unimportant. In fact, the car painter declined the compadre's offer of a room within her house as he did not want to risk damaging their relationship. This materially very poor dwelling was extremely well located for the family at that time; the form of tenancy was ideal, giving them security without commitment and the freedom to move at short notice; and the shelter itself provided all the essentials at minimum cost. The shack was, therefore, an admirable support for their actual situation and a vehicle for the realization of expectations.[34]

As for the oppressive house, it was a nearby modern dwelling created through government programs, occupied by a sick and semiemployed mason, his unemployed wife, and their student son.

The provisional shack (19) of a car painter's family temporarily dependent on rag-picking in a garbage dump in Mexico City. Being rent-free and close to work, urban facilities and relatives, this materially very poor dwelling actually maximizes the family's opportunities for betterment.

The modern standard house (20) of a semi-employed mason, his unemployed wife, and their student son. This materially high standard dwelling, isolating the family from its sources of livelihood and demanding over half its income for the (subsidized) rent-purchase and utility payments, minimizes opportunities for betterment.

7.13   Contrasting photographs of the "supportive shack" and the "oppressive house" from John F. C. Turner's *Housing by People* of 1976. (Illustration courtesy Marion Boyars.)

The mason's modern standard house is disastrously unsatisfactory. Previously resident in a shanty town not far from their present site on the edge of the city, this family had been instrumental in pressing for rehousing when the existence of the shanty town was threatened by the government authorities. Before relocation . . . , the family supported itself from a small shop serving tourists and from the elderly husband's irregular employment as a semi-skilled mason. The family had a low income but with low housing and transportation expenditures, it was able to eat reasonably well and maintain a fair level of health. Their reported income during the period immediately before the move was about three times the subsistence minimum.

This family now lives in a vastly improved modern house, equipped with basic modern services and conveniences. However, this "improvement" is endangering the lives of the family members, and in human and economic terms has led to dangerous deterioration of their condition. Incredibly, the family is required to spend 55 per cent of its total income to meet the rent-purchase and utility payments. . . . This family's situation would not quite be so bad if, in addition to the dramatic rise of their expenditure, they had not also suffered a substantial reduction of their income through the loss of the vending business which is forbidden in their new location. This double loss is typical of "housing improvement" programmes for low and very low-income people.[35]

Extended consideration of these dramatic reversals of the conventional wisdom of modernist housing policies led Turner to the conclusion that "the vast majority of officials and professionals keep recommending the destruction of people's homes in order to solve those same people's 'housing problems' by providing them with alternatives neither they nor society cannot afford."[36]

exactly Seattle & USA's problems w/ the demolition of "substandard" S.R.O. housing)

A reexamination of the needs of dwellers from his own decentralist, anarchist viewpoint led Turner to a political condemnation of both capitalist and socialist attitudes to housing problems.

The obvious fact that use values cannot be quantified worries those who assume that housing can only be satisfactorily supplied by large-scale organizations. The immeasurability of use values is not in the least perturbing to the conventional capitalist. His value system can only admit the existence of market values in the sphere of commercial production, distribution and consumption. . . . The conventional socialist, on the other hand, has always been perturbed by the conflict of use and market values—and the more he or she clings to a faith in large organizations (and centralizing technologies) the greater the conflict becomes. On the other hand, those who do not believe that large organizations can supply all people with personal goods and services, those who have neither a capitalistic nor an authoritarian outlook, need find no conflict or paradox. Material quantities and market values can be useful, even essential, indicators of use value, or of harmonies and tensions between supply and demand. But this principle can only be of use to those who see that the role of central administrations must be limited to ensuring personal and local access to essential resources such as, in the case of housing, appropriate technologies, land and credit.[37]

Together with his colleague Sudra, Turner proposed that addressing "the real problem" of housing required a consideration of two sets of factors, monetary and non-monetary. Following a detailed review of both, he concluded:

It should now be obvious that no conceivable authority could possibly anticipate the immense variety of household situations, priorities and specific housing needs. The huge efforts and sums spent on surveying housing conditions without reference to people's situations and priorities and without any clear understanding of the housing process, has done, and can only continue to do, a great deal of harm.[38]

The effect of Turner's long-term studies of the provision of housing in the third world went well beyond the destruction of the "architectural belief system" described by Martin Pawley. For that matter, his investigations raise issues that go well beyond modern architecture, and lead us to examine aspects of Enlightenment rationality beyond those that have already been discussed. For example, his resolute conclusion that the phenomenon of housing must be seen first and foremost as a "human institution," rather than as *either* a commodity or a service, shows Turner's clear abandonment of the utopian aspirations of instrumentality. Perhaps even more shocking is the discovery of the profound importance, within third world housing practises, of the economic concept of "equity." Recognizing the importance of "security of tenure" as one of the dimensions of the "human institution" of housing, Turner noted how, in numerous examples of squatter settlements that endured for some period of time, residents gradually came to hold equity in their homes and thus contributed to the establishment of vigorous local economies. Through this important field discovery, Turner was impelled to rethink the historic conviction, shared by both anarchism and communism in the nineteenth century, that "property is theft."[39] Indeed, Turner's rediscovery of equity as a decisive mode of security of tenure recalls Arendt's reading of the importance of property in the political theory of John Locke. For Arendt, following Locke, the right to hold property is an essential precondition of the political dignity of citizenship.[40] *ownership = pride* Thus, Turner's acknowledgment of the importance of equity as a component of successful residential communities in the third world casts a dramatic and politically charged light back on the collectivist, or at least centralized, orientation to land tenure that typified all orthodox European modernist approaches to urbanism.

On the concatenation of ideas generally constituting modernism in architecture—utopian, reformist, technological, and reductionist—the series of postwar critiques stretching from Rowe to Turner had a devastating cumulative effect. By the time Rowe's critique had been absorbed, it was no

7.14   The concluding page of Vincent Scully's *American Architecture and Urbanism,* juxtaposing an overall view of downtown Denver, Colorado, with the newly completed Garden Towers in Cleveland, Ohio.

longer possible to accept without question the essential moral legitimacy of reductionism. Venturi's critique abetted Rowe's scorn for reductive essentialism, at the same time as it challenged the evidently technological orientation of modernism. By the time the radical sociopolitical critiques of Goodman, Pawley, and Turner were concluded in the seventies, it was profoundly difficult for architects to believe any longer in the reforming efficacy or the utopian aspirations of modernism. In fact, it is clear that, for architects, the events of 1968 completed the more or less total destruction of the social and philosophical premises of modernism as they had been understood for three decades.

The immediate consequences were quite dramatic in both Europe and North America. Schools of architecture on both continents had been the seedbeds of many of the damning critiques that had been mounted. So it should not be surprising that one early consequence was a student demand for the reorganization of the entire system of architectural education to reflect these critiques. In the United States, for example, major changes were made at such important schools as those at Harvard, Colombia, MIT, and Berkeley. In Canada, the curricula of the schools at the universities of Toronto and British Columbia were completely reconstructed. In France, the entire national system of architectural education was scrapped and replaced by a new series of *Unités Pédagogiques d'Architecture* intended initially to be made up of groups of like-minded faculty and students, many of whom chose to orient their new curricula to the contentious new sociopolitical issues thrown up by the critique of modernism.[41]

Less profoundly but more immediately, architectural publishing also changed direction. Vincent Scully's long-awaited *American Architecture and Urbanism* happened to come out in 1969, and Scully chose to conclude his historical overview of three centuries of work with an image of the courtyard of a brand-new low-cost housing cooperative in a black neighborhood of Cleveland.[42] In a similar vein, the important British magazine *Architectural Design* chose at this time to completely reorient its editorial policy to focus on the newly topical issues of low-cost housing, alternative techniques, tenants rights, protests against urban renewal, etc.

In the world of architectural practice, the changes called for were slower to occur, possibly because of the time lag involved in the dissemination of

INDIGENOUS HOUSING
Directory of Alternative Technology   Part 2
ARCHITECTURAL DESIGN VOLUME XLV APRIL 1975 60p

7.15   A typical cover of *Architectural Design* following its post-1968 change of editorial policy.

new architectural approaches but also—and far more important—because the practices of orthodox modernism that had come under such severe criticism were at that time deeply linked with major sectors of the European and North American economies, most particularly with their respective development industries. Nevertheless, the challenge to the widespread assumption by the modernist architects of the 1950s and 1960s—who had all been educated in the ambience deriving from the accounts of modernism promoted by Gropius, Giedion, and their colleagues—of the inherent normative benevolence of their actions had a disconcerting effect on most thoughtful practitioners. The moral justification of their professional activity having been so suddenly destroyed, they found it profoundly difficult to go forward unaffected. As a result, one saw on the one hand much effort devoted by activist young architects to challenge orthodox building proposals, in cities across both continents, that seemed antisocial and urbanistically irresponsible. At the same time, architects working for the large-scale public agencies and development corporations under attack found themselves, at the least, attempting revision after unexpected revision of their design proposals, in hopes of gaining the approvals of residents and tenant groups that were becoming increasingly necessary. In short, between 1968 and the mid-1970s the new critique of modernism gained throughout the western world a decisive moral victory.

What an extraordinary historical development, then, that this critique should turn out, in present retrospect, to have had so few years of ascendancy. Newcomers to architecture today have great difficulty developing any adequate sense of the force of the critique in the late sixties and early seventies, and I believe this is largely due to the fact that its impact is currently so difficult to discern.

For example, the years immediately following 1968 saw a quick growth of interest among young architects in the kind of partisan professional action on behalf of disadvantaged groups on which radicals such as Robert Goodman had pinned their hopes, and which, for a time, became well-known under the rubric of "advocacy planning." Yet with astonishing speed, this important new mode of professional practice found itself moving farther and farther away from architecture itself, and closer and closer to a form of community-based politics. Indeed, many of the most thoughtful young architects who had chosen to become "advocates" began to see architecture as increasingly marginal. In a related development, *Architectural Design*, which only a few years earlier had made itself a vehicle for the dissemination of the newly politicized architectural ideas of the late sixties, suddenly in the mid-seventies dropped its political orientation altogether. Significantly enough, it commenced instead a new series of issues focusing on a group of young designers, theoreticians, and historians who were beginning to work in Europe and in North America, and who manifested a renewed and quite intense interest in formal and historical questions.

One of the first centers of such new ideas was Paris, which of course had been one of the key world centers of ferment in 1968. Yet even there—perhaps even especially so there—new ferment broke out, and one of the most important of the new *Unités Pédagogiques* (the teaching units that had succeeded the ateliers of the now abolished Ecole des Beaux-Arts) split in two. This was UP6 (according to the new nomenclature), which in the heady excitement following the May events had been the most politically active of all the new, self-formed groups of students and teachers. Yet in September of 1969, internal disputes respecting the appropriate relationship of political commitment to architectural praxis led to the secession from UP6 of a group of dissidents, including the important activist and intellectual Bernard Huet. Notwithstanding their respect for political "engagement," the dissidents decided that their former colleagues had become so totally absorbed in politics as to have effectively abandoned architectural praxis altogether. As Huet said in a 1971 conversation with Martin Pawley and Bernard Tschumi, "We do not wish to be concerned with planning social systems because that is a political problem to be solved by politicians. What we ask for is a framework, defined by politics, within which we can work."[43] Thus was formed one of the second generation of *Unités Pédagogiques* in Paris, UP8. In a text originally drafted by Huet and the collective of his students in 1970 and published in 1978 as an introduction to a program of studies, UP8 attempted to make its revisionist position clear.

politically
active
architecture
short-lived
by archit.
who would
rather
"just design"

> A school of architecture cannot be a small, isolated cell within the body of society, and the teaching which goes on there mustn't under any circumstances abstract itself from the mode of production and from the development of the productive forces of society. The specific production of the architect inscribes itself within the larger field of production of built objects; the architectural intervention cannot define itself without recourse to an analysis of the totality of that production, leading to a critical realization of what is taking place, not only during the architect's intervention, but also before and after it.[44]

Turning to the more specifically architectural objectives of the program, the statement explicitly challenged the partisans of the original UP6:

> We reject a teaching which is based on the illusion that it is possible to invent an architecture or a construction which is radically different from those which are currently produced in France, as regards their final results. Similarly, we reject a mode of teaching which is based solely on a negative "ideological critique" that denies consideration of any production which it sees as susceptible to "co-optation," by definition.[45]

In the English-speaking world as well, the first half of the 1970s saw the growth of a renewed interest in formal and historical issues in architecture. Indeed, it is interesting to note how the ongoing critique of orthodox modern architecture in the United States and England, in promoting the new movement that Charles Jencks named postmodernism, gradually came to incorporate less and less of the political content of the 1968 events. For example, in his famous polemic of 1977, *The Language of Post-Modern Architecture,* Jencks declared a specific date upon which modern architecture could be said to have died.[46] This was July 15, 1972, the date of the demolition by dynamiting of one of the blocks of the notorious Pruitt-Igoe public housing project in St. Louis, which had been created, from 1952 to 1955, to the designs of an architect who was one of the leaders of American architectural modernism, Minoru Yamasaki, and which in its time had attempted to implement many of the ideas of modernist urbanism from CIAM. In his text, Jencks employed Pruitt-Igoe to launch his critique of what he saw as modernism's architectural failure. Jencks, however, did not note that the same project had already been used by Robert Goodman in *After the Planners,* before the dramatic public incident of its demolition, to introduce the much more sweeping and political critique he had entitled "The Architecture of Repression." This interesting omission should perhaps

return to formalism

PART ONE
The Death of Modern Architecture

Happily, we can date the death of modern architecture to a precise moment in time. Unlike the legal death of a person, which is becoming a complex affair of brain waves versus heartbeats, modern architecture went out with a bang. That many people didn't notice, and no one was seen to mourn, does not make the sudden extinction any less of a fact, and that many designers are still trying to administer the kiss of life does not mean that it has been miraculously resurrected. No, it expired finally and completely in 1972, after having been flogged to death remorselessly for ten years by critics such as Jane Jacobs; and the fact that many so-called modern architects still go around practising a trade as if it were alive can be taken as one of the great curiosities of our age (like the British Monarchy giving life-prolonging drugs to 'The Royal Company of Archers' or 'The Extra Women of the Bedchamber').

Modern Architecture died in St Louis, Missouri on July 15, 1972 at 3.32 p.m. (or thereabouts) when the infamous Pruitt-Igoe scheme, or rather several of its slab
3   blocks, were given the final *coup de grâce* by dynamite. Previously it had been vandalised, mutilated and defaced by its black inhabitants, and although millions of dollars were pumped back, trying to keep it alive (fixing the broken elevators, repairing smashed windows, repainting), it was finally put out of its misery. Boom, boom, boom.

Without doubt, the ruins should be kept, the remains should have a preservation order slapped on them, so that
4   we keep a live memory of this failure in planning and architecture. Like the folly or artificial ruin — constructed on the estate of an eighteenth-century English eccentric to provide him with instructive reminders of former vanities and glories — we should learn to value and protect our former disasters. As Oscar Wilde said, 'experience is the name we give to our mistakes', and there is a certain health in leaving them judiciously scattered around the landscape as continual lessons.

Pruitt-Igoe was constructed according to the most progressive ideals of CIAM (the Congress of International Modern Architects) and it won an award from the American Institute of Architects when it was designed in 1951. It consisted of elegant slab blocks fourteen storeys high with rational 'streets in the air' (which were safe from cars, but as it turned out, not safe from crime); 'sun, space and greenery', which Le Corbusier called the 'three essential joys of urbanism' (instead of conventional streets, gardens and semi-private space, which he banished). It had a separation of pedestrian and vehicular traffic, the provision of play space, and local amenities such as laundries, crèches and gossip centres — all rational substitutes for traditional patterns. Moreover, its Purist style, its clean, salubrious hospital metaphor, was meant to instil, by good example, corresponding virtues in the inhabitants.

Good form was to lead to good content, or at least good conduct; the intelligent planning of abstract space was to promote healthy behaviour.

3 MINORU YAMASAKI. *Pruitt-Igoe Housing*, St Louis, 1952–55. Several slab blocks of this scheme were blown up in 1972 after they were continuously vandalised. The crime rate was higher than other developments, and Oscar Newman attributed this, in his book *Defensible Space*, to the long corridors, anonymity, and lack of controlled semi-private space. Another factor: it was designed in a purist language at variance with the architectural codes of the inhabitants.

4 PRUITT-IGOE AS RUIN. Like the Berlin Wall and the collapse of the high-rise block, Ronan Point, in England, 1968, this ruin has become a great architectural symbol. It should be preserved as a warning. Actually, after continued hostilities and disagreements, some blacks have managed to form a community in parts of the remaining habitable blocks — another symbol, in its way, that events and ideology, as well as architecture, determine the success of the environment.

9

7.16   The highly polemical opening page of part one of Charles Jencks's *Language of Post-Modern Architecture* of 1977.

be seen as an instance of the discernible weariness of explicitly politicized discussion that came to characterize most ongoing North American polemics about architecture in the second half of the seventies. For example, while both Michael Graves and Robert Stern became well known for the energetic attacks on orthodox modern architecture with which they so consistently preceded the presentation of their own projects in lectures during those years, they too eschewed the intensely politicized discussions of the late sixties, confining their objections to what they saw as modernism's inhumane and unrefined accommodations of human activities, and its muteness as a possible mode of symbolic discourse.

IV

The Architecture of Repression

As an architect, if I had no economic or social limitations, I'd solve all my problems with one-story buildings. Imagine how pleasant it would be to always work and plan in spaces overlooking lovely gardens filled with flowers.

Yet, we know that within the framework of our present cities this is impossible to achieve. Why? Because we must recognize social and economic limitations and requirements. A solution without such recognition would be meaningless.[1]

—Minoru Yamasaki, an architect for the Pruitt-Igoe Public Housing Project in St. Louis

92

THE GRAND CENTRAL STATION area in New York City is one of the most congested business districts in the world. It seethes with the congestion caused by real-estate speculation, the subways are jammed, and few rays of sunshine ever make it to the nearly impassable streets. In 1968 Marcel Breuer, a "world-renowned" architect, designed a 55-story 2,000,000-square-foot building to be perched on top of the existing Grand Central structure. Coincidentally, a week after the design was presented, Breuer received the Gold Medal of the American Institute of Architects, its highest award.

In some ways, Breuer's design is not so absurd as it may seem. Our economic system has traditionally reduced the

93

Pruitt-Igoe Public Housing Project, St. Louis

7.17 Facing pages from the opening of chapter IV in Robert Goodman's *After the Planners* of 1971; a parallel not remarked on by Charles Jencks in his subsequent work.

Meanwhile, in Europe, a dramatic gesture occurred that, much more fundamentally than any Anglo-American discussion, redefined the terms on which the possible relationship of politics to architecture could be considered. The gesture in question was made by Bernard Huet, who by this time had become the editor of the long-established French journal *L'Architecture d'aujourd'hui*. In an April 1977 editorial introducing recent projects from Italy, Spain, and the Ticino, which Aldo Rossi had grouped under the rubric of the "Tendenza,"[47] Huet traced the evolution of a line of thinking about architecture that had proceeded in Italy in the years following the Second World War, an evolution he had witnessed firsthand as a student of Ernesto Rogers in Milan in the late 1950s. Huet saw it as having begun in a reconsideration by the Italian intelligentsia of the problematic legacy of Fascism. From it, according to his argument, proceeded the important movement in the Italian cinema of the 1950s that came to be known as neorealism, together with an inventive series of related interpretations of realism in other arts, interpretations which, in their turn, influenced thoughtful Italian architects:

> For once, architects followed the lead of others. Burned by the regime of Mussolini which had first fascinated and subsequently repelled them, they lost their illusions in regard to the salvation and the progressivism supposedly offered by modern architecture. They were the first in Europe to recognize the ambiguity of the "formalism" of the International Style, to question the utility of "avant-gardes," and to disabuse themselves of utopias which were reductive of reality.[48]

As a result of this particular historical experience, as Huet saw it, the succeeding generations of Italian architects were in a better position than many others to face up to the broad implications of the crisis that occurred in 1968. As he put it,

> Two irreducible positions then confronted one another: the first, giving primacy to "content," predicted the death of architecture, and denied it any disciplinary specificity; the other, "formalist," put forward a cynical and opportunistic professionalism and exploited the confusion of "styles" (kitsch) for commercial purposes.

> Faced with these positions, certain architects formed the "Tendenza," which presented itself as a critical and operational alternative.[49]

As Huet saw it, this alternative entailed both an ideological critique of architectural history and a typological critique of architecture as a part of the historical process of the formation of cities. In fact, he saw the Tendenza has having achieved a quite fundamental transformation.

> The "Tendenza" proposed . . . to reconstruct the discipline of architecture. To the functionalism of modern architecture it opposed an "enlightened" rationalism, whose form yielded an idea of architecture as an instrument of knowledge. The irreducible specificity of architecture, and its disciplinary autonomy, reside in its capacity to produce "typical" forms of a general and popular bearing, which require a precise knowledge: a "metier." For the "Tendenza," architecture finds its only justification in its very "being"; it is invested with no content, with no redemptive value, and can express nothing by itself. . . . In a word, it is "realist."[50]

And this line of argument led Huet to his provocative conclusion:

> According to Brecht, "realism is not a matter of form." One is inclined to paraphrase him, and to state that formalism also is not a matter of form. One has to advance beyond the crude simplifications of a certain "formalist" critique. There is no Fascist or Stalinist architecture in "form," there is only the architecture of the Fascist, or of the Stalinist period.[51]

Some four years later, Leon Krier published in *Oppositions* his indignant defense of Albert Speer's projects for Berlin cited at the head of the text.

"Architecture is not political; it is only an instrument of politics": it is true that Krier's statement was deliberately polemical, designed to bring to a head the critical dissension then raging in regard to the possible boundaries of acceptable architectural classicism in our time, and in this sense it should perhaps be taken with a grain of salt. But Huet's earlier and more carefully considered conclusion is one that commands at least partial assent. As he was able to point out in the heated exchange of opinion following the publication of his remarks, any argument that claimed to see architecture as straightforwardly and unequivocally political would prove unable to sustain either prolonged or close critical scrutiny.[52] Returning us once again to the problematic question of the political status of modernism in Italy in the 1930s and 1940s, Huet commented provocatively: "If we continue to admire the architecture of Terragni, we do in spite of his active allegiance to Fascism, right up to the time of his death."[53] Conversely, he had in his original text already objected to the inclination of modernist critics of socialist realism in the Soviet Union to justify their stylistic critique on the grounds that it had been historically implemented through a bureaucratic codification, and through the Stalinist cult of personality. According to this line of argument, he complained, "it ends up that the monuments share the virtues and the vices of the regime that produces them."[54]

In fact, Huet's statement denies that the alleged "Fascism" or "Stalinism" of so-called Fascist or Stalinist architecture lies in architectural "form" itself. This is surely true. Yet it does not seem to me that this fact is sufficient to enable him to proceed, without qualification, to the subsequent statement that "there is only the architecture of the Fascist, or of the Stalinist period." For insofar as the progress of his commentary—from the original negation to the subsequent assertion—has entailed a shift of ground sufficient to permit the entry into the discussion of the concept of a historical "period," then it is surely also true that the same shift has the related consequence of moving the consideration of architecture away from "form," and back into the realm in which its propensity to acquire social and political connotations is inescapable. In this regard, we need only recall Walter Benjamin's well-known statement; "Architecture has always represented the prototype of a work of art the reception of which is consummated by a collectivity in a state of distraction."[55] Benjamin's conception of "a collectivity in a state of distraction" was one of the major intellectual influences on the semiological investigations of the first half of the 1960s, investigations that led this observer, like many others, to the conclusion that social readings of architectural artifacts proceed simultaneously on both conscious and unconscious levels. And if this is true, then it seems to me impossible that a denial of any inherent "politicality" of architectural "form" itself can legitimately proceed to a denial of the "politicality" of an identified historical period of architecture. Once architecture situates itself within a given social context, it inescapably forsakes the autonomy it possesses in its hypothetical status as pure "form."

To take the semiological reprise one step further, we may note again the fundamental distinction posited by semiotics between the signifier and the signified, the first of which is an arbitrary "form" (in Huet's sense) having no meaning "in itself," and the second of which is the referent, to which the first refers, by virtue of its understood role within the social construction that the semiological system as a whole constitutes. It seems to me that the principles of semiotics, as they apply to architecture, may be particularly useful in the discussion of the efforts of various protagonists to deal with architecture and its putative politicality.

We may begin with the matter of the opposed unconscious and conscious levels of "consummation" of meaning in architecture. A particularly apt contemporary instance of "unconscious" social consummation—one that Benjamin, with his keen appreciation of the phenomenon of shopping in late nineteenth-century Paris, would have savored—is the modern shopping center. The public at large has little awareness of the fact, but architects familiar with this quintessentially contemporary building type know well the characteristic plan forms employed by shopping center developers to subtly manipulate the patterns of movement of their customers. To start with, parking areas and parking structures have typically been disposed in relation to shopping areas proper so as to ensure as even a distribution as possible of customers to all areas of the center. Then too, major and minor anchors have usually been placed strategically to take customers past secondary retail facilities, so as to encourage impulse buys. This by now well-established pattern of the architecture of retail marketing has had the effect of maximizing overall sales revenue per square foot. And it has profound effects on the millions of users of such facilities, well below any threshold of awareness we could call conscious. In that sense, the contemporary shopping center seems to me a classic instance of Benjaminian collective consummation that is entirely unconscious.

At levels of consciousness that we might call intermediate we encounter such classically architectonic considerations as the representation of major and minor points of entry on the facades of building complexes. Such representations will sometimes be subconsciously grasped by users, but sometimes they will enter decisively into the realm of conscious perception and social appropriation. Another example of intermediate consciousness is that of the "architectural promenade," particularly in its Corbusian format. In this case, unlike that of the shopping center, the design is intended to stimulate the user's gradually unfolding conscious understanding of the complex spatial sequence of the building.

Finally, at the most conscious level of appropriation of meaning in architecture, we encounter what I, following terminology devised by Erwin Panofsky, would call iconography.[56] At this level of supraconscious perception, we depart significantly from the model of "distraction" as set out by Benjamin. Iconography, comprising all those matters respecting symbolic representation in the vertical plane of the facade, has historically speaking also been the most common locus of contention in regard to the attribution of political meaning in architecture. That is to say, in the same way that we have been taught to read the representation of the eagle as "standing for" the United States, and the lion for Great Britain, so also has it been suggested that we might read "transparency" in architecture as symbolic of "openness in government," as in the famous instance of Hannes Meyer's and Hans Wittwer's 1927 project for the League of Nations.

We may characterize the levels of socially appropriated meaning in archi-

7.18 A view of a typical shopping center of the 1970s: Scarborough Town Centre, outside Toronto. Note how the parking lots are sloped up and/or down so as to distribute customers equally over the lower and upper levels of the mall. In this case, it cannot be said any longer that there is such a thing as a "main floor," and this is a deliberate intention of the designers.

tecture as semiologically ordered in another, complementary way. The most unconscious modes of appropriation—those having at the most basic level to do with our sheer sensorimotor movement through space—can be read as the least arbitrary, and conversely the most conscious ones—those having to do with maximally explicit symbolic icons—as the most arbitrary. Such a schema would be quite compatible with the principles of semiotics, in that it would characterize the least conscious modes as the least susceptible to analysis according to a linguistic analogy, and the most conscious ones—that is to say the most iconic ones—as being the most susceptible to such analysis.

This last proposition may serve to clarify and even to justify Huet's understandable impatience with crude and oversimplified ascriptions of political significance to particular architectural artifacts. For if we agree that it is the most conscious modes of symbolic representation in architecture that are both the most capable of and the most susceptible to expression in political terms, and that these very modes of expression are also the most arbitrary ones, then we may also see why the iconographic level of possible social meaning in architecture is the most labile one. Just as the eagle stands for the United States in one context, it may easily stand for something else in a different one: in the context of anthropomorphic myths of the wilderness, for example, for the domination of species of which it is the predator. So too, the architectural "transparency" intended to connote "openness in government" may come instead to seem to stand for "anonymous and nonaccountable bureaucracy."

It is true that once situated in a given social and historical context, any architecture will both assume and express meanings on most or all of these levels of consciousness simultaneously. I owe to Antoine Grumbach a report of an episode in the Communards' battle to gain control of the various *quartiers* of Paris in 1870, which illustrates the import of architecture's fundamentally ambiguous social role with compelling force.[57] According to Grumbach's report, the Communards in a particular *arrondissement* had managed to gain control, and in the hours and days following their victory turned their thoughts to the necessity to secure and consolidate it, not least in the eyes of the population of the *quartier,* whose ongoing confidence the Communards most particularly wished to retain. Part of any successful effort to do so, they supposed, would entail the establishment of some clearly and publicly visible evidence of the existence and the operational efficacy of their new regime. The need for this focused specifically on a possible base for their ongoing deliberations. Since timing demanded that such public evidence of their effectiveness would need to be quickly apparent, they were compelled to consider only buildings that already existed. Of those, the most obvious possibility was the *hôtel de ville* of the *arrondissement,* the former occupants of which they had just defeated.

The consideration of this possibility presented the Communards with a classical dilemma of the kind that we face, in more general terms, in this discussion of architecture and politics. Some argued, for example, that the public symbolism of an occupation by the new regime of the very seat of the just defeated one would be utterly wrong. It might well suggest to the population of the *quartier,* in Arendt's rueful characterization, a political victory that "would not result in changing the world (or the system), but only its personnel."[58] Yet the sheer exigencies of the moment indicated to others the urgent need for some palpable public evidence of the stability and durability of the regime of the Communards, who had, indeed, up to that point been victorious, but who did not yet think themselves perceptible as a constituted government. In short, in circumstances in which the symbolic options open to them were problematically few, the Communards found themselves compelled to choose between the image of stability and one of a clean break with the old regime.

Surely any discussion of architecture and politics in the twentieth century must acknowledge two related conclusions drawn from the semiological work of the early sixties. On the one hand, it would seem to be clear, notwithstanding the Italian reformulation during those same years of architecture's "autonomy" as architecture, that architecture in society will nevertheless always remain capable of readings in particular political terms. On the other hand, it would seem to be equally clear that there will also continue to be sufficient fluidity in the possible political readings of any particular architectural motifs for architects to presume a considerable (albeit socially bounded) scope of praxis open to them in these matters. Absent the haste that history required of the Communards in Grumbach's fateful narrative, they may be confident of the possibility of seeking to constitute, through what they build, what they politically intend. By the same token, they must also recognize that the more politically iconic their work attempts to be, the less likely their own political interpretations of those efforts will be the ones that ultimately govern. In this regard, we may paraphrase Karl Kraus's famous observation about his own and Adolf Loos's efforts to "provide culture with elbow room." For it seems to me that the effect of a semiological reconsideration of the possible relationship of architecture and politics in our time may be, in a parallel way, to provide architecture with the elbow room it requires, politically speaking, in order to continue to exist as a viable mode of social praxis.

In light of this theoretical interlude, let us return to our two episodes of explicit politicization of architecture, that of the 1930s and that of the 1960s. We face, in these terms, a history of the politics of modernism in which a first political critique of modernism is made from the right, followed some 30 years later by a second political critique from the left. The second critique, notwithstanding that its explicit political orientation is very different, bears many substantive similarities to the first one, including allegations of modernism's "sterility," "inhumanity," and utopian aspirations to a technological universality, as well as its failure to respond to particularities of climate, geography, and local social custom.

We are now in a position to make two new kinds of observations of the politics of this strange double episode. First of all, it would now seem clear that many of the grosser and more specific political allegations that have been hurled back and forth are simply misplaced, politically speaking, on account of the relatively limited and also quite labile nature of many of what we have hitherto thought of as the more explicit modes of political representation in architecture. Secondly, the striking parallelism of the two

1930's   1960's ✗
right & left
criticism of
modernism on
similar pts.

7.19   A view of Fire Station No. 4 in Columbus, Indiana, from 1966, one of the brilliantly ironic early projects of Robert Venturi, when his interests in pop art—particularly that of the American painter Jasper Johns—seemed to sustain him in an astonishingly rigorous exploration of then extant Americana. (Illustration courtesy Venturi, Scott Brown & Associates.)

7.20   A "house in Maine" by Venturi, Scott Brown & Associates, from 1989. This may serve as an example of the loss of ironic distance, and of the sad more recent reabsorption of the firm of Venturi and his colleagues into a much more socially complicit mode of designing. (Photograph: Matt Warburg.)

critiques would also seem to suggest that insofar as they possess substantive historical grounding (going beyond polemics internal to architecture and its avant-gardes), it will be true that their long-term import will also go well beyond architecture, and will begin to encompass further reconsideration of the legacy of Enlightenment rationality, such as has already been predicted in chapter five. In its turn, of course, this larger philosophical reconsideration will inevitably have its own large political consequences.

To develop such a discussion, we may, for instance, essay a provisional analysis of the evolution of the recent (and ostensibly apolitical) architectural movement now known as postmodernism. Following the publication of Jencks's *Language of Post-Modernism* in 1977, the movement enjoyed a considerable critical and popular success. Indeed, not only Robert Stern and Michael Graves but a whole generation of architects succeeded polemically in launching their careers in its name. Yet before the movement even consolidated its historical position, evidence of cultural insecurity within its evolution became apparent.

To begin with, we may cite the important founding role of Robert Venturi, and of his keen interest in the cultural phenomenon of irony. This interest was a seminal contribution to the development of postmodernism, especially in North America, yet, significantly, Venturi himself, notwithstanding the strength of his profoundly ironic sensibility, has had great difficulty in sustaining an ironic posture in his and his collaborators' own recent corpus

7.21   Sketches of two adjacent houses for Livermore, California, by Thomas Gordon Smith, from 1979.

of work. Many of his followers have long since ceased even to attempt to sustain a posture of irony vis-à-vis contemporary culture as part of their philosophical orientation to architectural praxis. As Venturiesque irony has begun to dissipate, it seems to me that postmodernism has begun to move inexorably in one of two problematic directions.

For one strand within the movement, the tendency has been ever more consistently in the direction of a new and increasingly literal historicism. Robert Stern, for example, may be seen as far more literally historicist in his orientation than his mentor Venturi; Thomas Gordon Smith may be seen as even more literally historicist than Stern; and Quinlan Terry as more literally historicist than Smith.[59]

The second strand, also proceeding from the work of Venturi, has led farther and farther in the direction of a postmodernism of popular consumption. One can trace a consistent trajectory of this sort in the work of Charles Moore over the past two decades, from the Kresge College campus through the notorious Piazza d'Italia to his more recent works.[60]

This gradually polarizing evolution has had two key significances for the movement overall. As postmodernist historicism has become ever more literal-minded, it has concurrently become ever more preoccupied with correctness, with propriety, and with a strictness of representation of "traditional values." Conversely, consumerist postmodernism during the same period grew progressively more closely preoccupied with widespread popular response. It is not coincidental that this strand of postmodernism should now have become so closely associated with the phenomenon of the theme park.

As a result, then, notwithstanding the ostensible apoliticality of the architectural movement in the first instance, its two main strands have turned out to serve appropriately to symbolize the two main strands of neoconservative thought. It is hardly surprising that the historicism of a figure such as Quinlan Terry would have been considered as a possible vehicle for the symbolic representation of Britain under Prime Minister Thatcher, deeply concerned to assert traditional values and to reconstitute what it saw as appropriate decorum in the world.[61] In short, historicist postmodernism turned out to be the architecture of traditional neoconservatism. Consumerist postmodernism, on the other hand, we may see as having a loose but nevertheless highly appropriate association with the populist mode of neoconservatism, combining interest in grass roots initiatives, supply side economics, and a somewhat libertarian amorality.

To be sure, even though the force of the postmodernist tendency has by now waned significantly, neither of these two emergent political alignments is as yet all that clearly evident. Indeed, my the picture of them may be complicated further by the polemics of yet other observers of the present disarray of architectural culture.

7.22   A drawing by Quinlan Terry of a project for St. Mary's Church, Paddington, from 1973.

St. Mary's Church at Paddington Green, 1973

7.23   A view of the Faculty Club at the University of California at Santa Barbara by Charles Moore, from 1968.

7.24   A view of a part of the large complex in Pasadena, California, called Plaza Las Fuentes, recently completed by the firm of Moore Ruble Yudell.

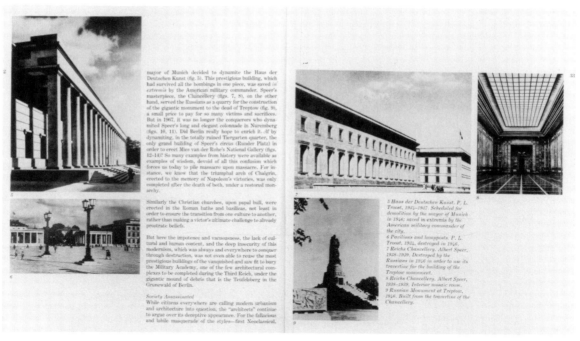

7.25 Facing pages from a 1981 text by Leon Krier in *Oppositions,* calling for the preservation of fragments of the work of Albert Speer, still surviving—but under threat of demolition—in Berlin at that time.

I have already noted how a progressive disillusionment with the direction of European modernism eventually led a critic such as Leon Krier to a defense of the wartime Berlin buildings of Albert Speer. In his defense, Krier opposed to the products of meretricious modernism precisely the same Albert Speer designs for the public spaces of imperial Berlin that Robert Goodman had employed in *After the Planners* to suggest the latent totalitarian tendencies of corporate modern architecture.[62] For Krier, his antipathy to the vocabulary of modernism in its technocratic manifestation outweighed any fear of possible commonalities with totalitarianism. Indeed, together with his ally Maurice Culot, Krier increasingly moved toward yet another new literal historicism, chiefly distinguished by its opposition to both consumerism and technology, which, for Krier, were indissolubly combined in the modern society he abhorred. The anomalous conjunction of cultural values that his work thus came to represent makes any political reading of his work highly ambiguous.

We may also turn to the related polemic of the Anglo-American critic Kenneth Frampton. For Frampton, the reduction of architecture to a phenomenon of social consumption was as troubling as it was for Krier. But Frampton remained committed to an older vision of modernism that was anticonsumerist and antiestablishment. In a series of arguments culminating in his *Modern Architecture: A Critical History* of 1980, Frampton continued to

sense of community and shared conviction—has been impaired, has atrophied in our time because of the retreat from architecture and public buildings as a conscious element of public policy and a purposeful instrument for the expression of public purpose.[9]

According to Moynihan, the inability of political leaders to insist on right kinds of architecture has led to:

. . . a steady deterioration in the quality of public buildings and spaces, and with it a decline in the symbols of public unity and common purpose with which the citizen can identify, of which he can be proud, and by which he can know what he shares with his fellow citizens.[10]

Some years earlier, another person in another country

Architecture of the Third Reich, Munich

Proposed architecture for U.S. government buildings, Washington, D.C.

who was also to become a public figure wrote about a similar concern:

. . . our cities of the present lack the outstanding symbol of national community which, we must therefore not be surprised to find, sees no symbol of itself in the cities. The inevitable result is a desolation whose practical effect is the total indifference of the big-city dweller to the destiny of his city.[11]

That was Adolf Hitler describing his views on city design in *Mein Kampf*. For government leaders, struck with a vision of the historic purpose of architectural propaganda, a major theme of building design is symbolic monuments to commemorate the present glory to future generations. According to Moynihan:

The task of this less than all-powerful nation is to show to the world and to ourselves that, sensing our limitations, we know also our strengths. The surest sign of whether we have done this will reside in the buildings and public places which we shall build in our time, and for which we will be remembered or forgotten in history.[12]

105

7.26   Facing pages from Robert Goodman's *After the Planners,* employing the same image of street-lamps in the Tiergarten later used by Krier.

defend the reformist position of first-generation modernism.[63] Believing with Jürgen Habermas that modernity remains "an incomplete project,"[64] he opposed both the historicist and the consumerist modes of postmodernism. Thus, Frampton's and Krier's positions, viewed first from a stylistic perspective and second from a political one, constitute problematic mirror images of one another. Sharing both a politics of the left and a strong commitment to the traditions of western European high culture, they both deplore the consumerist tendencies of modern Western society. Yet for the one a purified modernism remains the solution, as against two distinct modes of postmodernism that are viewed as reactionary and/or meretricious. For the other, modernism itself is seen to be hopelessly enmeshed in a technocratic consumerism, and the only hope is seen to lie in a return to a purified historicism. In such circumstances, it is hardly surprising that the most effective polemicist of postmodernism—Robert Stern—should have been as contemptuous of Frampton's puritanism as he was indifferent to Krier's doctrinaire historicism.[65]

While I believe that a broad political realignment of architectural positions is a likely result of the ongoing reconsideration of Enlightenment rationality, the complex pattern of stylistic and political forces I have just outlined makes the form any such realignment will take unclear. Even within the postmodernist camp, for example, stylistic allegiances might suggest the emergence of a new axis between, say, Leon Krier and Quinlan Terry. But this would constitute a surprising alignment of a somewhat puritanical leftist historicism with a highly idiosyncratic rightist one. Moralist commitments to reform and opposition to consumerism might suggest an axis between Krier and Frampton, but this would require an improbable reconciliation of opposite stylistic preferences vis-à-vis modernism and historicism. Some might simply anticipate a resurgence of a generalized, neoconservative postmodernism.

But this also seems unlikely. Just as the traditionalist and populist wings of neoconservative political thought find themselves in a continuing uneasy alliance, so too the historicist and consumerist branches of architectural postmodernism find their differences too great to conceal, even for the sake of a broad political victory within the culture of architecture. Considered as a broad-based social phenomenon, neoconservatism wishes to be politically traditionalist yet economically and technologically modern. Thus, postmodernist architecture's wariness of technological expression compounds an ambiguity central to the politics of neoconservatism itself. In this regard, it is interesting to note how modern British neoconservatism has found itself attached at one and the same time to two alternative modes of symbolic architectural expression. On the one hand, architecture such as that of Quinlan Terry might have been taken up as an appropriate vehicle for the expression of traditional values. On the other hand, considerable appeal has also attached to the architecture of Norman Foster and Richard Rogers, seen to offer indisputably powerful images of cutting-edge technological modernity.[66] In this sense, neoconservatism appears to be proving, in cultural terms, to be as problematically situated within the contradictory web of modernism as were earlier political movements.

Taking the overall theme of this text one step further, I should like to propound a hypothesis respecting some of the ways in which the ongoing reconsideration of Enlightenment rationality, which is likely to redefine the politics of our time, might also redefine our view of the operative relationship between politics and architecture. The hypothesis takes as its point of departure the broad theoretical positions of three of the figures discussed here whose names and ideas have not customarily been very closely linked: Colin Rowe, John Turner, and Bernard Huet. In the broad historical perspective deriving from the work of Adorno, Arendt, and their contemporaries, together with certain of the more recent cultural critiques associated with poststructuralism, I believe it will be possible to formulate a hypothesis in respect to a possible future for architecture within which certain key ideas of these three are provocatively complementary.[67]

To begin with the case of Rowe, the most explicit summing up of his own—usually quite elliptical—view of the cultural politics of modern architecture occurred in his introduction to the book *Five Architects* of 1972. To give the full flavor of Rowe's position, I quote in extenso:

> In post World War I Europe, the combined promise and threat of "Architecture or Revolution" could seem to many important innovators to be a very real one; but, in the United States, the presumption that only architecture could turn a "bad" revolution into a "good" one, that only Wagnerian recourse to "total" design could avert social catastrophe, this could never seem to be very highly plausible. For in the United States, the revolution was assumed to have already occurred—in 1776, and it was further assumed to have initiated a social order which was not to be superseded by subsequent developments. In other words, with the revolutionary theme divested by circumstances of both its catastrophic and futurist implications, with this theme rendering retrospective, legalistic and even nationalist, an indigenous modern architecture in America deployed connotations quite distinct from its European counterparts. Its tacit assumptions were infinitely less grand. . . .

> But, if the Architecture-Revolution confrontation (whatever value is attached to either of its components) is one of the more obviously unexplored ingredients of modern architecture's folklore, and if any attempt to explore it would, almost certainly, meet with the most strenuous disavowal of its significance, and if it might be possible to demonstrate the action or the inaction of this fantasy, for present

purposes it should be enough simply to reiterate that the revolutionary theme was never a very prominent component of American speculation about building. European modern architecture, even when it operated within the cracks and crannies of the capitalist system, existed within an ultimately socialist ambience: American modern architecture did not. And it was thus, and either by inadvertence or design, that when in the Nineteen-Thirties, European modern architecture came to infiltrate the United States, it was introduced as simply a new approach to building and not much more. That is, it was introduced largely purged of its ideological or societal content; and it became available, not as an evident manifestation (or cause) of socialism in some form or other, but rather as a *décor de la vie* for Greenwich, Connecticut or as a suitable veneer for the corporate activities of enlightened capitalism. The ironies of a European revolution which, perhaps, tragically failed to make it, do not comprise the most gratifying of spectacles. When these are compounded with the further ironies of trans-Atlantic architectural interchange and their physical results, in America, Europe and elsewhere, we find ourselves confronted with an evidence—an adulteration of meaning, principle and form which is far from easy to neglect. The impeccably good intentions of modern architecture, its genuine ideals of social service, above all the poetry with which, so often, it has invested random twentieth century happening may all conspire to inhibit doubts as to its present condition, to encourage a suppression of the obvious; but, conspire as they may, and however reluctantly we recognize it, the product of modern architecture compared with its performance, the gap between what was anticipated and what has been delivered, still establishes the base line for any responsible contemporary production.[68]

Confronting the work of the architects to which his text served as introduction, Rowe insisted on what he saw as the only possible means of approaching it:

> We are here, once more, in the area where the physique and the morale of modern architecture, its flesh and its word, are again, not coincident; and it is when we recognize that neither morale nor physique, neither word nor flesh, was ever consistent with each other, that we might reasonably approach the architects whose work is here presented.[69]

And this led him to put a question that was, for him, surprisingly poignant in tone:

> Under the circumstances, what to do? If we believe that modern architecture did establish one of the great hopes of the world—always, in detail, ridiculous, but never, in toto, to be rejected—then do we adhere to physique—flesh or to morale—word?[70]

For Rowe's countryman John Turner, the answer must surely, in the first instance, have seemed obvious. For he didn't share Rowe's preoccupation with the "plastic and spatial inventions of Cubism" nor has he yet appeared ready to concede that the European revolution "failed to make it." Indeed, his own loyalties to the political traditions of anarchism continued to nourish his convictions as to the possibilities for architects to ameliorate the human condition. Nevertheless, the sheer logic of his own analysis of the failures of the applied social programs of modernism, combined with his growing interest in the decentralist and anti-Enlightenment projects of Ivan Illich, and of such colleagues of his as Paolo Freire, in Central and South America, drew him ever closer to nonprofessional concepts of local control and autonomy, and farther and farther away from the assumed reformist benevolence of mainstream modernism.[71] In fact, in the end I believe it can be said that Rowe's ironic and elegiac loyalty to what he called the "physique" of modernism, and Turner's slow, even reluctant abandonment of its morale," make the two of them unexpected allies, in the wake of all our disillusionment with the legacy of Enlightenment rationality.

Now, Bernard Huet. As I have already intimated, it might well be asked what possible relationship his ideas might have to an evolution away from Enlightenment rationality, such as is intimated in the juxtaposition of Rowe and Turner. Yet the evolution of Huet's thinking in recent years also reveals evidence of a profound reassessment of apparent first principles. In his case, the reassessment has had centrally to do with his views of contemporary European architectural education. From very early on, he had been led to doubt the promise of "modernism" as conventionally understood. In an interview with Maurice Culot in 1980, he acknowledged how profoundly conservative his ideas of a desirable social evolution for architecture had become: "Architecture and the city both situate themselves inside a body of conventions, and these conventions undergo a very slow evolution."[72] Two years before, he had written a progress report on the developments in architectural education in France between 1968 and 1978. It was not a very positive assessment.

> The reform of '68 which proclaimed itself "democratic," was made by an elite of opponents who, without calculation, and with the best political intentions, put in place a new elitist pedagogy. No one recognized very quickly the pernicious effects

of certain words which were more liberal than the liberators. To organize an entire system of teaching on notions of free choice and of self-discipline without giving students the means with which to make choices and the parameters of the discipline, was to foster among those who were culturally deprived a confusion which the teachers hastened to sanction. To base such a pedagogical project on an expression of differences, and on creativity, condemned to a sterile anguish and eventually to traumatizing blockages those who did not feel themselves touched by the grace of inspiration, or who lacked insufficient intellectual agility to capture the subtle breezes of fashionable rhetoric. To renounce the teaching of precise knowledge, and at the same time to be confident it had been learned, was to degrade the status of the diploma, and was to leave young architects to the so-called "natural selection" of familial and economic relations.[73]

Huet then outlined a view of the contemporary state of architecture circa 1978, which he saw as a context for his new proposals for architectural education.

> All the progressive currents of thought that preceded and followed 1968, notwithstanding their divergences, were at least in accord on one point: to declare the end of utopias, and the death of avant-gardes. . . . No one understood then that the death of avant-gardes did not entail that of architecture, but rather the *relative disappearance* of a form of architecture: that of the elite—which would probably never cease to exist in the sense that, in the hands of a minority, it plays an important role in the dynamic of the transformation of architectural language. It would therefore be absurd to deny this fact, but it is infinitely more important to recognize the change of character which has come to pass in architecture without architects having noticed.

> One is in effect witnessing a phenomenon of the "massification" of architecture in our societies, which it is important not to assimilate—as per certain simplistic theories—into the mass production of built forms by industry.

> To speak of the "massification" of architecture is, of course, to acknowledge a complex mutation of a quantitative kind, whose resultant qualitative effects are not yet entirely visible. "Quantity" should not be reduced to the simple mass produced, or to a simple transformation of the conditions of production. Which means that today, architecture encompasses all sectors of built production (even if architects themselves play a minor role in that production). It also means that the power of architecture has now totally eluded those who dwell in it, and is monopolized by specialists (not all of whom are architects). Finally it means that architecture has become an object of mass consumption, even to the derisory image given by a house in a catalogue.

> Architectural "quality" is no longer good or bad, it *is* henceforth simply a market term. As for the architecture of the elite, it has found its own new market, that of art galleries.[74]

This state of affairs constituting, on Huet's view, the contemporary context of architectural praxis, he then turned to a consideration of the formulation of measures that might be thought appropriate to deal with it. As one might imagine, he had no recommendations to make regarding what he had named "elite architecture." But he did express deep concern respecting what he saw as a quite urgent question: "the practical incapacity to resolve three kinds of problems posed by 'mass architecture': the urban question, mastery of construction techniques, and finally, the communication of architecture with its public."[75] And this led him in turn to consideration of what he saw as the currently urgent needs of architectural education. For a start, he stated his opinion that the institutions of such education that had been created in France in the wake of the 1968 events were inadequate to the challenge:

> Whatever their particular nuances, they still subscribe to the logic of an "elite architecture." Their teaching perpetuates avant-garde nostalgias and struggles vainly to bridge the gap which has opened up between architecture and its public. It is the general concept of the system which is in question, and the courageous efforts of some teachers who are aware of the problem cannot effectively change the situation.

> Today, whether one likes it or not, the teaching of architecture must change in order to survive; it must become mass education, in other words education which, in its content and in its pedagogy, reflects the profound and irreversible mutation which architecture has now sustained.[76]

Thus Huet came to propose a set of objectives for mass architectural education that would parallel his conservative ideas of architecture and the city.

Is it possible to attempt a synthesis of the ideas of the three figures just discussed? I think so. Here is an idea of a broad yet I think intellectually coherent territory of architecture for our time, based on the ideas of all three. It is a territory within which architecture will in large part undoubtedly constitute a social institution, just as both Turner and Huet would clearly see it do. And despite his evidently aristocratic and anarchist leanings, I do not even see Rowe opposing it.

Indeed, it is my view that until such time as it does once again do so, architecture will continue to forfeit any possibility of playing the kind of central cultural role it has had within innumerable preindustrial societies. Within the social and political perspectives deriving from ongoing postmodern cultural discourse, it is clear that the "territory" in question will not be a homogeneous one. In fact, the heterogeneity so highly valued by that discourse is likely to make it one that manifests considerable discontinuity. Yet it seems to me that even an explicit acknowledgment of such discontinuity would mark the commencement of the possible mapping of the new territory in question. For my own part, I imagine it as one comprising, for a start, a large area characterized, whether we like it or not, by just that phenomenon of social "massification" so perceptively delineated by Huet. There, especially, will the social institution of architecture be centrally reconstituted. But, heterogeneity being what it is, this does not mean that there will not also be important border areas, within some of which self-declared elites will continue to pursue their interests, and will also continue, in Huet's words, to "play an important role in the dynamic of the transformation of architectural language." In an opposite and socially far more extensive border area, a vast and diverse array of grass roots, para-architectural, and self-help initiatives will also unfold. Just as they have already done in the modern world, within such recognizable realms as cuisine, clothing, and popular music, these initiatives will also contribute to the ongoing transformation of language for what we may, for want of a better term, call the architectural mainstream.

In the event that some such heterogeneous territory were to come to be, one would not suppose that the "alienation" of men and women from "the world" and the corresponding degradation of "the things" that comprise it, which have been with us since the beginning of the European Enlightenment, would altogether vanish. From our present historical vantage point, such a prospect seems remote. Still, far short of such a utopian prospect, we might see the lesser but nevertheless deeply satisfying possibility of formulating an affirmative answer to an eloquent and haunting question posed by Colin Rowe in 1972. It is the question with which he chose to

conclude his quite uncharacteristically poignant text, the introduction to
Five Architects:

> Can an architecture which professes an objective of continuous experiment ever
> become congruous with the ideal of an architecture which is to be popular, intelli-
> gible, and profound?[77]

"The Space of Appearance"

> Action and speech create a space between the participants which can find its proper location almost any time and anywhere. It is the space of appearance in the widest sense of the word, namely, the space where I appear to others as others appear to me, where men exist not merely like other living or inanimate things but make their appearance explicitly.[1]

The passage from Hannah Arendt that has given this book its title also sets the stage for a particular consideration of the meaning of the term "public," as it has been applied to various kinds of urban spaces during architecture's evolution in the twentieth century. For Arendt, the term "public" signifies two closely related but not identical phenomena:

> It means, first, that everything that appears in public can be seen and heard by everybody and has the widest possible publicity. For us, appearance—something that is being seen and heard by others as well as by ourselves—constitutes reality. . . . Second, the term "public" signifies the world itself, in so far as it is common to all of us and distinguished from our privately owned place in it. This world, however, is not identical with the earth or with nature, as the limited space for the movement of men and the general condition of organic life. It is related, rather, to the human artifact, the fabrication of human hands, as well as to affairs which go on among those who inhabit the man-made world together. To live together in the world means essentially that a world of things is located between those who have it in common, as a table is located between those who sit around it; the world, like every in-between, relates and separates men at the same time.[2]

Moreover, the fact that the world "relates and separates men at the same time" is, for Arendt, one of the profound characteristics of the phenomenon of "plurality, the basic condition of . . . action." In my introduction, I have already cited her conviction that

> if men were not equal, they could neither understand each other and those who came before them nor plan for the future and foresee the needs of those who will come after them. If men were not distinct, each human being distinguished from any other who is, was, or will ever be, they would need neither speech nor action to make themselves understood.[3]

Some years after Arendt had formulated her almost transcendent conception of the public, Richard Sennett put forward a specific historical description of the relationship of the "public" and the "private," as it had evolved in western European society over the past four centuries:

> The first recorded uses of the word "public" in English identify the "public" with the common good in society. . . . By the end of the 17th century, the opposition of "public" and "private" was shaded more like the way the terms are now used. "Public" meant open to the scrutiny of anyone, whereas "private" meant a shel-

tered region of life defined by one's family and friends. . . . To go "out in publick" (Swift) is a phrase based on society conceived in terms of this geography. The older senses are not entirely lost today in English, but this 18th century usage sets up the modern terms of reference.

The meanings accorded "le public" in French show something similar. Renaissance use of the word was largely in terms of the common good and the body politic; gradually "le public" became also a special region of sociability. The theatrical public was referred to in the time of Louis XIV by the catch-phrase "la cour et la ville," the court and the city. . . .

The sense of who "the public" were, and where one was when one was out "in public," became enlarged in the early 18th century in both Paris and London. Bourgeois people became less concerned to cover up their social origins; there were many more of them; the cities they inhabited were becoming a world in which widely diverse groups in society were coming into contact. By the time the word "public" had taken on its modern meaning, therefore, it meant not only a region of social life located apart from the realm of family and close friends, but also that this public realm of acquaintances and strangers included a relatively wide diversity of people.[4]

Sennett's conception of "the public" led him to consider definitions of "a city":

The simplest is that a city is a human settlement in which strangers are likely to meet. For this definition to hold true, the settlement has to have a large, heterogeneous population; the population has to be packed together rather densely; market exchanges among the population must make this dense, diverse mass interact.[5]

Now Sennett's conceptions of the public and of the city remind us of a somewhat analogous view of social life in cities from a period early in our own century. Insofar as the group of persons making up Sennett's public comprises strangers, it emphasizes "heterogeneity" and "anonymity" more explicitly than Arendt's does. And such heterogeneity and anonymity are also the hallmarks of the conception of the "city" put forward just after the turn of the century by the American sociologist Robert Park. While it is analogous to Sennett's, Park's conception possesses a somewhat starker social coloration. As Morton and Lucia White described it, Park

had spent his early years in a small town, but like so many of his generation, he was personally attracted to the city as a social milieu where as he put it—"everyone is more or less on his own." In more theoretical terms he explained the attraction of the metropolis for masses of people as partly due to the fact that there they found, more than in a small community, the moral climate to stimulate their innate qualities and bring them to full expression. The big city uniquely rewarded eccentricity, according to Park: even the criminal, the defective, and the genius found more opportunities to develop their dispositions in a great city than in a small town. Among other enticements of the city, as compared with small town and country, Park noted the heightened element of change; and he speculated further that the lure of great cities arises perhaps from stimulation which directly affects the reflexes, "like the attraction of the flame for the moth."[6]

Park's sense of everyone being "on his own," and of the "heightened element of chance," are in their turn highly suggestive of the conception of modern urban life that was formulated a few years later by Walter Benjamin. Benjamin's conception was quintessentially represented in the figure of the *flâneur* he saw as characteristic of Baudelaire's Paris.[7] A more distanced and ironic figure than the rural migrant to the big city characterized by Park, the *flâneur* was defined in the first instance by his "gaze," which Benjamin saw as that of "alienated man."

> The *flâneur* still stood at the margins, of the great city as of the bourgeois class. Neither of them had yet overwhelmed him. In neither of them was he at home. He sought his asylum in the crowd.[8]

Now the intellectual positions cited thus far encompass a rather broad range of characterizations of the public and of "appearance" within it. To start with, there is Arendt's deeply engaged and highly affirmative conception of "action," one that constitutes an almost purely phenomenological mode of political praxis. In distinction to her "active" one, the contemplative conception represented by Benjamin's *flâneur* is one of disengaged alienation. Yet both Arendt's and Benjamin's conceptions, like those of Sennett and Park, rest on a fundamental commitment to the key social phenomena of heterogeneity and anonymity. Arendt's commitment is given its unique form of expression in her poignant juxtaposition of men's "equality" and "distinctiveness" as the twin characteristics of the "plurality" that was for her the "basic condition of action." Sennett and Park explicitly emphasize social diversity and anonymity as basic characteristics of urbanity. As for Benjamin, he goes so far as to characterize the anonymity of "the crowd" as "asylum."

Notwithstanding their varied emphases, then, we may see this constellation of positions as forming a relatively unified intellectual whole. To demonstrate this conclusively, one need only compare these positions with the quite different and problematic conceptions of "intentional" and "unintentional community" that were discussed in chapter six. The reader will recall the quite striking antipathy the latter shared to any social idea of heterogeneity—or to the presence of strangers, which is an unavoidable concomitant of anonymity. Indeed, throughout the nineteenth and twentieth centuries, organicist conceptions of community have attempted to maximize the social homogeneity of community, either by excluding or escaping from those who do not conform, or by deliberately instituting programs of homogenization. What is more, it is precisely because of organicism's wariness of strangers, and of urban anonymity, that its devotees have so consistently, for almost a century now, been among the bitterest critics of the modern metropolis.

In dramatic contrast, the more urbane thinkers I have joined together above have all decisively acknowledged the essential characteristics of the public, however diverse their respective sensibilities. Taken as a group, they yield a possible view of the modern city whose full implications for contemporary architecture and urbanism are as yet far from realized, even at this late date. Indeed, it is even possible to contend that their views have formed an implicit backdrop to a whole series of discussions of urban space that have proceeded in architectural circles since the Second World War, and which remain unresolved.

Implicit, I say, since the explicit terms of the discussion have varied somewhat from the conceptual characterization of "the public" set out above. "Plurality" and "heterogeneity" do in fact turn up under their own names, even if "anonymity" rarely does. What is more, all three of these turn up, powerfully if indirectly, under the quintessentially modern rubric of "mobility." Then there is the matter of "history"—or to be more precise, the status that ought to be ascribed to the form of the "historical European city." Among all the urbanist debates of our century, this has surely been the bitterest recent one. And if it has sometimes been supposed that the status of the "historical city" has had nothing necessarily to do with any modern idea of the public, such a supposition has proceeded only in sad

why "organicism" is incompatible w/ heterogeneity

ignorance of the convictions of Arendt cited above: that, above all, the "public" signifies "the world itself"; and that "the world" is related to "the human artifact, the fabrication of human hands, as well as to affairs which go on among those . . . who have it in common." One way and another then, it is my view that "plurality," "mobility," and "history" have been hallmarks of debate about architecture and urbanism in Europe and North America since the end of the World War II.

Broadly speaking, it may be said that the debates in question have occurred in three stages, and that each of those stages has taken the form of an argument between an older and a younger generation. To begin with, we may note how, in the years immediately following the cessation of hostilities in Europe, the architects of CIAM had an unprecedented opportunity to implement the urban ideas they had been developing since the 1920s. These ideas were newly welcome to governments seeking to rebuild their cities; between the end of World War II and the middle of the 1950s, city after European city developed proposals for reconstruction following the principles of CIAM.[9] Thus, a surprisingly simple intellectual schema of urbanism came to have a profound effect on postwar urban Europe. The principles developed in the 1930s had entailed the clear-cut segregation, within the overall urban fabric, of what had been designated the four basic urban functions: work, living, recreation, and circulation. Thus postwar new towns were laid out in forms embodying such sharply demarcated land uses, and existing cities were subjected to quite radical urban surgery, intended to bring them also, to the maximum extent feasible, into line with the new planning principles. (The reader will recall Martin Pawley's acerbic slogan cited in chapter seven: "Bombers are a plan's best friend.") It is of particular significance to note how, as part of this process, circulation attained, for the first time in the history of city planning in Europe, a decisive land use status of its own. It was as a corollary of this pivotal event that circulation became dissociated from the historic urban form of the street, that "landscaped open space" acquired such a central new urban importance, and that a much more dispersed urban fabric than had previously been advocated came to be characteristic of urban reconstruction in Europe during this period. In fact, the momen-

8.1   A drawing of the Piazza San Marco by Saul Steinberg, used on the flyleaf of the 1952 publication of the proceedings of the 8th CIAM conference, focused on the subject "The Heart of the City."

tum of CIAM urbanism was so powerful that it continued largely unchallenged right up until the mid-1960s.

While the principles that had been developed by the members of CIAM prior to World War II formed the point of departure for almost all postwar developments, from a very early period limited modifications of the basic ideas were made. The four basic functional postulates of urbanism, as they had been defined in the 1933 Athens Charter, were consciously expanded at CIAM conferences after the war. In 1949, at Bergamo, the concept of the "historic center" was put forward for new consideration. In 1951, at Hoddesdon, the theme was the "urban core" more generally. Here, for the first time, the group devoted itself to a consideration of the phenomenon of the core, whether of a new town, such as St. Dié in France or Stevenage in England, or of an existing city, such as Coventry or Basel. By 1951, the views of the CIAM group had moderated to the point that they were even prepared to qualify the imperatives of the old functional grid, conceding that a mixture of functional activities was appropriate to this particular part of the urban territory. Indeed, in his introductory comments to the 1951 meeting, José Luis Sert, then president of the organization, went so far as to cite a now familiar passage from Ortega y Gasset's topical book of the period, *The Revolt of the Masses:*

> The "urbs" or the "polis" starts by being an empty space, the "forum," the "agora," and all the rest are just means of fixing that empty space, of limiting its outlines. The "polis" is not primarily a collection of habitable dwellings, but a meeting place for citizens, a space set apart for public functions.[10]

Despite this evidence of new interest in public space, CIAM did not then come seriously to grips with the issues of the historic fabric of existing urban cores, or with new issues arising out of the ever-growing phenomenon of mobility. Less still did it manage to come to grips with the more elusive social conception of plurality—this, of course, being one that had played no role at all in the original formulations of CIAM. Proposals from the 1951 meeting illustrate how high-handed the group remained in regard to such questions. A project for New Haven prepared by a group of students at Yale University, for example, deferred to the historical fabric only in retaining the three churches on the green, as well as a series of houses—eighteenth-century ones exclusively—facing it.[11] Everything else on two entire sides was to be removed. What is more, the proposed new construction actually penetrated into the green from one edge, eroding the clarity of its original nine-square geometry. Indeed, the whole emphasis of the New Haven proposal was on the segregation of pedestrian and vehicular traffic, with all vehicles removed from the central nine squares and diverted to a peripheral ring road.

In Europe, this growing inclination to deal with the expanding use of the automobile by segregation was received readily enough; there, of course, the historic cores of cities had been developed before the automobile's invention. But the fifties generation of CIAM applied it as well to the proposals for such cores as those of new towns throughout Europe, and even (the case cited above) in North America, where resistance to the idea remained quite strong. Here, pre-automobile urban cores were less common, the postwar increase in the use of the automobile had been most rapid, and the suburban model of urban development outstripped the abilities of European-oriented planners and architects to contain it.

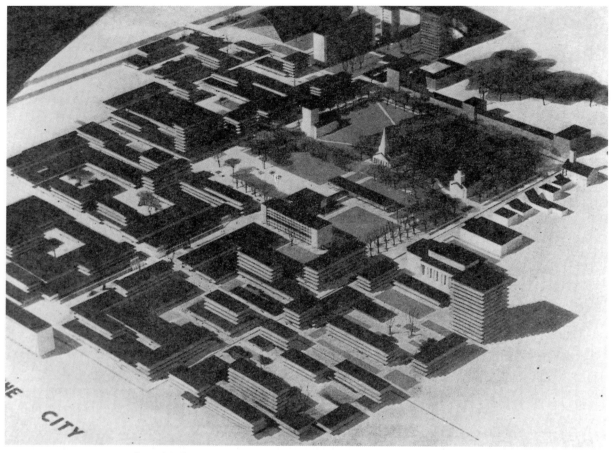

8.2   A view of a model of a student project for the redevelopment of downtown New Haven, Connecticut, included as one of the exemplars of appropriate new planning in the proceedings of the 8th CIAM conference.

In the early 1950s, the proponents of CIAM were still only tentatively beginning to face the challenges entailed by the implementation of the 1930s generation's thinking. Younger observers at CIAM conferences from 1951 onward grew increasingly restive. They not only saw a failure to live up to the origin vision of the "Radiant City" as it had been depicted in the 1930s by Le Corbusier; they also wanted to put new issues on the agenda for discussion. In 1955, for example, Peter and Alison Smithson, who were members of the younger generation critical of CIAM, published a text in the magazine *Architectural Design* in which they deplored the "mechanical" limitations of the modern movement as it had developed in the

1930s. By the mid-1950s such a mechanical approach no longer seemed adequate. Even the amendments to the original CIAM grid seemed to the young to be less than the situation required. According to Reyner Banham, "the young were for root-and-branch rejection of all the Athenian categories, which they frequently damned as 'diagrammatic.'"[12] By 1956, the cumulative impact of a series of attacks on the ideas and personalities of the older generation finally took its toll. As even Le Corbusier had by then acknowledged the force of the progressive revolt of the young, the leading figures of CIAM decided simply to disband the entire organization.

Following this dramatic turn of events, the members of the younger group of critics known as Team 10—found themselves in a position to promote their revisionist ideas with new effectiveness. In 1956, the Smithsons summed up their view of their professional responsibilities:

> We are still functionalists and we still accept the responsibility for the community as a whole, but today the word functional does not merely mean mechanical as it did thirty years ago. Our functionalism means accepting the realities of the situation, with all their contradictions and confusions and trying to do something with them.[13]

With these references to "realities" that entail "contradictions" and "confusions" as part of the urban situation, we see an acknowledgment of new circumstances that had been virtually imperceptible to the assured protagonists of CIAM only a few years previously. And while such acknowledgments do not quite constitute a full-fledged recognition of the phenomena of pluralism or of heterogeneity, these tentative observations are nevertheless among the early indicators of a new appreciation of the possible impact of such phenomena on the design of the contemporary city. Indeed, the evolution of the Smithsons' ideas in this regard could be traced back to the 1953 exhibition they had organized with the photographer Nigel Henderson and the sculptor Eduardo Paolozzi, entitled a "Parallel of Art and Life." Paolozzi's and Henderson's works were exhibited in a fashion that paid homage to the so-called anti-art of such painters as Jackson Pollock in the United States and Jean Dubuffet in France. Indeed, the terms *art brut* and *art autre* were being employed at the time to characterize these efforts to escape the orthodoxy of modernism, declaring a dis-

8.3 A view of the installation of the 1953 ICA exhibition "A Parallel of Art and Life," in London. (Photograph by permission, from David Robbins, *The Independent Group,* MIT Press.)

tinctive new curiosity about such ephemera of modern life as advertising, American consumer products, and comic books, not to mention that perhaps more consequential one that focused on the internal dynamics of the psyche.[14]

It is significant to note here, I think, how all these revisionist activities were proceeding in a larger cultural context marked by the growing anger of "angry young men" in Britain, and by the newly sophisticated modes of contemporary "alienation" that were coming to be associated with the new philosophical movement of existentialism, as it was emerging during those same years in France. Clearly, in circumstances involving such newly skeptical cultural praxes, the simple and normative social affirmations of CIAM orthodoxy no longer seemed adequate.

In their initial efforts to respond to such new influences yet sustain the heroic affirmation of modernism at the same time, the Smithsons began to develop a new terminology: "We have to create an architecture and a town planning which—through built form—can make meaningful the change, the growth, the flow, the 'vitality' of the community."[15] With this talk of "change" and "growth," the Smithsons, like their Continental colleagues Candilis, Josic, and Woods, introduced concepts into the discourse of modern urbanism that eventually became highly influential. Indeed, such concepts were fundamental to the revisionist architectural movements that came to be known as the "new brutalism" and "metabolism."

But if evidence of a new interest in plurality and heterogeneity can be seen in these important preoccupations of the fifties, an interest in mobility is more visible still. In the same text, the Smithsons specified the nature of the new urban propositions they were developing:

> The general idea . . . is the concept of the Cluster. The Cluster,—a close-knit, complicated, often-moving aggregation, but an aggregation with a distinct structure. This is perhaps as close as one can get to a description of the new ideal in architecture and planning. . . .
>
> . . . It is traditionally the architect's job to create the signs or images which represent the functions, aspirations and beliefs of the community, and create them in such a way that they add up to a comprehensible whole. The cluster concept provides us with a way of creating new images, using the techniques for example of road and communication engineering. Many solutions have been put forward to deal with the problem of traffic—motorways joining population centres, urban motorways within communities, peripheral controlled parking round the old centre, out-of-town shopping centres, off-motorway factories and residential dormitories; solutions which either disperse the energies of communities or integrate them in an entirely new way.[16]

Here the issue of mobility came strikingly to the fore. For the Smithsons themselves, these ideas crystallized in their famous entry to the 1958 competition for a new plan for the rebuilding of Berlin, the so-called Hauptstadt proposal, which accepted as givens both the existing road network

8.4   Peter and Alison Smithson's Hauptstadt competition proposal for Berlin, from 1957.

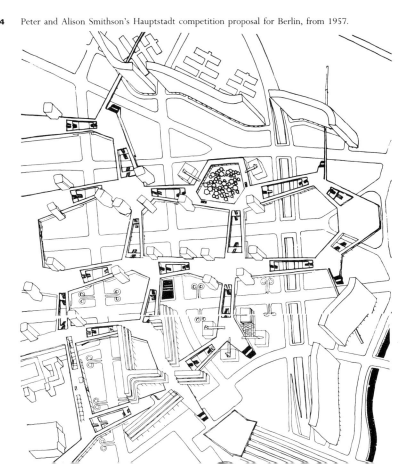

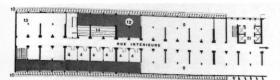

Plan d'aménagement des services communs (niveau 8)

  4 Boutiques   12 Vide
  9 Studios ou ateliers   13 Salon de lavage
10 Les lamelles brise-soleil 14 Brise-vue
11 Ascenseurs

Plan d'aménagement des services communs (niveau 7)

  1 Escalier de secours   6 Magasin d'alimentation
  2 Hall d'entrée   7 Lavabos
  3 Club des locataires, salons de lec-   8 Promenade publique
     ture, de musique et projections   9 Studios ou ateliers
  4 Boutiques   10 Les lamelles brise-soleil
  5 Alimentation (dépôt)   11 Ascenseurs

Le hall. Combinaison de la lumière artificielle et naturelle

8.5   The concept of the *rue intérieure,* as implemented in the *unité d'habitation* in Marseilles, completed in 1952; explained by Le Corbusier in volume 5 of the *Oeuvre complète.*

and a proposed new expressway network intended to create the kind of ring road around the core described in the text cited above. What was so noteworthy about the project was that it laid over both the existing and proposed road networks an entirely new, multilaterally continuous, upper-level walkway system, a system, moreover, that assumed a rather free-form geometry, departing from the rigid CIAM geometries the Team 10 members had long deplored. And this was still not the end of the new image of mobility. As Reyner Banham noted:

> the "image" of "Hauptstadt Berlin" was not only an irregular network of upper pedestrian walks as seen on plan; . . . it was also the means of vertical circulation that connected the old, ground-level grid with the new one above it. This was to be an escalator city, in which vertical transportation was to be almost more the norm than horizontal movement. This was both the image of the new elements, and the image of the old that had been transformed, for the urban meaning of the streets at ground level would clearly be quite different now that the main circulation of the city had moved up in the air.[17]

note how similar this "elevator" vertical city is related to Rem Koolhaas' Delerious NYC ideas.

Closely related to the concept of the cluster, for the Team 10 group, was the concept of the street. Not the street of historic European urban form, to be sure. Revisionist as they were, the members of Team 10 still held fast to the critique of the historic form of the street that had so forcefully been made by Le Corbusier, some two decades before, in his influential book *The Radiant City*. In a now notorious section of his 1933 polemic, Le Corbusier had declared the "death of the street," arguing instead for the most generalized relationship of circulation to urban fabric, which became a basic tenet of CIAM orthodoxy. Still, Le Corbusier himself, in his *unité d'habitation* at Marseilles (one of the early icons of brutalism), had put forward the idea of a new sort of street, a *rue intérieure,* which was intended to play a role as a key "social condenser" within the large ensemble of the building as a whole. In their 1952 competition entry for the Golden Lane Housing project in London, the Smithsons took Le Corbusier's *rue intérieure* and moved it to the building edge, where, in the form of the "street deck," it established a precedent that profoundly influenced housing projects around the world.[18]

When the street deck was linked to the cluster, there resulted the further new urban idea of "grain." This concept is probably best represented in two projects for universities in Germany by the Smithsons' colleagues in Team 10, Candilis, Josic and Woods. These projects are the competition entries for Bochum University from 1962 and Berlin Free University from 1964. In both of these cases, a three-dimensional urban grid was created, which allowed for a considerable degree of growth and change within the interstices of the system.[19]

Team 10's concept of grain was a very powerful one. Perhaps the most telling evidence is its influence on a late design by the first-generation modernist who, of all his contemporaries, had had far and away the greatest influence on Team 10 itself: Le Corbusier. In a provocative project for a new hospital in Venice from 1964–1965 that marked a dramatic change of design direction, Le Corbusier set out a proposal that married a historic idea of local neighborhoods (Venetian parishes) to the new urban idea of grain. The resulting planform was a complex, syncopated matrix in two

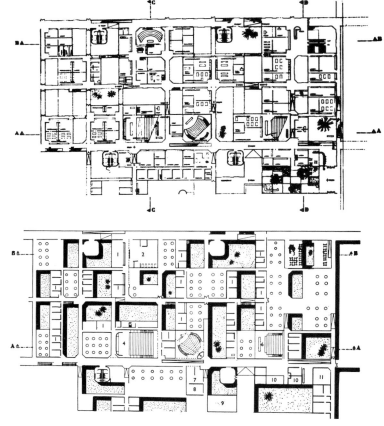

8.6   Plans of the winning competition entry for the proposed new Free University of Berlin, by Candilis, Josic and Woods, from 1964.

8.7   A photograph of the model of Le Corbusier's 1965 project for a new hospital for Venice, showing the influence of the ideas about the design of cities, and of major urban institutions, that had recently been promulgated by the younger generation of architects in Team 10, with whom Le Corbusier was then in close contact.

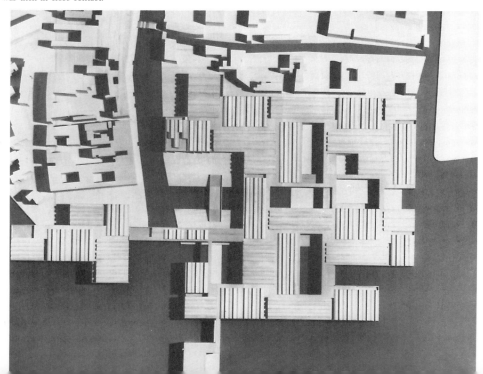

8.8   A photograph of the main open space in the Dogon community of Ogol, in the central Sahara, chosen by Aldo van Eyck to illustrate his essay in the 1969 anthology *Meaning in Architecture*. (Photograph by permission, Aldo van Eyck.)

dimensions, representing a modern and a historic urban idea at the same time.[20] Like the slightly earlier projects of the Smithsons and of Candilis, Josic and Woods, Le Corbusier's Venice Hospital was a bellwether. The cluster, the street, and grain all pointed in the direction of growing concern for mobility and plurality, in the evolving ideas of modernity within western European society as a whole.

At the same time that the part of Team 10 represented by the Smithsons and by Candilis, Josic and Woods was pursuing this particular line of investigation, another member of the Team had already formulated a revisionism of his own, this one in respect to history and to a poetic dimension of modernity that seemed to have been long lost sight of. Where the Smithsons and their European colleagues looked forward to emerging social issues of heterogeneity and mobility, Aldo van Eyck in Holland looked instead to the artifacts of primitive societies, and to the metaphors that had so consistently typified literary—as opposed to architectural—modernism, for new sources of inspiration.[21]

In this regard, it is not surprising that a radically revisionist essay on urbanism written in those years by Joseph Rykwert, "The Idea of a Town," first appeared in 1963 in a special issue of the magazine *Dutch Forum,* edited by van Eyck.[22] Rykwert did not just propose a modification of the instrumentalist urbanism of CIAM, such as was characteristic of the mainstream evolution of Team 10. Rather, he proposed an entirely different point of departure for intellectual discourse on urban form, one rooted in historical and anthropological myths of origin. Predictably, perhaps, Rykwert's provocative hypothesis had no great immediate influence on the evolving thinking about modern urbanism; it would have to await the onset of the broader reconsideration of Enlightment rationality in architecture, discussed in chapter five. For the mainstream of Team 10, as of the mid-1960s, such far-reaching historical reconsideration had not yet become a critical issue.

Even the more localized and more immediate issue of the status of the existing fabric of the historical cities of Europe was not yet a subject of fundamental concern, despite the tension it aroused as early as a 1959 meeting of the group at Otterlo. A telling dispute broke out on that occasion between Peter Smithson and the Italian architect Ernesto Rogers over projects being presented by each to the conference.[23]

The Smithsons presented part of the work of their London Roads Study, a project that took as given a proposal to cut a series of motorways through the fabric of inner London, in connection with which the Smithsons were proposing precise road alignments as well as the construction of new buildings in adjacent zones. Peter Smithson described the relationship of these buildings to the proposed new motorway system:

> When you examine an enlargement of such an area and look at what you have done to it, in terms of the new scale, it becomes obvious that if you have to rebuild or adjust because of the motor-way situation then you have to start thinking of a new sort of building. . . . Like the road pattern, the pattern of the new thing is a combination of ways that present themselves, because of dereliction and so on, and a general theory. The general theory is to connect where you have a take-off. You also have the bus stop of the rapid-transit system and these are the points of connection for the pedestrian system and connect to the old main routes, that is Regent Street, Leicester Square, Oxford Street, and Plymouth Street, and so on, the main places in London.

This is a solution which applies to this area which is Soho. But it extends into the whole shopping area which has still a long life and continuing validity, so there is no reason to destroy it. The life has to continue but the buildings have to change. We only keep the things which are urbanistically and constructionally valid.[24]

Following the initial presentation of their project, the Smithsons found themselves under extremely critical scrutiny from Rogers. The Italian architect began with an enquiry as to their conception of the existing streets: "I understood that you accept the main directions, what you call the streets. But then do you accept the streets only as directions?" Smithson attempted to answer, explaining the functional hierarchy of traffic flows which they had presupposed, but Rogers insisted on pursuing his point in

8.9   An illustration of the project called London Roads, excerpted from the proceedings of the 1959 CIAM conference at Otterlo.

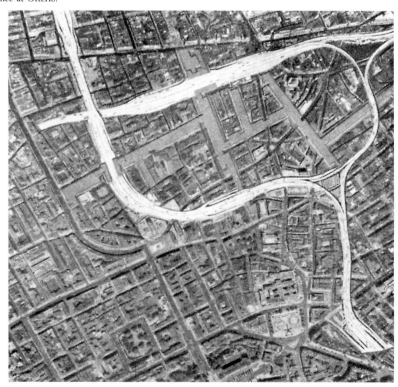

8.10   A view of the controversial project for the Torre Velasca, as presented by Ernesto Rogers to the 1959 CIAM conference at Otterlo.

respect to the existing fabric of the precinct:

> Excuse me for bringing up the controversial Soho area again. It seems to me that you are destroying everything but the directions. If you destroy the context, the context of Soho, why do you bother to conserve the directions? What in fact do you conserve and what do you destroy?

To this, Smithson replied:

> In the end we would probably destroy everything, stage by stage. But as you know cities are not rebuilt like that. The way it would actually work is this: you have a general objective of making a connected system of buildings, that is clear, but the immediate objective would be such that because of the construction of the motorway, certain parts would no longer be valid in their old use. They would acquire a new land value and in consequence there would be a need to change.

And to this Rogers made his final critique, attacking what he saw as the Smithsons' failure to understand imperatives respecting the preservation of the fabric of the historical city:

> My point is that your proceedings are a completely new dimension in town-planning construction and something which, with your permission, is historical. But I think that your contribution to history destroys history completely. I think in your capacity and with your ideas, you are being much too drastic; much too free.

The counterpoint to this discussion occurred at the same conference, when Rogers presented his recent project for a mixed-use tower block in downtown Milan, the controversial Torre Velasca. Following Rogers's presentation, Smithson returned to what he called "this question of history."

> I agree with you that it is no longer possible to take up an anti-historical position. You spoke about the position taken by the creators of modern architecture. Now, they may have taken up an anti-historical position but they took up a moral position as well as an artistic one. I think we find ourselves in the same situation. In making such a building you bring upon yourself the responsibility of not only doing this thing in this situation but it is also a model—an example—of a method. Now I suggest that you, in a way, created a model here which has included certain consequences which, if you had been aware of your position in society and your position in the development of things, you would have seen are dangerous. Such a development contains the possibility of other people's doing similar things in a worse way.

This tense disagreement in respect to the appropriate degree of contemporary deference to "history" was not resolved at the 1959 meeting. Indeed, I have cited it as an important precursor of debates that were to rage bitterly indeed, a decade and a half later, when a younger generation again would challenge the assumptions of the generation of Team 10, and would put against the concerns of mobility, and of growth and change, the newly rediscovered imperative of the form of the historical European city.

For most of the first half of the 1960s, discussion continued to revolve primarily around mobility, growth, and change, and around their implications for the appropriate form of urban space in the modern city. Perhaps the culmination of Team 10's activities was the realization of a project for a new city of 100,000 population, the competition for which had been won in 1962 by Candilis, Josic and Woods. This was Toulouse-le-Mirail, a vast undertaking between 1964 and 1971 that created a satellite city to the existing southern French city of Toulouse,[25] where most of the Team 10 urban interventions were implemented. An elevated pedestrian deck formed a spine that constituted the functional and symbolic organizational scheme of the entire settlement, within a vast ring road vehicular movement system. Access or street deck housing blocks lined the edges of the elevated deck, and secondary pedestrian walkway systems led onward to neighborhoods of lower-density housing and to special functional buildings such as schools and recreation buildings. As a built realization of Team 10's

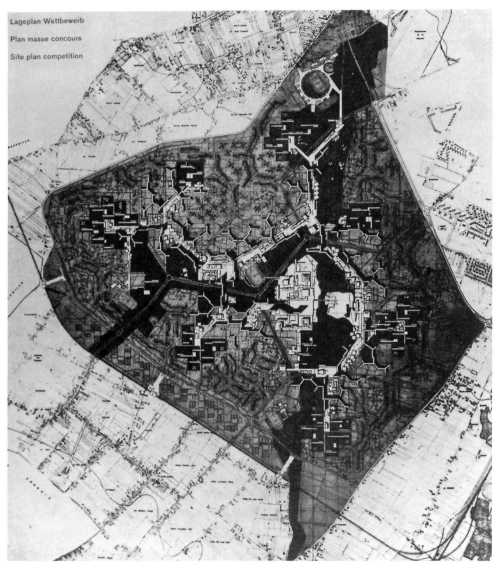

Lageplan Wettbewerb

Plan masse concours

Site plan competition

8.11   The site plan of the winning submission by Candilis, Josic and Woods in the 1962 competition for a new town in the south of France, to be called Toulouse-le-Mirail.

Anordnung umbauter Räume am
Fußgängernetz

Superposition des volumes bâtis
sur le réseau des piétons

Superposition of volumes built on
the pedestrian network

8.12 A detailed drawing showing the organization of the various highly integrated systems of pedestrian circulation in the scheme for Toulouse-le-Mirail. In this plan, white represents the ground plane, gray built form, and black the various proposed forms of pedestrian movement. At the outer limits of the drawing, the winding black pedestrian paths are on the ground. Closer in, where they become more rectilinear, they are elevated above vehicular routes, which pass under them.

ambitions, Toulouse-le-Mirail could hardly have been more complete. Thus when, only a few years after its occupation, it became in its own time a considerable sociological controversy, it put the urban theories of this generation under severely critical scrutiny. But this, too, is to anticipate events.

During the period when the Candilis, Josic and Woods project was being conceived and constructed, ever greater divergences were beginning to be evident between the European and American members of the same generation, in respect to the great issues of mobility and the public realm. As noted above, the principles of vehicular/pedestrian segregation, which had been among the principles taken over by the Team 10 generation from the CIAM generation, had been very slow to take hold in North America, where the association of the free movement of the automobile with individual initiative had been so long established. Only Victor Gruen's incorpo-

8.13 A view of one of the pedestrian courtyards forming part of the design of Victor Gruen's first shopping center: Northland in suburban Detroit, from 1954.

ration of such segregation into his early 1950s concept of a new building type—the suburban shopping center—gave the idea any significant North American currency.[26] But in this form, of course, the idea grew extremely powerful over the course of the late 1950s and 1960s. Indeed, the result of the hybridizing of such segregation with the economic function of merchandising and with the urban social role of a center made the shopping center probably the most consequential typological innovation in urban architecture during the twentieth century. Moreover, it is not unimportant that in the early development of their own ideas of "clustering," Peter and Alison Smithson paid explicit homage to the early ideas on neighborhood planning, and on vehicular/pedestrian segregation, that had been developed by Victor Gruen for Fort Worth, Texas.[27] But as the phenomenon of the shopping center grew in complexity and in social and economic power, the twin notions of social center and of mass-scale mobility began to radically outstrip those of cluster and of grain. And this fact, combined with the central function of the shopping center as a mechanism of consumption, began to trouble European observers.

To be sure, even in the 1950s when the Smithsons' interests in American consumerism were at their peak—"Today We Collect Ads" was the somewhat Americanophile title of an essay of theirs from 1955—this interest had been a somewhat distanced one. Indeed, for most of the period of its active existence Team 10 consistently opposed architectural proposals that uncritically accepted American social mores.[28] So widespread was this characteristic opposition that the only American architect to escape altogether the scorn of the Team 10 moralists during those years was Louis Kahn. One may gain a sharp sense of European disdain for American usages in modern architecture in a polemic that appeared as late as 1964, Team 10 member Colin St. John Wilson's "Letter to an American Student":

> I do not wish to go on raging at the latest phase of architecture in the United States. It seems that by now the conflict in judgement between European and American critics upon this subject needs understanding rather than exacerbation; and certainly as I sat and listened to the contributors to the Columbia symposium *Architecture in the 1930's,* I began to understand for the first time that there is a fundamental difference between American and European interpretation of the role of architecture in society. For the modern architecture of which these contributors spoke was almost unrecognizable to me. It was supposedly defined by some point of purely stylistic maturity called the International Style deeply indebted to Neo-Classicism and quite detached from the problems of its society. No Athens Charter, no "ilot insalubre," no echo of the cry "architecture or revolution," nothing of the search for new standards, of the fervour of groups such as CIAM and MARS to bring architecture to the attention of the people: art for art's sake, amen.
>
> Now in Europe, the notion of a new architecture was always a polemical one, in which, for better or for worse, a whole body of ideas was at stake.[29]

St. John Wilson's demurral was soon seconded by Reyner Banham, as well as by other European commentators who objected strenuously to the stylistic innovations being promoted by Philip Johnson, Eero Saarinen, and others. Then, too, just as this new European critique was taking shape, American attitudes to "the public realm" were moving in a direction that would prove even more troubling.

In 1965, volume 9/10 of *Perspecta*, the Yale architectural journal, was published under the editorship of Robert A. M. Stern, who was a student at Yale at the time. As one might expect at that date, the work of Louis Kahn loomed large in the issue. But even more pertinent, for my present purposes, was the second article in the issue, Charles Moore's "You Have to Pay for the Public Life." Moore had been asked to prepare a commentary on architecture on the American west coast from the perspective of "monument" and "place." As he put it:

> Perspecta's editors suspected, I presume, that I would discover that in California there is no contemporary monumental architecture, or that there is no urban scene (except in a sector of San Francisco), or, more probably, that both monumental architecture and the urban scene are missing. Their suspicions were well founded; any discussion from California in 1964 about monumental urban architecture is bound to be less about what we have than about what we have instead.[30]

Interestingly enough, Moore even cited the same passage on urbanity from Ortega y Gasset that had been quoted by José Luis Sert at the 1951 CIAM conference. But while he was prepared to concede to east coast prejudice that his discussion of California public space would revolve around "what we have instead," he nevertheless refused to concede that public space simply didn't exist there. Indeed, having commenced a detailed critique of the "placelessness" characteristic of recent modern work in the state, he took a strategic turn in his argument:

> Even in the few years of Yankee California's existence, this kind of placelessness has not always been characteristic. During the '20s and into the '30s, with what was doubtless an enormous assist from the Hollywood vision in the days of its greatest splendour, an architectural image of California developed which was exotic but specific, derivative but exhilaratingly free. . . . What came of this was architecture that owed something to Spain, very little to the people who were introducing the International Style, and a great deal to the movie camera's moving eye. . . . The act of recalling another quite imaginary civilization created a new and powerful public realm.[31]

As examples, Moore discussed in some detail Shepley, Rutan and Coolidge's old campus at Stanford University from 1887 (seen as a precursor) and William Mooser's Santa Barbara County Courthouse from 1929. Reaching the climax of his argument, Moore continued:

> More recent years have their monuments as well. Indeed, by almost any conceivable method of evaluation that does not exclude the public, Disneyland must be regarded as the most important single piece of construction in the West in the past several decades. The assumption inevitably made by people who have not yet been there—that it is some sort of physical extension of Mickey Mouse—is wildly inaccurate. Instead, singlehanded, it is engaged in replacing many of those elements of the public realm which have vanished in the featureless private floating world of southern California, whose only edge is the ocean, and whose centre is otherwise undiscoverable (unless by our revolution test it turns out to be on Manhattan Island). Curiously, for a public place, Disneyland is not free. You buy tickets at the

Sadly?

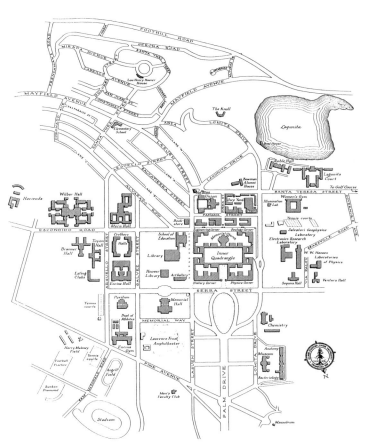

8.14   A plan of Shepley, Rutan and Coolidge's old campus for Stanford University in California from 1887, as illustrated in Charles Moore's polemical essay "You Have to Pay for the Public Life," published in *Perspecta* in 1965.

8.15   A plan of William Mooser's Santa Barbara County Courthouse, from 1929, also published by Charles Moore in his 1965 essay in *Perspecta*.

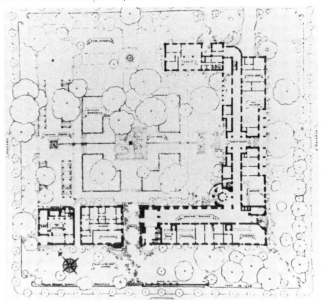

8.16   Main Street at Disneyland, illustrated as the finale in Charles Moore's 1965 essay in *Perspecta*.

gate. But then, Versailles cost someone a great deal of money, too. Now, as then, you have to pay for the public life.

Disneyland, it appears, is enormously important and successful just because it recreates all the chances to respond to a *public* environment, which Los Angeles particularly does not any longer have. It allows play-acting, both to be watched and to be participated in, in a public sphere.[32]

These inflammatory remarks led to a detailed, commendatory commentary on Disney's creation, as well as to the first extensive portfolio of photographs of Disneyland in any serious architectural magazine. With this encomium of a major enterprise of American consumerism, Moore brought European-American critical tensions to a new height, and these have not altogether abated up to the present day. But that was not all. Insofar as the shopping center had been the link between new urban theories in Europe and North America in the early 1950s, the inevitability of the evolution from the shopping center to the theme park put new stress on European convictions about the respective roles of pedestrians and vehicles in urban centers in the first place. And finally, in its characteristically Californian shamelessness about style, Disneyland brought stunningly to the forefront of discussion the relationship of the difficult new concepts of plurality and mobility to the third term of the emerging cultural crisis, that of history. For above all else, Moore argued, Disneyland successfully reconnected the popular American imagination to a mythic past, just as the movies had already done.

Interestingly enough, yet another intellectual trajectory—admittedly not a precisely parallel one—began to emerge in the later 1960s and 1970s, leading in Europe to yet another full-fledged intergenerational crisis in respect to the desirable form that urban life should take. One may trace this crisis back to a figure pivotal to the evolution from the generation of Team 10 to that of the European Rationalists who eventually attacked it. This is O. M. Ungers, who had been an important younger figure in Germany in the late 1950s and 1960s, prior to his move to the United States. In 1959, for example, Ungers had constructed a house for himself in Cologne that placed him in a rank with the Smithsons and with James Stirling in Britain, all of them influenced by the Maisons Jaoul of Le Corbusier.[33] But by the mid 1960s, notwithstanding his regard for his seniors in Team 10, Ungers's position began to shift. In an influential series of student projects undertaken under his leadership at the Technical University of Berlin, Ungers began to promote a strong current of formality, and a sharp urban definition, that contrasted noticeably with the "open aesthetic" of visual informality being promulgated by the Smithsons and others in Team 10. In a key project from 1964 done with a team of associates including the young Rob Krier, Ungers even went so far as to elaborate a scheme of types, organized together to create a formally distinctive and highly recognizable morphology for the Cologne district of Grunzug South.[34]

By the early 1970s, Ungers had moved to a position sufficiently distinct from that of the older generation to be included among the new and largely younger group by then coming to be known as the rationalists. In 1969, in another significant European linkage, Rob Krier's brother Leon went to work for James Stirling; in the years during and after Krier's stay in the Stirling office, Stirling's work too shifted ground, beginning to manifest an increasingly strong preoccupation with history, both in the form of recognizable if subtle historical references, and in his increasingly deferential attitude to existing urban fabric in the vicinity of his building projects.[35]

By the late 1970s, the delicate European consensus around the emerging issues of plurality, mobility, and history exploded completely. Probably the battle can be said to have been launched with Maurice Culot's and Leon Krier's compendium of 1978, *Rational Architecture,* with its highly polemical subtitle *The Reconstruction of the European City.* In this important document, another new generation turned dramatically on its seniors, challenging the

8.17   An axonometric view of the project for Grünzug-süd in Cologne by O. M. Ungers, assisted by F. Oswald and R. Krier, from 1964.

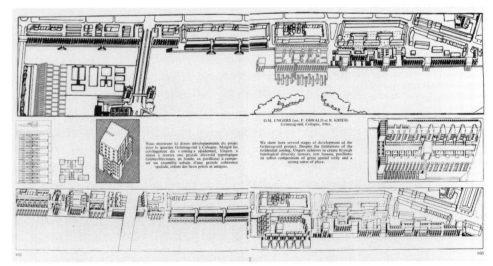

G. GRASSI, A. MONESTIROLI, R. RAFFAELE CONTI   Maison d'étudiants à Chieti   Students house in Chieti   1976

Les bâtiments ne forment pas un espace
descriptible. L'espace public est acci-
dentel.

The buildings do not form a describable
space, the public space is accidental.

59

8.18   A page from the publication *Rational Architecture* of 1978, contrasting the form of the project
for student housing at Chieti in Italy by G. Grassi, A. Monestiroli, and R. Raffaele Conti with generic
forms of housing recognizable from the polemic as being those of Team 10.

ideas that had sustained their vision of the city. Where the Team 10
generation had accepted the motorway as a new dimension of urban form,
the Rationalists fundamentally challenged it. In a preface to a series of
proposals for Stuttgart, for example, Rob Krier compared the damage done
to that city by "land speculation" and by "motorway construction" with
the damage done by Allied bombardments during the war.[36] Where Team
10 had developed a metaphor of the street, in connection with its idea of
the street deck, the Rationalists reasserted the historical street in its literal
form as the primary organizational principle of urbanism. Where the generation of Team 10 had conceived of the metaphor of urban grain, the
Rationalists argued for the primacy of the fabric of the historical European
city as it was, and argued that new interventions should defer to it. Where

Team 10 had argued for the development of an open aesthetic of building that was informal, subject to change and randomness, the Rationalists re-asserted the importance of formality in the urban vision, rejecting the traditions of both Team 10 and CIAM in favor of a reexamination of the urban planning principles of such then forgotten figures as Camillo Sitte, Otto Wagner, and Eliel Saarinen.[37]

Indeed, the Rationalists put forward a series of propositions that were radically conservative by comparison with those of the immediately preceding generation. They argued strongly for the importance of the principles of historical European urban morphology, and they claimed that the historic forms of the street, the square, and the block were fundamental to it. The public spaces of the city, they held, should be conceived in the first instance in purely formal terms; following the principles of Sitte, they put forward new lexicons of such spaces. They argued that the primary obligation of housing design was not individual dwelling amenity, but rather the overall urban relationship of unit type to local urban morphology; they argued that the form of new housing located in existing neighborhoods should be determined by the existing morphology of that neighborhood. Finally, they reasserted what they saw as the absolute primacy of the urban monument, in a perceived dialectical relationship with the fabric of the historical city.

Now this dramatic, internally consistent, and conservative series of propositions constituted the most important challenge yet to the ascendancy of the Team 10 generation. Moreover, it was a challenge that coincided with the public growth of serious doubts about the long-term social effectiveness of such major works of the previous decade as Candilis, Josic and Woods's Toulouse-le-Mirail in France, and Werner Duttmann, Hans Müller, and Georg Heinrich's Markisches-Viertel in West Berlin.[38] Both these major urban enclaves had been occupied for some years, and significant evidence of urban ennui and alienation was coming to be evident in them.

These citizen dissatisfactions fanned the flames of dispute between the older and younger generations. The late seventies and early eighties saw a series of increasingly acrimonious quarrels in which the young accused the older generation of betraying the long-standing traditions of European civilization in the creation of such unlivable urban precincts, while the old accused the young of betraying the principles of modern liberal democracy and seeking a return to the traditional social and political structures of prewar Europe. Leaving aside the grosser political allegations, it was nevertheless true that the proposals of the young did indeed cast a whole new light on the relationship among plurality, mobility, and history, which had formed such a continuous substratum of debate since the end of the war. For the Rationalists, of course, history, which had received the least attention from Team 10, was now placed in a position of absolute priority. As for mobility, it was seen as one principal rationale for the destruction of the European city that had been so extensive in the 1950s and 1960s. Thus it was radically displaced from the high priority it had enjoyed in the urban theories of Team 10. Indeed, the attitude of the Rationalists to mobility, and to the phenomenon of the automobile, remains obscure to this day.

As for the last of our three interrelated themes, that of plurality, it had always been somewhat elusive in the work of Team 10 and had never received the attention mobility had. Similarly, for the Rationalists, plurality per se has not been an issue, as the historical form of the city surely has been. To be sure, fragmentary evidence can be found in the Smithsons' early interest in the heterogeneity of London street life and in the aleatory provocations of Dubuffet and of advertising, as in Leon Krier's pleas for the reconstruction of the "quarter" as a new basis of everyday urban life. But striking evidence of the difficulties faced by both generations may be demonstrated in two projects of the 1970s by representatives of the opposing factions: Herman Hertzberger's Centraal Beheer Insurance Headquarters Building in Apeldoorn, Holland, from 1972, and Leon Krier's competition entry for housing for Royal Mint Square in London, from 1974.[39]

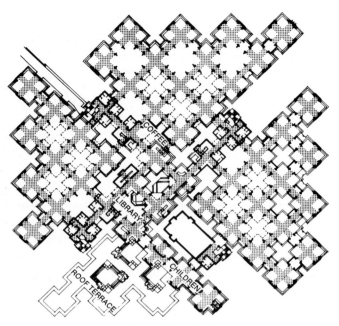

8.19   The plan of the Centraal Beheer at Apeldoorn, Holland, by Herman Hertzberger, from 1974.

Hertzberger is an interesting intergenerational figure, too young to have been a member of Team 10 proper but a protégé of Team 10 member Aldo van Eyck. By the mid-1970s Hertzberger had developed his own significant position as representative of the affiliated movement of Dutch structuralism. The office building in Apeldoorn was generally regarded as his most accomplished project up to that date. Basically, it is an office building to house the administration of a governmental insurance organization. Given his strong social orientation to architecture, Hertzberger was very interested in the potential programmatic symbolism of the building, but for him this symbolism was necessarily far more poetic and elliptical than institutional and monumental. Indeed, Hertzberger's almost psychoanalytic orientation to the creation of built form was so individualistic, in its point of departure, that he saw it as the obligation of his building to be anti-institutional, and to establish its intended systems of social meaning exclusively from the individual outward, as it were.

Thus the form of Apeldoorn is a cellular system of modules, grouped roughly into four and canted to 45 degrees, so that a fractured edge of a series of working trays abuts to a multistory route moving diagonally through the building as a whole. This route, of course, belongs to the Team 10 tradition of the street deck, and is surely intended, in some deep

8.20 A view along the interior spine of the Centraal Beheer of Hertzberger.

sense deriving from the heroic modernism of the twenties, to act as a "social condenser." But for Hertzberger the route is not conceived of as having any overriding collective symbolic force. Rather, its fractured profile, its character as the resultant of a series of cellular modules butted against it, and the manifest circumstantiality of the conditions of overlook created are all intended to preclude any such dominant meaning.

For Hertzberger, the constitution of the public realm can only proceed from the individual act cumulatively outward to the *resultant* collectivity. According to his politics, any preconstituted collective image would necessarily be authoritarian. So we should not be surprised that the external profile of the complex is an even more circumstantial resultant in its visual character than the interior profile of the trays against the route. Indeed, the honeycomb of the exterior presents no unified reading at all. Growing out of the Team 10 tradition, the Centraal Beheer manifests instead a commitment to the constitution of a human plurality that is radically individualist and decentralist, and that cannot tolerate any predetermined representation of collectivity.

Krier's proposal for a housing precinct at Royal Mint Square is not an institution at all but an extensive insertion into an existing residential quarter. Like Hertzberger's scheme, Krier's involves a diagonal route across the plan form of the proposal, but where Hertzberger's seeks to avoid collective symbolism at all costs, Krier's sets out equally deliberately to achieve it. In his case, the diagonal route is quite formally and axially

8.21   A plan of Leon Krier's 1974 competition entry for housing at Royal Mint Square in London. (Illustration: Leon Krier.)

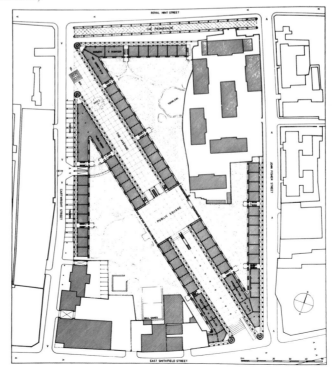

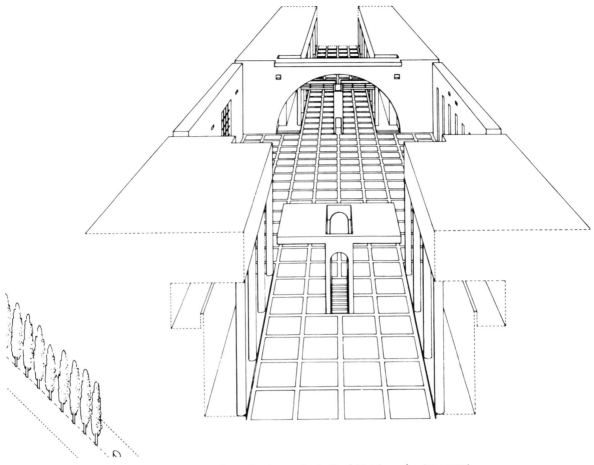

8.22 A view of the public spine of Leon Krier's entry for the Royal Mint Square housing competition. (Illustration: Leon Krier.)

organized and the fabric of the adjacent housing is formally welded together to monumentalize the route. At the midpoint of the route across the site, Krier located a collective focal space to serve the new quarter created by the project as a whole. According to his poignant description of the project, the opposite faces of the formally defined square were created by facades for community institutions that did not yet exist. Thus, this designer's political commitment to plurality and to the public committed him to rely on the pure iconographic power of the facade to constitute a new public realm.

In Hertzberger's case, we may conclude, the power of architecture to symbolize "the human artifact" in itself was consciously eschewed, while in

8.23 A photograph of one of the focal points of the interior of West Edmonton Mall, in Edmonton, Alberta. (Photograph: Jim Dow.)

Krier's such power was surely invoked, but in a manner that limited itself to pure iconography, thereby forsaking any possibility of human action in spontaneous terms, independent of a conscious intellectual appropriation. Given Benjamin's apt characterization of architecture as a phenomenon generally "appropriated by a collectivity in a state of distraction," Krier's exclusively iconographic gesture toward the *res publica* seems to me far too disembodied to be able to attain any compelling social reality. In short, it is my view that the two key projects, taken together, aptly crystallize a crisis of symbolic representation of "the public" that must be seen to be quintessentially characteristic of their period.

Perhaps a certain historical distance from the recriminations of the Team 10 and Rationalist generations will eventually permit further reconsideration of this crisis. For the moment, however, we may conclude this account by returning to North America, and noting a further hybridizing of ideas of the sort that contributed to the European/American debates of the 1960s. I have already noted how powerful the twin European ideas of pedestrian-vehicular segregation and of the center became in North America when they were combined by Victor Gruen in the form of the generic shopping center. I have also noted the inflammatory fashion in which Charles Moore linked the ideas of "history" and of "public life" in his complimentary account of the phenomenon of Disneyland. In the past decade or so we have witnessed a further hybridizing of types, in which the generic shopping center as conceived by Gruen and the theme park invented by Disney have themselves been combined. The controversial Canadian project West Edmonton Mall is a well-known example of this increasingly common new metropolitan phenomenon.[40] In a related development, the shopping center has been calculatedly hybridized with a Disney-style model of urban history, yielding new urban enclaves such as South Street Seaport in New York City, in which a real historic precinct has been transformed into a "themed" simulacrum of itself.

These astonishing urban phenomena of the end of the twentieth century as yet await their Walter Benjamin. To be sure, very recently efforts at serious critical analysis have begun. In a recent volume entitled *Variations on a Theme Park,* a group of authors including Margaret Crawford, Trevor Boddy, M. Christine Boyer, and Michael Sorkin have tackled the question vigorously.[41] Still, most of these commentators fall to the "pessimistic" side of cultural theory, as I characterized it at the end of chapter five. Certainly none attempts an optimistic apotheosis of the shopping center/theme park such as Lyotard's for information technology. In this sense, the negative critical tradition stretching from Debord to Jameson can be seen to hold fast. For it, the historically "themed" shopping center stands as a particularly apt manifestation of the dismaying ability of late capitalism to manipulate the symbolic discourse of contemporary society for its own purposes. What is more, the interpretation of the phenomenon by Sorkin and his colleagues, in specifically architectural terms, is marked to significant degree by a moral indignation reminiscent of the 1964 lament of St. John Wilson, discussed above.

An "other" interpretation of the phenomenon, one that is not indignant, is that of Jean Baudrillard, also discussed in chapter five. Indeed, in employing the term "simulacrum of itself" to describe South Street Seaport, I have borrowed a strategic usage from Baudrillard's influential essay "The Precession of Simulacra." In that text Baudrillard turned his attention to Disneyland.

> Disneyland is a perfect model of all the entangled orders of simulation. To begin with, it is a play of illusions and phantasms: Pirates, the Frontier, Future World, etc. This imaginary world is supposed to be what makes the operation successful. But what draws the crowds is undoubtedly much more the social microcosm, the miniaturized and *religious* revelling in real America, in its delights and drawbacks. You park outside, queue up inside, and are totally abandoned at the exit. In this imaginary world the only phantasmagoria is in the inherent warmth and affection of the crowd, and in that sufficiently excessive number of gadgets used there specifically to maintain the multitudinous affect. . . .

> The objective profile of America, then, may be traced throughout Disneyland, even down to the morphology of individuals and the crowd. All its values are exalted here, in miniature and comic strip form. Embalmed and pacified. Whence the possibility of an ideological analysis of Disneyland . . . : digest of the American way of life, panegyric to American values, idealized transposition of a contradictory reality. To be sure. But this conceals something else, and that "ideological" blanket exactly serves to cover over a *third-order simulation:* Disneyland is there to conceal the fact that it is the "real" country, all of "real" America, which *is* Disneyland. . . . Disneyland is presented as imaginary in order to make us believe that the rest is real, when in fact all of Los Angeles and the America surrounding it are no longer real, but of the order of the hyperreal and of simulation.[42]

It is this mode of cultural analysis that led Baudrillard to the proposition:

> When the real is no longer what it used to be, nostalgia assumes its full meaning. There is a proliferation of myths of origin and signs of reality; of secondhand truth, objectivity and authenticity. There is an escalation of the true, of the lived experience; a resurrection of the figurative where the object and substance have disappeared. And there is a panic-stricken production of the real and the referential, above and parallel to the panic of material production: this is how simulation appears in the phase which concerns us—a strategy of the real, neo-real, and hyperreal, whose universal double is a strategy of deterrence.[43]

An interesting comparison can be drawn between this distinctive mode of interpretation of "themed" urbanity developed by Baudrillard and the tradition of cultural criticism represented by Sorkin and his colleagues. The latter surely have seen this sociocultural phenomenon as an objectionable

8.24   An image of Leon Krier's Atlantis project, designed for Tenerife. (Illustration: Leon Krier.)

one, but their alienation from the phenomenon has never been so extreme as to cause them to place its "reality" in question. Indeed, one can say that for those critics it has been the palpable reality of the phenomenon that has generated the moral indignation sustaining their continuing critique. As I have already indicated in chapter five, Baudrillard's characteristic mode of interpretation embodies a far extremer alienation on the part of the observer. Rather than indignantly attacking the phenomenon in question, Baudrillard has chosen instead to bracket its putative reality in such a way as to place the critic in a posture of radically ironic distance. From such an aloof cultural posture, indignation would of course be altogether misplaced.

We can nevertheless see it as indicative of the degree of destabilization of the status of the public that a figure such as Leon Krier would recently have published a project that appears suspended somewhere between the two modes of critical discourse just outlined. The project to which I refer is his Atlantis, a community proposed to be built on the island of Tenerife.[44] Viewed from the perspective of Krier's own earlier work, stretching from the St. Quentin-en-Yvelines school discussed in chapter three to the Royal Mint Square housing discussed in this chapter, and from the perspective of the critique of consumer society he has shared with Kenneth Frampton, discussed in chapter seven, Atlantis would appear to be another in the brave series of urban propositions Krier has put forward for the purpose of reestablishing the historic "quarter" as the social and formal basis of a reformed urbanism for our time. Up to a point, Atlantis can indeed be read in this way, thereby seeming to confirm a position for its author within the by now familiar moral critique of consumer society.

Yet Atlantis can, in my view, equally readily be read in a quite different way. It is, after all, in the first instance a resort, not a quarter in any traditional sense. And it thereby places its author's increasingly historicist formal vocabulary at the service of a recreational consumerism that cannot be conclusively detached from the values of Baudrillard's Disneyland. Indeed, it is difficult not to see Atlantis as a latent further hybrid of the sort I have discussed above. Except that this time, the hybrid would be of the urban quarter, as Krier has so eloquently argued for it in the past, and the resort, one of the quintessential commercial development programs of our time. The "theme," in this case, would be classicism itself.

The fact that it is possible to conjure up so readily so disconcerting a reading of a work by Krier suggests to me that neither the moral indignation of the traditional critique nor the hyper-irony of the current one is ultimately going to prove adequate to deal with the controversies that lie ahead. The most they will be able to accomplish, I fear, will be to precipitate a whole new series of angry accusations of "false consciousness" on the one hand and ever more ironic postures of distance on the other.

For my own part, I hope for a far more fruitful theoretical exploration of our predicament than this acrimonious bifurcation, one that would look again to the related concepts of "plurality" and of "action" as they were propounded by Arendt in the late 1950s. Such a line of exploration will undoubtedly continue to sustain a significant component of irony—but my guess is that it will be a mode of irony such as was typical of much of the cultural critique of that earlier era, an irony suffused by passion and engagement such as we associate with such compelling figures as Camus and Pollock, rather than by the more recently typical aloof and rarefied distance.

Were such a line to be pursued, I further suspect that one might see an effort to reformulate a conception of the public for our time, and that the reformulation would comprise some as yet undefined hybrid of the citizen as characterized by Arendt and the *flâneur* so familiar from Benjamin. One might further suppose that the definition of such a hybrid could begin with a reexamination of the phenomenon of action in all its complex historical nuances. It is already quite clear, for example, that action in our time will not be able to be innocent, ahistorical, or even unconstructed.

Richard Sennett's thought-provoking account of the eighteenth-century argument between Diderot and Rousseau in regard to "man the actor" can instructively be reviewed in this context. For Diderot, the concept of "man the actor" arose out of earlier social analogies between the world and the stage such as that put forward by Henry Fielding.

> If, in general, man as actor relieved himself of the burdens of innate sin by divorcing his nature from his acts, 18th century common sense concluded that he thus could enjoy himself more. Tied in public neither to the realm of nature nor to the Christian duties of the soul, his playfulness and pleasure in the company of others could be released.[45]

But Diderot pressed the matter further, arguing that insofar as one spoke of "acting" as theatrical performance, "playfulness and pleasure" could hardly be considered adequate motivations. As he himself put it:

> If the actor were full, really full, of feeling, how could he play the same part twice running with the same spirit and success? Full of fire at the first performance, he would be worn out and cold as marble at the third.

This led the French philosopher of the theater to conclude that "acting," in this sense, must be considered an entirely artificial and repeatable construct: "I am talking to you of a work of Art, planned and composed—a work which is built up by degrees, and which lasts."[46]

Rousseau, in response, mounted a basic indictment of the idea of city as theater. For, as he saw it, if it were true that the emerging urban setting of the eighteenth century really was a "stage," and that "acting—not just performance on stage" but, by extension, "visits in cafes, walks and promenades, etc."—really were entirely artificial, then the large city, as it was already beginning to exist in the eighteenth century, was

> an environment wherein you cannot tell what kind of man a stranger is in a given situation by finding out how he survives. The situations, indeed, in which you are likely to meet him are those in which you are not meeting for some functional purpose, but meeting in the context of nonfunctional socializing, of social interaction for its own sake.[47]

And this, in turn, led Rousseau to see his fellow citizens as increasingly preoccupied—through the sheer pleasure of contact with others in public—with becoming "actors" of a special sort:

> scheming, idle people without religion or principle, whose imagination, depraved by sloth, inactivity, the love of pleasure, and great needs, engenders only monsters and inspires only crimes; . . . where *moeurs* and honor are nothing because each easily hiding his conduct from the public eye, shows himself only by his reputation.[48]

To be sure, any reformulated concept of action for our own time can be expected to encompass the artificial construct of "reputation," just as surely as it already did for Rousseau. What is more, its evident artificiality will surely continue to elicit, in response, the ironic gaze of the anonymous urban observer we have come to know as the *flâneur*. Yet even on so tentatively reconstituted a public realm as one based simply on reputation and irony, the passion and the engagement of Arendt's more ample model of action will not be precluded. Acting does, after all, on her own view, constitute in the first instance "the affairs which go on among those who have [the world] in common." In this sense, she is allied with Diderot, and against Rousseau, in recognizing artifice in the experience whereby "I appear to others as others appear to me."

Yet her conception of action nevertheless stops well short of the sort of pure artifice represented by Diderot's characterization of theater. As she puts it:

> In acting and speaking, men show who they are, reveal actively their unique personal identities and thus make their appearance in the human world. . . . This disclosure of "who" in contradistinction to "what" somebody is—his qualities, gifts, talents, and shortcomings, which he may display or hide—is implicit in everything somebody says and does. It can be hidden only in complete silence and perfect passivity, but its disclosure can almost never be achieved as a wilful purpose, as though one possessed and could dispose of this "who" in the same manner he has and can dispose of his qualities. On the contrary, it is more than likely that the "who," which appears so clearly and unmistakably to others, remains hidden from the person himself, like the *daimōn* in Greek religion which accompanies each man throughout his life, always looking over his shoulder from behind and thus visible only to those he encounters.[49]

The constructedness of reputation and the distance of irony notwithstanding, then, the newly public realm I am attempting to imagine for our time will not be an altogether conscious construct. It seems to me almost certain that it will be fabricated, in part, of known historical models, but those models will have been fragmented and reconstituted in newly affirmative ways. It will also be rhetorical in its explicit taking up of public positions, but the concatenation of those positions will itself be heterogeneous—not to say pluralistic. And its formation will disclose evidence of many an engaged hand in the process of its fabrication.

To be sure, within its tentatively demarcated territory, no protagonist is going to be able to claim authenticity unquestionably for himself. Indeed, while it is likely that many of its manifestations may readily be dismissed as inauthentic, such dismissal will not legitimate any overall retreat—whether puritanical, Rousseaesque, or whatever—from the large social and economic forces or the ephemeral products of the postmodern world, out of which material it will perforce have to be made. We can hope, however, that it will constitute a world of passionate symbolic reinterpretations, the precise social meaning of which we will not be able to determine by ourselves, or in advance. Indeed, following Arendt, we may say that as architects, we will not to be able to see altogether clearly the consequences of these efforts of our own, but will be able to rest confident that they will "appear clearly and unmistakably to others."

NOTES

Introduction

EPIGRAPHS   Hannah Arendt, *The Human Condition* (Chicago: University of Chicago Press, 1958), 180.

Theodor Adorno, "Functionalism Today: An Address to the 1965 Meeting of the *Deutscher Werkbund*," *Oppositions* 17 (Summer 1979): 38.

1   Wolfe's best-known text in this area is *From Bauhaus to Our House* (New York: Farrar Straus Giroux, 1981). The Prince of Wales's widely disseminated views on architecture and urbanism have formed the basis of both books and television programs. A broad summary and discussion of his critique is in Christopher Martin and Charles Krevitt, "Prince Charles and the Architectural Debate," a special issue of *Architectural Design* (1989).

2   Moore's project was the subject of an extensive discussion by a diverse group of commentators, including myself, published in *Places: A Quarterly Journal of Environmental Design* 1, no. 2 (Winter 1984).

3   Barthes first became known for a provocative series of critical essays, *Mythologies* (Paris: Seuil, 1957). Later he published the seminal text *Elements of Semiology* (London: Jonathan Cape, 1967), followed in turn by the works that made him famous outside of France: *Système de la mode* (Paris: Seuil, 1967), *La Chambre claire* (Paris: Seuil, 1980), etc. The work that launched the influence of Lévi-Strauss outside anthropology was probably *La Pensée sauvage* (Paris: Plon, 1972), though his *Structural Anthropology* (New York: Basic Books, 1963) was widely known, as was his inaugural lecture at the Collège de France, published in English as *The Scope of Anthropology* (London: Jonathan Cape, 1967).

4   Charles Jencks, *The Language of Post-Modern Architecture* (London: Academy Editions, 1977).

5   A representative text of Lyotard is *The Postmodern Condition: A Report on Knowledge* (Minneapolis: University of Minnesota Press, 1984). Representative texts of Derrida include *Speech and Phenomena* (Evanston: Northwestern University Press, 1973); *Writing and Difference* (Chicago: University of Chicago Press, 1978); and *The Truth in Painting* (Chicago: University of Chicago Press, 1987). For Baudrillard, see "The Ecstasy of Communications," reprinted in Hal Foster, *The Anti-Aesthetic* (Port Townsend: Bay Press, 1983); "The Precession of Simulacra," in *Simulations* (New York: Semiotext(e), 1983); and *America* (London: Verso, 1988).

6   The battle can be seen engaged in the catalogue of the exhibition *Deconstructivist*

Architecture, curated by Philip Johnson and Mark Wigley (Boston: New York Graphic Society, 1988).

7   A late revisionist work of Stern is *Modern Classicism* (New York: Rizzoli, 1988).

8   Fredric Jameson, "Postmodernism, or the Cultural Logic of Late Capitalism," *New Left Review* 146 (1984): 80.

9   Anders Stephanson in conversation with Cornell West, in Andrew Ross, *Universal Abandon? The Politics of Postmodernism* (Minneapolis: University of Minnesota Press, 1988), 176.

10   Albrecht Wellmer, *The Persistence of Modernity* (Cambridge: MIT Press, 1991), viii.

11   For evidence of Wellmer's debt to Habermas see Wellmer, *The Persistence of Modernity,* 36–94.

12   Ross, *Universal Abandon,* x.

13   Yet another terminological ambiguity, one whose theoretical implications are pursued in chapter seven, also merits reference here. For over a decade now, in the larger realm of discussion outside architecture, a key set of critical oppositions has been employed by cultural theorists of various persuasions. These have typically taken the form "modern" versus "avant-garde," and "high" culture versus "low."

The first of these two sets of conceptual oppositions was introduced by the German critic Peter Bürger in his *Theory of the Avant-Garde* of 1974, and has more recently been expanded to encompass the latter as well by Andreas Huyssen, in his *After the Great Divide* of 1986. Huyssen summarized the relationship of the two oppositions as follows:

> The historical avantgarde aimed at developing an alternative relationship between high art and mass culture, and thus should be distinguished from modernism, which for the most part insisted on the inherent hostility between high and low. Such a distinction is not meant to account for each and every individual case; there are modernists whose aesthetic practise was close to the spirit of avantgardism, and one could point to avantgardists who shared modernism's aversion to any form of mass culture. But even though the boundaries between modernism and avantgardism remained fluid, the distinction I am suggesting permits us to focus on sufficiently discernible trends within the culture of modernity. More specifically, it allows us to distinguish the historical avantgarde from late-nineteenth-century modernism as well as from the high modernism of the interwar years. In addition, the focus on the high/low dichotomy and on the modernism/avantgardism constellation in the earlier twentieth cen-

tury will ultimately provide us with a better understanding of postmodernism and its history since the 1960s.

What I am calling the Great Divide is the kind of discourse which insists on the categorical distinction between high art and mass culture. In my view, this divide is much more important for a theoretical and historical understanding of modernism and its aftermath than the alleged historical break which, in the eyes of so many critics, separates postmodernism from modernism. The discourse of the great divide has been dominant primarily in two periods, first in the last decades of the nineteenth century and the first few years of the 20th, and then again in the two decades or so following World War II. (*After the Great Divide* [Bloomington: Indiana University Press, 1986], viii)

Huyssen sees the present state of affairs as changing rapidly, with the key consequence that the "Great Divide," as he has characterized it, is

increasingly challenged by recent developments in the arts, film, literature, architecture and criticism. This second major challenge to the canonized high/low dichotomy goes by the name of postmodernism; and like the historical avantgarde though in very different ways, postmodernism rejects the theories and practises of the Great Divide. Indeed, the birth of the postmodern out of the spirit of an adversary avantgardism cannot be adequately understood unless modernism's and postmodernism's different relationship to mass culture is grasped.

Huyssen's schemas are particularly suggestive for ongoing research in architecture, not least due to the particular instances of historical avant-gardism that he has cited: "Its most salient manifestations were expressionism and Berlin Dada in Germany; Russian constructivism, futurism and the proletcult in the years following the Russian Revolution; and French surrealism, especially in its earlier phase." Given architecture's inherently social characteristics as an art form, the context of such avant-garde precedents as those cited by Huyssen offers the possibility of a richer model of architectural theory for the present time than any presently extant. Indeed, this book can in certain respects be seen to pursue such a possibility.

But this doesn't mean that the terminological ambiguities have been resolved, for the terminological schemas of Bürger and Huyssen, subtle though they may be, are not universally accepted in current discourse either. In fact, yet another significant body of ideas stands in flat contradiction to the "avant-garde/modern" schema propounded by Bürger and Huyssen and implicitly appropriated by Andrew Ross. The body of ideas in question was given expression in a polemical text from the late 1970s by the Italian architect Giorgio Grassi, who mounted a highly disparaging attack on the idea of an architectural avant-garde entitled "Avant-garde and Continuity," *Oppositions* 21 (Summer 1980), 24. According to Grassi, there were, in any discussion of an architectural avant-garde, two basic issues: (1) that avant-garde architecture itself is of minor importance. It is always marginal to any decisive change—despite the fact that its importance has been exaggerated to an absurd degree by militant criticism, and even though it has been take seriously by many, both in the past and today; (2) that the avant-garde position in architecture contradicts the very definition of architecture; that is to say, it is contrary to architecture's most specific characteristics; factors which cannot be over-looked in the projection of architecture, not even when the contradiction between architecture and the city, or between humanity and the reality of its product, is as much in evidence as it is today.

Where Bürger, and following him Huyssen and Ross, have seen the "avant-garde" as the stream within modernism that was anti-elitist and speculatively open to "contamination" by mass culture, Grassi has characterized the "avant-garde" within modern architecture as the part of it that was the most rarefied and the least social in its orientation.

14 For a detailed account of the apparatus of semiotics as applied to architecture, see Charles Jencks and George Baird, eds., *Meaning in Architecture* (New York: Braziller, 1969).

15 Tschumi's project has now been extensively documented. An example is *Progressive Architecture,* November 1989.

16 Eisenman's Wexner Center has been published in *Progressive Architecture,* October 1991.

17 For this tendency, see Baudrillard, "The Precession of Simulacra."

18 Bourdieu's influence on Ross is evident in a number of essays in his *No Respect* (New York: Routledge, 1989).

19 My argument here is in significant debt to that of Andreas Huyssen, "In the Shadow of McLuhan, Jean Baudrillard's Theory of Simulation," *Assemblage* 10 (December 1989): 7.

20 Walter Benjamin, "The Work of Art in the Era of Mechanical Reproduction," in *Illuminations* (New York: Harcourt, Brace & World, 1968), 241.

21 Maurice Culot, "Conversation avec Bernard Huet," in Bernard Huet, *Anachroniques d'architecture* (Brussels: Archives d'architecture moderne, 1981), 172.

22 Ross, *Universal Abandon,* x.

23 Arendt, *The Human Condition,* 305 (including a quotation by her from Henri Bergson). In a dense and pessimistic text of 1944 by two other European emigrés in America, Max Horkheimer and Theodor Adorno, one finds perhaps the earliest extant expression of the loss of confidence in the Enlightenment rationality underpinning modernism, by thinkers who had begun their careers within its traditions. Written in the darkest years of the middle of the war, Horkheimer's and Adorno's *Dialectic of Enlightenment* showed the acute disillusionment of its authors with the Enlightenment's once-supposed indisputable beneficence. They had found themselves driven to the conclusion that it had to be held complicit in the hitherto unimaginable events taking place in Europe in the late 1930s and 1940s:

> We are wholly convinced . . . that social freedom is inseparable from enlightened thought. Nevertheless, we believe that we have just as clearly recognized that the notion of this very way of thinking, no less than the actual historic forms—the social institutions—with which it is interwoven, already contains the seed of the reversal universally apparent today. If enlightenment does not accommodate reflection on this recidivist element, then it seals its own fate. If consideration of the destructive aspect of progress is left to its enemies, blindly pragmatized thought loses its transcending quality and its relation to truth. In the enigmatic readiness of the technologically educated masses to fall under the sway of any despotism, in its self-destructive affinity to popular paranoia, and in all uncomprehended absurdity, the weakness of the modern theoretical faculty is apparent.

the Horman Ezleen aspect

Horkheimer and Adorno, *Dialectic of Enlightenment* (New York: Continuum, 1988), xiii.

24 Arendt's disavowal by thinkers of a Marxist persuasion probably sprang originally from her publication in 1951 of *The Origins of Totalitarianism* (my edition is New York: Harcourt Brace Jovanovich, 1968), the first text that treated Nazi Germany and Stalinist Russia as more or less equivalent political regimes. Her parting of the ways with conventional American academic propriety culminated with the publication in 1958 of *The Human Condition.* Her extremely acrimonious split with the representative groups of American Jewry followed from the publication of *Eichmann in Jerusalem* (New York: Viking Press, 1963).

25 Mary McCarthy's and Hans Jonas's relationships to Arendt are well documented in Elizabeth Young-Breuhl's *Hannah Arendt: For Love of the World* (New Haven: Yale University Press, 1984); Young-Breuhl is also represented in Melvyn Hill, ed., *Hannah Arendt: The Recovery of the Public World* (New York: St. Martin's Press, 1978). Michael Denneny went on to become an editor of *Christopher Street,* the New York-based gay literary magazine.

Frampton's position on Arendt has been given what I think may be considered a definitive expression in his *Modern Architecture and the Critical Present* (London: Architectural Design and Academy Editions, 1982), conceived by him as a compilation of texts that would document, frame, and serve as his response to the overall critical reception of his *Modern Architecture: A Critical History* (New York: Thames and Hudson, 1980). Frampton opened *Modern Architecture and the Critical Present* with a text entitled "The Status of Man and the Status of His Objects: A Reading of the Human Condition," a reworked version of a paper he had delivered in Arendt's presence, at a conference convened in her honor at York University in Toronto in 1972 (see Hill, *Hannah Arendt,* 101).

"The Status of Man" seems to me definitive, insofar as it addresses itself quite fundamentally to the concepts of "labor" and "work," as Arendt characterizes them, and explores their potential import for our understanding of architecture. The reader who compares Frampton's commentary on these matters with the more detailed one of my own in chapters three and four will find no significant difference of opinion between us in this regard. Indeed, the specific architectural debates that I underpin with Arendt's arguments can readily be seen as a fleshing out of the more general historical arguments Frampton outlines in his essay.

At the same time, it may be in an account of Arendt's view of the relationship of "action" to architecture that my departures from Frampton's arguments can be articulated most clearly. While it gives an utterly cogent account of the import of the concepts of labor and work in architecture, Frampton's essay does not similarly pursue her concept of action. To be sure, "the world" is for her an impassioned object of love, but as I understand her, it is so only as a frame to provide the "shining brightness" of action. Not only is this emphasis central to Arendt's work, it seems to me that it is in large measure because of it that her contribution to political theory is so contentious. Her perceived role as a maverick; her contrarian intellectual tendencies; her aversion to categorization as conservative or radical; all these are, in my view, manifestations of the complex conception of action she managed to forge from a heteroclite reading of Augustine, Dante, Heidegger, Machiavelli, and Marx.

I have been struck, in this regard, by a rereading of the proceedings of the 1972 conference I attended along with Frampton. While his emphasis in that early period of our joint interest in her ideas was as I have described it above, my own, judging from the published commentaries, already appears itself to have been much more contrarian. I noted, for example, that a number of left-liberal political economists and sociologists in attendance pursued her with questions that implicitly disparaged the absence of any substantive "engagement" in her political thought. As this discussion was proceeding, I took it upon myself to ask her whether, in the

[margin handwritten note:] Baird & Frampton similar

circumstances of such criticism, it might not be worthwhile for her to respond by expanding upon her notorious commendation of Machiavelli for teaching men "how not to be good"—or to underscore what I had taken to be her basic characterization of political action, not to "do good" but to "seek glory." Sure enough, she took up my invitation enthusiastically (Hill, *Hannah Arendt,* 310). Later in the same discussion, Arendt was interrogated by Albrecht Wellmer as to the appropriateness of politics as a vehicle for the solution, say, of the "housing problem." Here again I reminded her of the fascinating sociological discoveries that were then beginning to be made, whereby it appeared that so-called "housing experts" were condemning as "inadequate" housing the actual occupants of which found perfectly acceptable as accommodation. Here too, Arendt happily seized on the "anarchistic" thrust of my intervention, to disparage still further what she saw as the lamentable "instrumentalization" of political praxis that seemed to be implicit in conventional left liberalism (ibid., 318).

This anecdote seems to me worth recounting since it encapsulates so concisely my own sense of the very broad implications for architecture that might be drawn out of Arendt's remarkable concept of "action," and of the ways in which they differ from those that Frampton has identified. Given the startling "Machiavellianism" of her orientation to politics, it seems to me that she would deeply resist the well-known political "good intentions" of orthodox modern architecture that Frampton continues to admire.

If chapters three and four pursue implications of "labor" and "work" in Arendt that are parallel to Frampton's, I believe the reader will find equally potent and quite distinct implications of my reading of her concept of "action" in chapters one, five, six, seven, and eight.

Moreover, this different emphasis leads me to quite different conclusions than his about the overall implications of Arendt's thinking for architecture. I can point, for instance, to the projects with which Frampton saw fit to conclude *Modern Architecture and the Critical Present,* and which, he agreed, might consistently be seen as demonstrating "resistance to the mono-valent propensity of consumer culture" (Frampton, *Modern Architecture and the Critical Present,* 86). While this may be so, I am at a loss to see how most of them could be seen to derive from "action" in Arendt's sense. Two of them—housing projects by Gwathmey Siegel and Henri Ciriani—are indisputably paternalist projects of the sort I criticize in chapters six and seven for their problematic tendency to dissipate, rather than to focus, public life. The last one—a City Hall for San Bernardino by Cesar Pelli—comprises merely a stylistically acceptable repackaging of a by then historically questionable building program. Indeed, of the five, only one—a housing project from Berlin by Josef Kleiheus—would seem to me to be sufficiently engaged with the actual political realities of its historical situation to manifest any redemptive political potential, such as I have attempted to articulate in chapter seven.

In turn, this sharp difference of orientation in respect to the architectural applicability of Arendt's ideas—which it seems to me my text as a whole represents—may enable me to cite here what I see as the major limitation to Frampton's alternative reading. Surely it is indicative that "The Status of Man and the Status of His Objects" begins with a quotation from Adorno and ends (more or less) with others from Marcuse and Habermas (ibid., 7, 19). Thus Frampton (admittedly not without some trepidation) virtually assimilates Arendt to the Frankfurt School. I think it is his unyielding preoccupation with consumerism that causes him to do this, but it has the disappointing effect, as I see it, of rendering his architectural prescriptions either overly utopian or unnecessarily bleak.

While not denying parallels between Arendt and the Frankfurt School (I have, after all, quoted Adorno myself), I am equally interested in reading her as allied to the anarchist, libertarian political tradition associated with revolutionaries such as Rosa Luxemburg, student leaders such as Daniel Cohn-Bendit, social critics such as Ivan Illich, and housing activists such as John F. C. Turner—not to mention the legions of minority and gay activists who have, over the years, been so inspired by her.

Surely what makes Arendt so distinctive among the major political and cultural theorists of our time has been precisely the contrarianism that enables her to span so provocatively from the aloof cultural critique of the Frankfurt School to the intense, phenomenologically engaged activism of the sixties.

As much as the Arendt who is the defender of "the fabrication of the human artifice," it is the Arendt of "action" whom I have attempted to honor in the arguments that follow. For if I understand her correctly, "the space of appearance" will need to evoke the second as much as the first.

26 *Hannah Arendt/Karl Jaspers Correspondence, 1926–1969* (New York: Harcourt Brace Jovanovich, 1992).

27 See especially Claude Lefort, *Democracy and Political Theory* (Minneapolis: University of Minnesota Press, 1988).

28 Reiner Schurmann's *Heidegger on Being and Acting: From Principles to Anarchy* (Bloomington: Indiana University Press, 1990) is dedicated to the memory of Arendt.

Further evidence of the expanding current interest in Arendt's ideas may be found in Bonnie Honig, *Political Theory and the Displacement of Politics* (Ithaca: Cornell University Press, 1993) and in a forthcoming text on Arendt by Seyla Benhabib.

29   Jean L. Cohen and Andrew Arato, *Civil Society and Political Theory* (Cambridge: MIT Press, 1992). See especially chapter 4, "The Normative Critique: Hannah Arendt."

30   Arendt, *The Human Condition,* 198–199.

31   Ibid., 95

32   Ibid., 95–96.

33   Ibid., 88.

34   Ibid., 98–99.

35   Ibid., 89.

36   For a detailed account of the primacy of life see *The Human Condition,* part III, "Labor."

37   For an excellent account of the political influence of Spencer, especially in North America, see Richard Hofstadter, *Social Darwinism in American Thought* (Boston: Beacon Press, 1955), especially chapter 2, "The Vogue of Spencer." Mumford's published body of work is vast; the influence of organicism on it can be seen in *The Culture of Cities* (New York: Harcourt, Brace and Company, 1938). See also Donald Miller's biography *Lewis Mumford: A Life* (New York: Weidenfeld & Nicolson, 1989).

Lukács's views in this matter are of particular interest in that he was also responsible for the formulation of a highly influential model of "reification," in his *History and Class Consciousness* of 1923. To be sure, in doing so he began, like Arendt, with reference to Marx, citing a passage from *Capital* with which to elucidate what he called specifically the "reification of work":

> The products of labour become commodities, social things whose qualities are at the same time perceptible and imperceptible by the senses. . . . It is only a definite social relation between men that assumes, in their eyes, the fantastic form of a relation between things.

For Lukács, following Marx, it is this "fantastic form of a relation between things" that, in the first instance, constitutes "reification." Yet as his argument proceeds, the continuing influence upon him of the late nineteenth-century sociologist of *Gemeinschaft und Gesellschaft* Ferdinand Tonnies becomes ever more apparent, and Lukács can be seen increasingly consistently to set up an opposition between the evidently "alienated" and "atomized" products of such labor as characterized by Marx, and those other, earlier ones that, according to his view, more "organically" emerged within precapitalist societies. Here his evident bias in favor of "organicism" and the "life process," and his unqualified rejection of "reification," become correspondingly more sweeping both at the same time.

History and Class Consciousness, of 1923, is Lukács's major work. I have consulted the 1971 translation published by Merlin Press, London, in which the passage from Karl Marx is quoted on p. 86. Tonnies's influence on Lukács is described in Michael Lowy, *From Romanticism to Bolshevism* (London: New Left Books, 1979).

38   Arendt, *The Human Condition,* 173.

39   Ibid., 169. Having fought for most of her intellectual life an unfashionable battle for the acknowledgment of the necessity of reification, Arendt must have been struck, late in her career, to receive belated support from a key figure in the anti-Heideggerian camp in modern cultural theory. This is Theodor Adorno, who late in his own intellectual career came to a guarded and thoughtful view of reification that bears close comparison to Arendt's. In a passage close to the end of his *Negative Dialectics* of 1966, for example (New York: Continuum, 1987, 374)—a passage knowledgeable readers have even seen as a retrospective criticism of Lukács— Adorno ruminated that "the category of reification, which was inspired by the wishful image of unbroken subjective immediacy, no longer merits the key position accorded to it." In fact, Adorno took a position on reification that was surprisingly compatible with Arendt's, observing in a late essay on Aldous Huxley ("Aldous Huxley and Utopia," *Prisms,* Cambridge: MIT Press, 1982, 106):

> Humanity includes reification, as well as its opposite, not merely as the condition from which liberation is possible but also positively, as the form in which, however brittle and inadequate it may be, subjective impulses are realized, but only by being objectified.

Small wonder then that, looking back over a century of controversy on this difficult question, Adorno concluded (*Negative Dialectics,* 374) that "pure immediacy and fetishism are equally untrue." It would appear that Adorno and Arendt, proceeding from rather different intellectual starting points, arrived at a position of notable concurrence with respect to the hoary question of reification.

40   Arendt, *The Human Condition,* 175–176.

41 Ibid., 176, 179.

42 If none of Arendt's philosophical predecessors has matched her passion for the "world," it is equally true that none of them has manifested any interest at all in the potentiality of "action." Given their quite Hegelian teleologies, we would probably not have expected such interest of Marx or of Lukács. Yet, interestingly enough, one finds none in Adorno or in Heidegger either. In both their cases, a temperamental inclination toward the *vita contemplativa* rather than the *vita activa* (as Arendt would characterize the two modes of living) is probably the cause. By contrast, and notwithstanding her own interest in contemplation, she also stands amongst her philosophical peers as an almost unique example of a thinker with a "passionate"—for some observers even "embarrassing"—engagement with the phenomenon of "action."

43 Arendt, *The Human Condition,* 180

44 Among the many graduate students from Arendt's days at the University of Chicago who have subsequently distinguished themselves in these areas are the rock critics Robert Christgau and Greil Marcus, not to mention those already cited, Elizabeth Young-Breuhl and the gay activist Michael Denneny.

45 Arendt, *The Human Condition,* 57.

Chapter One
Life as a Work of Art

EPIGRAPH   Hannah Arendt, "Isak Dinesen: 1885–1963," in *Men in Dark Times* (New York: Harcourt, Brace & World, 1968), 109.

1 Adolf Loos, "The Story of a Poor Rich Man," in Ludwig Münz and Gustav Künstler, *Adolf Loos: Pioneer of Modern Architecture* (New York: Praeger Publishers, 1966), 223–224.

2 Ibid., 225.

3 Adolf Loos, "Ornament and Crime," in Münz and Künstler, *Adolf Loos,* 226.

4 Theodor Adorno, "Functionalism Today: An Address to the 1965 Meeting of the *Deutscher Werkbund,*" *Oppositions* 17 (1979), 33.

5 Adolf Loos, quoted in Münz and Künstler, *Adolf Loos,* 17.

6 Ibid., 16.

7 Ibid., 19.

8 Robert Breuer, "Peter Behrens," *Werkkunst* 3 (9 February 1908): 145–149.

9 Henry Van de Velde, "Extracts from His Memoirs: 1891–1901," *Architectural Review,* 112, no. 669 (September 1952): 153.

10 Walter Benjamin, "Paris: Capital of the Nineteenth Century," *Perspecta* 12 (1969): 169.

11 Van de Velde, "Memoirs: 1891–1901," 151.

12 Ibid., 152.

13 William Morris, in a letter quoted in Nikolaus Pevsner, *Some Architectural Writers of the Nineteenth Century* (Oxford: Clarendon Press, 1972), 281.

14 Van de Velde, "Memoirs: 1891–1901," 151.

15 Benjamin, "Paris: Capital of the Nineteenth Century," 169.

16 Van de Velde, "Memoirs: 1891–1901," 146.

16 Benjamin, "Paris: Capital of the Nineteenth Century," 169.

18 Arendt, "Isak Dinesen," 109.

19 Robert Clark, "The German Return to Classicism after Jugendstil," *Journal of the Society of Art Historians* 29 (October 1970): 273.

20 Ibid.

21 On the evolution of Behrens's career see Tilmann Buddensieg, *Industriekultur: Peter Behrens and the AEG* (Cambridge: MIT Press, 1984).

22 Peter Behrens, quoted in Stanford Anderson, "Behrens' Changing Concept," *Architectural Design* (February 1969): 77.

23 Gropius's well-known project has been extensively documented in numerous texts. See, for example, Leonardo Benevolo, *History of Modern Architecture* (Cambridge: MIT Press, 1971), 383–387.

24 Hermann Muthesius, quoted in Benevolo, *History of Modern Architecture,* 381.

25 Hermann Muthesius, quoted in Nikolaus Pevsner, *Pioneers of Modern Design* (1936; reprint, Harmondsworth: Penguin Books, 1960), 37.

26 Henry Van de Velde, quoted in Pevsner, *Pioneers of Modern Design,* 18.

27 Pevsner, in his *Pioneer of Modern Design* of 1936, was the first writer to introduce the concept of "matter-of-factness" explicitly into theroetical architectural discourse in the English language. For further discussion see chapter two below.

28 It is interesting in retrospect to compare the circumstances of these images with those outlined in Philippe Boudon's sociological account of the transformations made by long-term inhabitants to Le Corbusier's pioneering housing project in Pessace, near Bordeaux, roughly contemporary with the Esprit Nouveau pavilion. Looking at successive transformations of plans, elevations, and roofs, Le Corbusier commented to Boudon: "It's amazing the things they have done."

29 Chris Welles, "How It Feels to Live in Total Design," *Life* (29 April 1966): 59.

30 These projects of Michael Graves are all documented in Karen Vogel Nichols, Patrick J. Burke, and Caroline Hancock, *Michael Graves Buildings and Projects 1982–1989* (Princeton: Princeton Architectural Press, 1990).

31 Silva's provocative project is illustrated in Elizabeth Diller, Diane Lewis, and Kim Shkapich, *The Education of an Architect* (New York: Rizzoli, 1988).

Chapter Two
Early Struggles in the Phenomenology of Modernism

EPIGRAPH   Hannah Arendt, *The Human Condition* (Chicago: University of Chicago Press, 1958), 10.

1 Nikolaus Pevsner, *Pioneers of Modern Design* (1936; reprint, Harmondsworth: Penguin Books, 1960), 38, 32.

2   F. T. Marinetti, quoted in Reyner Banham, *Theory and Design in the First Machine Age* (London: Architectural Press, 1960), 125.

3   Pevsner, *Pioneers of Modern Design,* 211.

4   Banham was probably the first English-speaking historian of modernism to reassert the claims of the futurists so forcefully. See Banham, *Theory and Design in the First Machine Age,* 98.

5   Robert Lebel, *Marcel Duchamp* (New York: Grove Press, 1959), 35.

6   Pevsner, *Pioneers of Modern Design,* 32.

7   Hermann Muthesius, *The English House* (New York: Rizzoli, 1979), 149.

8   Streiter's views are discussed in Harry Malgrave's introduction to Otto Wagner, *Modern Architecture* (Santa Monica: Getty Center, 1988), 33.

9   Events in German architectural circles during this period are discussed in detail in Marcel Franciscono, *Walter Gropius and the Creation of the Bauhaus in Weimar* (Urbana: University of Illinois Press, 1971).

10 Hannes Mayer, "The New World," in Claude Schnaidt, *Hannes Meyer: Buildings, Projects and Writings* (London: Alec Tiranti, 1965), 91.

11 Hannes Meyer, "building," in Schnaidt, *Hannes Meyer,* 95.

12 Karel Teige, "Mundaneum," *Oppositions* 4 (October 1974): 89, 91.

13 Le Corbusier "In Defense of Architecture," *Oppositions* 4 (October 1974): 95.

14 Ibid., 96.

15 Ibid., 106.

16 Ibid., 105.

17 For a broad if partisan overview, see John Willet, *Art and Politics in the Weimar Period: The New Sobriety, 1917–1933* (New York: Pantheon Books, 1978).

18   Barbara Miller Lane, *Architecture and Politics in Germany, 1918–1945* (Cambridge: Harvard University Press, 1968), 130.

19   Ibid., 130, 132.

20   Johannes Duiker, "Dr. Berlage and the *Nieuwe Zakelijkheid*," in E. J. Jelles and C. A. Alberts, "Duiker 1890–1935," *Forum voor architectuur en daarmee verbonden kunsten* 5, 6 (January 1972): 132.

21   Ibid.

22   Berlage, quoted in ibid., 132.

23   It is interesting to map this astute if anecdotal observation of Berlage's against the larger critique of instrumentality in human affairs mounted by Hannah Arendt in her *The Human Condition* of 1958. Berlage's characterization of functionalism as potentially *expedient* is the first reference of this kind in modern architectural theory that I know.

24   Henry-Russell Hitchcock and Philip Johnson, *The International Style* (New York: W. W. Norton and Company, 1966), 92.

25   Ibid., 91.

26   This reference to "the data alone" is very telling, in that it evokes so strongly the bid to revive a purely rationalized orientation to design that arose later on, in the wake of the collapse of "establishment modern architecture" in the sixties. Among the many symptomatic reactions to that collapse in those days were one that arose in Germany at the Hochschule für Gestaltung and one in Britain at the Bartlett School of Architecture, where powerful movements were oriented—yet again—toward expunging subjectivity from design altogether, and toward rendering it instead a purely inductive process of empirical data gathering, possibly even one that could, in principle, be accomplished entirely by computer. Significantly enough, one of the early products of this tendency was a text by the then young theoretician Christopher Alexander, entitled "Notes on the Synthesis of Form."

27   Johannes Duiker, "The House of Dr. d'Alsace in Rue St. Guillaume in Paris," in Jelles and Alberts, "Duiker 1890–1935," 143.

28   Ibid.

29 Ibid.

30 It is important to note here that only a year before the first presentation in Paris of the famous text "The Author as Producer," Benjamin had written a fascinating commentary entitled "Experience and Poverty" in which he made a strong case for a modern life of an abstemious restraint, such as might readily be associated affirmatively with the *sachlich* tendency. Significantly enough, however, the praise of restraint and of straightforwardness embodied in the 1933 text has, as its explicitly posited negation, the mindless bourgeois self-satisfaction of the pre–World War I era. If one is to read "Experience and Poverty" of 1933 and "The Author as Producer" of 1934 at face value, it would seem that in the short span of a year or so, Benjamin moved from a sympathy for the *Sachlichkeit* tendency (characterized as opposed to bourgeois complacency) to an opposition to it (based on a certain complacency it was itself capable of being seen to embody, only one year later).

31 Sergei Eisenstein, quoted in Peter Wollen, *Signs and Meaning in the Cinema* (London: Secker & Warburg, 1969), 32.

32 Wollen, *Signs and Meaning,* 27–28.

33 Walter Benjamin, "The Author as Producer," in *Understanding Brecht* (London: New Left Books, 1973), 94.

34 Ibid.

35 Ibid., 96.

36 Ibid., 99.

37 Georg Lukács, "Reportage or Portrayal?," in *Essays on Realism* (Cambridge: MIT Press, 1981), 45.

Chapter Three
"The Labour of Our Body and the Work of Our Hands"

EPIGRAPH John Locke, *The Second Treatise of Government* (Indianapolis: Hackett, 1980), 19.

1 Adolf Behne's essay was published in an English translation: "Art, Handicraft, Technology," *Oppositions* 22 (Fall 1980): 96–104.

2   Francesco Dal Co, "The Remoteness of *die Moderne*," *Oppositions* 22 (Fall 1980): 74–95. This essay summarizes some of the critical hypotheses in the first part Dal Co's book, *Abitare nel moderno* (Milan: Feltrinelli, 1981).

3   Behne, "Art, Handicraft, Technology," 96.

4   Ibid., 97.

5   Ibid., 98.

6   Ibid., 99.

7   Ibid., 101.

8   Ibid., 102.

9   Ibid., 103–104.

10   In part, according to Dal Co, this is a result of a theoretical vantage point newly available after the end of the First World War, from which the central theoretical interests of the Werkbund took on a different appearance than they had in 1914. The openness, typicality, and restraint that have been associated with the theories of Adolf Loos, and that had at that time been counterposed to the perceived excesses of the Secession, had by 1920 taken on a somewhat different cast. Dal Co has gone so far as to claim that the Werkbund group still shared with the generation of the Secession a strong conviction of the necessity for artists to resist what they still saw as the tendency of modern civilization to fragmentation and dispersion. Against this artists were expected, by means of design acts, to develop a new "harmonious culture," and the basis of this culture—*Wohnkultur,* a culture of habitation—was, for the protagonists of the Werkbund, the house.

For them architecture was "a fragile bridge which mediates between the infinite multifacetedness of the contemporary world, its endless possibilities, its indefatigable dynamism, and that point of tranquility, of subjective withdrawal, represented by the house, by habitation, the place where the human being can again find his roots" (Behne, quoted in Dal Co, "Remoteness," 82). Thus the new interest in standards, in practicality, and in technique was still radically qualified by a powerfully felt commitment to quality. And this commitment maintained a scrupulous distance, according to Dal Co, from the everyday practices of technology and industry:

In the more serious theories of *die Moderne,* the "style of the age" is not at all a metaphor for qualities such as "functionality," "technology," "industrial forms," etc., or for the harmony of forms and functions, to use a customary expression—it is on the contrary the expression of the effort to harmonize the most functional characteristics of modern civilization—which is in itself functional and anti-decorative—with the values of a harmonious and subjective mode of habitation. (Ibid., 88–89)

Not only is there evident here a strong reservation regarding technology and industrialization; an integral component of the culture of habitation was a commitment to traditional precepts of craftsmanship:

From the theories of the Werkbund there emerged, often overwhelmingly, a hypothesis which posited the design function as the basis for the harmonizing power of artistic work: this function not only guarantees the survival of certain forms of labour which would otherwise be destined to disappear, it also restores meaning to handicrafts, safeguarding the fundamental value preserved by artisan "harmonious culture." (Ibid., 89)

This commentary of Dal Co's seems to me to place Behne's text in an apt position in the historical evolution of mainstream modernism.

11 John Ruskin, quoted in Nikolaus Pevsner, *Studies in Art, Architecture and Design* (London: Thames and Hudson, 1968), 2:105.

12 Mathew Digby Wyatt, quoted in Pevsner, *Studies in Art, Architecture and Design,* 2:104.

13 John Ruskin, quoted in Raymond Williams, *Culture and Society* (Harmondsworth: Penguin Books, 1961), 146–147.

14 Karl Marx, *Capital* (New York: Vintage Books, 1977), 1:483.

15 Sigfried Giedion, *Mechanization Takes Command* (New York: Oxford University Press, 1948).

16 Giedion, *Mechanization Takes Command,* 482.

17 Ibid.

18 Ibid.

19 Ibid.

20 Hannah Arendt, *The Human Condition* (Chicago: University of Chicago Press, 1958), 96.

21   Ibid., 136–137.

22   Ibid., 101.

23   Ibid., 306–307.

24   Ibid., 123–124.

25   Adam Smith, *The Wealth of Nations* (London: Penguin Classics, 1986), 112.

26   Arendt, *The Human Condition*, 126.

27   William Morris, *Collected Works* (London, 1910–1915), 22:40.

28   The episode is documented in the interview between Krier and Colin Davis published in Leon Krier, *Drawings 1967–1980* (Brussels: Archives d'Architecture Moderne, 1980), xxiv.

Chapter Four
Instruments and Monuments

EPIGRAPHS   Adolf Loos, "Architecture," in Tim Benton, Charlotte Benton, and Dennis Sharp, *Architecture and Design 1890–1939* (New York: Watson-Guptill, 1975), 45.

Karel Tiege, "Mundaneum," *Oppositions* 4 (October 1974): 83.

1   Karl Kraus, quoted in Allan Janik and Stephen Toulmin, *Wittgenstein's Vienna* (New York: Simon and Schuster, 1973), 89.

2   Teige, "Mundaneum," 89–91.

3   Hannah Arendt, *The Human Condition* (Chicago: University of Chicago Press, 1958), 153.

4   Ibid.

5   Ibid., 294–295.

6   Ibid., 305.

7   Le Corbusier, "In Defense of Architecture," *Oppositions* 4 (October 1974): 98.

8   Ibid.

9   Ibid., 96.

10 Henry-Russell Hitchcock and Philip Johnson, *The International Style* (1932; reprint New York: W. W. Norton and Company, 1966), 80.

11 Ibid., 94.

12 Lewis Mumford, "The Death of the Monument," in J. L. Martin, Ben Nicholson, and Noam Gabo, *Circle: International Survey of Constructive Art* (1937; reprint, London: Faber and Faber, 1971), 264, 265–266.

13 Ibid., 266.

14 Ibid.

15 Ibid.

16 Ibid., 267. Interestingly enough, in taking such an uncompromising stance Mumford effectively ruled out in advance any of the approaches to the "recycling" of historical buildings that have recently become so well established, as well as any complex reworking of their forms as is typical, for example, of the work of Carlo Scarpa.

17 The first version of Giedion's text was published in Paul Zucker, *New Architecture and City Planning* (New York: Philosophical Library, 1944), 549ff.

18 Gregor Paulsson, Henry-Russell Hitchcock, William Holford, Sigfried Giedion, Walter Gropius, Lucio Costa, and Alfred Roth, "In Search of a New Monumentality: A Symposium," in *Architectural Review* 104, no. 621 (September 1948).

19 Ibid., 126.

20 Ibid., 124.

21 Ibid., 123.

22 Giedion, in "In Search of a New Monumentality," 126.

23 Ibid.

24 See Le Corbusier, *Oeuvre complète,* vol. 3 (Erlenbach-Zurich: Editions d'Architecture, 1946), 82–89.

25 Sigfried Giedion, *A Decade of New Architecture* (Zurich: Editions Girsberger, 1951), 116.

26 Lewis Mumford, "Monumentalism, Symbolism and Style," *Architectural Review* 105, no. 628 (April 1949), 174.

27 Mumford's curious group of citations also posits a quite sweeping and speculative association from the British arts and crafts at the end of the nineteenth century, to the expressionism of the 1920s, to the revisionist modernism of the 1930s.

28 Mumford, "Monumentalism, Symbolism and Style," 174.

29 Ibid., 180

30 This now recognizable cliché was in those days a popular distillation of ideas expressed in major texts by Pevsner, Giedion, and of course by Le Corbusier himself.

31 Colin Rowe, "The Mathematics of the Ideal Villa," reprinted in *The Mathematics of the Ideal Villa and Other Essays* (Cambridge: MIT Press, 1976), 14.

32 Rudolf Wittkower, *Architectural Principles in the Age of Humanism* (1949; reprint, London: Alec Tiranti, 1962), 1.

33 Rowe, "Mathematics of the Ideal Villa," 24.

34 Vincent Scully, "Doldrums in the Suburbs," *Perspecta* 9/10 (1966): 289.

35 Reyner Banham, *Theory and Design in the First Machine Age* (London: Architectural Press, 1960), 325.

36 Buckminster Fuller, quoted in ibid., 325.

37 Banham, ibid., 327.

38 Ibid., 329.

39 Reyner Banham, *The New Brutalism* (London: Architectural Press, 1966), 134–135.

40 Ibid., 135.

41 For information on these groups, see various issues of the British architectural magazine *Architectural Design* from the middle 1960s through the early 1970s.

42 George Baird, "La Dimension Amoureuse in Architecture," in Charles Jencks and George Baird, eds., *Meaning in Architecture* (New York: Braziller, 1969), 78.

43 Included in Reyner Banham, "The Architecture of Wampanoag," in Jencks and Baird, *Meaning in Architecture,* 109.

44 Ibid.

45 Ibid., 111.

46 Ibid.

47 Christopher Alexander, *Notes on the Synthesis of Form* (Cambridge: Harvard University Press, 1964).

48 The Ulm episode is briefly discussed in "Place, Production and Architecture: Towards a Critical Theory of Building," in Kenneth Frampton's *Modern Architecture and the Critical Present* (London: Architectural Design and Academy Editions, 1982).

49 Arendt, *The Human Condition,* 157.

50 Ibid., 154.

51 Ibid., 157.

52 Ibid., 158–159.

53 Colin Rowe, introduction to *Five Architects: Eisenman, Graves, Gwathmey, Hejduk, and Meier* (New York: Wittenborn and Company, 1972).

54 See, for example, Peter Eisenman, *House X* (New York: Rizzoli, 1982).

55 Peter Eisenman, introduction to Rafael Moneo, "Aldo Rossi: The Idea of Architecture and the Modena Cemetery," *Oppositions* 5 (Summer 1976): 1.

56   Moneo, "Aldo Rossi," 3. It is interesting to note how decisively this position of Rossi both challenges and answers the naive concern of Lewis Mumford in respect to "petrification," cited above.

57   Ibid., 6.

58   Aldo Rossi, quoted in ibid.

59   Moneo, ibid., 18.

60   Ibid.

61   Eisenman, introduction to Moneo, "Aldo Rossi," 1.

62   Moneo, "Aldo Rossi," 19.

Chapter Five
Panopticism

EPIGRAPH   **Jeremy Bentham, quoted in Gertrude Himmelfarb, "The Haunted House of Jeremy Bentham," in *Victorian Minds* (New York: Alfred Knopf, 1968), 33.**

1   Barbara Kreis, "The Idea of the *Dom-Kommuna* and the Dilemma of the Soviet Avant-Garde," *Oppositions* 21 (Summer 1980): 53.

2   Ibid.

3   Ibid., 67.

4   Ibid., 69–70.

5   Ibid., 71.

6   I. Kuzman, quoted in Anatole Kopp, *Town and Revolution* (London: Thames and Hudson, 1970), 153.

7   Hannah Arendt, *The Human Condition* (Chicago: University of Chicago Press, 1958), 305.

8   Quoted in Peter Wollen, *Signs and Meaning in the Cinema* (London: Secker & Warburg, 1969), 27.

9 V. I. Lenin, quoted in Harry Braverman, *Labor and Monopoly Capital* (New York: Monthly Review Press, 1974), 12.

10 Ibid., 112, 113.

11 Ibid., 118.

12 William Morris, quoted in Raymond Williams, *Culture and Society* (Harmondsworth: Penguin Books, 1961), 154.

13 Charles Dickens, *Hard Times* (London: Collins, [1906]), 33.

14 Ibid., 23.

15 Ibid., 8.

16 Williams, *Culture and Society,* 105.

17 See A. W. N. Pugin, *Contrasts* (reprint, Leicester: Leicester University Press, 1969).

18 Samuel T. Coleridge, quoted in Williams, *Culture and Society,* 73.

19 Le Corbusier, "In Defense of Architecture," *Oppositions* 4 (October 1974): 106.

20 Max Horkheimer and Theodor Adorno, *Dialectic of Enlightenment* (New York: Continuum Books, 1988), xii.

21 Michel Foucault, *Madness and Civilization: A History of Insanity in the Age of Reason* (London: Tavistock Publications, 1965).

22 Michel Foucault, *Discipline and Punish* (New York: Vintage Books, 1979), 216.

23 Ibid., 218.

24 Ibid., 221.

25 See Braverman, *Labor and Monopoly Capital,* and Sigfried Giedion, *Mechanization Takes Command* (New York: Oxford University Press, 1948), especially their respective discussions of work that followed historically from Taylor's, such as that of Frank and Lillian Gilbreth.

26 The work of the situationists has been recently documented in Elisabeth Sussman, ed., *On the Passage of a Few People through a Rather Brief Moment in Time* (Cambridge: MIT Press, 1989). "Advocacy planning" is described, albeit in a highly partisan fashion, in Robert Goodman's *After the Planners* (New York: Simon and Schuster, 1971), to be discussed in detail in chapter seven.

27 Debord's seminal text is *Society of the Spectacle* (Detroit: Black and Red, 1983). Jameson is the author of numerous key texts in recent cultural theory, of which the most pertinent to this point is his *Postmodernism, or the Cultural Logic of Late Capitalism* (Durham: Duke University Press, 1992). My understanding of Maldonado's position is derived from Frampton, *Modern Architecture and the Critical Present* (London: Architectural Design and Academy Editions, 1982).

28 See Lyotard, *The Postmodern Condition: A Report on Knowledge* (Minneapolis: University of Minnesota Press, 1984), and Bruce Sterling, *The Hacker Crackdown* (New York: Bantam Books, 1993).

29 Lyotard, *The Postmodern Condition,* 67.

30 Shoshana Zuboff, *In the Age of the Smart Machine* (New York: Basic Books, 1988). See especially chapter 4, "Office Technology as Exile and Integration."

31 Constance Penley and Andrew Ross, eds., *Technocultures* (Minneapolis: University of Minnesota Press, 1991), xii.

Chapter Six
Organicist Yearnings and Their Consequences

1 It is interesting to note that between the publication of "The Death of the Monument" in *Circle* in 1937 and its incorporation into his book *The Culture of Cities* in 1938, Mumford modified his text quite significantly, revising a number of the more startling claims from the 1937 version quoted here. The original appeared in J. L. Martin, Ben Nicholson, and Noam Gabo, *Circle: International Survey of Constructive Art* (1937; reprint, London: Faber and Faber, 1971). I owe to my Harvard colleague Werner Sollois the realization that this sequence of extreme statement on this subject, followed by partial recantation, is foreshadowed in opinions of the character Holgrave in Nathaniel Hawthorne's *The House of the Seven Gables*. Mumford would, of course, have known this novel.

2 Ibid., 265–266.

3 Ibid., 268.

4 Edmund Burke, quoted in Raymond Williams, *Culture and Society 1780–1950* (Harmondsworth: Penguin Books, 1961), 30.

5 *Coleridge's Essays and Lectures on Shakespeare,* ed. Ernest Rhys (London and Toronto: J. M. Dent and Sons, 1926), 46.

6 For my understanding of Tonnies I have relied on Harry Liebersohn, *Fate and Utopia in German Sociology 1870–1923* (Cambridge: MIT Press, 1988).

7 Morton White and Lucia White, *The Intellectual versus the City* (Oxford: Oxford University Press, 1977), 150.

8 Frank Lloyd Wright, "Organic Architecture," in *Frank Lloyd Wright on Architecture,* ed. Frederick Gutheim (New York: University Library, 1935, Grosset & Dunlap, 1941), 178.

9 Ibid., 181.

10 S. T. Coleridge, quoted in Williams, *Culture and Society,* 82.

11 William Morris, "The Revival of Architecture," reprinted in Nikolaus Pevsner, *Some Architectural Writers of the Nineteenth Century* (Oxford: Clarendon Press, 1972), 323.

12 Liebersohn, *Fate and Utopia in German Sociology,* 28, 29.

13 Arthur O. Lovejoy, *The Great Chain of Being, A Study in the History of an Idea* (New York: Harper and Row, 1965), 52.

14 Hannah Arendt, *The Human Condition* (Chicago: University of Chicago Press, 1958), 106.

15 Lewis Mumford, "Introduction," in Ian McHarg, *Design with Nature* (Garden City, New York: Doubleday & Company, 1971), vii.

16 McHarg, *Design with Nature,* 1

17 Richard Hofstadter, *Social Darwinism in American Thought* (Boston: Beacon Press, 1955), 4.

18   Ibid., 41.

19   John D. Rockefeller, quoted in Hofstadter, *Social Darwinism in American Thought,* 45.

20   Hofstadter, *Social Darwinism in American Thought,* 115.

21   Ibid., 50.

22   Arendt, *The Human Condition,* 157.

23   Ibid., 307–309.

24   Ibid., 96.

25   It is interesting to note that even Mumford's deeply supportive recent biographer Donald Miller concedes that the great theoretician "never adequately described" what he meant by a "normalized standard of consumption." See Donald L. Miller, *Lewis Mumford: A Life* (New York: Weidenfeld & Nicholson, 1989), 296.

26   Arendt, *The Human Condition,* 126.

27   Ibid.

28   William Morris, *News From Nowhere,* in *Three Works by William Morris* (New York: International Publishers, 1967), 211.

29   Francesco Dal Co, "From Parks to the Region: Progressive Ideology and the Reform of the American City," in Giorgio Ciucci, Francesco Dal Co, Mario Manieri-Elia, and Manfredo Tafuri, *The American City from the Civil War to the New Deal* (Cambridge: MIT Press, 1979).

30   Giorgio Ciucci, "The City in Agrarian Ideology and Frank Lloyd Wright: Origins and Development of Broadacres," in Ciucci et al., *The American City,* 317.

31   Dal Co, "From Parks to the Region," 179.

32   Ibid., 165.

33   Ibid., 241.

34   McHarg, *Design with Nature,* 38, 110.

35 Shades of this difference of opinion can also be discerned in the celebrated debate between Mumford and Jane Jacobs on the occasion of the publication of Jacobs's *The Death and Life of Great American Cities* in 1961.

36 Ciucci, "The City in Agrarian Ideology," 307.

37 Ibid., 311.

38 Ibid., 321.

39 Ibid., 362.

40 Ibid., 352.

41 Arendt, *The Human Condition,* 117–118.

42 Goran Schildt, *Alvar Aalto: The Decisive Years* (New York: Rizzoli, 1986), 148.

Chapter Seven
Architecture and Politics

EPIGRAPHS   Le Corbusier, *Towards a New Architecture* (London: Architectural Press, 1946), 269.

Leon Krier, "Vorwärts, Kameraden, wir müssen zurück," *Oppositions* 24 (Spring 1981): 37.

1 I use the qualifying phrase "in many ways" since, despite the famous statement itself, Le Corbusier was far from being the most politicized of modern architects. Recent scholarship has shown how hard he worked to persuade governments of various political persuasions of the merits of his architectural ideas, from the 1920s right through the difficult 1930s, on into the period of reconstruction after World War II. To employ an ironic paraphrase of Krier, one might say that over his career he attempted as much to use politics as an instrument to *achieve architecture* as to effect political change *through* architecture. Unlike such an unfortunate contemporary as Hannes Meyer, Le Corbusier never found himself impelled to reject on political grounds an earlier architectural position of his own.

2 For Germany, see Barbara Miller Lane, *Architecture and Politics in Germany, 1918–1945* (Cambridge: Harvard University Press, 1968); for Italy, see Diane Ghirardo, "Italian Architects and Fascist Politics: An Evaluation of the Rationalist's Role in Regime

Building," *Journal of the Society of Architectural Historians* 39 (May 1980); for the Soviet Union, see Anatole Kopp, *Town and Revolution: Soviet Architecture and City Planning, 1917–1935* (London: Thames and Hudson, 1970) and "Foreign Architects in the Soviet Union during the First Two Five Year Plans," in *Reshaping Russian Architecture: Western Technology, Utopian Dreams,* ed. William C. Brumfield (Washington: Woodrow Wilson Center; Cambridge: Cambridge University Press, 1990).

3   Ghirardo, "Italian Architects and Fascist Politics," 117.

4   Lane, *Architecture and Politics,* 136.

5   Quoted in Lane, *Architecture and Politics,* 162.

6   Quoted in Kopp, *Town and Revolution,* 94, 95.

7   Hans Schmidt, "1932: The Soviet Union and Modern Architecture," in El Lissitzky, *Russia: Architecture for a World Revolution,* appendix III (London: Lund Humphries, 1970), 218.

8   Ibid., 219.

9   Ibid., 220.

10 Il Gruppo Sette, "1926: Architecture," *Oppositions* 6 (Fall 1976): 89.

11 Ibid., 90.

12 Ghirardo, "Italian Architecture and Fascist Politics," 112.

13 Ibid.

14 Ibid., 120.

15 Thomas Schumacher, *Danteum: A Study in the Architecture of Literature* (Princeton: Princeton Architectural Press, 1985). See especially chapter 2, "Terragni and His Sources."

16 See Franco Borsi, *The Monumental Era: European Architecture and Design, 1929–1939* (New York: Rizzoli, 1978), 114.

17   In this regard, see the discussions of the aspirations of the Vienna Secession, as well as of Adolf Loos's critique of them, in chapter one above.

18   Sigfried Giedion, *Befreites Wohnen* (Zurich and Leipzig: Orell Fussli Verlag, 1929).

19   Sigfried Giedion, *A Decade of New Architecture* (Zurich: Editions Girsberger, 1951), 116.

20   Rowe's two essays were originally published in the British magazine *The Architectural Review* in 1947 and 1950.

21   Robert Venturi, *Complexity and Contradiction in Architecture* (New York: Museum of Modern Art, 1966).

22   Robert Goodman, *After the Planners* (New York: Simon and Schuster, 1971), 7.

23   Ibid., 126.

24   Ibid., 130.

25   Ibid., 181.

26   Ibid., 188, 190, 208, 209.

27   Martin Pawley, *Architecture versus Housing* (New York and Washington: Praeger Publishers, 1971), 45.

28   Ibid., 81.

29   Ibid., 82.

30   Ibid.

31   John F. C. Turner and Robert Fichter, eds., *Freedom to Build* (New York: Macmillan Company, 1972), and John F. C. Turner, *Housing by People* (London: Marion Boyars, 1976).

32   Colin Ward, preface to Turner, *Housing by People,* 5–6.

33   Turner, *Housing by People,* 35, 47, 47.

34 Ibid., 56.

35 Ibid.

36 Ibid., 61.

37 Ibid., 65.

38 Ibid., 71.

39 The celebrated statement was made by Pierre-Joseph Proudhon in his 1840 book *What Is Property?,* cited in George Lichtheim, *The Origins of Socialism* (London: Weidenfeld and Nicholson, 1968), 84.

40 Hannah Arendt, *The Human Condition* (Chicago: University of Chicago Press, 1958), especially 109.

41 See the special September 1971 issue of the British magazine *Architectural Design.* This issue, entitled "The Beaux Arts Since '68," was written by Martin Pawley and Bernard Tschumi.

42 Vincent Scully, *American Architecture and Urbanism* (New York: Praeger Publishers, 1969), 255.

43 Bernard Huet, quoted in Pawley and Tschumi, "The Beaux Arts Since '68," 554.

44 Bernard Huet, *Anachroniques d'architecture* (Brussels: Archives d'Architecture Moderne, 1981), 81.

45 Ibid., 83.

46 Charles Jencks, *The Language of Post-Modern Architecture* (London: Academy Editions, 1977), 9.

47 Bernard Huet, "Formalisme-Réalisme," in *Anachroniques d'architecture,* 53.

48 Ibid., 56.

49 Ibid.

50 Ibid., 57.

51 Ibid.

52 Bernard Huet, "Le Temps des malentendus" in *Anachroniques d'architecture*, 76.

53 Huet, "Formalisme-Réalisme," 55.

54 Ibid., 57.

55 Walter Benjamin, "The Work of Art in the Era of Mechanical Reproduction," in *Illuminations* (New York: Harcourt, Brace & World, 1968), 241.

56 Erwin Panofsky, "Iconography and Iconology: An Introduction to the Study of Renaissance Art," in *Meaning in the Visual Arts* (Garden City, New York: Doubleday Anchor Books, 1955), 26.

57 I have recently discussed the source of this story with Grumbach, who cannot recall it. He reports he suspects the story may be apocryphal.

58 Hannah Arendt, *On Violence* (New York: Harcourt, Brace & World, 1970), 21.

59 A range of examples of characteristic works of these figures may be found in Robert A. M. Stern, *Modern Classicism* (New York: Rizzoli, 1988).

60 A good account of a range of early works of Moore, up to the Piazza d'Italia, is in *L'Architecture d'aujourd'hui*, 184 (March/April 1976).

61 For an account of the work of Quinlan Terry see Frank Russell, ed., *Quinlan Terry* (London: Architectural Design and Academy Editions, 1981).

62 Goodman, *After the Planners*, 104.

63 Kenneth Frampton, *Modern Architecture: A Critical History* (New York: Oxford University Press, 1980).

64 Jürgen Habermas, "Modernity—An Incomplete Project," trans. Seyla Ben-Habib, in *The Anti-Aesthetic: Essays on Postmodern Culture*, ed. Hal Foster (Port Townsend, Washington: Bay Press, 1983).

65 See Robert A. M. Stern, "Giedion's Ghost," a review of Frampton's *Modern Architecture: A Critical History*, in *Skyline, The Architecture and Design Review* (October 1981).

66 As examples see "Norman Foster: 1964–1987," *A+U* (May 1988, extra edition), and *Richard Rogers + Architects* (London: Architectural Monographs, 1985).

67 It is interesting to sketch a map of certain key correspondences and oppositions among the ideas of the three figures, especially in light of the two broad theoretical schemas developed in note 13 of the introduction to this text. These are, first, the "high culture/low culture" or "high culture/mass culture" opposition, which has been put forward by Andreas Huyssen, and second, the "avant-garde/modern" or "avant-garde/continuity" oppositions put forward by Bürger and Grassi respectively.

In the case of Colin Rowe, his basic loyalty to the high culture of modernism will be evident enough to the reader in the passage from "The Mathematics of the Ideal Villa" that was quoted in chapter four. While this is true, one can also readily enough describe Rowe, in Huyssen's terms, as having an "aesthetic practise close to the spirit of avant-gardism." This has been manifest, to cite only one particularly relevant instance, in Rowe's enduring enthusiasm for Le Corbusier's frequent deployment of *objets trouvés* within his overall formal systems of design.

As for the avant-garde/modern opposition propounded by Bürger, Rowe would have to be seen as neutral in respect to it. Indeed, I can recall no passage in his work that would even bring such a schema to mind. However, when we come to Grassi's opposition of avant-garde to continuity, I think that Rowe, if forced to choose, would surely come down on the side of elitist innovation as against the sort of social "continuity" given primacy by Grassi. His inclination toward a sort of Burkean individualism—not to say, in more modern terms, toward an aristocratic anarchism—would undoubtedly dispose him to take a stand against Grassi's distinctly collectivist social bias.

Moving to the case of Turner, I think it is reasonably clear at the outset that Huyssen's schema of high culture as against low is not one of any overriding urgency for him, given the fact that his central preoccupations have not been with cultural production per se. He ought probably to be seen in these terms as having a temperamental inclination to favor the products of low or mass culture over those of high but without holding any particular opposition to the latter. Faced with Bürger's opposition of avant-garde and modern, on the other hand, it seems to me likely that we would see Turner's sensibility become decidedly more engaged. Given his generic commitment to grass roots social praxes, he would undoubtedly share with Huyssen's "historical avant-garde" an interest in "developing an alternative relationship between high art and mass culture." As for Grassi's schema of avant-garde and continuity, I think we may surmise that Turner would in the first instance refuse to acknowledge it out of loyalty to the so-called historical avant-garde characterized by Huyssen—especially in its frequently individualistic if not anarchist inclinations. Yet this would not, in my view, be a simple matter for Turner. On further consideration, Turner would surely ascribe substantial validity to Grassi's position, particularly since the concept of continuity that is so central to it shares a great deal with Turner's own eventual formulation of the important idea that housing is first and foremost a "social institution."

For Huet, at the outset he should probably be seen as being as neutral with respect to the high culture/low culture opposition as Rowe was with respect to the avant-garde/modern one. This is not to suggest any lack of interest in either on the part of the French architect. On the contrary, the neutrality I ascribe to him is really an acknowledgment of the breadth and depth of his interests in, and knowledge of, many strands of both.

When we come to Huyssen's avant-garde/modern opposition, on the other hand, clear difficulties would arise. As I have already noted, Huet is a close enough ally of Grassi's to be committed to some such opposition of avant-garde and continuity as that propounded by his Italian colleague. And this necessarily makes Huet an opponent of the alternative schema proposed by Bürger and Huyssen. Indeed, Huet's scorn for avant-gardes in architecture—which he has often portrayed as "elitist"—appears to be a basic tenet of his theoretical position. His strong convictions in this matter are clearly evident in the passages from his writings on architectural pedagogy, and on the Tendenza, that I have quoted above. Like Turner, Huet has become fundamentally committed to the idea of architecture as a social institution; his strong convictions in this respect are explored in further detail below. However, unlike the English theoretician of self-help housing, Huet has not manifested any individualist let alone anarchist sympathies in this regard. On the contrary, he has moved in recent years to the view that it is only within the context of a decisive acknowledgment—however reluctant a one—that architecture has now inescapably become a mass cultural phenomenon, that contemporary praxis can any longer possess the kind of broad-based significance it held in the societies of the past.

68 Colin Rowe, introductin to *Five Architects* (New York: Wittenborn & Company, 1972), 3.

69 Ibid.

70 Ibid.

71   The influence of Illich on Turner is cited in Colin Ward's preface to Turner, *Housing by People.*

72   Maurice Culot, "Conversation avec Bernard Huet," in Huet, *Anachroniques d'architecture,* 172.

73   Bernard Huet, "Point de vue sur l'enseignement," in *Anachroniques d'architecture,* 90.

74   Ibid., 90.

75   Ibid., 92.

76   Ibid., 93.

77   Rowe, introduction to *Five Architects,* 7.

Chapter Eight
"The Space of Appearance"

1   Hannah Arendt, *The Human Condition* (Chicago: University of Chicago Press, 1958), 198–199.

2   Ibid., 50, 52.

3   Ibid., 175.

4   Richard Sennett, *The Fall of Public Man* (New York: Vintage Books, Random House 1978), 16.

5   Ibid., 39.

6   Morton White and Lucia White, *The Intellectual versus the City* (London: Oxford University Press, 1977), 158.

7   It is interesting to note that Benjamin's concept of the *flâneur* has a quite different cast from Baudelaire's (from whom he took it over). Where Benjamin cites the "gaze of alienated man," Baudelaire refers instead to "the immense joy" the perfect *flâneur* feels, "to set up house in the heart of the multitude, amid the ebb and flow of movement, in the midst of the fugitive and the infinite." Charles Baudelaire,

"The Painter of Modern Life," in *The Painter of Modern Life and Other Essays,* translated and edited by Jonathan Mayne (New York: Da Capo Press, 1986), 9.

8   Walter Benjamin, "Paris, Capital of the Nineteenth Century," *Perspecta* 12 (1969): 170.

9   Definitive expositions of the fundamental urban principles of CIAM can be found in Le Corbusier, *The Athens Charter* (New York: Grossman Publishers, 1973); and in Martin Steinmann, ed., *CIAM Dokumente 1928–1939* (Basel and Stuttgart: Birkhauser Verlag, 1979).

10   José Ortega y Gasset, quoted in José Luis Sert, "Centres of Community Life," in J. Tyrwhitt, J. L. Sert, and E. N. Rogers. *The Heart of the City* (London: Lund Humphries, 1952), 3.

11   Ibid., 146.

12   Reyner Banham, *The New Brutalism* (London: Architectural Press, 1966), 71.

13   Alison Smithson and Peter Smithson, quoted in ibid., 72.

14   See ibid., especially chapters 5.1 and 5.2.

15   Alison Smithson and Peter Smithson, quoted in ibid., 72.

16   Ibid., 73.

17   Ibid., 74.

18   See Alison Smithson, ed., *Team 10 Primer* (London: Studio Vista, 1965), 76.

19   Ibid., 9 and 61.

20   Le Corbusier, *Oeuvre Complète,* vol. 7 (Zurich: Editions d'Architecture, 1965), 140.

21   See Aldo van Eyck, "The Interior of Time," and Aldo van Eyck, Paul Parin, and Fritz Morgenthaler, "A Miracle of Moderation," in Charles Jencks and George Baird, eds., *Meaning in Architecture* (New York: Braziller, 1969), 172.

22   Joseph Rykwert, "The Idea of a Town," originally published in *Dutch Forum* 17, no. 3 (1963), and later as a book (Princeton: Princeton University Press, 1976).

23 Virtually the entire proceedings of the conference were published in Oscar New-man, ed., *CIAM at Otterloo, 1959; Arbeitsgruppe für die Gestaltung soziologischer und visueller Zusammenlagen* (Stuttgart: Karl Kramer Verlag, 1961).

24 Smithson, in Newman, *CIAM at Otterlo,* 76. The following excerpts are from ibid., 76–77.

25 See Georges Candilis, Alexis Josic, and Shadrach Woods, *Toulouse le Mirail: Birth of a New Town* (Stuttgart: Karl Kramer Verlag, 1975).

26 Victor Gruen, *Centers for the Urban Environment: Survival of the Cities* (New York: Van Nostrand Reinhold Company, 1973). See especially chapter 3.

27 Ibid., 192.

28 Banham, *The New Brutalism,* 62.

29 Colin St. John Wilson, "Two Letters on the State of Architecture," *Journal of Architectural Education* 25 no. 1 (Fall 1981): 9.

30 Charles Moore, "You Have to Pay for the Public Life," *Perspecta* 9/10 (1965): 58.

31 Ibid., 60.

32 Ibid., 65.

33 Banham, *The New Brutalism,* 125 and 144.

34 The project for Grunzug South is illustrated in Maurice Culot and Leon Krier, *Rational Architecture: The Reconstruction of the European City* (Brussels: Archives d'Architecture Moderne, 1978), 102.

35 Projects from the Stirling office including the competition entries for Siemens AG in Munich and for the Derby Town Centre from 1970 are examples of this. See Peter Arnell and Ted Bickford, *James Stirling: Buildings and Projects* (New York: Rizzoli, 1984), 155 and 170.

36 See Rob Krier, *Stadtraum: Theorie und Praxis* (Stuttgart: Karl Kramer Verlag, 1975).

37 Saarinen's urban thinking is expounded in his *The City: Its Growth, Its Decay, Its Future* (New York: Reinhold Publishing Corporation, 1943). Sitte's seminal work (its influence on Saarinen, not to mention the Krier brothers, has obviously been profound) was his *City Planning According to Artistic Principles.* The edition I have consulted is translated by George Collins and Christiane Craseman Collins (New York: Rizzoli, 1986). Wagner's urban ideas were put forward in his *Die Grosstadt: eine Studie über diese* (Vienna: Anton Schroll, 1911).

38 An early, brief, and favorable account of the later harshly criticized Markisches-Viertel can be found in Gunther Feuerstein, *New Directions in German Architecture* (New York: Braziller, 1968), 70.

39 For the project of Hertzberger, see Alan Colquhoun, "Centraal Beheer," *Architecture Plus* (September/October, 1974), 48–55; for that of Krier, see Antoine Grumbach, "Les Frères Krier; le retour du refoule," in *L'Architecture d'aujourd'hui* 179 (May–June 1975): 69.

40 See Ian Pearson, "Shop Till You Drop," *Saturday Night Magazine* (May 1986), 48–56; and Peter Hemingway, "The Joy of Kitsch," *The Canadian Architect,* March 1986, 32.

41 Michael Sorkin, ed., *Variations on a Theme Park* (New York: Hill and Wang, 1992).

42 Jean Baudrillard, "The Precession of Simulacra," *Art & Text* no. 11 (September 1983), 261.

43 Ibid., 257.

44 Leon Krier, "Atlantis Tenerife," *Domus* (May 1988), 45.

45 Sennett, *The Fall of Public Man,* 110.

46 Denis Diderot, quoted in ibid., 111, 112.

47 Ibid., 118.

48 Rousseau, quoted in ibid., 112.

49 Arendt, *The Human Condition,* 179–180.

INDEX